PIONEER COACHES OF THE NFL

PIONEER COACHES OF THE NFL

Shaping the Game in the Days of Leather Helmets and 60-Minute Men

John Maxymuk

ROWMAN & LITTLEFIELD
Lanham • Boulder • New York • London

Published by Rowman & Littlefield
An imprint of The Rowman & Littlefield Publishing Group, Inc.
4501 Forbes Boulevard, Suite 200, Lanham, Maryland 20706
www.rowman.com

6 Tinworth Street, London SE11 5AL

British Library Cataloguing in Publication Information Available

Library of Congress Cataloging-in-Publication Data

Names: Maxymuk, John, author.
Title: Pioneer coaches of the NFL : shaping the game in the days of leather helmets and 60-minute men / John Maxymuk.
Description: Lanham : Rowman & Littlefield, [2019] | Includes bibliographical references and index.
Identifiers: LCCN 2018059680 (print) | LCCN 2019004572 (ebook) | ISBN 9781538112243 (electronic) | ISBN 9781538112236 (cloth : alk. paper)
Subjects: LCSH: Football coaches—United States—Biography. | Football—Coaching.
Classification: LCC GV939.A1 (ebook) | LCC GV939.A1 M3896 2019 (print) | DDC 796.3320922 [B]—dc23
LC record available at https://lccn.loc.gov/2018059680

∞ ™ The paper used in this publication meets the minimum requirements of American National Standard for Information Sciences Permanence of Paper for Printed Library Materials, ANSI/NISO Z39.48-1992.

Printed in the United States of America

As always, for Suzanne,
who encouraged me to start another book project,
knowing full well the consequences

CONTENTS

Preface ix

Acknowledgments xiii

Introduction: Emerging from the Shadow of College Football xv

1 Player-Coach: Guy Chamberlin Shows the Way 1

2 Taking Flight: Curly Lambeau and LeRoy Andrew Work the Passing Game 19

3 T Men: George Halas, Dutch Sternaman, and Ralph Jones Open Up the "Regular Formation" 47

4 Almost Famous: Potsy Clark Writes the Book on the Pro Game 67

5 Smash Mouth: Steve Owen Wins with Defense and the Kicking Game 87

6 Wing Man: Ray Flaherty Masters the Tried and True 109

7 Big Man Off Campus: Jock Sutherland Finds a New Challenge 131

8 T-Men II: Halas, Jones, and Clark Shaughnessy Go All In 149

9 Players' Coach: Jimmy Conzelman's Championship Charm 177

10 Counterpunch: Greasy Neale Defenses the T 195

Epilogue: Paul Brown: Modern Pro Football Coach 215

Afterword: Fritz Pollard's Dream Deferred 223

Postscript: Equivalencies 227

Notes 231

Bibliography	257
Index	265
About the Author	279

PREFACE

Coaches are the means by which the National Football League evolved and grew from meager and hardscrabble origins almost 100 years ago to assert itself as the most popular spectator sport in the United States. They are the men who devised, adapted, and altered the on-the-field stratagems that developed the game into the dramatic televised spectacle it has become.

How did the game grow, evolve, and prosper in the crucial first 30 years of the league? What role did the head coach play in this transformation? How did the pro coach's rise in stature lift the play-for-pay game to new heights? These are the larger questions *Pioneer Coaches of the NFL* confronts as it traces the evolution of playing rules, game equipment, and coaching strategies. Coaches shaped the game's changes and began to cultivate an audience of their own through their actions on the practice and playing fields, in addition to their interactions with the press. Today, there is no one more important to a team's success than the head coach.

Football coaching at the pro level is a fascinating, multilayered job. Coaches are personnel managers in an extremely pressurized position. They need to work well with upper management to get the players they want and with the players themselves to get the best performance on the field. They are not hired to coach, but to win games; team failure leads to coaching unemployment.

Seven years ago, I wrote *NFL Head Coaches: A Biographical Dictionary, 1920–2011*, in which I give thumbnail biographical, career, and statistical information on the 466 men who had served as head coaches in the NFL up to that point. My intention with each coach was to explain who he was, his coaching approach and style, and his accomplishments. In the course of researching that book, I continually was impressed by how much the early coaches advanced the game as a whole; however, even the most influential and innovative of these pioneers are largely forgotten today.

In this current book, my focus is on those coaching ancestors, the ones who shaped the profession. Starting as little more than on-field captains who also ran practices—if there was time for practice—coaches in the first three decades of the game established many of the procedures, conventions, and protocols that the modern football coach still uses. In particular, my attention is devoted to 13 men who, in my view, had the most lasting impression on the game and its history. It was this group of coaches who initially devised the basic repertoire of plays and alignments, as well as passing routes, blocking schemes, line splits, shifts, motion, and substitution patterns. These men morphed defensive alignments from seven- to six- to five-man lines, introduced the four-man secondary, conceived zone and man-to-man coverage mixes, used double teams in both coverage and blocking, and concocted linebacker and safety blitzing. These pioneers presented later coaches a rich palate with which to imagine and create an even greater game.

The break point for the dawn of the modern game of pro football is 1950, when unlimited substitution was permanently instituted. Free substitution enabled the creation of two-platoon football and initiated an ever-increasing gyre of specialization that required more players with more focused and complex assignments, which, in turn, demanded more centralized strategic control from the coach.

Paul Brown also came to the NFL in 1950, although he had already coached for four years in the rival All-America Football Conference after World War II. Brown was the first modern pro football coach. He was the first to call all the offensive plays, the first to hire an extended full-time staff, and the first to make classroom teaching a regular part of the players' day, as well as being the instigator of several strategic firsts.

While Brown turned the job into a profession, he did not emerge out of thin air. Although he never played or coached under any of the early coaches profiled in this book, he built on the foundation they had established throughout the previous three decades.

The chapters fall roughly in chronological order, so the story of the 13 coaches here relates the narrative of the pro game's first 30 years, when it positioned itself to surpass college football and then Major League Baseball in popularity. Aside from biographical and career details for these coaches, my emphasis is on their strategic approach to the game and their impact on its history and that of the coaching profession. Chapters are divided into three main sections: life and career; coaching keys (what they contributed to the evolution of the coaching profession); and pivotal games (highlighting postseason and other significant games in which these men matched wits on the field so as to explore the contrasts between them and demonstrate how they advanced the game).

I created figures to illustrate basic offensive and defensive formations, as well as the occasional significant play. The back matter of the book includes an afterword about the long, hard road African American coaches have traveled, along with a bibliography. I was able to watch game film of the teams of each of these coaches, with the exception of our starting point—Guy Chamberlin. That film study was illuminating in bringing to life the written record, and I hope it makes this text clearer and more useful.

The coaches included here are long dead, but their work lives on in today's game. I hope this book indicates how.

ACKNOWLEDGMENTS

This book would not have been written without the friendship and fellowship of Chris Willis, librarian at NFL Films. Chris passed on my name to Rowman & Littlefield acquisitions editor Christen Karniski. Christen and I tossed around several ideas for potential projects before she amalgamated parts of our discussion into the idea of a book on the evolution of NFL coaching in the league's formative first three decades.

It was also through Chris that I was able to access the film library of NFL Films to get a full picture of how the coaches in this book approached the game. That film study informs the other research I conducted to give me a fuller understanding of the origins of today's game. Also of great assistance in this regard were several fellow football historians and friends who shared resources and insights about the early game. Foremost of all, was Coach T. J. Troup, who is always generous with his time, but abundant thanks are due to Nick Webster, John Richards, Evan Bass, Eric Goska, and Rob Stevens as well.

Another friend, historian, and accomplished writer, Jeff Miller, was kind enough to read the manuscript and offer a wealth of excellent suggestions.

Jon Kendle, the archivist of the Pro Football Hall of Fame, helped me navigate archival resources at his site, greatly expanding the scope of my research.

I am also indebted to Dal Andrew, son of one of the most unjustly forgotten coaches included in this book, for his recollections of his father. Likewise, the day I spent with Jim Conzelman Jr. and his daughter, Shelley Burger, was enlightening for not only the interview, but also the two-foot-by-three-foot laminated scrapbook Jim created about his father. And thanks to Mike Moran, son of early star player Hap Moran, for getting me in touch with Dal. Mike also served as my resident genealogist, gathering family tree info on several coaches via Ancestry.com.

Finally, I would like to thank my colleagues at the Paul Robeson Library at Rutgers University–Camden for their support while I undertook this project. Above all, my wife Suzanne is the rock of my life and the reason I wake up fairly happy every day.

INTRODUCTION

Emerging from the Shadow of College Football

When the National Football League began as the American Profession-al Football Association in 1920, it was a disrespected, ragtag organization trying to capitalize on the mass popularity of the college version of the sport with its postgraduate variety. College football was king, was grow-ing, and was disdainful of any pretenders to the throne. Michael Oriard writes in his book *King Football*,

> It was the growth of college football into a spectator sport to rival Major League Baseball that most importantly marks the years between the two wars. Given the relatively low percentage of Americans who attended college—8 percent of 18 to 21 year olds in 1920, increasing to only 12 percent in 1930, a little less than 16 percent in 1940 (still not quite 30 percent in 1950, despite the thousands attending on the GI Bill)—college football's broad appeal is remarkable. Attendance at college football games increased 119 percent in the 1920s, exceeding 10 million by the end of the decade, slightly more than for Major League Baseball. Both as cause and effect of the tremendous new enthusiasm for football, a stadium-building boom in the 1920s planted huge concrete and brick bowls in landscapes throughout the Midwest, South, and Far West in the 1920s. By 1930, there were 74 concrete stadiums, 55 of them built since 1920, 6 of them with a seating capac-ity exceeding 70,000, including the Rose Bowl in Pasadena (1922), the Los Angeles Coliseum (1923), and Soldier Field in Chicago (1924). About 60 percent of the attendance at college football came from some

40 institutions whose teams played in these massive structures. Eight Big Ten universities built or expanded their football stadiums in the 1920s.[1]

An offshoot of the college game, pro football was born in the 1890s, when independent teams sprung up mostly around industrial towns in Ohio and Pennsylvania, and spread throughout the Midwest in the first two decades of the 20th century. The so-called Ohio League was the best-known loose association of teams in that period. It was dominated in the early years of the century by the Massillon Tigers and, in the later teens, by their rivals, the Canton Bulldogs. Several of the teams from that tentative grouping, including Canton (but not Massillon), joined the fledgling APFA in 1920, but none of those teams would survive into the 1930s.

In contrast to their college counterparts, pro football teams in the 1920s typically played in unenclosed fields (Rock Island Independents and Green Bay Packers), high school grounds (Muncie Flyers and Pottsville Maroons), minor league baseball fields (Milwaukee Badgers and Minneapolis Marines), and even a bicycle cycledrome (Providence Steam Roller). Luckier teams got to play in Major League Baseball stadiums (Chicago Bears and Chicago Cardinals), while the Frankford Yellow Jackets were unique in having their own pro football stadium in Philadelphia.

Before 1925, pro football crowds of at least 10,000 were rare. Red Grange drove up attendance in games in which he was involved after joining the Bears, and attendance began to inch into five figures more often in the latter part of the decade; however, the league's average attendance, according to NFL vice president Carl Storck, was still just 6,000 in 1929.[2]

College football was a serious business run by revered legends of the game. Yale man Walter Camp was known as the "Father of American Football," as he led the national rules committee and picked the main All-America team for decades. Camp was responsible for the scrimmage line, 11 men per side, a system of downs to define a team's possession, and set plays, although he resisted the legalization of the forward pass in 1906, when the game was under fire for its brutality.

Camp coached both Amos Alonzo Stagg and Henry L. Williams at Yale. Beginning in the 1890s, Stagg coached college football for more than 50 years, mostly at the University of Chicago; Williams became known for his offensive strategy called the "Minnesota shift" while coaching at that state university from 1900 to 1921. In 1893, the two collaborated on an early classic book of football strategy whose very title indicated the seriousness of the college game: *A Scientific and Practical Treatise on American Football for Schools and Colleges*. This instructional manual includes a voluminous playbook of 69 plays, and most of them were run from the "regular formation," which later became known as the T formation. Walter Camp may indeed be the sport's father, but Stagg's influence was massive. Many features of modern football have their origins with him—the direct pass from center, presnap shifts, man-in-motion, unbalanced lines, flankers, end-around, and hidden-ball plays—to name just a few.

Stagg's strongest competition as an innovator was Cornell-educated Glenn "Pop" Warner. Warner wrote several instructional books on football after inventing the single wing, the sport's dominant offensive alignment of the first half of the 20th century, while at the Carlisle Industrial School in 1907. At Carlisle, he would later coach the great Jim Thorpe and also devised a second major formation, the double wing. Warner was something of a coaching nomad, leading teams at eight different schools, some concurrently, from 1895 to 1938. At Stanford in the 1920s, he employed his double wing with another legendary player, Ernie Nevers, and in 1929, he lent his name to a pee wee football organization still around today, Pop Warner Football.

However, the college coach who made the greatest impact on the public-at-large in this halcyon period was Notre Dame's Knute Rockne. Rockne was not the innovator the previous two coaches were, although his Notre Dame shift would prove to be influential throughout both the college and pro game in the coming decades. Rockne freely admitted that Stagg invented the shift and credited both Stagg and Henry Williams as the "great masters of the evolutions and gyrations of the shift."[3] Rockne's influence was spread in two ways. First was the force and engaging quality of his personality in the press and to the greater public. He was charming, witty, and astoundingly successful; Notre Dame was 105–12–5 from 1918 through 1930, before his tragic death in a plane crash. Second, former players under Rockne took up coaching in both college and the pros in large numbers, spreading his system throughout the nation.

No coach had more of his acolytes working as head coaches in the early NFL than Rockne, with seven (Norm Barry, Joe Brandy, Marty

Brill, Jack Chevigny, Frank Coughlin, Harry Mehre, and Curly Lambeau). In addition, nine more former Rockne players would helm pro teams in the coming decades (Dutch Bergman, Joe Bach, Hunk Anderson, Clem Crowe, Jim Crowley, Buck Shaw, Clipper Smith, Adam Walsh, and Chile Walsh). Five more pro coaches either played with Rockne at Notre Dame or under him when he assisted head coach Jess Harper in the teens (Gus Dorais, Jimmy Phelan, Cap Edwards, Stan Cofall, and Jack Meagher).

The only other college coach to have a similar influence on the early NFL was Bob Zuppke of Illinois. Zuppke's seven former players who became pro coaches were George Halas, Dutch and Joey Sternaman, Potsy Clark, Russ Daugherty, Jack Depler, and Wally McIlwain. Zuppke was a free thinker and the popularizer of the huddle, who tailored his offense to the players he had on hand, so he might use the single wing, the I formation, the spread, or the T in any particular season. His key role for pro football, however, is that he taught George Halas the T, and Halas brought it to the NFL.

These men and several others were viewed as giants of college football. Fielding Yost of Michigan, John Heisman of Georgia Tech, and Dana X. Bible of Nebraska and Texas won more than 180 games in their coaching careers. George Woodruff, who played for Camp; Howard Jones, who played for Stagg; Jock Sutherland, who played for Warner; Gil Dobie, who played for Williams; Frank Leahy, who played for Rockne; and Dan McGugin, who played for Yost, carried on the legacy and continued to burnish the honored image of the sagacious and virtuous college football coach.

Most of these early coaches scorned the pro game and extolled the virtue of amateurism. Pop Warner sniffed in *Football for Coaches and Players* in 1927, "The game as played by the colleges and schools is free from all suspicion of crookedness, and there is always such keen rivalry between the teams playing that there is a snap and dash about the game which is usually absent from professional sports, especially professional football."[4]

Rockne, who had played professionally himself while he worked as an assistant coach at Notre Dame, generally was not so puritanical; however, even he echoed Fielding Yost by calling the pro game a "menace" in 1922, when his Notre Dame program was threatened because three of his players were found to be playing professionally under assumed names.[5]

Another of his players, Hunk Anderson, was playing professional base-ball on the side and suspended from athletics during his senior year of 1922. Nonetheless, that fall Hunk began playing professionally for the Chicago Bears, while simultaneously serving as Rockne's line coach, so Knute couldn't have been too troubled about professionalism. Anderson would later succeed Rockne as coach of the Fighting Irish in 1931.

Stagg, however, was the real Simon Pure of pro football critics. In his 1927 volume *Touchdown!* Stagg disparages the handful of Chicago alumni who opted to play professionally:

> There is nothing intrinsically dishonorable about it, but a boy who has earned a college degree and his letter ought to have an equipment of character, knowledge, and fight worthy of a man's size job, instead of snatching at the first roll of soft and easy money in sight. I never did a wiser thing than refusing the $4,200 a season offered me by the New York Nationals in the '80s when the sum just about represented the national wealth to me.[6]

Stagg then gets much more moralistic:

> I have argued all along that football is a sport distinct in character. There is no reason why a man can't play baseball or tennis or run the 220-high hurdles as well for money as he can for love of his college and the sport; but they have no such emotional basis as football, nor do they demand a like physical condition.

He concludes, "Football on such terms is a travesty, a Shetland pony rodeo, a vegetarian guzzle."[7]

The ironic thing is that recent research of archival materials by John Kryk for *Stagg vs. Yost: The Birth of Cutthroat Football* makes clear that Stagg was more than a bit of a phony; the *Detroit Free Press* at the time referred to him sneeringly as "Great-I-Am." In trying to best the audacious Michigan upstart Fielding Yost, Stagg imported ringers and used ineligible players, while accusing Michigan of the same.[8]

Still, in *Touchdown!* Stagg avers the nobility of his work, the coaching profession:

> The day is past when a coach can be any kind of an old rake and hold his job. Good character, right living, good example, clean sportsmanship, along with good coaching, are more and more being insisted

upon by all our colleges. College faculties are demanding that the coach be interested in the development of the manhood of the boys, as well as in creating football players. Unsportsmanlike conduct and dirty tactics are now pretty generally taboo among our best institutions.[9]

The coaching role in the nascent NFL was quite different in both function and perception from that of college coaches and from more modern times. Coaches did not have playbooks or do film study or even call the plays. Their major function was running practices. The game on the field was directed by the captain and/or signal caller. At the outset, pro coaches were not extolled in the press as being anything like the paragons of the college game.

In a piece by Jim Campbell for the *Coffin Corner* in 1995, 1920s tackle John Alexander ran down what coaches could and couldn't do in the first decade of the NFL:

The coach, during the game, was really not much of a factor in those days. There was no coaching from the sidelines—you couldn't yell instructions, you couldn't even signal in plays. That would have been a 15-yard penalty if you got caught. The game was really played on the field by the 11 men you had out there. The captain was the key man on game day. He called the signals. He kept order and discipline. Not the coach. Coaches worked with us in practice, and when the game came around they'd say, "I did all I could. Now, you go out and play. I'm going to watch and enjoy the game." There was a lot of truth to that. There were few timeouts. When there were, we didn't go to the side-line to discuss the upcoming plays. There were even rules in effect that kept the game on the field rather than on the sidelines. Did you know that if a substitute came into the game—and there weren't many times that happened—an official went right into the huddle with him to make sure he didn't convey any messages from the coach to his team-mates?[10]

As such, it made sense for the coach to be on the field. Add in the shoestring financial picture and it's not a surprise that most teams hired player-coaches in the early days. In fact, in the early 1920s, there was a rudimentary salary cap structure governing player earnings. So if a team could pay a star both a noncapped supplement as coach and a relatively low salary as a player, it was to its benefit.

I did some calculations. From 1920 to 1932, 117 different men served as NFL head coaches. A total of 82 of them, 70 percent, were player-coaches at least part of that time. Since 1933, only 10 of the roughly 400 NFL coaches have been player-coaches. In the 1930s, Al Jolley, Algy Clark, Jap Douds, Milan Creighton, Dutch Clark, Art Lewis, and Johnny Blood were the last of the player-coaches. After Blood was fired in 1939, the only player-coaches were a trio of Chicago Rockets who led that All-America Football Conference team on an interim basis for a half-dozen games in 1946.

But many of these early player-coaches continued coaching in the pros after retiring as players. In the 1920s, 74.3 percent of teams were led by current players, 6.2 percent by ex-players, 5.3 percent by former college coaches, and 14.2 percent by team owners. In the 1930s, that breakdown evolved to 25.3 percent current players, 29.5 percent ex-players, 38.9 percent former college coaches, and 6.3 percent owners. By the 1940s, the backgrounds of noninterim coaches were 41.6 percent ex-players, 51.9 percent former college coaches, 3.1 percent previous pro assistant coaches, and 3.4 percent owners. These figures count George Halas as one-half an owner and one-half either a player-coach or ex-player.

On the other hand, pro coaches in the 1920s had greater say in player recruitment in a time of chaotic player movement, as well as in the promotional and payroll aspects of the sport—particularly in road games. Away from home, the coach often would try to goose the gate by engaging with the local media and was regularly charged with collecting and distributing the visiting team's take of the gate receipts.

The pro game in the 1920s would be unrecognizable to anyone raised on the modern game. It was one-platoon football; everyone played both offense and defense. Rosters in the 1920s were limited to 16 to 18 players, and if a player left the game, he could not return until the next quarter. Alexander recalled, "You see, in those days, linemen would just put their heads down and charge straight ahead. The game was almost a tug-of-war in those days, without a rope. The teams were really bunched up, and nearly every play was a running play, although the forward pass was certainly legal."[11]

There were no hashmarks on the field, so the next play began where the last ended. If a team ran wide and got tackled near the sideline, five or six linemen might be on one side of the center on the next snap because the ball was spotted so close to the edge of the field. The offense would have to waste a play just to get back to the middle of the field. Alexander added, "Coaches put a lot of emphasis on playing mistake-free football. Be conservative, and let the other team make a mistake. That's why a lot of coaches would elect to kick off if their team won the toss of the coin."[12]

Field position was key. Teams often punted on third down or even earlier to mitigate possible bad center snaps or misplays and allow a possible second try on fourth down. Also, teams did not want to risk fumbling the ball deep in their own territory and allowing an easy score. Alexander remembered,

> If you received a punt inside your own 20-yard line, you usually punted it back to the other team on first down—not even run one play. Sometimes the safetyman who fielded the punt would simply punt it back. That's right, he'd just catch the ball and give it a boot right back. Not even down it or return it and run a play before punting. Just punt the thing right back where it came from. That was legal.[13]

The ball was fatter and harder to throw, and the rules also discouraged the passing game. Passes had to be thrown from at least five yards behind the line of scrimmage. Incompletions in the end zone were considered touchbacks that gave the opposing team the ball. Alexander further recalled,

> The rules in the 20s provided for a five-yard penalty if you threw two consecutive incompletions. If you threw a pass that was incomplete out of bounds, it was the other team's ball where it went out. If an ineligible receiver caught a pass—I guess I should say forward pass, because in those days they were always termed forward passes—the ball was given over to the defense at the spot where it was caught.[14]

These factors created a slow, low-scoring, ground-and-pound pro product. In the decade of the 1920s, the average points-per-game ranged from a low of 7.6 in 1926, to a high of 10.4 in 1924. Fifty-seven NFL games in the 1920s ended in 0–0 ties. That's 7.2 percent of the decade's contests producing *zero* points. Although the college game was played according to the same rulebook, such factors as more professional coaching and more practice time to hone the offensive attack resulted in a much lower 2.4 percent of games ending 0–0. From my tabulations, the low scoring continued into the 1930s with the average points-per-game for pro teams running 10.6, 9.9, and 8.2 from 1930 to 1932, respectively. It was time for a change; it was time to break away from the college rule-book.

On the one hand, NFL president Joe Carr defended his league in 1932:

> The crowd goes to a football game for the thrills, and the pros are giving the customers as many sensational plays as the college gridders. In a college game, you see stars in two or three positions on the team, while in a professional contest, every man needs to be a star to retain his place on the team. This is why pro football is a more finished product than the amateur sport. [15]

On the other, he admitted,

> We are primarily interested in developing a spectacular scoring game. We haven't the pageantry that goes with college games, so as a substitute we must offer wide open play, with frequent scoring. Then, too, we are not committed to throwing a tight wall of protection around our players. They are more mature, more experienced than collegians and thus are better able to protect themselves. [16]

The 1932 NFL season provided the impetus of change. It ended with the Bears and Spartans tied for first, with 6–1–6 and 6–1–4 records, respectively (each a .857 winning percentage), and the Packers trailing them with a 10–3–1 record (a .769 winning percentage). Ties didn't count then in figuring the winning percentage. According to today's rules of a tie counting .5 win and .5 loss, the Bears would have been at .692 and the Spartans at .727. The Packers, at .750, would have won their fourth consecutive NFL title, with the Spartans second and the Bears third. To break the tie in the actual standings, however, the Bears and Spartans agreed to have a playoff to determine the champion. Although that game would count in the regular-season standings, it really was the first post-season playoff game in league history.

Because of a snowstorm, the game was played indoors at Chicago Stadium, a venue that only allowed a field 60 yards long and 45 yards wide (rather than 100 by 55 of the standard football gridiron). A number of accommodations to the rules were instituted because of this. Most notable was the creation of hashmarks, 10 yards in from the sidelines, to place the ball after wide plays. The game was won on a touchdown pass from Bronko Nagurski to Red Grange in the fourth quarter, although the

Spartans bitterly contested the legality of the play because they contended that Nagurski was not the required five yards behind the line when he threw the ball.

Besides providing an exciting winner-take-all conclusion to the season, which the league decided to continue by dividing into two divisions for the upcoming campaign, four other major changes were instituted. Three of those changes were derived directly from that same playoff game. First, hashmarks, or inbounds lines, were established 10 yards from the sidelines; second, passes were permitted anywhere behind the line of scrimmage; and third, the goalposts were moved from the end line to the goal line. Coupled with the official NFL ball being slimmed more than an inch to make it easier to throw, the pro game finally began to open up and reach the public.

Not everyone agreed with the changes. Ed Pollock, sports editor of the *Philadelphia Public Ledger*, lamented in 1933,

> The decision of the pros to break away from the college game is in my opinion the worst mistake the league has made since the outlawed practice of raiding college squads for material. Football is distinctly a college game. The collegians get the crowds and have the better opportunity to educate the spectators to their rules. Disagreements in the professional code will merely lead to louder outcries against the lawmakers and the officials who must enforce the rules. It makes no difference whether the changes made by the professionals are good or poor. For the sake of uniformity, understanding, and progress they should not have been made.[17]

But scoring average would increase to 15.4 by the end of the 1930s and then to 22.5 by the end of the 1940s. After slowly gaining a foothold in the 1920s, pro football began to climb in the 1930s and 1940s before scrambling past the college game in the 1950s and Major League Baseball in the 1960s to become the leading sport in the nation for the past 50 years. In the early growth period from 1920 to 1950, the role and bearing of the pro football coach evolved, and these coaches, in turn, developed the game itself. Slowly, pro football coaches began to draw the same respect previously only accorded their college brethren.

The college game remains immensely popular today but trails the NFL in power and influence. There are clear differences. The college game is a training ground for the pros; its athletes aspire to reach the top level, the

NFL, but most will not. And that is true for coaches as well. Rare is the coach who succeeds in both pro and college football, as Jimmy Johnson, Pete Carroll, and Jim Harbaugh have. The differences in the players and the style of play often derail a coach going from one to the other. Nick Saban struggled in the pros, it seemed, because his authoritarian style did not mesh with pro athletes. Chip Kelly failed in the pros because his flashy college offense was defensed within a year or so in the pros. Bruce Arians and Dennis Green, meanwhile, struggled with the recruiting requirements in the colleges but had success in the pro game.

By the 1950s, the pro football coach had emerged from the persistent shadow cast by the popular image of the college coach to be his own man; the men profiled in this volume invented, so to speak, the modern pro football coach.

The first to make a name for himself as a pro coach, ironically, has been largely forgotten today: Guy Chamberlin (58–16–7, with four NFL championships). Chamberlin played end for the 1921 champion Chicago Staleys under George Halas and Dutch Sternaman before signing with the Canton Bulldogs as player-coach in 1922. The Bulldogs won the NFL title in both 1922 and 1923, then were sold, resurfaced as the Cleveland Bulldogs in 1924, and won a third straight championship. Chamberlin then moved on to Philadelphia's Frankford Yellow Jackets and, in his second season as player-coach, won his fifth title in six seasons, fourth as a coach. After one more season as the player-coach for the Chicago Cardinals in 1927, Chamberlin left football for good. Although elected to the Pro Football Hall of Fame in 1965, he is unknown to contemporary football fans.

Earl "Curly" Lambeau (226–132–22, with six NFL championships) began his 29-year career as a player and coach with his hometown Green Bay Packers, a team he helped found, and was the earliest proponent of the passing game in the league. Throughout his lengthy tenure as the team's coach, his offense almost always featured a star passer and deep threat receiver, even as the game began to pass him by in the late 1940s. LeRoy Andrew (51–27–4) coached the league's first great passer, Benny Friedman, in three different cities—Cleveland, Detroit, and New York— and battled the Packers for league supremacy at the close of the NFL's first decade.

Chicago Bears co-owners and cocoaches George Halas (318–148–31, with six NFL championships) and Ed "Dutch" Sternaman learned the game's oldest formation, the T, from their college coach, Bob Zuppke of Illinois, and were one of few NFL teams to use it in the 1920s, although they also used the single wing. When a rift developed and deepened between Halas and Sternaman, they agreed to bring in Ralph Jones (24–10–7) as coach in 1930. Jones had coached the two in basketball and freshman football at Illinois. He developed the man-in-motion and other changes to open up the T formation and won a championship before Halas, now sole owner, reclaimed the coaching slot in 1933.

The quarterback of the Fighting Illini when Halas was a freshman was George "Potsy" Clark (64–42–12, with one NFL championship). Clark was a sharp operator who fashioned a 40-year career in coaching and administration at both the college and pro levels. His greatest success came coaching the Portsmouth Spartans/Detroit Lions in the 1930s. Clark was a frequent author on football and wrote the first book by a pro coach on the pro game in 1935.

Former NFL tackle Steve Owen (151–100–17, with two NFL championships) took over the New York Giants in 1931, lasting 23 years as the team's coach. Playing in New York, he was lauded in the press for his stratagems and known as the best defensive coach in the game. He liked a low-scoring affair, and his teams consistently featured a quality kicking game.

Ray Flaherty (80–37–5, with two NFL championships) was a three-time All-Pro end who spent his final five years as a player on Owen's Giants and the last three as the team captain and an assistant coach. He retired as a player in 1936, and immediately was hired as coach of the Redskins. He ran the single wing and was noted for his unique substitution patterns in the one-platoon game. Flaherty continued to run the single wing exclusively through the end of the 1940s, when only one other pro team was still running that offense. His successful coaching career ended abruptly in 1950, because no one was looking for someone coaching an outdated offense.

Another single wing proponent, dour Jock Sutherland (28–16–1), had led multiple Pitt Panthers teams to national championships before becoming the most successful college coach to move to the pros in 1940. The hiring of the renowned Sutherland by first the Brooklyn Dodgers and later the Pittsburgh Steelers was benchmark in the rising status of the pro coach, and his double team blocking schemes were a leading feature of Vince Lombardi's power sweep in the 1960s.

With the changes to the old-style T instituted by Ralph Jones at the beginning of the 1930s growing stale, Halas, Jones, and Clark Shaughnessy (14–7–3) turbo-powered the offense at the end of that decade. In 1940, the Bears went all in and started using the modern T formation exclusively and subsequently won four NFL titles in seven years. Shaughnessy took the T to Stanford and transformed a 1–7–1 team to Rose Bowl winners in one year in 1940. The trio then feverishly promoted the offense to both the pros and colleges throughout the 1940s, and the T has been the standard offense ever since, although with many variations.

Halas's rival coach of the Chicago Cardinals, Jimmy Conzelman (87–63–17, with two NFL championships), who had once won a NFL title with the Providence Steam Roller in 1928, was an early convert to the T. He was a renaissance man of many interests and talents with a sunny personality unlike most coaches. Jimmy made his mark in the late 1940s, winning a second NFL championship 19 years after his first, before suddenly retiring in 1949, as an early victim of coaching burnout.

Greasy Neale (63–43–5, with two NFL championships) took over the Eagles in 1941, and was the earliest convert to the T. He borrowed the films of the Bears 73–0 1940 championship game win against the Redskins and copied the Bears' offense for Philadelphia. He also developed an effective defense to counter the T with his 5–2–4 Eagle defense, which also would spread through the league, as his Eagles would conclude the 1940s with consecutive shutout victories in the NFL title games of 1948 and 1949.

I selected these coaches for their general impact on the pro game, but it is interesting that this group won nine of the first 12 league championships. Furthermore, beginning with the 1932 de facto title game, there were 18 NFL postseason championship games from 1932 to 1949, as well as three other postseason conference playoffs (1941, 1943, and 1947). Of these 21 games, 18 featured a pair of these coaches matching wits, and two other contests included one of them on the sideline (counting the 1942 and 1943 title games coached by Halas's assistants while he was in the U.S. Navy). The only postseason game in which none of these coaches took part was the 1945 championship, which pitted Adam Walsh's Rams against Dudley DeGroot's Redskins, and was the first NFL championship that featured both teams running the T formation.

Both of these men only spent two seasons coaching NFL football, however.

One other coach is included regrettably as an afterword. Despite a brief NFL coaching resume, star signal caller Fritz Pollard for decades served as a beacon for African American coaching aspirants. He only spent parts of four seasons as a pro head coach, but he had a full career outside the NFL. Although Pollard lived to 92, he did not survive long enough to see the second black NFL coach, Art Shell, take the reins with the Raiders three years later in 1989. Since then, the employment market for black coaches has improved markedly.

As a group, these coaches paved the way for the first, and possibly still the greatest, modern pro football coach, Paul Brown (213–104–9, with seven professional championships), to materialize in the postwar era. Fittingly, Brown began his career in the rival All-America Football Conference in 1946, and faced off in the first two AAFC title matches against the only NFL coach to defect to the new league—single wing devotee Ray Flaherty. Once the two-platoon era began in 1950, the pro game rose to new heights, and several coaches led the way as the game grew to a colossus. From Brown, Buddy Parker, and Sid Gillman to Vince Lombardi and Tom Landry to Don Shula and Chuck Noll to Bill Walsh and Joe Gibbs to Jimmy Johnson and Bill Belichick, coaching giants continue to push the pro game forward. The mansion they have built, renovated, and expanded, however, was constructed on the foundation laid by the coaches profiled in this book.

I

PLAYER-COACH

Guy Chamberlin Shows the Way

George Halas might seem the logical starting point in any sort of historical treatment of the National Football League; he was a dominant, driving force in the league from its founding meeting in 1920 until his death in 1983. Halas played end for nine years and was named to the NFL's All-Decade team for the 1920s. He coached his team for 40 years and won a record six NFL titles. Above all, he owned and operated his franchise for more than 60 years, outlasting his original contemporaries by decades.

Papa Bear was indeed the patriarch of the NFL, but for the story of pro football coaches, we start with one of his players on the original Decatur/ Chicago Staleys, which became the Chicago Bears in 1922—Guy Chamberlin. Chamberlin played the end opposite Halas on the Staley line in 1920 and 1921, and George later said of losing him, "Over 30 years of coaching, I've made my share of mistakes, but one of the biggest was my failure to sign Chamberlin again for the 1922 season."[1]

We start with Chamberlin because he embodies his era, the very beginning of the NFL, in several ways. First, he used the prevailing offense of the time, the single wing, but made it his own and was very successful against like competitors. Halas, by contrast, went his own way with the T formation, which we explore in chapter 3. Second, the success he had in a short time frame has never been equaled in the almost 100 years of league history. Chamberlin, or "Champ" as he came to be known, coached four league championship teams in five years, including three consecutively.

And he did so with three different franchises. While Curly Lambeau and Vince Lombardi both won three consecutive titles, neither coach was able to win a fourth within another season, and both won those titles for just one franchise.

Finally, he was a player-coach, the standard operating model of the period. He expertly melded two distinct functions for his team to lead it to triumph. Having first won a championship playing under Halas, his record as a player was even more impressive in that he played on four consecutive champions and five in six years. As pointed out in the introduction, player-coaches were the norm in the 1920s, with 74 percent of teams using them in the decade. As the league matured and the game diversified and became more complicated, that percentage dropped to 25 in the 1930s and zero ever since. Of the coaches in this book, five were player-coaches in the 1920s. Halas, Lambeau, LeRoy Andrew, and Jimmy Conzelman excelled, but Guy Chamberlin was the best of them.

LIFE AND CAREER

Berlin Guy Chamberlin was born on a family farm outside of Blue Springs in Gage County, Nebraska, on January 16, 1894. His father, Elmer, had moved from Salem, New York, in 1885, with his four brothers, to work the rich land of the Midwest. At some point, either Elmer or his father, William, shortened their surname of "Chamberlain" to "Chamberlin" so to better fit on grain bags and help the family business. Guy's mother, the former Anna Tobyne, whose family came to Nebraska from Illinois via covered wagon, named her third son after the old-world city to celebrate her German heritage, but the boy was always known simply as "Guy."[2] Anna inherited her family's farm, and Elmer kept adding land until it reached almost 1,000 acres.[3]

Chamberlin had two older brothers, Warren and William, a younger brother, Truman, and twin younger sisters, Frances and Ramona. Guy grew up doing his farm chores and driving a buggy to school with his brother Bill, but the small local high school did not field a football team. Instead, he told reporter Wally Provost years later, "Neither Blue Springs nor Wymore had high school teams, but we'd play choose-up at a park on the edge of Wymore." He added,

We wore plow shoes and overalls. Occasionally somebody would scrounge around and find an old pair of football pants. There would be a few helmets, but mostly we were bareheaded. One year, mother sewed some pieces of padding into the elbows and around the shoulders of an old sweater. We were a nondescript outfit. When you got into college from a small town like I did, and got some half-decent shoes and equipment, you were so proud you played all the harder.[4]

Guy's brother Bill enrolled at Nebraska Wesleyan when Guy was a senior in high school and made the school's football team, which sparked Guy's interest. A year later (1911), 17-year-old Guy enrolled at Wesleyan, although Bill had transferred to the University of Nebraska by then. At Wesleyan, Guy became a multisport star, competing in track and field and baseball, as well as football. Chamberlin played end and halfback under coach Bill Kline. Kline, who later wrote a mail order instructional on how to play football, was a former sprinter at the University of Illinois and taught Chamberlin to run more erect and lift his knees higher, which improved his speed. As a freshman, Guy received All-State notice after Wesleyan's undefeated season and attracted interest from University of Nebraska coach Ewald "Jumbo" Stiehm; however, Guy continued at Wesleyan in 1912, and had another impressive season, although the team did lose twice. He then transferred to Nebraska in 1913.[5]

As a transfer student, Chamberlin had to sit out one season, but he practiced with the Cornhusker freshman squad against the varsity. Originally taunted by upperclassmen as "that star from Wesleyan," Guy's rugged play in practice won over the varsity, and he moved seamlessly onto the squad in 1914. That year, he scored nine touchdowns and led Nebraska to 7–0–1 record. Stiehm was a hulking former lineman from Wisconsin, but his offense relied more on speed, quickness, and deception, featuring highly choreographed plays that depended on precise timing. As a senior in 1915, Chamberlin upped his scoring to 15 touchdowns, earning him consensus All-America honors, and the team achieved a perfect 8–0 record.[6]

In his posthumously published autobiography, legendary coach Knute Rockne recalled his first encounter with Chamberlin in 1915. Rockne was then an assistant at Notre Dame under Head Coach Jess Harper and scouted Nebraska before a showdown between the Fighting Irish and the Cornhuskers. Rockne reported back two keys for his players to watch: Chamberlin never cut back on his runs, and he always licked his fingers first if he was going to pass the ball. In the game, however, Chamberlain scored twice on cutback runs and tallied the third and winning score in the 20–19 game by tossing a touchdown pass without first licking his fingers. Harper forgave Rockne, saying, "That fellow's a demon, strong as a dozen men and fast as a sprinter. When those long legs start to pound, you might know what's comin' but it don't do any good."[7]

Chamberlin received his B.A. in political economy in June 1916. He signed a baseball contract with Wichita of the Western League in March but was cut in April. Pro football was not a serious option at that point, so Chamberlin accepted a coaching position at Doane College in Crete, Nebraska, for the fall. The following autumn, he coached a high school in Lexington, Nebraska. In May 1918, with the United States having entered World War I, he enlisted in the U.S. Army and was commissioned a second lieutenant. He was teaching artillery to cavalry units at Camp Kearny, California, when the war ended on November 11, 1918, and then stayed on as the camp's athletic director until September 1919.[8]

In the meantime, he married Lucille Lees on January 3, 1919. Lees had graduated from Nebraska a year after Chamberlin. Her father, James Thomas Lees, was a noted Greek scholar who also served as department head and provost at Nebraska. Guy and Lucille would later divorce but had an accomplished daughter, Patricia, who graduated from Nebraska and won a scholarship to Columbia's prestigious journalism school in 1945.[9]

The decision to leave the army in 1919 was prompted by Jim Thorpe recruiting Chamberlin to join the Canton Bulldogs, one of the top professional football teams in the country. The Bulldogs had won at least a share of the informal Ohio League championship in 1915, 1916, and 1917, before most teams disbanded for World War I in 1918. With the end of the war, the Bulldogs reformed, stronger than ever. Before he signed, however, Chamberlin wired team owner Ralph Hay to say he had a higher offer from another team, and Hay upped the ante to bring Guy to Canton. The speedy, solidly built, 6-foot-2, 200-pound Chamberlin joined a backfield that included the aging Thorpe, Joe Guyon, Pete Calac, and Cecil "Tex" Grigg. Guy often took Thorpe's place when Jim needed a rest, and he remembered Thorpe as the greatest player he ever saw. As a coach, Guy recalled, "He was bright, and he could coach a football team. I won't say he was the smartest I ever saw, but his plays were credible and he could work his backs and linemen well."[10]

The 1919 Canton Bulldogs went 9–0–1, featuring two victories over the Massillon Tigers—their traditional rivals, and won another Ohio League title. It was Chamberlin's first taste of winning as a pro. The following August, several football moguls gathered in the Hupmobile showroom of Bulldogs owner Ralph Hay and formed the American Professional Football League, which would be renamed the National Football League two years later. The Bulldogs wanted to retain Chamberlin, who was living in town and playing semipro baseball for the Canton Noakers after having played basketball with the local Knights of Columbus that winter; however, players were free agents in that era, and Guy received a better offer from George Halas to join the fledgling Decatur Staleys. He took a job at the Staley starch works in Decatur and joined the company football team.

In Decatur, Chamberlin encountered a higher level of commitment. He later recalled,

> With Canton in 1919, the players would start gathering on Saturday night. We'd have our only full-squad practice the morning of the game—usually Sunday at 10 o'clock or whenever the last fellow got in. Invariably, the play was ragged. There just was no opportunity to develop precise teamwork. George Halas was the first man to really organize a team. [11]

With the Staleys, Guy's string of success continued. The team finished in second place in 1920, with a 10–1–2 record, and won the league title in 1921 by going 9–1–1. On the Staleys, Chamberlin held down right end, with Halas at left end, and won All-League notice in his first year. A rivalry naturally developed between the two, not only on the gridiron, but also at company picnics when the two would compete in races and other events. Chamberlin downplayed it, saying, "There was a little jealousy in the background, but neither one of us would let it show." But in July, the *Akron Beacon Journal* reported that Hay was considering Bill Steers, University of Oregon All-America, and Chamberlin for the Bulldogs' coaching slot. In August, Hay offered Guy the job of player-coach, and he jumped at the chance to take charge of his own team. Reportedly, Chamberlin was paid $2,500 per season in Canton, but he recalled, "The program concession was part of the pay, and I made about as much out of that as I did the regular salary." [12]

Chamberlin worked with the owner to rebuild the team, keeping only seven players from the 1921 squad that had finished 5–2–3 and bringing in 15 new players, one of which was Guy himself. Canton kept four core starters—tackle Pete Henry, guard Duke Osborn, end Bird Carroll, and back Harry Robb—but brought in seven new ones, and the Bulldogs won the NFL title with a 10–0–2 record. The strength of the team was the line, led by two Hall of Fame tackles in Fats Henry and Link Lyman, and two talented guards in Osborn and Tarzan Taylor. Describing his tackles, Guy once said,

> Lyman stood 6-foot-2 and weighed about 257. When he hit you, he hit you for good, and he didn't care who you were. Henry was shorter: weighed 245. He was very active in the line and was one of the finest punters of all time. A lot of people said they were responsible for our success . . . and they were about right. [13]

The 1922 Bulldogs scored 184 points and gave up just 15. They did not allow a touchdown until the fifth game of the year, against the Bears, and it was another six weeks until they gave up another. Chamberlin himself was providing heroics from both sides of the ball throughout the year and was celebrated regularly for his kick coverage excellence. Reading through the game stories in the local newspapers gives a flavor of Chamberlin's impact. He had a 10-yard end-around rush against Thorpe's Oorang Indians in week three. The Bulldogs held Akron to zero first downs in week four, and Guy was singled out for his defensive brilliance that day, including a forced fumble/fumble recovery that led to a Bulldog field goal. The following week against the Bears, the reporter noted that Chamberlin was triple-blocked on the lone Bears touchdown, demonstrating his importance on defense.

The next week, the Bulldogs were held to a 0–0 tie by the Toledo Maroons, partly due to quarterback Wooky Roberts being knocked "batty" by a kick in the head: "He kept calling signals which are not in the code, but neither Chamberlin nor the other Bulldogs realized why until they assembled in the dressing room after the tussle. Roberts still had mice in the garrett." [14] In a rough battle with the Buffalo All-Americans two weeks later, Guy had a 16-yard run that set up the only score of the 3–0 victory. Late in the fourth quarter, he ran down Buffalo receiver Luke Urban from behind after a 68-yard pass play and then led the ensuing goal-line stand to clinch the game. In a showdown with the 6–1 Chicago

Cardinals, the Bulldogs trailed 3–0 going into the fourth quarter, when Chamberlin took command. He blocked a punt to lead to the first touchdown, intercepted a Cardinals pass and returned it 19 yards for the second touchdown, and then intercepted a second pass and returned it 18 yards for the final touchdown. Three touchdowns in four minutes was shocking for the low-scoring era. The next week, he blocked another punt against Akron, recovered it, and scored. In a 40–6 beating of the Milwaukee Badgers, Chamberlin scored two touchdowns rushing, one of which was set up by his 50-yard pass reception. In the season finale against Toledo, his 50-yard reception led to one score, and he caught his own touchdown pass later in the game.

For the season, he has been credited unofficially with 10 receptions for 258 yards, 18 rushes for 160, 5 interceptions, and 7 touchdowns scored.[15] It was a remarkable performance for both Chamberlin and the team. The Bulldogs' finances were not so healthy, however. Attendance was insufficient to cover expenses, and Hays sold the team to a consortium of Canton businessmen, ending his successful five-year tenure as owner.

Under new management, Chamberlin was still in charge on the field and set about to improve the unbeaten defending champions in 1923. Eight of the 20 Bulldogs that season were new to the team. Two, guard Rudy Comstock and center Larry Conover, moved in as starters and made the Canton line, offensively and defensively, even stronger. As such, the team posted another undefeated season of 11–0–1 and outscored their opponents, 246–19. They allowed just one touchdown the entire season.

Again, Chamberlin led his team with big plays throughout the year. In the opener against the Hammond Pros, he blocked a punt and caught a pass for a 30-yard gain. The next week against the Louisville Brecks, he caught a 44-yard touchdown pass. In week three, he intercepted a pass as the Bulldogs held the Dayton Triangles to a single pass completion for the game. In week four, the Bulldogs posted their fourth consecutive shutout, beating the Bears, 6–0, on two fourth-quarter field goals.

The Akron Pros were the first team to score on Canton but lost, 7–3, as Chamberlin blocked a field goal, forced a fumble, and had three tackles for loss, including one of Dutch Hendrian for minus-five yards on a fourth and goal in the fourth quarter. The following week, the Cardinals managed a field goal but lost to Canton, 7–3, with a Chamberlin 45-yard pass reception leading to the game's only touchdown.

Against Buffalo on a muddy field, Canton allowed just three first downs but trailed, 3–0, until Guy blocked a punt in the game's final minute to set up the tying dropkick field goal in the closing seconds. He later recalled, "We called timeout, got down on our knees, and pawed a six-foot circle about six to eight inches deep, down to dry ground. We wiped off Fats Henry's shoe, and he kicked the tying field goal."[16] The Oorang Indians came to town the next week to give the Bulldogs a breather. Guy caught one touchdown pass, and his 28-yard reception led to another in a 41–0 laugher. The following week, Canton traveled to nearby Cleveland to pound the Indians, 46–10, giving up their only touchdown of the year and impressing Cleveland owner Sam Deutsch.

Canton finished their 1923 season with three consecutive shutouts: 28–0 against Toledo, 14–0 against Buffalo, and 10–0 against Columbus. The rematch with Buffalo was interesting for three reasons. First, newspaper accounts noted that the Bulldogs were forced to huddle on offense because the All-Americans knew their signals, indicating the rarity of the practice of huddling at the time. Normally, the plays were called at the line of scrimmage. Second, Chamberlin's 40-yard reception set up the second touchdown, and he also recorded a sack in the game. Finally, Guy injured his leg and missed the finale against Columbus a week later.

While the Bulldogs finished their December on the East Coast with exhibition wins against Frankford and the Melrose Athletic Club, the financial picture had not improved from the previous season. Chamberlin represented the Bulldogs at the league meetings in January and June, but in August, Sam Deutsch, a Cleveland sports promoter and, as noted earlier, owner of that city's Indians franchise, purchased the Bulldogs with the intention of restocking his Cleveland team with the top players from Canton. Although there was a public outcry from Cantonians, the league approved the deal. Deutsch offered to sell the deboned Bulldog franchise back to Canton interests, but there were no takers. So, for the 1924 season, Deutsch owned two NFL franchises. He operated the Cleveland one with a transfusion of Bulldogs players, let the Canton franchise sit vacant, changed the Cleveland franchise name to Bulldogs, and hired Chamberlin to manage it.[17]

Of the 21 men who appeared with the Cleveland Bulldogs in 1924, eight came from Canton, four were former Indians, and nine were new imports. Six of the primary starters were from Canton, one came from

Cleveland, and four were new—most notably rookie tailback Hoge Workman from Ohio State.

Despite losing tackle Pete Henry, center Larry Conover, and back Harry Robb to the independent Pottsville Maroons, the Bulldogs were still formidable but no longer invincible. Chamberlin guided the team to a 7–1–1 record, good enough for a third straight Bulldog league crown, while outscoring opponents by 229 to 60; however, allowing 60 points in nine games, up from 34 in the 23 games from the two prior seasons, indicates a decline in dominance.

Cleveland's opening day 16–14 triumph against the Bears, the third straight victory for Chamberlin against Halas, was the only time the Bulldogs beat a winning team throughout the year. In week two, they held the Frankford Yellow Jackets to a 3–3 tie and then bested four straight losing teams: Akron, 29–14; Rochester, 59–0; Dayton, 35–0; and Akron again, 20–7.

Frankford next came to Cleveland for a rematch and handed Chamberlin his first loss as a coach, and his first as a player since he played for the champion Staleys in 1921. Frankford won, 12–7, and opened up the race for the NFL title. Cleveland then beat Columbus, 7–0; hosted Milwaukee on Thanksgiving in Canton; and won easily, 53–10, and cancelled their final scheduled game on November 30, against Buffalo, due to a blizzard. At that point, the NFL season officially ended with the Bulldogs holding an .875 winning percentage, better than the 6–1–4 Bears, at .857, and the 11–2–1 Yellow Jackets, at .846.

However, the third championship was thrown into doubt when the Bulldogs agreed to travel to Wrigley Field to play the Bears again on December 7. In a lackluster performance, Cleveland was upended, 23–0, and Halas claimed the NFL title as the Bears' property. The problem with that claim was that the game was a postseason exhibition not sanctioned by the league; so, at the league meeting in January, Cleveland was officially crowned the champion.[18]

Chamberlin related an interesting coda to the story many years later when he told the *Omaha World-Herald* that Deutsch wanted to cancel the game because bad weather would make the take from the gate too small to pay for the trip. Chamberlin claimed that he called the players together and told them if they would take the risk of paying their own way, they would split the receipts among themselves. Game day turned out to be sunny, and a good crowd was on hand. Guy left the game early to claim the Bulldogs' take and was given $12,000 in cash. He was escorted back to his hotel in a Brinks truck and divvied up roughly $900 to each of the players who made the trip. When he returned to Cleveland, Deutsch asked for his cut, but Chamberlin shut him out, saying, "He cried on my shoulder: 'You can't do this to me.' We did though."[19] Guy knew his way around a dollar.

Deutsch sold the dormant Canton franchise back to Canton interests in 1925 and held on to a depleted Cleveland franchise, as Guy moved on to take over the third-place Frankford Yellow Jackets that season. He arrived in September and said of his players, "They'll all have to fight for their jobs, and that includes me."[20]

Chamberlin brought just three Bulldogs (tackle Link Lyman and backs Lou Smyth and Ben Jones) with him to Frankford, but he added 21 new faces to the seven holdovers from the successful 1924 team. Unfortunately, Guy's first Frankford team took a step backward, dropping to sixth in the league, with a 13–7 record, and only outscoring the opposition by 190 to 169. The team started the season 9–1 and only gave up 30 points in those first 10 games, but Chamberlin broke his shoulder blade in that 10th game against Akron. He missed the next several weeks before returning late in the year, and the team's performance suffered. The season was also marred by Chamberlin suspending star tackle Bull Behman in December for indifferent play.[21]

After the season, Chamberlin also inserted himself into the controversy swirling about Red Grange, who had joined the Bears to finish their season and continued on a lucrative postseason barnstorming tour as soon as his college eligibility expired. Guy was quoted in the *Canton Daily News* on December 21 as saying,

> The day that the famous Illinois star stepped in the professional field is one that will be regretted a long time by followers of the commercial game. Grange broke down morally and physically because more was asked of him than any human being could perform. The pro players on other teams were affected by the Grange splurge, and the public is disillusioned.[22]

A day later, however, the *Canton Repository* reported that Guy and Link Lyman were heading south to join Grange and the Bears for the tour. So much for disillusion.[23]

Healthy again in 1926, the 32-year-old Chamberlin appeared in all 17 games for the Yellow Jackets and led the team to 14–1–2 record and his fourth championship as a coach. The offense improved to first in the league with 236 points and the defense to second, allowing just 49. Chamberlin brought in two more former Bulldogs (guard Rudy Comstock and back Wooky Roberts) but lost Link Lyman to the Bears. He also brought in 13 new men to augment the 12 players who carried over from 1925.

Frankford tied the Akron Indians on opening day and then won six straight games by shutout before losing to the Providence Steam Roller, 7–6, on Saturday, October 30. They then beat the Steam Roller, 6–3, on Sunday, the following day, in Providence, illustrating why the Philadelphia outfit played so many games. Pennsylvania "blue laws" did not allow sports contests on Sundays, so the Yellow Jackets often played a home game on Saturday and an away game with the same team the next day. The Yellow Jackets did not lose again in 1926, beating the Bears, 7–6, on Saturday, December 4. Chamberlin blocked both a field goal and an extra point in that game, defeating Halas again and essentially delivering the championship to Frankford. The Jackets finished the season by shutting out the Steamroller, 24–0, on December 11, and tying a rugged Pottsville squad at zero on December 18.

Despite winning a fourth title in five years and building a strong roster, Chamberlin was not retained by the Frankford management in 1927, and no definitive reason was ever given. The main presumption is that Guy wanted more money than Frankford was willing to pay; he had proved to be a stiff negotiator throughout his career. But the Chicago Cardinals team that had signed him was not particularly flush with cash at that point, so money may not have been the only factor.

The *Philadelphia Inquirer* reported that all was not well at the team's postseason celebration dinner. Chamberlin was said to be upset with how he had been treated by management and the fans, and by how one of his men, Wooky Roberts, had been released without Guy's consent. The story noted that Chamberlin and his players were dissatisfied with their salaries as well.[24] An editorial in the *Frankford Yellow Jacket News* for April 1927 hinted at management's discontent: "There were times and conditions continually arising during the past season when the humiliation and sacrifice and closing our eyes to things that were not exactly nice made us more than once ask one another—WHAT PRICE CHAMPION-

SHIP." The team's directors, who penned the piece, followed up with, "We must have been very tolerant and charitable toward the coach at the close of the 1925 season to choose him to lead our team in 1926. But this is where we learned that an unsuccessful leader in the first year was an entirely different proposition to a successful leader in the following year."[25]

Nonetheless, Chamberlin moved on to the Cardinals and tried to remake that squad by bringing in four former Frankford players and 10 newcomers to join 11 Chicago holdovers. This time the magic was gone. The team limped to a 2–6–1 start before team owner Chris O'Brien pulled the plug on Guy prior to the Thanksgiving game against the crosstown Bears.[26] The 33-year-old Chamberlin appeared in six games for the Cardinals but was no longer a starter.

Chamberlin never coached in the NFL again. He worked as a salesman in Cleveland for the next four years and even played for and coached the semipro Cleveland Collegians in 1928. Cleveland finished their season playing the Canton semipro entry at Lakeside Park in Canton, and Guy remarked, "I'm especially glad to play my last game right here where I started my professional career. You don't know how proud I was of those old Bulldogs, and it was my connection with them that caused me to play my farewell game here."[27]

Years later, Guy told the *Canton Repository*, "I had a chance to go into college coaching. Colgate approached me, but I didn't want to take on additional worries."[28] In 1932, he returned to the family farm in Nebraska and worked it until 1948, when he finally sold the property. Throughout his post-pro football career, he sometimes was mentioned as a possible head coach for his alma mater and expressed interest in that possibility, but nothing ever came of it. His niece remembers Chamberlin returning to the farm in 1932, down and out, depressed and drinking, before he eventually regained his footing on the farm. Guy married his second wife, Bernyce Weeks, on June 12, 1941. From 1948 to 1953, he ran a Ford farm implement business in Nebraska City, but after he developed heart trouble, he took a position in Lincoln as the agricultural supervisor at the state reformatory in 1954. Guy retired from there in 1964, at the age of 70.[29]

In his later years, he was elected to the Helms Foundation Hall of Fame in 1962, and to the Pro Football Hall of Fame in 1965, before he passed away on April 4, 1967, in a Lincoln hospital. Posthumously, the

University of Nebraska created the Guy Chamberlin Trophy in 1967, to honor annually the senior football player who best exhibits the "qualities and dedication of Guy Chamberlin to the Cornhusker tradition."[30] In an interview after being elected to the Pro Football Hall, Chamberlin maintained,

> Several of these games we won . . . either we got a break or at a critical moment, one of our plays proved a success that gave us those winning points. Well now, I had won so much of the time, I felt so sorry for those losing teams—who were really as good as we were, but we were a little more fortunate—that I never was one to gloat over winning too much because I felt you're lucky. You're very fortunate to go that far so long.[31]

COACHING KEYS

So what did Guy Chamberlin contribute to the coaching profession? Years later, he recalled accepting his first coaching assignment with Canton in 1922, stating,

> As soon as I'd said yes, I asked myself, "What business have I got coaching?" I thought back over my career . . . back to Wesleyan and Coach Kline, to Nebraska and Coach Stiehm, to Thorpe and Halas. I took the best I knew from every source. I evolved a style of play no one team ever had used before. But at the same time, it was football that everybody used.[32]

From Kline, he acquired the value of conditioning and training; from Stiehm, he learned to employ deception and precision; from Thorpe, he discovered the importance of leading by example; and from Halas, he learned to stress organization.

Above all, Chamberlin's teams relied on physical conditioning, rigorous practice, and exacting teamwork. Cleveland Bulldogs guard Ralph Vince recalled, "Before Chamberlin came to Cleveland, we just met on Sunday afternoon, ate lunch, and played the game. He made us start practicing every day." As such, one rule that Guy instituted upon taking the position in Canton was that every team member must reside in town during the season so they could attend daily practice.[33]

At his first training camp with the Bulldogs, Chamberlin started the team "throwing and catching forward passes, falling on the ball, punting and sprinting, winding up the work by circling the field." The second week commenced with "signals and formations." He also introduced a "charging and pushing machine, another innovation of the professionals here."[34]

Presumably, that charging machine was a blocking sled, and a few days later, the team was reported to be drilling with a tackling dummy.[35] Three years later, when he took over in Frankford, the *Philadelphia Evening Bulletin* reported,

> Several innovations at the Yellow Jacket training base, including the installation of tackling dummies and the construction of a new charging machine, built after specifications planned by him [Chamberlin]. The new mentor will make excellent use of the cinder track, as he is a firm believer in track work as a conditioner for football players.[36]

Three-and-a-half-hour practice sessions were not unheard of for Chamberlin squads, and in the case of rain, the team might have a two-hour blackboard drill instead.[37]

Former Canton guard Duke Osborn remembered of Chamberlin, "As a coach, he was the greatest organizer I ever knew." Yellow Jackets guard Bill Hoffman recalled, "He was a taskmaster like Lombardi. He kept us on the field for hours, even in the bitter cold. We couldn't complain, though, because he was out there practicing with us as a two-way end." Hoffman added, "We became like a family because we lived together, and the people of Frankford supported us because we were their friends and neighbors."[38]

On the field, Chamberlin emphasized the running game, like almost all of his contemporaries. The newspapers of the time called it "straight football," as opposed to the aerial attack. He liked to keep things simple, saying, "When I started to coach pro ball, Andy Smith of California said to me, 'Son, you want 10 or 12 plays. Three or four plays from three or four formations and that's all you can master in one season. The trick is not the play but how well you execute it.'"[39]

Bill Hoffman attested to that with the Yellow Jackets, stating, "We only had a dozen plays. A couple of off-tackle runs and sweeps. Four or five passes, including a screen. A reverse and an end-around. That was it, but we practiced those plays over and over until we could run them in our sleep." While Chamberlin used the standard single wing formation (see figure 1.1), he employed it with a twist. "Guy's guards lined up side by side behind the center, and the quarterback behind them. On signal, the guards went into the line right or left but stayed together. 'This permitted a lot of weak-side plays if the opponent shifted quickly,' he related. 'I never basically changed that at all.'"[40]

Canton tackle Link Lyman recollected,

> We had this play where [Guy] came around on an end-reverse, and sometimes he would get the ball on an end sweep, or we'd fake it to him and hand it to the fullback up the middle. Other times, our full-back Louie Smyth would drop back and hit me on a tackle-eligible play down the field.[41]

A tackle would be eligible to touch the ball if the end on his side lined up on the other side of the line, making the tackle the de facto end. Indeed, Chamberlin liked this wrinkle. In 1922, Fats Henry ran the ball 15 times for 79 yards; in 1923, he and Lyman ran the ball eight times for 37 yards

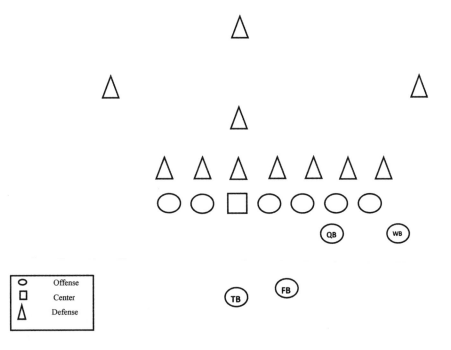

Figure 1.1. Single wing offense and seven-diamond defense

and caught three passes for 109 yards and two scores according to incomplete compiled statistics. Lyman also caught a 50-yard touchdown in 1924.[42]

Chamberlin was not dogmatic about his approach, however. He adopted different game plans for each contest depending on the strengths and weaknesses of his opponent. According to the *Philadelphia Inquirer*, "Against some teams Chamberlin sends his men in to batter their way to victory by straight football. Other opponents, boasting lines that stand out far above the ordinary, have been vanquished by his highly developed forward-pass attack."[43]

PIVOTAL GAMES

Each championship team coached by Guy Chamberlin was followed closely in the standings by the same runner-up, the Chicago Bears, coached by partners George Halas and Dutch Sternaman. In each case, beating the Bears was essential for winning the title.

In 1922, the Bulldogs and Bears met in week five with both teams undefeated. The *Canton Repository* built up the game: "It is doubtful whether any professional game in the last 10 years has seen two such powerful machines collide as will battle at Chicago this afternoon."[44] Emphasis was placed on the weight advantage of the Bears. Despite the Bulldogs featuring a large and powerful line, Chicago's was even bigger. In the game, Canton lost several scoring chances due to questionable calls by the referee, who was a "personal friend and business associate of the Bear captain" (George Halas). The Bulldogs scored in the first quarter following an interception by Tarzan Taylor. A pass reception by Bird Carroll took the ball to the Chicago five, and then Pete Shaw punched it in from there and booted the extra point. In the final period, a couple of long passes by the Bears led to a touchdown run by Joey Sternaman, on which Chamberlin was triple-teamed by Chicago interference; however, a heavy rush caused Sternaman to miss the extra point and preserve the slim 7–6 Bulldogs victory.[45]

A year later, the two teams met in week four, again in Chicago, but this time only Canton was undefeated. Again, the buildup stressed Chicago power versus Canton team play and strong passing and kicking games. The *Canton Repository* also noted the rivalry of Chamberlin and Halas, which they attributed to "acts by Halas that were not fair to the Bulldog chieftain."[46] This time, the Bulldogs outplayed the Bears from start to finish, completely shutting down the Chicago offense. Canton's Fats Henry dropkicked two fourth quarter field goals of 15 and 20 yards to provide the 6–0 margin.

In 1924, Chicago hosted Cleveland in the season opener. Now relying on the passing talents of rookie Hoge Workman, the Bulldogs measured out a 16–14 victory on the strength of a field goal, a rushing touchdown, and another touchdown on a blocked punt. Joey Sternaman scored twice for Chicago—on a pass reception and a 70-yard punt return.

The last significant meeting of Chamberlin and Halas occurred in Philadelphia in 1926. Three weeks before the end of the season, the Bears were in first place, with an 11–0–2 record, while Frankford trailed with a 12–1–3 record. A back-and-forth defensive battle remained scoreless well into the fourth quarter until Chicago's Bill Senn broke free for a 62-yard touchdown run. Guy blocked the extra point to try to keep the score 6–0. He had earlier blocked a field goal attempt as well. Frankford got the ball with five minutes to play and went to the air. Passes from Houston Stockton moved the Yellow Jackets from their own 25 to the Bears 27 with a little more than a minute to go. On fourth-and-three, Stockton dropped back 10 yards to elude the Bears rush and launched the tying score to 5-foot-4 back "Two Bits" Homan. Tex Hamer's extra point gave Frankford the 7–6 victory and the path to the championship two weeks later.

Chamberlin once remarked, "Coaching pros was easy although my approach to the game was wrong. I led by example rather than actually coaching."[47] That was the style of the time, but Guy was being modest. He excelled as a player, yes, but also as a coach. Cleveland's Ralph Vince concluded, "Chamberlin was a playing coach. We all had a lot of respect for him as a player and as a coach."[48] Another smart coach covered in this book, Steve Owen, extolled Guy as the "shrewdest opportunist I have ever seen," adding,

> He was uncanny in "smelling out" a play or mistake. His shrewdness could beat the other team in every which way which is possible. He was the fellow who invariably came up with the fumble, the blocked kick, the interception, as well as the pass thrown by his own man, which would win the game.[49]

Chamberlin epitomized the player-coach model and demonstrated the arrangement's strengths and limitations. A recent book by Sam Walker champions the idea that the key to any great dynasty in any team sport is not the coach, but the captain on the field. The captain is not necessarily the greatest player, but he is the one who completes the unsung necessities for victory and provides the example that his teammates willingly follow to advance team goals. Guy took pride in every aspect of play away from the ball: blocking, mucking around on the defensive line, hustling on kick coverage, and displaying a knack for blocking kicks. He was the team leader. While Walker's thesis is needlessly hostile to the contributions of coaches, it does provide the key to Chamberlin, the greatest player-coach. [50]

However, once his playing career was over, he never coached again. Unlike the other five coaches in this book who began as player-coaches, once Chamberlin could no longer perform on the field, he did not make the transition to the sidelines. Perhaps he just didn't have it in him to care as much once he was removed from the gridiron. He concluded, "I was an easy goin' sort of guy except when I was in a football uniform." [51] Playing the game helped make him a successful coach.

2

TAKING FLIGHT

Curly Lambeau and LeRoy Andrew
Work the Passing Game

As already established, pro football in the 1920s was a tough slog. Opponents generally were mirror images of one another: a single wing power ground attack on offense and the ubiquitous 7–1–2–1, or "seven diamond," defense. Most teams were led by a player-coach who adhered to the simple dictates of "straight football," to keep hitting the opposing line until it broke. Two player-coaches went against the grain, however, and strove to open up the game with the aerial attack. Curly Lambeau in Green Bay and LeRoy Andrew in Cleveland, Detroit, and New York followed their own paths to find a better way to win football games.

Analyzing the unofficial and incomplete league statistics for the period from 1920 to 1931, compiled from contemporary game accounts by Neft, Cohen, and Korch, it is clear who the dominant passing teams were. Lambeau's Packers led the league in passing yards four times (1923, 1924, 1926, and 1931), finishing second four other seasons, third once, and fourth once. Andrew coached for only seven full seasons, but his team finished first in the league in passing yards the last four of them (1927–1930) and led the league in points each of those years. It should also be noted that teams coached by Guy Chamberlin twice led the league in this period and finished second once and third once.[1] Passing was difficult and erratic, but the better teams demonstrated its value.

Lambeau and Andrew were the two coaches most devoted to the air game, but they were drawn to it for different reasons. For Curly, it was a more natural inclination in that the Packers' player-coach was the original passing star for the team as its tailback. He passed the ball because he liked to play that way and saw its potential for creating a winner. He told sportswriter Lee Remmel, "I always loved to pass. I used to practice passing in the spring. The ball was harder to throw then—it was bigger around." He added, "I don't think we would have gotten into the National Football League without passing. We took advantage of the defense, and it paid off."[2]

LeRoy Andrew also began as a player-coach but usually played in the line. At his first NFL coaching stop in Kansas City (with the Blues in 1924 and the Cowboys in 1925–1926), he did not have a strong passing attack; however, Andrew jumped at the chance to sign Benny Friedman, the best passer in college football, once the franchise moved to Cleveland in 1927, and gladly let Friedman air it out on offense. LeRoy was flexible enough to change his approach to accommodate the special talents of his best player, and he stuck with Friedman and the passing attack as they moved from Cleveland to Detroit to New York.

In addition to their shared proclivity for the pass, the other striking similarity between these two coaches is that they both started teams and had to find financial sponsors or backers to enact their gridiron dreams. Lambeau found his initial backing from his employer, the Indian Packing Company. Later, the team was supported by a handful of Green Bay's leading citizens, who set up public ownership of the franchise. Andrew was the driving force to establish pro football in Kansas City and found investors for the new team, too. He then was instrumental in the subsequent sale of the franchise and players to Cleveland and then Detroit and finally New York. For both coaches, this led to them operating their teams with a great deal of independence and ensuring things unfolded the way they envisioned. Andrew's almost-complete franchise control ended once he joined Tim Mara's Giants, and that would lead to his ouster. By contrast, Lambeau enjoyed autonomy in running the community-owned Packers for a much longer period and had a more extended sad denouement to his celebrated coaching career.

LIVES AND CAREERS

Despite winning more games (51) than any other coach from the first dozen years of the NFL, aside from Hall of Famers Halas, Lambeau, Chamberlin, and Conzelman, LeRoy Andrew's career rests almost entirely in obscurity. Let's begin with the name. In virtually every reference source, he is called "Andrews." In fact, that frequently was the case in contemporary newspaper notices and game programs as well. According to his son, however, the name is singular, "Andrew," just as it was when the family arrived in this country from Scotland in 1871, and his father signed his name as "LeRoy Andrew" or "L. B. Andrew."[3]

LeRoy was born on a farm in Osage, Kansas, on June 27, 1896. In 1910, at the age of 14, he left the farm by mule and rode 15 miles to the nearest town, Pittsburg, Kansas, with the $50 he had to his name. His aim was to further his education, against his father's will, and he arranged to live in a loft above a grocery store in exchange for sweeping out and cleaning the store each day. He enrolled at the State Manual Training Normal School in Pittsburg, where he completed high school in 1914, while earning All-Conference honors on the football team. LeRoy continued at the same institution—today known as Pittsburg State University—for his college education. He played guard and tackle under coach R. O. Courtright in 1915 and 1916, and put the shot on the track team. But he did not return for his senior year in 1917, a decision that would have implications for his career later in life.[4]

Instead, Andrew married Zelda Holt, a fellow student at Pittsburg, and coached football at Cherokee County High School, where his wife taught. The following year, he did some farming and ranching in Girard, Kansas, until he enlisted in the military and joined the Great Lakes Naval Training Station football team, which broadened his world. Playing with future NFL luminaries George Halas, Paddy Driscoll, and Jimmy Conzelman in 1918, Andrew faced off against All-America talent, including Rutgers star Paul Robeson and Notre Dame legend George Gipp (and perhaps Fighting Irish freshman Curly Lambeau). He also met the undersecretary of the U.S. Navy, Franklin Roosevelt, when the team played at Annapolis. The 6–0–2 Bluejackets then defeated the Mare Island Marines in the 1919 Rose Bowl, but Andrew missed the game because he was quarantined on the base due to illness.[5]

After the war, LeRoy worked as a bank cashier in Englevale, Kansas, in 1919, but he missed football. In 1922, Andrew tried out unsuccessfully for the Rock Island Independents but the following year made the St. Louis All-Stars, a one-year entry in the NFL led by Ollie Kraehe. Kraehe was a St. Louis native who grew up with Jimmy Conzelman and played guard for Rock Island in 1922, before forming the optimistically moni-kered All-Stars.[6] St. Louis finished just 1–4–2, with Andrew starting four games in his introduction to the NFL, whetting his appetite for more.

Curly Lambeau's family also came to this country in the 1870s. His grandfather, Victor, arrived in Green Bay from Belgium at the age of 19, in 1873. Victor, a building contractor, and his wife, Marie, had six chil-dren, including Curly's father, Marcel, but then tragedy struck in 1891. Victor accosted his wife on a Green Bay street corner, shot her in the neck, and then took his own life. Marie, who the *Green Bay Press-Gazette* reported spoke only French, survived the shooting, and when Earl Louis (Curly) Lambeau, the first child of Marcel and Mary, was born on April 9, 1998, she became his godmother.[7]

Marcel, like his father, was a contractor who built houses, but the family kept on the move. Curly had two brothers and a sister, and the four siblings were born in different houses in town during a six-year period. Curly was a natural athlete who played baseball and lettered for four years in football at Green Bay East High School. He graduated in 1917 and considered attending the University of Wisconsin but never enrolled. A year later, he did enroll at Notre Dame and played fullback as a fresh-man on Knute Rockne's first team alongside the aforementioned George Gipp, as well as future coaches Hunk Anderson, Norm Barry, Clipper Smith, and Eddie Anderson. But Curly dropped out of school at the end of his first semester. Many reasons have been floated to explain his abrupt departure: He had tonsillitis, his grades weren't good, Rockne didn't renew his scholarship, he ran out of money, or some combination thereof. The full truth remains a mystery.[8]

Curly returned to Green Bay in 1919; started working at Frank Peck's Indian Packing Company; and married his high school sweetheart, Mar-guerite Van Kessel, that August. Five days before his wedding, he helped found the Green Bay Packers at a meeting in the editorial offices of the *Green Bay Press-Gazette*, along with *Press-Gazette* editor George Whit-ney Calhoun. Peck's Indian Packing Company agreed to sponsor the team. Lambeau was elected captain and Calhoun manager. The team later hired Green Bay West High School coach Bill Ryan as coach, and Lambeau served as cocoach of Green Bay East High that year as well. The original Packers were an independent outfit who tore through local competition, going 10–1 in 1919 and 9–1–1 in 1920. They played their home games at Hagermeister Park, a sandlot field that did not have a fence or bleachers until 1920.[9]

In December 1920, Curly and Marguerite had a son they named Don, and he would be their only child. That same month, the Acme Packing Company bought out Indian, but Lambeau managed to interest Acme's owners, John and Emmett Clair, in not only continuing the sponsorship, but also underwriting the team's entry into the American Professional Football Association in 1921. The Clair's sponsorship did not last long, however. The team had a moderately successful first season, with a 3–2–1 record in league games, which is still credited to captain Lambeau; however, the 1921 team was actually coached by former University of Wisconsin star Joe Hoeffel, according to contemporary newspaper accounts uncovered by journalist Cliff Christl in 2001.[10]

Of more importance, the Clairs surrendered the franchise at the league meeting on January 28, 1922, after it was determined that Green Bay had used three college players—playing under assumed names—in a non-league game in December. Lambeau rounded up the $250 needed to have the franchise reinstated in his name at the league meeting in June 1922, and took over as coach of the team, as well as the captaincy, that season. Again, the Packers were moderately successful on the field, with a 4–3–3 record, but nearly perished when bad weather wiped out a game and the team's finances late in the year. At this point, Andrew Turnbull, publisher of the *Press-Gazette*, stepped in to lead the team's first stock sale that December and turned the Packers into a publicly owned corporation. Now on more solid financial footing, the Packers posted consecutive seven-win seasons and began to recruit a higher quality of talent, bringing in Nebraska star Verne Lewellen in 1924. On the field, the Packers led the league in passing yards both years, with Curly throwing for 752 yards in 1923 and 1,094 yards in 1924. He also threw 11 touchdown passes and 46 interceptions in that time, demonstrating that he didn't always make the wisest choices with the ball.

Lambeau had established a solid team and took another big step forward in 1927, when he acquired two former Marquette stars: end Lavvie Dilweg from the Milwaukee Badgers and quarterback Red Dunn from the

Chicago Cardinals. Dilweg was a star on both sides of the ball and received All-Pro notice in eight of his nine seasons in the NFL; he and Guy Chamberlin were likely the best ends of the 1920s. Dunn was an expert signal caller and a more reliable lead passer than Lambeau. In five seasons with the Packers, Dunn threw for 31 touchdowns and 36 interceptions. The team became a real contender and finished in second place in 1927, followed by fourth in 1928.

A year later, Lambeau upgraded the Packers to championship status by importing three future Hall of Famers: tackle Cal Hubbard from the Giants, guard Mike Michalske from the Yankees, and wingback Johnny Blood from the Pottsville Maroons. The Packers would dominate the league for the next three seasons and win three consecutive championships with records of 12–0–1, 10–3–1, and 12–2. That is a run of 34–5–2, scoring 723 points and allowing just 220—an average of 17.6 points scored to 5.4 allowed per game. Green Bay's runner-up in the first two years of that run was the Andrew-led New York Giants, who finished 26–5–1 from 1929 to 1930, scored 620 points, and allowed 186—an average of 19.4 points scored to 5.8 allowed per game. LeRoy took a more meandering path to the top of the league.

Andrew began his coaching career in Kansas City, where he got together with his friend, Cameron Reed, to round up investors for a new NFL franchise that Andrew obtained at the league meeting in January. The team was called the Blues and was set up as primarily a road team since few league teams were willing to travel that far west for a doubtful payday. Andrew was player-coach of the Blues and stocked the team mostly with players from the Midwest, but the squad posted a paltry 2–7 record in 1924. Future Giants coach Steve Owen was a member of that first Kansas City team and recalled in his autobiography that Andrew "ran the club on a shoestring," adding, "but to my knowledge he never beat a boy out of a quarter." Owen remembers Andrew borrowing money from players to pay immediate operating expenses and then repaying them as cash flow improved.[11]

The team was renamed the Cowboys in 1925, and attracted attention by arriving in each city decked out in chaps, cowboy hats, and cowboy boots. Owen remembered, "Our outfits and background were a good selling point for publicity when Andrews [sic] talked business."[12] LeRoy's son, Dal Andrew, explained, "Dad recognized the importance of the promotion aspect to the multifaceted role of a pro football coach in the twenties." He added, "In addition to playing and being the coach, everything I see indicates he was very much the general manager, recruiter, the scheduler, and everything else that went with running a football team in the 1920s, especially a road team." Dal chuckled when recalling that his father told him he had two envelopes of money on the team's road trips. One—the dry money—was stashed away while the team played a game. The other—the wet money—was the gate receipts for the game that Andrew retrieved at halftime and had nowhere else to store but in his jockstrap for the rest of the contest. Wet money was used to purchase train tickets from disgusted train station cashiers. [13]

Dal notes that his father had a very comfortable yearlong schedule in those days. "During spring and summer, he would play golf and recruit football players. Come the fall, he would put the golf clubs away and play football. In winter, he'd return to the [family] farm."[14] In three years, LeRoy built up the Kansas City franchise to an 8–3 team that finished fourth in the league in 1926. In those 11 games, however, the Cowboys scored just 76 points and gave up 53. All three losses were by shutout, while their wins included three shutouts, two 7–2 games, and one 7–3 win. They were a thumping and thrashing outfit.

But the traveling team was not making money, and LeRoy's son avers, "The people that had the franchise got tired of it. They found someone in Cleveland who would buy them out. It was pretty much an economic move." The "someone" they found was Sam Deutsch, itching to try again in the NFL after his failure with the 1924 NFL champion Cleveland Bulldogs. The new Bulldogs signed a local boy to generate excitement, and Andrew took charge. Said Dal, "I don't know when Dad made contact with [Benny] Friedman, but supposedly Friedman had an appreciation for the Cowboys winning games. Dad had enough savvy to recognize what he could do with Friedman."[15]

Savvy indeed. Cleveland native Benny Friedman was a consensus two-time All-America tailback at Michigan under renowned coach Fielding Yost and was considered the best passer in the nation by far, college or pro. He was a national figure and would write the first football book devoted to the pro game, *The Passing Game*, in 1931. Benny was a charter member of the College Football Hall of Fame in 1951, but his abrasive egotism alienated voters of the Pro Football Hall, and he was not elected to Canton until 2005, 42 years after its founding and 23 years after his death. Andrew supplied Friedman with an able supporting cast and allowed him to run the offense the wide-open way he liked. Dal asserts, "The statistics speak for themselves. He had a passer, and he modified the team's approach to exploit the capabilities of the passer for the benefit of the team."[16]

The 1927 Bulldogs actually held training camp at Excelsior Springs, Kansas, due to Andrew's regional background and may have been the first NFL team to hold training camp outside its local area.[17] The camp was rigorous and featured two practices a day, as well as nighttime classroom sessions. The team was successful on the field, finishing in fourth place, with an 8–4–1 record, and outscoring opponents 209–107. That year, LeRoy played in his last two games for the Bulldogs. Off the field, however, it was the same old story for Deutsch—little fan support and a financial loss. Once again, Sam wanted out. Some Detroit investors, led by Elliott Fisher, bought the Bulldogs, figuring Friedman's Michigan ties would attract fans. Thus, the Detroit Wolverines were born in 1928. Andrew's new team, the first on which he was not a player, moved up to third in the league, with a 7–2–1 record, and outscored opponents 189–76. But as part of a familiar pattern, they were not a financial success.

Fisher was approached by Tim Mara of the New York Giants, a team coming off a down year both on the field and at the gate. Mara was looking for an exciting superstar to turn both aspects around, and he focused on Friedman for his crowd-pleasing talent and because Benny's Jewish background could prove an attraction in New York City. Andrew argued against a trade of his star player, as it would cripple the team and make it worth less. Fisher wanted to sell Friedman's contract to the Giants but ran into a snag, according to Dal Andrew.

> Friedman's contract was not Fisher's to sell. Friedman's contract had dad's name on it. It was a personal service contract. Dad was always a negotiator, looking to see what could advance the team. He was always very team-oriented. I'm sure it was a four-way [Fisher, Mara, Friedman, Andrew] agreement because dad had a pretty good rapport with Benny Friedman initially.[18]

While there is no proof of Friedman's contract being a personal services contract, it would explain why Mara purchased the entire franchise—players and coach—to obtain Friedman. The investment paid off, as the Friedman-led Giants, coached by Andrew, were a hit both on the field and at the box office. Andrew brought eight players from Detroit; kept seven Giants from the 1928 season, one of whom was tackle Steve Owen; and acquired seven new players to produce one of the top two teams in the league. A player he did not sign, however, would play a large role in his future.

Andrew was tasked with signing local collegiate hero Ken Strong of New York University by Mara and Harry March, the team's treasurer and quasi-general manager. The numbers differ according to who is telling the story, but the gist is that when Andrew met with Strong, he offered him half of what Mara and March authorized him to offer, so Strong took a higher offer to sign with the Staten Island Stapletons instead. His son asserts that LeRoy made the initial low offer as a negotiating ploy and expected the negotiations to continue later. In any case, Andrew misread the situation.

In New York, Andrew did not have the same status as before. He was mentioned in the *New York Times* holding two practice sessions a day at the Giants' 1929 training camp in Asbury Park, New Jersey, but is not mentioned in the paper's game account of the team's home opener in October. Benny Friedman's notoriety completely eclipsed the coach.[19]

After stumbling to a 0–0 tie with the lowly Orange (New Jersey) Tornadoes in the opener, the Giants thundered to the top of the standings. By late November, the league had two undefeated teams—the 8–0–1 Giants and the 9–0 Packers—who were headed for a showdown at the Polo Grounds on November 24. Just a day before the game, the *Honolulu Star-Advertiser* ran a letter LeRoy Andrew wrote to the Honolulu paper's sports editor saying that should his team win the NFL title, he was taking them on a West Coast tour and would like to include Hawaii if a game could be arranged between the Giants and a local team;[20] however, the Giants lost to the Packers that Sunday, and it was the only loss either team would suffer the entire year. The Packers won the title two weeks later.

The 1930 season again pitted the Giants and the Packers as favorites for the flag. The teams first met on October 5, in Green Bay, and the Packers triumphed again in a close contest. A 70-yard touchdown pass from Red Dunn to Johnny Blood in the fourth quarter proved the winning score in the 14–7 game. The Packers remained undefeated until losing to the Cardinals on November 16, one week before the rematch with New York at the Polo Grounds. The 8–1 Packers were in the sights of the 10–2

Giants. In another hard-fought battle between the NFL's two heavy-weights on November 23, the Giants prevailed in a game highlighted by a 91-yard run by halfback Hap Moran. The Giants .846 winning percentage (the determinant of the championship) now outdistanced that of the .800 Packers and put the New Yorkers in first place. It was the high point of LeRoy Andrew's coaching career. Just one week later, the Packers would be two games ahead of the Giants.

The following Thursday, Thanksgiving, the Packers beat Frankford, while the Giants lost to Ken Strong and the Staten Island Stapletons. On Sunday, November 30, Green Bay whipped Staten Island by 30 points, while New York lost to Brooklyn. The Packers were now 10–2, with the Giants in second place, at 11–4. Friedman had an injured leg and did not play in the loss to Brooklyn. He did not play a week later in a win against Frankford, either, and that spelled the end for Andrew in New York.

According to Giants historian Barry Gottehrer, Friedman and Owen went to the Maras and complained that their coach was so obsessed with facing Knute Rockne in an upcoming exhibition game against a team of Notre Dame All-Stars that Andrew was out of control. Friedman himself would repeat that story in later years; however, the thought of the rough and tough Andrew going to pieces concerning an upcoming charity exhibition while his team was chasing a NFL title seems ridiculous. A small news item on December 8 indicates that Andrew was fired as coach and that Friedman and Owen would finish the season as cocoaches. At that point, the Giants had already won their final game against Brooklyn to end up in second with a 13–4 record. When the change became effective is not clear, but Gottehrer contended it was the morning after the Frankford game, but then he had the Brooklyn game a week after Frankford rather than the next day, as it occurred. [21]

A more important factor in Andrew's firing was alluded to by Gottehrer immediately after he floated the Rockne story:

> When the Giants returned to their dressing room trailing Frankford, 6–0, Andrews [sic] started to berate his players, threatening fines and even firings. He made considerable noise but little sense, and suddenly he turned to Friedman, who, with Cagle, had been held out of the game because of injuries. "And you, Friedman," Andrews shouted, "can lose your money just like anyone else." [22]

While Gottehrer's point was that Andrew was frazzled and out of control, one also could say that Andrew was trying to treat everyone equally.

Dal Andrew agreed that the aforementioned story sounds like his father.

> Team morale and discipline held together quite well for the first year, but things started to come apart in 1930, with regard to discipline— players not staying in shape, players not making it to practice to the point where in one game one of the players never even showed up for the ballgame. Dad, in the tradition of [his role as] coach and general manager, said, "Okay, you don't get a check this week." The Maras did not back him up.

He added, "I remember Dad expressing sensitivity about All-Stars and prima donnas on the team."[23]

A coach who has just posted back-to-back 13-win seasons should be a hot commodity, and LeRoy was. Dal remembers his father saying that he was up for the coaching position at Columbia University in 1930, but he lost out to Lou Little because he did not have a college degree. It is unclear whether he would have tried to coach both teams that season or simply left the Giants. On the market in 1931, LeRoy was a finalist in Portsmouth but lost out on the Spartans job to Potsy Clark. He also was mentioned as a potential coach for a Milwaukee group bidding for a NFL franchise, but nothing came of that. On August 26, 1931, Andrew signed to coach the Chicago Cardinals, led by star Ernie Nevers, who had been the team's player-coach the prior season.[24]

The Cardinals switched from Nevers's double wing to Andrew's pre-ferred single wing attack and won their two preseason games against local semipro outfits. In the season opener in Portsmouth on September 23, however, the Cardinals lost, 13–3. Four days later, Andrew was in Green Bay scouting the Packers, who were the Cardinals' next scheduled opponent, albeit not until October 11. Interviewed at the game, Andrew asserted that the Packers' new 6–2–2–1 defense was flawed, stating, "I predict their defense will not get by against other Packer foes—and certainly not against us."[25] He would not get to prove that. On October 6, the *Chicago Tribune* reported his resignation. The same piece noted that 17 Cardinals players had gone to the team owner the previous week to complain about Andrew's offense and wanted Nevers reinstated. Andrew is quoted as denying Nevers had anything to do with the insurrection because Ernie was "one of my best friends."[26] However, Dal Andrew commented, "Apparently, he and Nevers never got along that well."[27]

LeRoy would never coach again in the NFL. Similar to Guy Chamberlin, Andrew's fall from grace was swift after reaching the pinnacle of his career. In 1932, he interviewed to be the first coach of the Boston Braves (now Washington Redskins). A letter from Lou Little to his old University of Pennsylvania teammate, Bert Bell, claimed that owner George Preston Marshall told Little he had decided on Andrew as coach but that Little talked him into hiring another former Penn teammate, Lud Wray, instead. In 1933, Andrew was a finalist for the coaching post for the expansion Cincinnati Reds franchise but lost out to Al Jolley.[28]

While he attempted to get back into coaching, LeRoy worked as a repo man for GMAC in Detroit from 1931 to 1934, and then moved to Texas, where he sold insurance, before returning to Kansas to work construction. In the late 1930s, the divorced Andrew married Helen Hampson and had three sons, Dal, Mack, and Len, between 1939 and 1943. After the war, he ran a cabinet shop in Neodesha, Kansas, until he bumped into his old friend, Cameron Reed, who operated a pioneering united funds business called Waddell and Reed with partner Chauncey Waddell. In 1949, Reed convinced Andrew to move into the investment business and take over the Arkansas region for the firm, which he did until he retired in the early 1960s. In retirement, he continued with his love of golf and reconnected with old friend Cal Hubbard for bird hunting trips. LeRoy Andrew, forgotten coaching pioneer, died of congestive heart failure in July 1978.

Curly Lambeau played his last game in 1929, and reached his coaching peak in winning three consecutive NFL championships from 1929 to 1931. Unlike Andrew, his coaching career did not seriously falter at that point. As noted in the introduction, he almost led the Packers to a fourth consecutive title in 1932, but Lambeau was done in by the league's policy of not counting ties in figuring winning percentage. Signal caller Red Dunn retired after the 1931 season and was replaced by a new passing star in local boy Arnie Herber. Herber had a different skill set than Dunn, so Lambeau changed the offense accordingly. Still, the team slipped to a losing record in 1933, and nudged to just over .500 in 1934, before Lambeau made the biggest signing of his career in 1935, with whippet end Don Hutson. He saw Hutson play on his annual postseason scouting trip to California. Curly also brought home a second wife, Susan Johnson, a former Miss California that year; he and first wife Marguerite had divorced in 1934.

Hutson starred in Alabama's 1935 Rose Bowl victory against Stanford and, in the last year before the NFL instituted its player draft, signed contracts with both Lambeau and Shipwreck Kelly's Brooklyn Dodgers. According to lore, he was awarded to the Packers because his Packers contract was postmarked 17 minutes earlier than his Dodgers contract when they were sent to the league office. That decision was fortuitous for Green Bay, Lambeau, and Hutson himself, since Hutson was going to a better team in Green Bay and a coach who favored the passing game in Lambeau. Don would go on to lead the league in receiving touchdowns nine times, receptions eight times, receiving yards seven times, and scoring five times. When he retired after an 11-year career, he held virtually every career receiving record for the NFL. Many still consider him the greatest Packers player in history.

Hutson broke in with a bang. On the first play of his second game, he and Johnny Blood ran companion deep routes, and when the safety went with the well-known Blood, Hutson was all alone for an 83-yard touchdown that proved to be the only score in a 7–0 win against the archrival Bears. He caught 18 passes as a rookie before leading the league in 1936, while spurring the Packers to a fourth world championship, beating Ray Flaherty's Redskins. In 1938, Lambeau drafted Cecil Isbell from Purdue and had two ace passers. Green Bay returned to the title game against Steve Owen's Giants in each of the next two seasons, losing in 1938 and winning a fifth title in 1939.

Lambeau's team had won five championships in 11 years from 1929 to 1939, and the coach was widely celebrated in the national media as the pass-oriented genius who brought a little town into the limelight. In that decade, Green Bay was featured in *Time* and *Newsweek*, as well as regularly covered by sports columnists John Kieran and Arthur Daley of the *New York Times*. *Collier's* magazine ran a feature article on the team in 1937, and the *Saturday Evening Post* did so in 1940. Curly also arranged for the 1936 champion Packers to shoot a short film in Hollywood with Pete Smith, who peppered his movies with a wisecracking voice-over. The 10-minute film *Pigskin Champions* debuted in theaters in August 1937, and brought more prominence to the league's smallest market.

In 1940, the Bears unleashed the full fury of the modern T formation and ruled the league for the first half of the decade. Curly's Packers, who would be one of the last teams in the league to switch to the T, started a slow decline. After having beaten the Bears in 14 of 27 games in their 11-year glory era, the Packers would go just 4–16–1 against them in the last decade of Lambeau's time in Green Bay. The 1941 Packers were the second-best team in the league and tied the Bears for the West crown with a 10–1 record, but they were trampled in the playoff. Green Bay finished second to Chicago in 1942 and 1943, before winning one more NFL title in 1944, in the depths of the war years, beating Steve Owen's Giants—led by former Packer Arnie Herber—in the title game.

Lambeau cut Herber in 1941, and Cecil Isbell shockingly retired after the 1942 season, leaving the passing to lesser lights like Irv Comp. Even with Hutson, the Packers never again had a top passing game. From 1943 to the end of the decade, the Packers finished 3rd, 4th, 5th, 10th, 7th, 9th, and 10th in passing yards, respectively. Lambeau, the passing pioneer, reverted to a running game but with steadily diminishing success. From 1932 to 1945, Hutson's last season, the Packers ran the ball 3.2 percent less than the league average; from 1946 to 1953, Curly's teams ran the ball 6.7 percent more than the league. Curly's last winning season was 1947, when he switched to the T. Green Bay finished 3–9 in 1948 and 2–10 in 1949. In 1949, Lambeau retreated to the press box after the first game and left the coaching of his clearly undermanned Packers to his assistant coaches. Curly, a relentless womanizer, was now on his third marriage, the team was financially in trouble, and the board of directors was aiming to exert more control when Curly quit and took the head coaching position with the Chicago Cardinals in January 1950.

After two losing seasons in Chicago, Curly quit again. Walter Wolfner, the Cardinals managing director, charged that "Lambeau hasn't even spoken to one of his assistants for the last three weeks. This feeling can be attributed to Lambeau's alibiing after losing games. He always blamed his assistants for the defeats."[29] Nonetheless, Lambeau was hired by George Marshall to coach the Redskins in 1952. He led them to a 4–8 season that year and 6–5–1 in 1953; however, stars Gene Brito and Eddie LeBaron signed with Canadian teams rather than continue playing for Lambeau, whom they did not respect. Oddly, the end came when Marshall grew upset that Curly was allowing his team to drink beer in the hotel in the 1954 preseason. A loud argument between the two hotheads resulted in Lambeau's firing.[30]

The next year, Curly signed on to coach the College All-Stars and led the team to a 30–27 victory against the champion Cleveland Browns in August. Lambeau coached the All-Stars two more years but lost both games. Although there was some talk of bringing Curly back to coach the flailing Packers in 1959, the board made a much more intelligent choice and hired Vince Lombardi. Curly claimed that he was working on an autobiography to be titled *40 Years of Mistakes*, but the alleged manuscript was lost in a fire.[31] He remained close to Don Hutson and spent most of his time in Wisconsin and California. He was dating a young woman named Mary Jane Van Duyse, who was a majorette at Packers games, and stopped to help her father cut the grass on June 1, 1965, only to collapse dead from a heart attack.

Upon Lambeau's death, old rival George Halas wrote, "He did it so well that he kept beating the Bears. You know that was the greatest thing that could have happened to us. He kept beating us until he started such a rivalry that I couldn't hope would end."[32] Curly and Halas were charter members of the Pro Football Hall of Fame when it opened in 1963, but upon his death, Lambeau received an even more prominent honor when the Packers—despite the objections of current coach Vince Lombardi—renamed new City Stadium after him. It was a fitting honor for the team's most essential man, the man who put his small hometown on the map. Lambeau Field also was an old idea, however. In October 1937, a man named Homer Maes Jr. wrote a letter to the *Green Bay Press-Gazette* proposing that the original City Stadium be renamed Lambeau Field. In 1965, it was an idea whose time had come.[33]

COACHING KEYS

Clearly, Curly Lambeau had a greater impact on football during the long haul of his career than LeRoy Andrew, who coached just seven full seasons, but both were instrumental in the promulgation of the aerial attack in the pro game. Andrew's influence is tied to his connection with Benny Friedman, a connection he cultivated as long as he was able.

In the view of George Halas's partner, Dutch Sternaman, Friedman was the league's "first great passer."[34] Halas concurred many years later, writing, "Until Friedman came along, the pass had been used as a desperation weapon in a long yardage situation on third down—or when your team was hopelessly behind. Benny demonstrated that the pass could be mixed with running plays as an integral part of the offense." Halas also asserted that the league's rules committee slenderized the ball in 1931 and 1934, to encourage others to mirror Benny's airborne success.[35]

Sternaman's notes also indicate that the Bears realized the only way to stop Friedman was to "hit him hands high," in other words rough him up and not allow him time to pass the ball.[36] Friedman, who wrote several pieces on football for *Collier's* in the 1930s and 1940s, recalled those tactics, in particular as used by Bears lineman Bill Fleckenstein, in a 1932 article and was sued for libel by Fleckenstein. Fleckenstein ultimately won his lawsuit but was awarded just six cents in damages because the jury felt that the general sense of the article was accurate.[37]

Giants end Ray Flaherty commented, "Benny was not a good long passer. He didn't throw the ball too well long, but he was a very good short passer. So quite a few of our passes were cross-field patterns or some other patterns of that kind, breaking in or out."[38]

Friedman also was an able runner who led his team in both rushing and passing each year under Andrew. As a passer, he was breaking new ground, including a then-unheard of 20 touchdown tosses in 1929, when the second-best total in the NFL was 11. Dal Andrew said his father was proud of the "role that Friedman had in changing the game." He added that his father "was quite willing to innovate, and the statistics show it."[39]

In Friedman's book *The Passing Game*, published in 1931, Benny mentions his Michigan coach Fielding Yost but not his pro coach, LeRoy Andrew. He diagrams four plays—two from his days at Michigan, one of a fake punt pass play perpetrated by Green Bay on the Giants, and one from a Giants game against the Bears that illustrates Benny's willingness to throw the ball from his own seven-yard line. While Friedman was, no doubt, the engine of the offense, Andrew's contribution should not be slighted. A 1931 article correctly categorizes Andrew's teams: "His teams have always been colorful on attack and barrier-like on defense, but above all that, they have always been showmen, a spectacle to delight the eye of the spectator."[40] In fact, once Andrew left, Friedman was only a part-time player who tossed 13 touchdowns and 23 interceptions for mediocre teams that finished 19–26–2 in four years. He only lasted one more season in New York because he tried to persuade Tim Mara to make him a part-owner of the Giants and then left after Mara refused. Friedman had his best years with the winning team built and run by Andrew.

Years later, LeRoy told a reporter, "I coached fundamental football without didoes. We didn't try the fancy stuff—doesn't work. All the other teams knew our plays, some of them even knew our signals, but the plays still worked." He added, "The greatest deception possible comes from starting all plays of any certain type, exactly alike." He also maintained, "The biggest single improvement that could be made in football would be in the delivery of forward passes. Benny Friedman, greatest of passers, had a follow-through like a baseball pitcher or a golfer."[41]

George Halas felt that the developments set in place by Friedman made possible the emergence of the "swift, slender, sure-fingered end from Alabama named Don Hutson";[42] however, the Packers were leaders in the passing attack well before Hutson came along to perfect it. The basis for Lambeau's offense was the Notre Dame shift he learned in his one season under Knute Rockne (see figure 2.1). The offense would line up in a T formation with a balanced line, a guard, a tackle, and an end on both sides of the center. On signal, the backs would shift into a box that resembled a single wing backfield, and the ends might flex out a bit from the tackles. In the box, the left halfback, fullback, and quarterback shifted laterally, while the right halfback moved toward the line and to the right, lining up as a slotback or wingback. The shift could go either to the right or the left (see figure 2.2).

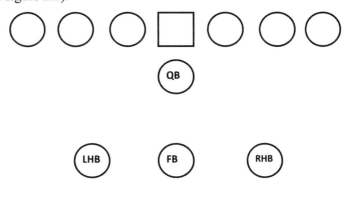

Figure 2.1. Notre Dame box offense preshift

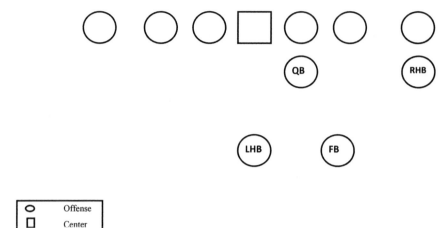

Figure 2.2. Notre Dame shift at snap

From that basis, Lambeau's attack varied, depending on the talent he had on hand. In the early 1920s, he was the main back and would receive a deep snap from the center in the halfback position. Charlie Mathys, the 5-foot-7 Packers quarterback, was more of a receiver and blocker who caught a league-leading 33 passes in 1923, and topped the NFL again in 1924, with 30 catches. With the coming of Verne Lewellen and other talented backs in the mid-1920s, the offense grew more diverse, with more backs taking snaps. When Lambeau obtained Red Dunn at quarterback, however, his offense took into account what Dunn offered. Dunn was best at taking a short pass from center and distributing the ball, whether on a handoff to another back or via a pass. The quarterback did not always get the ball, but that exchange was much more prevalent with Dunn at the position. This version of the offense was sometimes referred to as a V formation because that's how the quarterback, left halfback, and fullback aligned, and this offense, which was attuned for quick opening plays, bore some similarities to a more modern T formation[43] (see figure 2.3).

But after Dunn retired Arnie Herber did not have the skill set to run that offense, nor did he possess the running ability that a traditional single wing tailback would have. What he did best was throw the ball deep, so that was his main function in the 1930s. Lambeau accumulated a host of multitalented backs to fit into his versatile 1930s attack: Clarke Hinkle, Bob Monnett, Joe Laws, Hank Bruder, and eventually Cecil Isbell—who did have the triple threat skill set of the ideal single wing tailback. Watch-

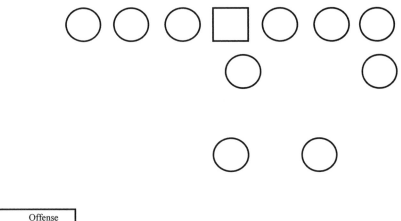

| ○ | Offense |
| □ | Center |

Figure 2.3.   Packers V formation

ing film of the Packers of the late 1930s and early 1940s, one sees backs moving between different positions and substituting fairly regularly. It should also be noted that Green Bay usually had one of the better place-kicking units in the NFL, finishing first or second in the league in field goals nine times between 1934 and 1947. Going back to the acclaimed punting of Verne Lewellen, Lambeau placed emphasis on the kicking game.

And then there was Hutson. Jimmy Conzelman claimed, "Hutson is the only football player who ever lived who forced an opposing coach to put two men against him." Jimmy saw Don's qualities as, "fourfold: speed . . . hands . . . judgment of a thrown ball . . . his big act."[44] That "big act" alludes to the pass patterns that Hutson frequently is credited with creating. Cleveland sportswriter John Dietrich memorably characterized the 1930s Packer attack as follows: "The Packers, shooting passes in all directions from their gyrating Notre Dame offensive, were the most air-minded outfit to pester Cleveland this year."[45] Charting nine game films from the 1940s provides additional insight into the air attack. In those games, Hutson flexed out at least a few yards on 67 percent of offensive plays, while other Packers ends did so just 17 percent of the time. By contrast, in the 1939 title game, Hutson was flexed less than one-third of the time. In support of this thought, Clarke Hinkle told Murray Olderman that in the 1930s, "The offensive formations of our day spanned about 12 yards because we did not have flankers and split ends. In addition, our offensive linemen were not spaced as loose. Result: The defensive formations were tighter, so it was harder to find a hole." Although it's an extremely small sample, the film I've seen makes me wonder whether the positioning of Hutson on offense evolved throughout time.[46]

On defense, his positioning distinctly changed when Lambeau brought in bruising Larry Craig as quarterback in 1939. Quarterback in that offense solely meant blocking back. Craig functioned like a fullback in more contemporary offenses; he was purely a lead blocker. His talent allowed Lambeau to make a major move to preserve the health of his greatest player. Instead of having Hutson line up at defensive end, Craig took that slot, while the ball-hawking Hutson became the team's leading interceptor in the secondary. This move was quite unique at the time. Two-way players did not shift around so freely. To Lambeau's credit, he was considering it as early as 1936, and did not hesitate to make the move when he got the right player to make it work in 1939.[47]

Lambeau claimed to be one of the first to move from a seven- to a six-man line in the 1930s, with the center dropping back to join the fullback as a second linebacker (see figure 2.4). Generally, his teams had strong defenses. His most famous strategic defensive move, however, came in 1941, when he switched the Packers back to a seven-man line to upend the mighty Chicago offense and beat the Bears, 16–14. Unfortunately, in the playoff at the end of the season, the strategic magic wore off, and the Bears crushed the Packers, 33–14. Perhaps what was really missing at that point was superstar linemen the caliber of Cal Hubbard and Mike Michalske from the 1929–1931 champions.

Not everyone thought highly of Curly's strategic acumen. Cal Hubbard told Ralph Hickok,

> Hell, sometimes Curly would design a new play, draw it up on the blackboard, and we just knew it wouldn't work the way he drew it. He'd have impossible blocking assignments, or the play would take too long to develop. The defense would mess it up before it got going. We'd have to tell him that, and one of the veterans would go right up to the blackboard and change it around. Most of the time, Johnny Blood was the spokesman because he was always ready to speak up to Curly.[48]

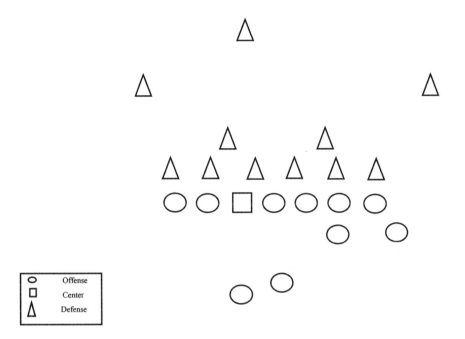

Figure 2.4.   6–2–2–1 defense

Mike Michalske partially agreed with Hubbard but added, "He really learned football from his players, and after a few years I think he knew as much as any coach in the game." Don Hutson, who came along a little later, felt differently, stating, "I was fortunate in having a creative coach like Curly Lambeau, one who really saw the merits of the passing game at a time when just about no one else did."[49]

And then there was his manner. An article in the *Milwaukee Journal* the day after the Packers won the 1936 championship was titled "Curley [*sic*] Spouts Advice; Nobody Pays Attention," and bemusedly depicts Lambeau's vocal antics on the sidelines during the game with the emphasis on the players disregarding him.[50] Guard John Biola remembered, "And how he would rant and rave. During a game, nobody would want to talk to him. You'd stay as far away as you could on the bench."[51] Clarke Hinkle stated, "I never really liked him. Didn't really respect him either." Hinkle did consider Lambeau a "great psychologist," however.[52] Center Charley Brock thought, "Curly never became too intimate with the players, and as the years progressed we realized it was because he didn't want to lose control of them."[53] Guard Buckets Goldenberg asserted, "He was a great salesman. He could sell oysters to a fisherman. It was this salesmanship that helped him develop so many stars."[54] Bob Snyder, an assistant coach at the end of Lambeau's tenure in Green Bay, told Cliff Christl, "I don't think players played out of respect for Curly as much as out of fear of Curly."[55]

By the late 1940s, the talent was gone, and Lambeau was out of ideas. He shifted the offense to the T in 1947, and imported a passer, Jack Jacobs, to run it. After one more mediocre season, everything fell apart. In 1948, he completely lost the team when he fined each player a full game check after they lost for the second time in week four. Once the team beat a tough Rams squad in week five to pull to 3–2, however, Lambeau infuriated the team by not rescinding the ridiculous fine from the previous week. He lost all authority and went 2–17 in his last 19 games in Green Bay.

Today we remember Lambeau for his glory days when he championed the passing game and led six teams to championships. Curly once told sportswriter Ollie Keuchle that his most satisfying game was the 1940 College All-Star Game, when the 1939 champs dismantled the college boys, 45–28, and displayed the awesome power of the air game. "We scored more points than the pros had scored in the six previous games combined and opened the eyes of those who for so long had refused to accept pro ball for what it was," he said.[56] It was his passing attack that brought that acceptance.

KEY GAMES

Six games shine a good light on these two aerial-minded coaches: three regular-season matches between Lambeau and Andrew, and three post-season championship games involving just Curly. Lambeau and Andrew had met three times on the field before LeRoy took over in New York in 1929, and Curly won all three. The Packers defeated Kansas City twice in 1924, and beat Cleveland in Friedman's first game as a pro in 1927. In New York, the teams were more evenly matched.

In 1929, both the Packers and Giants were undefeated when they met at the Polo Grounds on November 24. The eagerly awaited match in which the big-city Giants were rated 5–3 favorites over the small-town

Packers marked the first radio broadcast of a Green Bay game by WTMJ in Milwaukee. The Packers came into the game a bit banged up, with Red Dunn, halfback Eddie Kotal, and end Dick O'Donnell out of service. In fact, 10 Packers would play the entire 60 minutes, with only guard Jim Bowdoin having to leave in the last minute due to an injury. The dark footage of the game that exists reveals the Packers usually in a balanced line and running from the Notre Dame box, with some snaps going directly to the quarterback and some to the halfback. On defense, Green Bay lined up both in seven- and six-man lines, in which Hubbard roamed freely. New York's offense ran out of a mix of single wing and punt formations, with Friedman and Tiny Feather taking most of the deep snaps (see figure 2.5). Defensively, Steve Owen claims he lobbied Andrew to play a six-man line against Green Bay, but they did so only for the first play. On film, they are solely in a seven-man front.

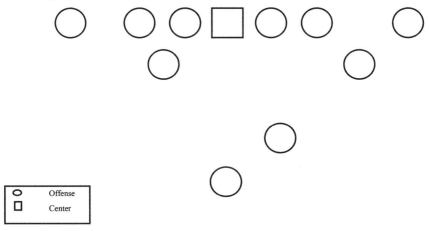

Figure 2.5. Short punt formation

Early in the first quarter, Johnny Blood recovered a Giants fumble on a punt at the New York 35. Eight plays later, on fourth and goal from the six, Bo Molenda tossed a touchdown pass to Herdis McCrary and then converted the extra point. New York struck back quickly on a 65-yard pass play from Friedman to Ray Flaherty that carried to the Green Bay 10. Two plays later, however, Blood intercepted a Friedman pass at the goal line to stop the threat. Both teams moved the ball some in the first half but without more points. The half ended with Friedman intercepting a pass by Lewellen at the Giants' three.

The first time the Giants got the ball in the second half they drove 66 yards for a touchdown. A 25-yard completion from Tony Plansky to Tiny Feather and a 16-yard touchdown pass from Friedman to Plansky highlighted the drive. The extra point was missed, so Green Bay still led, 7–6. From that point onward, New York lost 19 yards on its final four possessions, while the Packers scored again after Lewellen faked a punt and threw a 30-yard completion into Giants territory. The touchdown came 11 plays later on a one-yard buck by Molenda, making the score 14–6. Two plays later, Jug Earpe picked off Friedman at the New York 37, and a 12-play drive resulted in a Blood run for the final score in the 20–6 Packers victory. The Giants ran the ball 35 times for 46 yards and completed five of 14 passes for 157 yards; Green Bay ran 43 times for 117 yards and completed six of 12 passes for 105. Lewellen averaged 50 yards per punt in contrast to the Giants' 39-yard average.

The two teams tangled twice in 1930, providing two more dramatic games. The first, on October 5, at Green Bay, was tied 7–7 in the fourth quarter when Red Dunn hit a streaking Johnny Blood with a 15-yard pass that turned into a 70-yard touchdown. Green Bay scored its first touchdown on a pass from Dunn to Tom Nash, while New York scored on a pass from Friedman to Len Sedbrook. Again, Friedman was largely kept in check by an alert Green Bay defense. In the 1930 rematch on November 23, Andrew finally bested Lambeau, 13–7, with the New York touchdowns coming on a 22-yard touchdown pass from Friedman to Red Badgro and a three-yard run by Benny. Lewellen scored for the Packers, but two second-half goal-line stands secured the victory for New York and put them in first place. It was the acme of LeRoy Andrew's career; one week later they were back in second place. Two weeks later, Andrew was fired.

Lambeau's next championship came at the expense of the Boston Redskins on December 13, 1936, but the game was played at the Polo Grounds in New York since Redskins owner George Marshall had given up on Boston and would soon move the team to Washington. The Packers had led the league in scoring, while Boston had allowed the fewest yards—Chicago and Detroit allowed fewer points, however. The game hinged primarily on two big passes by Arnie Herber. On the Packers' second possession, Herber hit Don Hutson for a 42-yard touchdown. Leading 7–6 at the half, Green Bay took the kickoff and, propelled by a 55-yard strike from Herber to Johnny Blood, tallied a second touchdown to make the score 14–6. The Packers later notched an insurance touchdown after blocking a Redskins punt. While Herber was six of 15 for 134 yards and with Bob Monnett completing three more passes for 23 more yards, the Redskins hit on just seven of 27 passes for 91 yards. To respond, Flaherty knew he needed a passer, and the Redskins selected Sammy Baugh in the next year's college draft.

The Packers returned to the championship game in 1938, losing to Steve Owen's Giants. In a rematch in Milwaukee on December 10, 1939, an effective passing game was again key in a 27–0 Packers blowout. It was the largest title game point differential in history until the Bears beat Washington, 73–0, the following year. Lambeau's attack this time, however, was to rely more on a power running game. On a windy Wisconsin day, the Packers ran the ball 49 times for 138 yards and threw the ball just 10 times, completing seven for 96 yards, with three interceptions. The Giants ran 34 times for 72 yards and threw 25 passes but completed just eight for 94 yards and had six passes intercepted. Don Hutson was held to just two receptions for 21 yards, but his first catch for 15 yards set up a touchdown pass from Herber to Milt Gantenbein two plays later, with Hutson acting as a decoy.

Leading just 7–0 at the half, Green Bay took control in the third quarter, scoring 10 points, including a 31-yard touchdown pass from Cecil Isbell to Joe Laws to make the score 17–0, and making the fourth quarter a time of desperation for New York. The Packers intercepted two more passes and scored 10 more points to complete their win.

Five years later, Lambeau won his last title with a similar strategy against Steve Owen's Giants. The Packers won the coin toss but turned the tables on New York by electing to kick off, a regular practice of the defensive-oriented Owen. Once again, Owen threw all his resources into stopping Hutson—and largely succeeded—but he lost the game. With the Giants concentrating on Hutson, Green Bay ran the ball 49 times for 163 yards and threw the ball just 11 times, completing a mere three passes. All three completions were for more than 20 yards, however, and two came on the same drive—a 23-yard pass to Hutson was followed two plays later by a 26-yard toss to fullback Ted Fritsch for the score while three Giants were chasing Hutson. Fritsch had scored the first touchdown on a fourth-down, one-yard plunge earlier in the second quarter. Joe Laws led the way with 74 yards rushing. Years later, he told reporter Lee Remmel,

We ran as much as we did just because of the way the game developed. We were picking up yardage running, so why throw? If they'd have changed their defense, we would have thrown more. We were using Hutson as a decoy that day. They were putting three men on him, so that was always leaving something or somebody else open. [57]

The Giants, by contrast, ran the ball 30 times for 85 yards and threw 22 times, completing eight for 114 yards. The Giants passer was aging Arnie Herber, and the Packers stole four of his passes, with Laws accounting for three. New York scored one touchdown in the third quarter, but the Green Bay defense continually shut down Herber in the final stanza and secured the win.

That game was Lambeau's last hurrah, but he coached for another nine years in the NFL. He and LeRoy Andrew had essentially founded their original teams and ran the full operation as coaches and general managers. In a sense, Andrew was driven out of the game by the league maturing and becoming more stable on the management side. The coach's role was no longer as multidimensional as when he started. Dal Andrew stated,

It's important to recognize that relationship between Dad and Mara and the Giants. Here you had a coach who had built a very successful team over a period of five to six years and had succeeded with a very high degree of independence, decision-making, self-sufficiency, autonomy, and had been hired because of that success. He got to New York and wound up with a lot of help and support that he wasn't used to. For five to six years, he had made the decisions regarding hiring, firing, and what players were worth.

On top of that, "Dad was not known for low-intensity conflict resolution . . . he had a temper." [58]

Lambeau also had a temper; he was sometimes referred to as the Bellicose Belgian for his rants during a game, on the practice field, and in the locker room. With the Packers' unique ownership structure, however, he had help, but he didn't really answer to anyone. He was able to maintain near-total control of the franchise for decades—until he completely failed and the franchise needed to be rescued by its board of directors.

In the 1920s, both men played a large role in opening up the way the game was played on the field, making it more exciting and interesting to spectators and helping to grow the league and the pro game. Andrew lost out at that point, but Lambeau continued to influence the game strongly throughout the 1930s and even into the 1940s, when his moment began to wane.

3

T MEN

George Halas, Dutch Sternaman, and Ralph Jones Open Up the "Regular Formation"

While Curly Lambeau and LeRoy Andrew were playing key roles in opening up the pro game by exploring the possibilities of the aerial assault, a few other early coaches took a different route to enact change. George Halas, his partner, Edward "Dutch" Sternaman, and one of their former coaches at the University of Illinois, Ralph Jones, took the T formation, one of oldest schemes of the game, and modernized it to broaden the evolution of offensive strategy.

The T formation, so called because both halfbacks and the fullback align behind the center and quarterback like the crossbar of a capital "T," dates to the 1880s and was likely first drawn up by Walter Camp, often referred to as the "father of football" (see figure 3.1). In his book *American Football*, Camp referred to the T as the "original" formation. He instituted many bedrock rules changes to the early game. These changes included creating a line of scrimmage, using the center snap to start each play, and instituting a system of downs (originally three downs to make five yards, later amended to four downs to make 10 yards). The basic requirements of seven men on the line and four men in the backfield would not come until 1909; however, the T's design enabled the same sorts of mass power plays as the wedges that were also prevalent in the 19th century. In a wedge play, 10 teammates surrounded the ballcarrier, shoulder to shoulder, in a brutal attempt to trample the 11 defensive players opposite them. The flying wedge, in which two groups of five players each took a 25-yard running head start to converge around the ballcarrier and into the opposing team, was so deadly that it was outlawed in 1894, just two years after Harvard instituted it against Yale.[1]

In the early T formation, linemen also stood shoulder to shoulder, and every play was a running play, generally right up the middle. Once again, mass against mass. It was the main formation in use until two developments in the first decade of the 20th century—the legalization of the forward pass in 1906 and Glenn "Pop" Warner's creation of the single wing formation at about the same time. Camp referred to the single wing as the "Carlisle formation" because that is where Warner coached when he popularized it. In the single wing, the line is unbalanced with an extra guard or tackle on one side of the center; two backs are close to the line and two are deep in the backfield. The center snap usually went directly to a deep back. It allowed for endless variations and the ability to mass blockers for either inside or outside runs. The back taking the deep snap was already in position to pass the ball as well.[2]

By the time the American Professional Football Association began play in 1920, virtually every college and pro team was running either the single wing or a shift offense, the most popular shift being the Notre

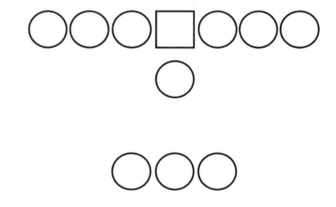

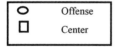

Figure 3.1. Early T formation

Dame shift, in which the offensive backs would move from a basic T formation behind a balanced line to being positioned roughly in the shape of a box. The Notre Dame shift also featured a center snap to a deep back. The one pro team that was still making extensive use of the T was the Decatur Staleys, who would become the Chicago Bears two years later. As we will see, the Staleys/Bears actually ran a varied offense that used several different formations, but they aligned most often in the T.

The earliest pro coaches generally ran the offense they had used in college, and the Halas–Sternaman partnership was no exception. They ran what they learned at Illinois under Bob Zuppke, a German-born, innovative iconoclast who coached the Fighting Illini from 1913 to 1941, and won four national championships. Zuppke was a thoroughly practical coach. He based his strategic approach on the abilities of the players he had in any one year. At various times, he used the T formation (which he called the "regular formation"), the single wing, the short punt, or whatever he thought would work best with the personnel on hand.[3] During his first decade in Champaign—when Halas, Sternaman, and Potsy Clark played under him—Zuppke had a clever assistant coach named Ralph Jones, who coached the basketball team as well. In this environment, Halas and Sternaman learned the game and, together with Jones, formed an Illinois triumvirate that kept the T vital. A second trio later would evolve the offense further to transform the game, as we will examine in chapter 8.

LIVES AND CAREERS

George Stanley Halas is arguably the most significant and influential man in NFL history. He was an All-League player, a coach for 40 years—in four 10-year spans separated by short sabbaticals—and the owner with the most sway in such league decisions as changing equipment, altering rules, hiring and firing commissioners, and charting the expansion of the league. Indeed, Halas was the face of the NFL for five decades. He was born in Chicago on February 2, 1895. His parents, Frank and Barbara, were emigres from the Czech/Bohemia region, and he had two older brothers, Walter and Frank Jr., and a sister, Lillian. Frank Sr. was a tailor who sold his business after having a stroke and bought a small apartment house with a grocery store on the ground level. After Frank's death in

1910, Halas and his siblings helped Barbara run the grocery store and maintain the apartments. [4]

Halas was undersized when he played on the junior varsity at Crane Tech High School, so when he graduated in 1913, he took a year off and worked for Western Electric in nearby Cicero, Illinois, where his childhood sweetheart, Minerva Bushing, also worked. He would marry Min in 1922, and they would have two children, a son George and daughter Virginia. After a year in the workforce, Halas enrolled as a civil engineering major at Illinois in 1914, and reported to freshman football coach Ralph Jones, who positioned George at right halfback. The following year, varsity coach Bob Zuppke moved Halas to end, but George broke his jaw and spent the season on the sideline. He did play basketball (under Jones, the Illini cage coach) and baseball, however, and excelled at both. In 1916, George broke his leg and missed another football season, but Zuppke hired him to manage the supply room. That same year, sophomore Dutch Sternaman joined the team at left halfback. [5]

Edward Carl "Dutch" Sternaman was born just a week after Halas, on February 9, 1895, in Springfield, Illinois. Dutch earned 13 varsity letters at Springfield High, in football, basketball, baseball, and track. As a high school senior, he was named All-State in basketball. He enrolled in the mechanical engineering program at Illinois in 1915, and lettered in football in 1916. [6]

In 1917, Halas and Sternaman both starred on the gridiron in Champaign, and Sternaman was elected team captain for his upcoming senior season of 1918, when World War I intervened, sending both men into the military. Sternaman was named athletic director at Camp Funston in Fort Riley, Kansas, and ran the football team there that fall. Decades later, he recalled, "With some Zup [Zuppke] formations and working with the huddle I formed some plays that were to become fundamental in my system for the next 10 years." [7]

Halas starred on the Great Lakes Naval Station team that trounced the Mare Island Marines, 17–0, in the 1919 Rose Bowl. On that team, Halas played alongside future NFL players and coaches LeRoy Andrew, Jimmy Conzelman, and Paddy Driscoll. In the Rose Bowl, Driscoll dropkicked a field goal and threw a 30-yard touchdown pass to Halas. George also intercepted a Mare Island pass and returned it 77 yards to the Marines' three-yard line, leading to the other touchdown in the game.

With the war over in 1919, Sternaman returned to Champaign for his senior year, while Halas, a speedy .350 batsman for the Illini baseball team as an undergraduate, reported to spring training with the 1919 New York Yankees. George hurt his hip while sliding that spring but still went north with New York. By July, however, he was batting just .091 and had appeared in just a dozen games. The Yankees released Halas, and he signed with St. Paul of the American Association before returning home to Chicago to begin work in the bridge department of the Chicago, Burlington, & Quincy Railroad. That fall, while Sternaman again was starring for Zuppke, Halas signed on with the Hammond Pros independent football team, where he teamed again with Paddy Driscoll and faced off against such pro stars as Jim Thorpe of Canton and Fritz Pollard of Akron.[8]

George liked the idea of making money doing what he loved most and recalled Coach Zuppke once lamenting, "Just when I teach you fellows how to play football, you graduate and I lose you."[9] Zuppke was a staunch opponent of professionalism in his sport and continually advised his players against turning pro, even as his most fervent acolyte, Halas, rose to the top of the postgraduate version of the game. So, when A. E. Staley of the Staley Starch Company in Decatur, Illinois, offered George a job working at the plant and organizing a pro football team, Halas eagerly accepted.

Sternaman later claimed that Staley had offered him that same opportunity during the 1919 Christmas vacation but that Dutch had turned him down.[10] Dutch did accept Halas's offer to join the new team in 1920, along with such stars as Guy Chamberlin of Nebraska, George Trafton of Notre Dame, and Jimmy Conzelman of Washington/St. Louis. Halas was also present at the famous meeting at Ralph Hay's Hupmobile dealership in Canton, Ohio, in September, during which the APFA was formed, with Decatur as a charter member.

The Decatur Staleys finished second in the league in that initial season, with Sternaman leading the team in scoring, rushing, and interceptions. Despite being a success on the field, the Staleys spent more money than A. E. was willing to lose. He met with Halas and offered to give George $5,000 in seed money to separate from the company and move to Chicago as long as the team was called the Staleys for one more season. Thus, the Chicago Staleys were born in 1921, with Dutch Sternaman as Halas's full partner. Halas reasoned,

> What I needed, I finally decided, was a partner. Our Staley halfback, Dutch Sternaman, seemed like an ideal choice. He was from Springfield, Illinois, and a top-notch ballplayer. By inducing Dutch to join the firm, I would reduce the administrative work by 50 percent and also lighten the payroll by $100 a game. Happily, the idea appealed to Dutch, so we joined forces.[11]

Again, Sternaman led the team in rushing and scoring in 1921. On Thanksgiving that year in Chicago, the Staleys met the tough Buffalo All-Americans team, led by quarterback/coach Tommy Hughitt, in a de facto title game between the league's two unbeaten teams. Buffalo prevailed, 7–6, but agreed to a rematch, again in Chicago, with the understanding that the game would be considered a postseason exhibition game. On December 4, the Staleys beat Buffalo, 10–7, and then claimed the title. The league backed Halas's 9–1–1 Staleys over the 9–1–2 All-Americans on the grounds that the most recent game counted as the tiebreaker.

Dutch's brother, Joey, another Illini alumnus, joined the newly christened Chicago Bears as quarterback in 1922, and developed into an outstanding player (and eventually a source of friction between the partners). But Joey left the Bears to operate the Duluth Kelleys in 1923, before returning in 1924. He left again in 1926, to form the Chicago Bulls in the competing American Football League, before returning to the Bears in 1927, for the remainder of the decade. The Bears, meanwhile, continued to excel on the field and finished second to Guy Chamberlin's Bulldogs in 1922, 1923, and 1924, attaining records of 9–3, 9–2–1, and 6–1–4, respectively.

The team dipped a bit in 1925, to 9–5–3, seventh in the 20-team league, but Halas and Sternaman made the biggest move in the league's early history by signing Illinois star halfback Red Grange immediately following the conclusion of his final game as a senior. Grange and the Bears set out on a 19-game, 67-day barnstorming tour arranged by Halas, Sternaman, and Grange's agent, C. C. Pyle. That tour included seven league games and 12 exhibitions, and ranged as far south as Florida and as far west as California. Grange joined the Bears for their league game against the Cardinals on November 26, and the tour concluded in Seattle on January 31, 1926. Along the way, Grange made more than $100,000 from his share of the profits, but it was a windfall for the Bears partners as well;[12] however, the two sides could not agree on a contract for 1926, since Pyle and Grange also insisted on a share of the team. When Halas and Sternaman refused, Pyle and Grange formed the rival AFL for 1926, with Grange playing for the league's flagship New York Yankees team. Grange's Yankees led the circuit in scoring but finished second to the Philadelphia Quakers in the standings, while Joey Sternaman's Chicago Bulls posted a mediocre 5–6–3 record.

One result of the financial pressures brought by the new league was the Cardinals dealing Paddy Driscoll to the Bears to keep him from signing with the AFL Bulls. The replenished Bears had an excellent 12–1–3 record in 1926. Yet, the squad also finished second to a Philadelphia team, Guy Chamberlin's Frankford Yellow Jackets, who recorded a 14–1–2 mark; however, the Halas–Sternaman partnership began to fray, with Halas questioning whether Dutch's loyalty was compromised by his relationship with his brother Joey, particularly regarding scheduling issues. During the next few years, the relationship between George and Dutch would deteriorate concerning several issues. Halas wrote in his autobiography,

> My biggest problem was personal. My relationship with Dutch Sternaman was worsening. Mutual trust had almost vanished. The split hurt the team. I developed plays. Dutch would drill them into the backfield, I into the line. I was steadily moving toward an open game with a 60–40 division between running and passing. Sternaman wanted a tight game. The consequence was that I would tell the team to do this and Sternaman would tell them to do that. [13]

A look at the archival Sternaman Collection at the Pro Football Hall of Fame clearly indicates that Sternaman was creating plays, too. It is also worth noting that if Halas was aiming for a 60–40 run/pass ratio in the 1920s, that would have been a very open game indeed. The league began keeping official statistics in 1932, and the overall ratio that year was 75–25. That year, the Packers of passing pioneer Curly Lambeau ran the ball 76 percent of the time; Lambeau would not get to a 60–40 run/pass split until 1942, and Halas not until 1947.

The Bears dropped to a 9–3–2 record in 1927, Dutch's last year as a player, and then to 7–5–1 in 1928, which marked the end of Halas's playing career. The bottom dropped out in 1929, with the Bears sinking to 4–9–2, ninth in a 12-team league. Halas later wrote, "The time had come for Dutch and me to stop coaching, or, more accurately, miscoaching. We had to put coaching under one mind." The one mind on whom the two easily could agree was Ralph Jones, who had coached both of them in basketball and freshman football at Illinois. Halas wrote, "Both Dutch and I had played for Ralph and had great confidence in his ability." Jones promised the partners a NFL championship within three years and delivered on that and much more for the game itself.[14]

Ralph Jones was a mere 5-foot-7, slight of build, and baldheaded, but he stands as a giant in pro football history—an unsung giant, however. Jones was born on September 22, 1880, in Marion County, Indiana, and grew up in Indianapolis, where he graduated from Shortridge High School. As a junior at Shortridge in 1900, he formed the basketball team, played on it, and coached it. He is said to be the first high school basketball coach in Indiana, less than a decade after the game was invented by James Naismith in 1891. At Shortridge, Ralph played football, basketball, track, and baseball. He coached the basketball team there from 1900 to 1901, then again from 1903 to 1904. In conjunction with this activity, he also coached at the local YMCA, where he was athletic director from 1901 to 1902, and at Butler University, where his team finished 2–2 in 1903.

In 1904, Jones was named basketball coach at Wabash College. Through the 1909 season, Jones led Wabash to an impressive 75–6 record, while also serving as athletic director there and at the Crawfordsville YMCA. He also coached that YMCA squad from 1905 to 1907. In 1910, Jones moved up a level to Purdue University, coaching the basketball and track teams, and assisting with the football and baseball teams. From 1910 to 1912, Jones led the Boilermaker basketball team to a 32–9 record and two Big Nine Conference titles.

Lured across the state line in 1913, Ralph took over as the basketball coach at Illinois, while also assisting Bob Zuppke with the football team and George Huff with the baseball team. In addition, Jones served as assistant athletic director under Huff and started a school for basketball coaches during his time at Illinois. From 1913 to 1920, Ralph's Illini cagers posted an 85–34 record, won two Big Nine titles, and were rated national champions in 1915. He also wrote *Basketball from a Coaching Standpoint*, a fairly popular instructional book that went through three editions in that time.[15] Jones is considered an early proponent of the fast break and recorded a 194–51 overall record as a college coach.

While Halas and Sternaman were breaking into pro football, Jones moved on again in 1921, taking over as the athletic director at the Lake

Forest Academy prep school. As part of his duties, he coached the basket-ball team to a 94–9 mark from 1921 to 1929, and on the gridiron lost just six football games in his tenure. In 1927, he was a finalist for the football coaching position at Northwestern but lost out to Dick Hanley.[16] Three years later, his former pupils came calling and hired Ralph as the Bears coach.

Under Halas and Sternaman, the Bears primarily ran the T formation just as they had learned it from Zuppke at Illinois; however, George's experience may have predated Champaign. A childhood friend of Halas wrote a letter to the *Washington Post* in 1942, indicating that they played in the T formation at Crane Tech under Coach Billy Meyers.[17] In any case, the Bears offense in the 1920s produced 12.5 points per game, better than the league average of 9.1. The team never led the league in scoring but twice finished second before dropping to a lackluster seventh in 1929.

Jones attempted to pump a little air into the offense with changes to player spacing, the center snap, and motion. In particular, he spaced the lineman further from one another, situated the two ends two yards out from the tackles, and moved the halfbacks wider, aligning behind the outside leg of the tackles. In addition, he moved the quarterback closer to the center to take a hand-to-hand exchange. Most important of all, Jones put the halfback in motion before the snap of the ball. Red Grange had returned to the Bears in 1929, as the team's left halfback, and became the first man in motion for the Bears' T, usually going in motion to the right. When Grange started mixing it up by going in motion to the left, that added more variety to the offense as well.[18]

Were the results immediate? That's debatable. The Bears improved to 9–4–1, third in the league and fifth in points scored in 1930; slipped to 8–5, again in third place but fourth in points scored in 1931; and then won the championship in 1932, with a 7–1–6 record, while leading the league in scoring. In terms of scoring, however, Chicago averaged 11.6 points per game during Jones's three-year tenure as coach, two points better than the league average of 9.6 but hardly revolutionary. Nonetheless, the com-bination of the changes to the T, the 1933 rules changes (allowing passing from anywhere behind the line of scrimmage, introducing hashmarks, and moving the goalposts to the goal line), and the slimming of the ball allowed the Bears offense to expand faster than the league average in the next six seasons from 1933 to 1938. In that time, the league average increased to 11.6 points per game, but the Bears shot up to 17.1, as they finished first or second in points in four of those six years.

But Jones did not remain to enjoy the fruits of his streamlined T because the ownership situation of the Bears changed. Both Sternaman and Halas had other jobs and investments aside from owning the Bears. Dutch sold insurance and sporting goods, in addition to owning gas stations, and business suffered during the Great Depression. In 1931, the two owners agreed that one would sell out to the other, with Sternaman conditionally agreeing to sell his interest in the team to Halas for $38,000, to be delivered in three installments, with the final payment due in one year's time. Halas later recalled that he was not able to raise the last $5,000 until the day the payment was due. Had he not raised the cash, Sternaman would have owned the Bears, and George would have been out of football. [19]

Dutch never again had any contact with professional sports, although he did coach Chicago's North Park College football team in 1936, 1937, and 1948, compiling an 8–8–4 record. Instead, he continued to operate his gas stations and heating supply company for the rest of his life. He died on February 1, 1973, but more recently Sternaman has become more prominent in football history after his family donated his extensive personal files, organized throughout the years by Dutch's wife, Florence, to the Pro Football Hall of Fame's archives, where the Dutch Sternaman Collection is now a treasure trove for researchers of the early pro game.

With Sternaman out of the picture and the Bears again a championship-caliber team, Halas returned to the coaching sidelines in 1933. The details of the coaching switch are murky. Halas wrote that Jones resigned to become athletic director at Lake Forest College and that he himself stepped in to coach, "For this year only!" Jones may have been forced out by Halas, or he may have simply gotten a better financial deal from Lake Forest than the thrifty Halas was offering. In any case, Halas was back at the Bears' helm in 1933. And as Red Grange once pointed out, "Nobody was outspoken with him because he owned the ballclub, too. And he had a pretty good break. Nobody could go over his head." [20]

At Lake Forest, Jones coached the football and baseball teams from 1933 to 1948. On the gridiron, Lake Forest posted a 52–31–10 record in that period. He also continued as a consultant with the Bears. Halas kept a number of "$1 a year" men on the payroll as advisors, and Ralph would continue to shape the Bears' T even after leaving the team. He also made the circuit at coaching clinics in the 1940s. Ironically, he pointed out in 1941 that he had used the T in only two of his eight years at Lake Forest up to that point because he didn't have the players to make the system work. He noted that the T needed "a halfback and fullback who can get off their marks quickly and drive hard, and a quarterback who is a master strategist, skilled passer, and leader."[21] A few years later, Jones complained that as more and more teams switched to the T, they weren't following his precepts, saying, "You would suspect coaches switching to the T at this late date would benefit by the Bears' experience, yet the bulk of them monkey around with their own ideas with sad results."[22]

At age 68, Jones retired to Estes Park, Colorado, and died there three years later on July 26, 1951. There were a few reminders of Jones's prominence throughout the years. He was inducted posthumously into the National Association of Intercollegiate Athletics Hall of Fame as a football coach in 1958, and the Indiana Basketball Hall of Fame in 2011. Chauncey Durden, the longtime sports editor of the *Richmond Times Dispatch*, wrote columns extolling the work of Jones and denigrating that of Clark Shaughnessy in the development of the T formation in 1945, 1947, 1950, 1963, 1967, and 1977. Most appropriately, Halas fully credited Jones as a brilliant coach who transformed the T in a *Saturday Evening Post* series in 1957, and in his autobiography in 1978.[23]

So, Halas took back the coaching reigns in 1933, and the team repeated as champions. He and Jones had built a strong squad. The team featured Carl Brumbaugh at quarterback; Bronko Nagurski at fullback; Grange and Keith Moleworth at halfback; Bill Hewitt, Luke Johnsos, and Bill Karr at the ends; and stalwart linemen like George Musso and Link Lyman on the forward wall. The Western Conference champion Bears then beat the New York Giants, winners of the Eastern Conference in the first official NFL title game, to repeat as league champions.

In 1934, the Bears were even fiercer, going undefeated, with a 13–0–1 record, leading the league in scoring and finishing second in points allowed. In the championship rematch with the Giants, however, Chicago lost, 30–13, on a slippery Polo Grounds field to the 8–5 Giants in a game known as the "Sneaker Game" because the Giants improved their footing in the second half when they switched from cleated shoes to sneakers. That 1934 team was powered by the infusion of rookie halfback Beattie Feathers, who became the league's first 1,000-yard rusher that season. He was particularly adept at following the blocking of fullback Bronko Nagurski, and the Bears would accommodate Feathers's talents by frequently lining up in the single wing, as well as the T.

Brumbaugh quit in a salary dispute in 1935, and the team slipped to 6–4–2 behind new quarterback Bernie Masterson. Brumbaugh returned in 1936, and the team improved to 9–3, although Masterson remained the primary signal caller for the next few years. A year later, Chicago returned to the title game, this time against rookie passing marvel Sammy Baugh and the Washington Redskins, but lost, 28–21, in an exciting contest of big plays through the air for both teams. When the team slumped to 6–5 in 1938, Halas acquired Columbia single wing tailback Sid Luckman through the draft, but not to run the offense that Sid knew. A new era of the T was about to start, but that is discussed in chapter 8.

COACHING KEYS

Any discussion of the coaching style of George Halas and, by extension, Dutch Sternaman must begin with their college coach, Bob Zuppke. Zuppke was an experimenter and an innovator, an adaptor and a tinkerer, who never was wed to any one system in his attack. One fellow coach anonymously said of him, "Zuppke probably will use this week whatever plays worked well against him in the game last week."[24] The 1920s Staleys/Bears followed that template in designing their offense.

One clue is given in a short notice published in the *Chicago Tribune* in 1921, regarding the upcoming game between the Staleys and the Detroit Tigers: "The Tigers have a heavy, powerful set of ends and tackles who smash up interference and nail the runner fiercely. To meet this type of a game Coach George Halas has been drilling the Staleys more along the open, forward passing game this week than the old-fashioned battering method."[25] In those scuffling days for the pro game, Halas would write his own game stories to try to get publicity for his team in the local papers; this piece sounds like something he may have planted and gives an indication of his aim to move beyond the "old-fashioned battering method."

Halas gave further insight into his offense in a series of *Chicago Daily Journal* pieces published in 1922, under his byline, and given the running title "Lessons in Football."[26] In article 3, "Explanation of Formations," he described the three main formations used in his system and gave each its own number: 16 for the regular (T) formation, 22 for the Harvard shift, and 32 for the Minnesota shift. In each formation, the players first arrange in three lines (two tackles and the center on the line of scrimmage, guards and ends behind them, and four backs behind the guards and ends) before shifting when the signal is called. For the Harvard shift, the team shifts into an unbalanced line with four linemen on one side of the center and two on the other. In the backfield, the quarterback moves behind the center, the left halfback behind him at T formation depth, and the other two backs at in-between depth. For the Minnesota shift, one side has five linemen and the other just the end, while the backs align similarly to the single wing.

In Dutch Sternaman's notes, he shows a different preshift formation for 1924, in which the interior linemen come to the line of scrimmage, the ends line up next to the quarterback, and the other three backs line up behind them. Sternaman wrote, "This formation is almost a complete circle with the Q.B. in the center. The reason for this is that the Q.B. can get the attention of his teammates, as well as not having to call the numbers so loud." The huddle was rarely used in those days, so players learned the play call at the line of scrimmage. Sternaman also outlined the signal-calling method in another handwritten note. Essentially, the Bears quarterback would call out three double-digit numbers. The first would be the step signal to indicate when the ball should be snapped—on the first or second "hep." The second number would indicate the formation, for example, 22 is Harvard shift right, while 23 is Harvard shift left. The third number would indicate the play, based on the numbering of the backs and the holes, and would be followed by one or two "heps" to start the play.[27]

Halas's series went on for more than a month and included several play descriptions, for instance, "Trick Fullback Line Buck," "Forward Pass from Harvard Formation," and "Criss-Cross Forward Pass from Punt Formation." Sternaman's notes also show plays from a formation labeled the "Penn State shift," which appears to be the same as the Notre Dame shift. From those notes, we can see that the team was still supplementing its T formation by using the Harvard shift in the mid-1920s and the Notre Dame shift in 1929, the last year Halas and Sternaman cocoached the team. On the other side of the ball, Dutch's notes evince that the Bears' defense used both man-to-man and zone coverage of the opposing passing game, which is interesting in that zone defense often is thought to be something more modern in origin. [28]

When Halas and Sternaman stepped aside in 1930, bringing in Ralph Jones to coach the Bears, Jones set about making the T a more modern form of attack. In his autobiography, Halas entitled his chapter on the coach "Ralph Jones: A Call for Brains," and Ralph proved a strategist of the first order. [29] In transforming the T, he widened the spacing between linemen and between backs, and honed the intricacies of the center–quarterback exchange, as discussed earlier. The addition of a halfback laterally in motion before the snap, however, is the most obvious improvement he made to the basic T (see figure 3.2).

Halas liked to say that the man in motion could do seven different things:

> He can block out the end as the play goes around. He can take out the halfback downfield. He can go down and take a flat pass. He can run and catch a long pass. He can go in motion a little deeper, take a lateral, and then forward pass. He sets up a quick kick for the tailback. He is a splendid decoy when the play goes the other way.

In essence, the man in motion gave defenses something else to worry about and caused them to shift personnel and create holes elsewhere. Halas also pointed out, "The vastly improved blocking angle—with the

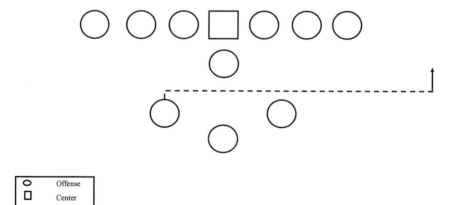

Figure 3.2.   Ralph Jones's widened T with the man in motion

man in motion coming back to hit the end from his blind side—made the T a balanced running attack. Now the backs could run outside as they hit up the middle on quick openers."[30]

Some dispute Jones's provenance on the man-in-motion tactic. Sol Metzger, a sportswriter and onetime college football coach and player, recalled in 1931 that Pop Warner had used a man in motion as a blocker in 1902. In 1953, Joe McKenney, a former Boston College player, claimed that his coach, Frank Cavanaugh, got there first, stating, "In 1922, Cav experimented with the present man-in-motion offense, but he used the end, Tony Comerford, as the man in motion, five yards back of the line of scrimmage, sending a back up to the line of scrimmage." Two letters from Amos Alonzo Stagg raise additional points. In one from 1949, Stagg discussed his use of the tactic in 1927: "A fourth contribution which I made to the T was the man-in-motion play, which I called a Pedinger because Mendenhall, my quarterback, gave it that name." In the second, from 1952, Stagg described seeing the Bears play in 1937:

> They used the Pedinger man-in-motion play from a T formation a few times in those games, but they got very little out of it from a passing standpoint. It was mainly a distracting maneuver for a buck. That was the first time I had seen the Bears play, and I was astonished at the simplicity of their use of the Pedinger.[31]

While there might be nothing new under the sun in football, it can be accurately said that Ralph Jones was the coach who made the man in motion a central element of the T formation. He was the coach whose tinkering with the basic creaky T jumpstarted its evolution into the base formation of football that it has been for the past 75 to 80 years. In a related vein, Halas also credited Jones with the expansion of the Bears' "streamliner" plays (i.e., quick thrusting plays in which backs squirt through holes open only momentarily, with the emphasis on speed—both in the line and in the backfield). Halas wrote that he learned this system from Zuppke at Illinois and that Jones "developed the system still further, adding man-in-motion plays. Today the Bears use streamliners as a foundation and as a springboard for lateral passes, forward passes, and even wide plays."[32]

When Halas returned as the Bears coach in 1933, he inherited a great team, a revised offense, and a new game with the loosening of passing restrictions, the institution of hashmarks to keep teams from being pinned to the sidelines, and the movement of the goalposts to the goal line to encourage field goals and decrease tie games. Halas took good advantage of this situation, and the Bears appeared in three championship games in the next five years, winning it all in 1933.

Halas maintained his interest in a varied offense during that time. Speedy halfback Beattie Feathers was ideally suited to the single wing, and Halas continued to use that as a supplement to his T. In 1936, college coach Dutch Bergman published a book of favorite plays from the best-known coaches in the nation, including a handful of pro coaches. Halas's entry in the book is a "full-spinner lateral forward lateral pass," a gimmick play run from the Notre Dame box. [33]

The best Bears game film available from the time matched Chicago against the Lions in Detroit on Thanksgiving Day 1936. In that game, the Bears used the T, with Carl Brumbaugh and then Bernie Masterson at quarterback, but they also switched to the single wing, with Keith Molesworth receiving the snaps at tailback quite a bit. With the Lions leading, 13–7, late in the game, the Bears switched to punt formation, the 1930s version of a shotgun spread offense, to unsuccessfully try to overcome the deficit.

Within a few years, Halas would find the keys to make the T so varied that it would become his only system. Throughout his long career as a coach and owner, Halas was not the innovative strategist that drove his team. Instead, he was smart enough to find people, like Jones, who were better than him at that, and he let them work. He was a practical man who knew how to run things, be it a business or a football team. Halas approvingly quoted his great fullback, Bronko Nagurski:

> Ralph Jones was a great strategist, but Halas has a talent for handling people. He has immense enthusiasm. He is a fighter. He is always out to win. He treated everyone in a different manner. Sometimes he'd take a player into a corner and talk to him quietly. Sometimes he'd chew a fellow out in front of everybody. He seemed to know how each person would respond. [34]

And, as Red Grange pointed out, he owned the team, so his players had nowhere to complain.

PIVOTAL GAMES

The Bears won two championship games in the 1930s, one coached by
Ralph Jones and one by George Halas. Let's examine each one. In 1932,
the Bears and Portsmouth Spartans tied for the league lead with 6–1–6
and 6–1–4 records, respectively—ties not counting in the standings at the
time. Chicago had tied its first three games, 0–0, and then lost game four
at home, 2–0, but during the span of the last nine games the team averaged 13 points per game; its rugged defense registered seven shutouts on
the season. The Spartans were never shut out but averaged just 10 points
a game and recorded four shutouts on defense. Both games between the
two had ended in ties, 13–13 and 7–7.

The teams agreed to a playoff in Chicago that technically is listed as a
regular-season game. Portsmouth's star player, Dutch Clark, had already
left the team to begin his offseason job as basketball coach at his alma
mater in Colorado. Because of the bitter cold weather in Chicago, the
game was moved indoors to Chicago Stadium, where it would be the
original *Sunday Night Football*, but without any cameras to cover it.
Exhibition games had been played indoors before, as noted in chapter 1,
and, in fact, the Bears had played a game against the crosstown Cardinals
for charity at Chicago Stadium two years earlier. Since the stadium floor
was 80 yards long with rounded, fenced-off edges, it could only accommodate a 60-yard playing field with two 10-yard end zones. Special rules
for the game allowed for no field-goal kicking and that the ball would be
moved in 10 yards on any play that ended at the sideline (although the
offense would lose a down in exchange).

During this weird game, the Bears recorded eight first downs to the
Spartans' five. Chicago completed three of 16 passes for 18 yards, and
Portsmouth completed two of 12 for 28 yards. The Bears intercepted five
passes and the Spartans three. There were only two touchdown opportunities, one for each team, and both followed interceptions. At the end of
the first half, Johnny Cavosie picked off a Bears pass at the Chicago 16
and raced to the six-yard line. Three rushes moved the ball to the two, but
Portsmouth failed to convert on fourth down. Later, with 11 minutes left
in the game, the Bears Dick Nesbit intercepted an Ace Gutowsky pass
and ran it back to the Spartan seven. The ball was moved in from the
sidelines, costing the Bears a down. Two rumbles by Bronko Nagurski
moved the ball to the two. On fourth down, Bronko got the ball again,

started to run, and then backpedaled and threw a jump pass to Red Grange, the man in motion, in the end zone for the game's only touchdown. Although Portsmouth protested vehemently that Nagurski was not the requisite five yards behind the line when he threw, the officials disagreed. Chicago recorded a clinching safety in the closing minutes when Mule Wilson, in punt formation, fumbled the snap out of the end zone. Ralph Jones's team won the championship on a pass play to the man in motion.

A year later, George Halas was in charge of the team again and took advantage of the several rule changes approved by the league after the Bears–Spartans playoff the year before. Those changes opened up the game. This Bears–Giants game was viewed as a toss-up by oddsmakers. The 10–2–1 Bears, winners of the new Western Conference, gave up the second-fewest points in the league, while the 11–3 Giants, winners of the nascent Eastern Conference, led the league by averaging 17.4 points per game behind tailback Harry Newman, the team's leading passer and rusher. The teams split their two regular-season contests, and this title match turned out to be one of the most exciting championship contests ever played.

The Associated Press's lede for their game account enthused, "In a sensational shower of forward passes, the Chicago Bears won the National Football League championship here today." The account later continued, "The game was a revelation to college coaches who advocate no changes in the rules. It was strictly an offensive battle with the professional rule of allowing passes to be thrown anywhere behind the line of scrimmage being responsible for nine-tenths of the thrills."[35]

The contest was a seesaw battle, with the lead changing hands six times. In the first quarter, an exchange of punts led to the Bears getting in position for a 16-yard field goal by Jack Manders. In the second quarter, Chicago added a second Manders field goal from the 40, but the Giants struck back on a 29-yard scoring pass from Newman to end Red Badgro before the intermission to take a 7–6 lead.

In the third quarter, another Bears drive resulted in a third field goal from Manders and another lead change. The Giants tried the hidden-ball trick, with center Mel Hein lining up on the end of the line to be eligible to take the pigskin back after snapping it to Newman and slipping down field with it. Keith Molesworth spotted Hein's deception, however, and the drive ended in a punt. The next time the Giants got the ball, Newman passed them down the field to the one, where Max Krause plunged over for a 14–9 lead. The ensuing Bears drive was powered by a pass from punt formation from George Corbett to quarterback Carl Brumbaugh for a 67-yard gain to the New York eight. On third down, Nagurski again faked a plunge and threw a jump-pass touchdown to Bill Karr to take a 16–14 lead after three quarters.

In the fourth quarter, Newman's air attack pushed the Giants down the field to the Bears eight. Newman then pitched to Ken Strong, who ran wide before ad-libbing a lateral back to Newman. Harry scrambled with the ball until he spotted Strong open in the corner of the end zone. The bullet touchdown pass gave New York a five-point bulge. The teams next exchanged punts, but Ken Strong's boot traveled only nine yards to his own 47. Following a first down at the 33, Nagurski tossed a short pass to Bill Hewitt, who lateralled to Bill Karr at the 20, and he ran free for a touchdown to give the Bears a 23–21 advantage with three minutes to play. On the Giants' final play, Newman, who completed 13 of 19 passes for 209 yards, connected with Dale Burnett at the Chicago 40. Mel Hein was trailing the play, and Red Grange was the only defender nearby. Only an expert wrap-up tackle by Grange kept Burnett from lateralling to Hein, and the game ended with the Bears on top.

Halas won his first championship game with trick plays and a wide-open offense. His T formation quarterback, Brumbaugh, threw just two passes, both incomplete. His other backs, however, completed seven of 14 passes for 150 yards, and probably not from the T. Halas would do whatever it took to win.

That 1933 championship pitted Halas against Steve Owen, the subject of chapter 5, and both were still early in their coaching careers. Yes, it was Halas's 11th year as a coach, but he had another 29 to go. Owen would introduce several innovations on both offense and defense in the coming years, and Halas's most fruitful years were still to come as well. He reached 1939 having had a highly influential career, but in the next decade he would reach his acme and truly change the game, both pro and college.

4

ALMOST FAMOUS

Potsy Clark Writes the Book on the Pro Game

Illinois coach Bob Zuppke's practical approach to football is demonstrated by the choices of his acolytes. George Halas and Dutch Sternaman used the T formation as the basis of their joint offense when coaching the pros, while Zuppke's favorite Illini signal caller, Potsy Clark, was a single wing man. Clark had a mind of his own. New York sportswriter Stanley Woodward claimed Clark used the Haughton system, which employed both the single wing and punt formations (taken from Harvard coach Percy Haughton) and the Zuppke defense. [1]

Potsy was a communicator and educator in the field of sports and regularly conducted coaching clinics throughout his career. In the early 1920s, he cowrote, with Big Ten commissioner Major John Griffith, a series of instructional books on football, basketball, boxing, and track and field that were compiled as the Wilson Athletic Library. Five of those titles were on football. He also served as athletic director at numerous institutions, demonstrating a talent for sports administration. Above all, Potsy was a football coach who guided several college teams both before and after his time coaching the pros.

Several prominent college coaches wrote books on the game in its first 60 years, including Walter Camp, Amos Alonzo Stagg, Harry Williams, Pop Warner, Bill Roper, Percy Haughton, Bob Zuppke, and Knute Rockne. Potsy, however, was the first professional coach to do so, with *Football: A Book for Players and Football Fans* in 1935. The book is a 32-

page, soft-cover, illustrated instructional guide that provides a good look at how the pro game was played in the 1930s. It was just the third book ever published on pro football, following passing star Benny Friedman's *The Passing Game*, from 1931, and Harry March's *Pro Football, Its Ups and Downs: A Lighthearted History of the Post Graduate Game*, from 1934. March had some involvement in the early Ohio League and was the de facto general manager of the New York Giants until being ousted in 1934. His book is a loose history of pro football, written mostly from memory.

The only other pro coaches to write a book on the game in the first half of the 20th century was the triumvirate of Halas, Ralph Jones, and Clark Shaughnessy in 1941; however, their "book," *The Modern T Formation with Man in Motion*, was really just the playbook that they used when teaching at coaching clinics. The first biographical treatment of a pro football coach would not come until 1952, when Steve Owen published his autobiography, *My Kind of Football*. Overall, the selection of titles on pro football through 1949 was slim—roughly 20 titles—and most centered on teams or players, not coaches.

Potsy Clark was a NFL forerunner in reaching the public through the written word, and his book offers a wealth of information about the game of the mid-1930s. One example is the two-page spread at the center of the book that depicts the common strategy map for the pro game, in which the gridiron is divided into defensive, intermediate, and offensive territories, and is similar to a map in Zuppke's book and text in Haughton's. From a team's goal line to the 15 was the "badlands," where it was recommended to punt on first down. From the 15 to the 40 was the area to punt on second or third down. Between the 40s, punting was reserved for fourth downs. From the opponents' 40 on in was the area for passing and field-goal kicking. From the 20 on in was the "scoring zone" (equivalent to today's red zone), where the advice was to avoid the fancy stuff and stick to basic plays. [2]

In another section, Clark diagramed a successful play from each of the teams in the NFL and in the text described their offensive system as a whole. The Giants, Redskins, and Eagles used the single wing with an unbalanced line; the Dodgers and Cardinals used the double wing with an unbalanced line; the Packers, Pirates, and St. Louis Gunners used the Notre Dame shift with a balanced line. The Redskins and Dodgers also used the punt formation at times. The Redskins, Dodgers, Gunners, Pirates, and Eagles called their plays in the huddle, while the other teams did so at the line. Oddly, Clark stated that the Bears employed the single wing, but their play diagram shows a T formation. Ultimately, he concluded, "There is no system in football that doesn't depend upon the hard and conscientious efforts of all the players."[3] Potsy had great success sticking to the fundamentals of blocking, tackling, and kicking, but it was discipline and teamwork that made him a winner.

LIFE AND CAREER

George M. Clark was born on a stock farm in Carthage, Illinois, on March 20, 1894. George was nicknamed "Potsy" at the age of six by the local veterinarian and went by that for the rest of his life. On the farm, he grew up doing chores, along with his four brothers, three sisters, parents, grandparents, and an uncle, who all lived on the property. When Potsy was 10, his father died of erysipelas, a skin infection that would also cause the death of baseball manager Miller Huggins years later. Clark entered Carthage High School four years later and led the team to consecutive unbeaten seasons in 1909 and 1910 as the squad's quarterback. He also starred at baseball, basketball, and track. The family moved from the farm into town in 1911, and during Potsy's senior year, the team lost only its season finale.[4]

Clark enrolled in William and Vashti College in Aledo, Illinois, in 1912, joining two of his brothers. Potsy later recalled, "I carried milk for my board and room at William and Vashti."[5] There the 5-foot-7, 147-pound quarterback and his two brothers formed the "Clark Trio," leading the team to an unbeaten season that culminated with Potsy being elected captain for the 1913 campaign. A year later, he enrolled at the University of Illinois, where he quarterbacked the Illini in Bob Zuppke's second season as coach.

Zuppke later wrote,

> The basic attack of the 1914 team was the balanced formation now known as the I formation. This was supported by the spread and the deep T—punt formation adapted to quick openings, wide-running plays, passes with the ever-present threat of the punt. This is the only team in all my career which had the necessary talent for that formation, and that is why I like to say that the 1914 team played the most modern

game yet attempted. Its decisive victories and the fact that it was my first great college team make me think it was the greatest of all my teams. Two of my greatest college backs played on this team, [Harold] Pogue and Potsy Clark. The third was [Red] Grange.[6]

That team won the Big Ten Conference championship. In 1915, Potsy and sophomore end George Halas both suffered broken jaws, but Potsy played anyway and led Illinois to a tie for the Big Ten Conference title with Minnesota. The athletically gifted Clark also played shortstop on Illinois' conference champion baseball team the previous spring and was offered a contract by both John McGraw of the New York Giants and Clark Griffith of the Washington Senators. Potsy stayed in school, however, and received his degree in 1916. That summer, he taught in a summer school for coaches before becoming assistant football coach at the University of Kansas in the fall.

With World War I raging in May 1917, Potsy entered officer training at Fort Riley, Kansas, and was commissioned as a second lieutenant. That year he coached the Camp Funston baseball, basketball, and football teams to service championships before going overseas in the summer of 1918. Clark saw combat in World War I, but with the cessation of hostilities, he quarterbacked the football team of the 89th Division to the American Expeditionary Force championship against the 36th Division in March 1919. In the title game, played in Paris, Potsy scored two second-half touchdowns to spur a 14–6 win with General John "Black Jack" Pershing watching from the stands. What was most significant about the team, however, is that it was coached by former Harvard player Paul Withington, who introduced Clark to the offense employed by Harvard coach Percy Haughton.[7]

After the war, Zuppke hired Clark as the school's baseball coach and his assistant football coach. Moreover, Potsy taught in the first four-year course for coaches at Illinois that year, also forming a partnership with Major John Griffith, then the publicist for the Illinois Athletic Department, who would serve as Big Ten commissioner from 1922 to 1942. The two started the *Athletic Journal*, which grew into the Wilson Athletic Library. Clark and Griffith cowrote 10 titles in that series.[8] Clark then took the job as head coach at Michigan Agricultural College (now Michigan State), where he led the Spartans to a 4–6 record in 1920. More important to Potsy was that he met Janet Mahon, a MAC coed whom he would marry during Christmas in 1921.

By the time the couple married, Clark had returned to the University of Kansas, where he coached the football team to a 16–17–1 record from 1921 to 1925. After that middling record, Potsy, his wife, and his daughters, Mary and Jane, moved to Minnesota, where he assisted Doc Spears with the football team for one year before being named athletic director and football coach at Butler University in Indianapolis, Indiana. In three years, Clark led Butler to a 19–5 record and oversaw the construction of a new 36,000-seat stadium and 15,000-seat fieldhouse; however, not everyone considered those positive developments.

In August 1930, Butler was dropped from the North Central Association of Colleges because of its emphasis on athletics rather than academics. The primary evidence of this misalignment of priorities was Potsy's $10,000 salary (larger than that of the college president) and the $750,000 spent on the two new facilities. Clark stepped down within days of the NCAC decision and began selling insurance.[9]

Clark, who was successful in the insurance field due to his loquacious nature and gift of persuasion, continued that line of work in the offseason even after he returned to coaching in 1931. Perhaps driven by the Butler experience, Potsy widened his horizons to pro football and applied for the open job as coach of the Portsmouth Spartans in January 1931. He was hired in March and soon thereafter wrote a letter to the *Portsmouth Times* in which he extolled the importance of local support: "Football is like war—there must be spirit behind the team. Football players, like women, are vain, and they play better or dress better when they know the public is watching." He added that he was looking forward to the change and gave a good indication of what he valued as a coach:

> I have been won over to professional football the past several years, especially when the league forbade the use of college players before graduation or the year of graduation period. Organized practice has improved the game more than any other thing, I believe. I saw several games last fall, and the teams showed drill, precision in their plays, hustle in the huddle and formations, players showed they were in fairly good condition, rowdyism by players and spectators has disappeared.[10]

Clark returned to Portsmouth in July and gave a series of speeches to local groups and businesses to drum up interest in the team. At a rally at the Masonic temple in town, Clark indicated he was the right man to run a team that was run on a shoestring. "I don't need so many players," he said. "The size of the squad never worries me. Just give me big, tough boys, boys with brains, and we'll get somewhere."[11]

Portsmouth and Green Bay were the last small towns with teams in the NFL, and the financial support for the Spartans was weaker than for the Packers. Portsmouth kept its roster size small but still frequently had trouble meeting the payroll. The team travelled by bus rather than train, and Potsy had the players keep a pair of football shoes on the bus so they could practice by the side of the road when the vehicle would stop.[12]

On the team's first day of practice, Clark threw Father Lumpkin, the star back from the 1930 squad, off the field for fooling around too much. Lumpkin apologized to Potsy the next day, and thus the coach had established discipline on the team.[13] The team itself was remade with an infusion of talent. With the demise of the independent Ironton Tanks came a handful of players, one of whom was star back Glenn Presnell. Clark signed two rookie linemen, Ox Emerson and George Christensen, who would make the NFL All-Decade team for the 1930s. Best of all, Potsy's brother Stu was coaching at the University of Denver and recommended a triple-threat back from Colorado College who had spent the 1930 season as an assistant coach at his alma mater—Dutch Clark. Dutch gave the Spartans one of the top players in the NFL and eventually wound up in the Pro Football Hall of Fame.

Portsmouth had finished 5–6–1 in 1930, but with several new faces coming in, Potsy made sure they stayed focused from the start. Before they took the field for the season opener against Brooklyn on a steamy day in early September, Clark told his troops, "The first man who says a word about the heat is a weakling and doesn't deserve to be on this ballclub. Forget about the heat and go out and win the game."[14] They did. In fact, Portsmouth won its first eight games, five by shutout. Rookie George Christensen attributed the start to Clark's college-style approach to practice, saying, "Our club, which did scrimmage and work in practice just like a varsity team, got off to a running start by outconditioning its opponents early in the season."[15]

In November, they lost back-to-back games to the Giants and Bears, won two more, and then lost to the Cardinals on November 22, with starting tackle Jap Douds being ejected from the game for cursing at the officials. Two days later, Clark suspended Douds and announced, "Douds was put out of the game for certain language that he used in addressing one of the officials. This is one rule that must be adhered to as long as I am coaching the team."[16] Douds never played for the Spartans again, but the team rallied to defeat the Bears, 3–0, in the season finale on November 29.

Except the Spartans did not consider that to be their season finale. The team had a tentative agreement with Green Bay for the Packers to finish the season in Portsmouth's Universal Stadium on December 13; however, once the Packers lost to the Bears on December 6, dropping Green Bay's record to 12–2, just one game better than Portsmouth's 11–3, Curly Lambeau decided not to risk the Packers' third straight NFL title with a finale in Ohio. Clark, the Spartans, and Spartans fans were incensed. The *Portsmouth Times* referred to the Packers as the "Yellow Bay Pikers," "Cheese Champs," and "limburger champions." Clark pleaded with league president Joe Carr, stating, "I don't see how a team can claim a pennant when they haven't played all the teams in the league."[17] The protest was to no avail; the league ruled that the Packers–Spartans game was never part of the official schedule, so Green Bay was under no obligation to play.

Still, it was a great season and a great coaching job by Clark in his first year as a pro coach. On the down side, the players were not paid their full salaries. One-quarter of their pay was withheld during the season to be paid in full at season's end, but the coffers were almost empty. At a May rally in support of the team's stock drive to raise money, the team president stressed that if the back salaries were not paid by August, those players would be free agents. Fortunately, enough cash was raised so that catastrophe was avoided. The other offseason priority was getting the Packers on the schedule, and a home-and-home series was arranged.

Portsmouth did not break out of the gate as fast in 1932. The team beat the Giants in the opener, then tied the Cardinals before losing, 15–10, in Green Bay on a fourth-quarter touchdown run by Clarke Hinkle. The loss to the despised defending champions was aggravating and mixed with controversy. Clark told Lambeau after the game, "The officials deliberately handed you the game and you know it, Curly." Curly replied, "We beat you here, and we can beat you any place, officials or no officials." Potsy countered with a challenge: "You remember this, when you bring your overrated 11 to Portsmouth, I'm going to beat you with 11 men. I'm not going to make a single substitution to prove to you just how strong your team really is."[18]

The optimistic Clark told the *Portsmouth Times*, "The Spartans have hit their stride, and the team is going to be hard to stop."[19] He was right. From that game onward, the Spartans would not lose another, tying Staten Island once and the Bears twice, and beating Staten Island, New York, Brooklyn, and Boston, leading to a scheduled finale against Green Bay. When Portsmouth demolished Green Bay, 19–0, on December 4, it vaulted the 6–1–4 Spartans into first place over the 10–2 Packers. A week later, Green Bay stumbled against Chicago, allowing the 6–1–6 Bears to tie Portsmouth for first place.

A championship game was hastily arranged for the following Sunday in Chicago, although the game would count as part of the regular season and not be considered a postseason game. Because of bad weather in the Windy City, the game was moved indoors to Chicago Stadium and played on a shortened field made of tanbark. Just when it looked as if the game was going to end in the third tie of the season between these two opponents, a turnover led to a controversial Chicago touchdown. The touchdown was disputed because it was argued that Chicago fullback Bronko Nagurski was not five yards behind the line of scrimmage (as mandated by league rules) when he connected with Red Grange in the end zone. A late safety made the final score 9–0. The Bears were champions, the Spartans dropped to third behind the Packers, and Potsy was again left sputtering about the unfair fate of his team.

The discontinuance of the five-yard rule was one of several changes made in 1933 to open up the game. Potsy, who was on the three-man rules committee with George Halas and Curly Lambeau, was in favor of the change since the rule was not enforced effectively anyway. The Spartans offense, despite being third in the NFL in scoring in 1932, had declined almost three points per game that season, and Clark drew criticism for the stodginess of his attack. Dutch Clark recalled,

> We ran from a single wing formation at Portsmouth—it would be years before anyone but the Bears used the T—and we had about nine running plays and nine passing plays. When we told Potsy we'd like to get a little fancy, he'd say, "Percy Haughton used only nine of each, and what's good enough for him is good enough for you guys."[20]

Looking at the run/pass ratio of the Spartans, it's hard to believe he had nine passing plays. Official statistics began in 1932, so from 1932 to 1936, Clark's teams ran the ball 78.4 percent of the time. Even in an era when the league as a whole ran the ball 72.9 percent of the time, Potsy's attack ran the ball 7.5 percent more than that—almost 80 percent of its plays were runs. In fact, in 1934 and 1936, Clark's offense did exceed 80 percent running plays.

The other Clark, Dutch Clark, the team's biggest star, delivered another blow to the offense in 1933, when he retired to take a coaching position at the Colorado School of Mines. Dutch was tired of waiting for the money due him as Portsmouth continued to struggle financially, so he took a surer paycheck. League scoring improved about 1.5 points per game with the rule changes, and Portsmouth bumped up a little more than that, with Glenn Presnell and Ace Gutowsky shouldering more of the burden with Dutch gone. Thus, the team remained a contender. After eight weeks, the 6–2 Spartans trailed only the 6–1–1 Bears in the new Western Conference. While Chicago finished the season on a 4–1 run, however, Portsmouth dropped its last three games, losing to the expansion Cincinnati Reds once and the Bears twice.

The Spartans finished second in the Western Division in 1933, but Portsmouth was done as a NFL city. Unable to pay its bills, the franchise was sold to Detroit radio mogul George A. Richards in the spring of 1934. One of his first acts was to re-sign Potsy as coach of the newly christened Detroit Lions. Clark had been courted by the University of Indiana and also the NFL's Pittsburgh Pirates in late winter but stuck with his team for the move to Detroit. Potsy was able to bring back Dutch Clark now that the team was on stable financial ground.

An upbeat Potsy told the *Detroit Times*, "If they know they're champions they will play like champions. Don't you think Mickey Cochrane [Detroit baseball manager] has his Tigers thinking they're champions? Of course he has, and look where they're headed."[21] The brand new Lions threatened to trample the rest of the league in 1934. With Dutch Clark guiding the attack, the team averaged more than 200 yards rushing per game and scored the second-most points in the league; however, it was on the other side of the ball that the Lions made history.

Detroit shut out its first seven opponents of the season, outscoring them 118–0. Only one team, the Brooklyn Dodgers, was able to breach Detroit's 20-yard line, and that was due to recovering a Lions fumble. Finally, in week eight against the Pirates, the Lions defense yielded. Safety Dutch Clark missed in trying to jump a pass route to intercept Harp Vaughan's first-quarter pass to Joe Skladany, and Skladany raced to the end zone with a 62-yard touchdown. Detroit countered with a 400-yard rushing attack and pummeled Pittsburgh, 40–7.

The Lions then beat the Cardinals and the St. Louis Gunners to improve to 10–0. Unfortunately, the Bears had the same record and were tied for first place in the West. In week 11, Detroit stumbled against the rebuilding Packers and lost, 3–0, on a 47-yard fourth-quarter field goal by Clarke Hinkle. That was Curly Lambeau's rejoinder to an earlier 3–0 loss to Detroit on Glenn Presnell's record-setting 54-yard field goal. The Lions found themselves one game behind the Bears with two games remaining, a home-and-home series against Chicago.

The first match came four days later, on Thanksgiving Day, in Detroit. The Lions built a 16–7 halftime lead but could not hold it. They gave up two field goals in the third quarter, and Nagurski ended the game in the fourth quarter with a two-yard touchdown pass to Bill Hewitt. Chicago had clinched the title with that 20–16 win and, three days later, ended the season undefeated with a 10–7 victory against the Lions. For the second year in a row, Potsy's team had dropped the final three games of the season to fall into second place. For the fourth year in a row, a successful season had a bitter end.

That 1934 team may have been Potsy's finest, and once again the coach found himself courted by a pro team—the Cardinals—and a major college—this time Harvard. George Richards short-circuited that talk by promoting Clark to coach and general manager of the Lions on January 10, 1935. The upcoming season started in frustrating fashion, as the team struggled to deal with injuries and setbacks but ultimately proved to be the most rewarding of Potsy's career.

The Lions ground-and-pound running attack continued to be effective, as the team scored the second-most points in the league. Surprisingly, however, the defense dropped to fifth in points allowed, and Detroit had difficulty establishing any momentum throughout much of the season. The Lions beat the Eagles, 35–0, in the opener but then were tied by the Cardinals and lost to the Dodgers. They beat the Redskins, then lost to the Packers, beat the Redskins and Cardinals, and then were embarrassed by the Packers, 31–7. Eight weeks into the season, the 4–3–1 Lions were last in the four-team Western Conference, behind the 6–2 Packers, 5–2 Bears, and 4–2–1 Cardinals.

Clark remained optimistic and encouraged his team with expectations of victory. On November 17, the Lions faced Green Bay for the third time that year and finally won, 20–10. Potsy exclaimed after the game, "We've lost our last game this season, and if we get a break the national professional football championship will be decided in Detroit in December."[22] Detroit tied the Bears on November 24, and then four days later, on Thanksgiving Day, beat Chicago, 14–2, while the Cardinals toppled the Packers, 9–7. The 6–3–2 Lions were now tied with the Cardinals for first, with the 7–4 Packers and 5–4–1 Bears trailing. In the last two weeks of the season, Detroit beat Brooklyn, 28–0, while Green Bay beat Philadelphia and the Cardinals tied, and then lost to the Bears to give the West to the Lions. Potsy had gotten his team to the title game against the Eastern Division champion Giants and prevailed, 26–7, in a dominant performance described later in this chapter.

The high point of Clark's professional career came in 1935. Not only did his team finally win the NFL championship, but also his book was published. But there was trouble in paradise. He and owner Richards often were at odds, and that worsened during the team's West Coast barnstorming trip after the 1935 season, when there were reports that Potsy was to be fired. Dutch Clark remembered, "Richards was a funny guy, you know. He and Potsy were always having trouble. Potsy quit a half-dozen times, and Richards fired him a half-dozen times. And Richards would offer me the job." In the offseason, Potsy and Richards worked out their differences again. [23]

Potsy was cheerful in July 1936, when he was in Boston to teach in a summer coaching school at Northeastern University. He told the press, "Right now I wouldn't swap this pro job for any college job in the country."[24] It would be an odd season, however. The Lions finished second in the league both in points scored and points allowed but were not much of a factor in the race. They started with three wins by a combined 76–7 margin but then lost the next three games to the Packers, Bears, and Giants, respectively, and dropped from contention. The Green Bay game featured four fourth-quarter lead changes, with the Pack prevailing, 20–18. The Bears game had three fourth-quarter lead changes, with Chicago winning, 12–10.

The Lions rallied by winning the next four games by a combined 93–17 score to reach the edge of contention, but a 26–17 loss to Green Bay ended any dreams for Potsy's men. But the season finale, a victory against the lowly Brooklyn Dodgers, signaled a new path for the coach. At season's end, Clark and Richards began negotiations for a new contract. Richards was offering a one-year deal, but Potsy wanted a three-year pact. Despite the regular disputes with the owner, Clark asserted, "Only the question of money could interest me in leaving Detroit."[25] In January, Dan Topping, owner of the Brooklyn Dodgers, offered Potsy the deal he wanted, and Clark left Detroit for Brooklyn.

Coming off a 3–8–1 season, Brooklyn was not a good team, so the highly regarded Clark was greeted with admiration and anticipation by the local press. Potsy, who was said to have been involved with selecting blue and silver as the Lions' colors in 1934, aided in the choice to switch the Dodgers from green and silver to carnation red and silver to herald the team's rebirth. Clark immediately fit into the local New York coaching fraternity—he and Steve Owen in the pros and such college coaches as Lou Little, Chick Meehan, Mal Stevens, and Jim Crowley—that regularly gathered socially on Saturday nights.[26]

Clark was said to have imbued the pro team with college spirit, and spirit was always a big part of his program. In Brooklyn, he invoked the same committee system he employed with the Lions. Clark didn't have an assistant coach until 1935, when Red Smith—later an assistant under Curly Lambeau and then Steve Owen—joined him for one year. Instead, Potsy relied on his veteran players to keep things running smoothly through a system of player committees on such things as housing, meals, and discipline.[27]

But Clark wanted things run his way both on and off the field, and that did not suit everyone. Talented halfback Joe Maniaci recalled,

> Potsy Clark was, in my mind, a great football coach, but he was very selfish. When it came to playing the game, when it came to defense work or anything, what he says goes. You had to play it . . . his way . . . if you had ability in football and . . . had something to say, it was against his principals.[28]

Dutch Clark was more attuned to Potsy and had a better relationship with him. "Potsy kept you ready. But he always had a few jokes," he said. "He was a little bit like Duffy Daugherty, who used to coach at Michigan State. He'd get you in the huddle and tell you jokes. But he'd work you hard. He got you ready for the ballgame."[29]

With the Dodgers, however, success was elusive. A 3–7–1 record in 1937 was highlighted only by the promise of rookie tailback Ace Parker in the last four games of the season. Several good rookies came on board in 1938, including guard Bruiser Kinard, end Perry Schwarz, and fullback Scrapper Farrell, and the team improved to a 4–4–3 record. But it was a deceptive record, since the team was outscored by 30 points throughout the season. The following year, the team was 4–3–1 after eight weeks but then lost the last three contests by a combined 98–7 score to the Packers, Redskins, and Giants. Essentially, the Dodgers could not beat a good team. Potsy told the *New York Times*, "Unfortunately, we don't have the men they do. Our roster contains 15 good players, whereas the Giants have nearly 30."[30] On December 1, 1939, Clark resigned as the Dodgers coach.

Potsy was not out of work for long, however. Fred Mandel, owner of a Detroit department store, purchased the Lions from George Richards on January 16, 1940, and announced he was hiring Potsy Clark to run the team. Clark had a new star tailback from Colorado in Byron "Whizzer" White, who he obtained from Pittsburgh, but he quickly learned that one can't go home again. White led the league in rushing, and Detroit finished a respectable 5–5–1, but they were not a strong club. Clark did manage to defeat the Packers and Bears once each, but the grind of the pro game was getting to him.

The Lions' season ended on November 24, and Potsy was announced as the new coach for the University of Grand Rapids five days later, which came as a surprise to owner Fred Mandel. Potsy reasoned, "This position represents security to me. I have two daughters approaching college age, and I shall be glad to have them at a growing institution. I myself will be happy to be in a situation that does not depend on my won and lost record."[31]

At the University, Clark added Gerald Ford, a former University of Michigan center, as his assistant coach. UGR posted a successful 6–2 record in 1941, but with the United States entering World War II, Potsy returned to the military. He enlisted in the U.S. Navy Reserve as a lieutenant commander in March 1942, and both he and Ford initially served at North Carolina Preflight. That fall, Clark coached the Pensacola service team to a 6–2 record. He was reassigned to St. Mary's Preflight in 1944, and went from there to the submarine force. He was discharged in July 1945, and took the coaching position at the University of Nebraska.

Potsy led the Cornhuskers to a 4–5 record that fall and then was moved back to Grand Rapids as athletic director and college administrator in 1946. Two years later, Nebraska rehired Clark as its football coach.

After a 2–6 record in 1948, Potsy was promoted to athletic director and left coaching. He worked in that capacity in Lincoln until 1953. In 1954, he was named athletic director for California Western and served for two years before leaving to enter the brokerage business in La Jolla, California, in 1956. Potsy retired a dozen years later and died of a heart attack on November 8, 1974, at the age of 80.

COACHING KEYS

Clark was an inspirational coach who strove to get his players to play together as a team and stay emotionally keyed up. He drew heavily on his own experience in the army to bolster his belief in the need for spirit on a winning club. At the time, the "old college spirit" was often invoked as a plus for the undergraduate game. One reporter asked Potsy why the pro game was superior. "Well, it's experience, for one thing and . . ." began Mr. Clark. "Don't be modest about it, Potsy," shouted one of his players from across the dressing room. "Tell him the truth. . . . It's the old army spirit!"[32] That anonymous player was citing Clark's military background as a big reason for his success.

Potsy had his teams practice long and hard. He fostered togetherness by keeping his team close, even off the field. In Portsmouth, the players lived in local rooming houses. When Clark got to Brooklyn, he set up a clubhouse. "Now my ideas are different from those of a lot of football coaches," he related. "We'll have a clubhouse somewhere near the field, and all the unmarried players will live there. I'll have to live outside because I'm married, and the married players can live within walking distance."[33]

Potsy only had an assistant coach for one season before he got to Brooklyn and did not have one in his first year there, so he got used to relying on his veteran players to help out on the field. He also had the veterans help off the field with his committee structure to run the clubhouse. He told the *New York Herald Tribune*, "We'll have an executive committee, a house committee, a gambling committee, a football rules committee, a reception and entertainment committee, and a 'wayward' committee."[34] He was empowering the players to govern themselves and, in turn, foster team spirit.

On the field, Clark was a conservative coach. In the pamphlet he cowrote with Major Griffith called *Football Offense*, Potsy spelled out three systems of football: straight or conservative, open or versatile, and wide open or fancy. Conservative emphasizes running and punting and relies upon a strong defense. Versatile features more passing and stresses offense over defense. Wide open attempts to spread the formation wide and force the defense to cover more ground, with more emphasis given to deception than to such basics as blocking and tackling.[35] Potsy always favored the conservative approach. On more than one occasion, he called the punt the most important play in football. As Glenn Presnell put it, "We just used mostly straight football. We worked hard. We had good blockers. We had a good offense."[36]

Clark generally ran his offense out of the single wing formation. Sportswriter Stanley Woodward described that approach as follows:

> On the offense Potsy's team lines up with 10 men in the positions they would normally occupy in single wing formation, with the end split and wing back in the hole. The 11th man, the quarterback, lines up two yards back of the short-side guard and shifts. He either hops up on the short-side wing, drops back into the tail position, gets under center, or runs out to become a flanker on the short side.[37]

There are similarities here to Haughton's attack.[38]

Potsy's 1935 book outlines the fundamentals of his offense in four plays, all from the single wing. The bedrock play is the off-tackle smash that uses double-team blocks on the defensive guard and tackle to create the hole. As Clark put it, "This is an *11-man* play. If one player on the team starts dreaming, Presnell [the runner] might just as well sit down and rest till it's all over. There won't be any touchdown."[39]

To keep the defense honest, Potsy recommended his close-end run, which goes through the hole on the other side of the defensive tackle. A second variation to these two plays is a pass to the end meant to look like a pass to the halfback coming out of the backfield and drawing the secondary's coverage. Clark says, "These three plays—off-tackle, close around end, and pass—will give you the foundation for an offense."[40] Potsy's attack was simple and relied on execution. Dutch Clark noted, "As for game plans and such, we had no such thing. We were going off tackle or we were spinning. The thing that was going the best for us was the thing we stayed with."[41]

In his book, Potsy adds one more play to the mix with the wide-end sweep. This play is also his contribution to Dutch Bergman's 1936 title *Fifty Football Plays*, although there it is called a single reverse.[42] It is an end sweep to the weak side of the formation with the strong-side wing back taking a handoff from the tailback and following the massed blocking of pulling linemen and lead backs to sweep to the other side of the field. It was clearly a forerunner to Vince Lombardi's famous power sweep, which was the foundational play of the Green Bay Packers 1960s dynasty.

That play diagram is shown from the double wing, but Potsy rarely used that formation. His offense was usually aligned in the single wing and sometimes in short punt. When he got to Brooklyn, he expanded his use of the short punt formation, most likely to take advantage of Ace Parker's passing skill. On film, one can see Parker lining up close to the center, taking a short snap, and dropping back on some plays or dropping back before the snap to take a deep pass from center on others. On still others, the fullback would get the snap instead. Parker could throw the ball to one of the ends, the right halfback going out on a pattern or the left halfback coming across the backfield to take a shovel pass. In Brooklyn, however, Clark did not have the talent he had in Portsmouth and Detroit, and the team foundered.

On the other side of the ball, Clark's teams usually aligned in a six-man line—either a 6–2–2–1 or a 6–3–2—but on rare occasions used a seven-man line. In either case, Potsy used a "cup" defense, with the outer linemen charging upfield and pushing in to funnel all plays to the middle of the line, where congestion was the heaviest. It was the basic defense run by Zuppke.[43] Glenn Presnell recalled, "We had a good defensive team. Of course, that wouldn't stand up today with the forward passing as it is and all that I'm sure. But most of the teams ran, and we had a real strong defense against the run."[44]

The *Detroit Free Press* described the Lion pass defense as "essentially a zone and man-to-man combination."[45] Dutch Clark adds,

> I played safety. We played a 6–2–2–1, that's all we ever played. That was a six-man line, two linebackers, two halfbacks, and a safety. I was the middle man, and we played more or less of a zone. Most teams at the time played seven-man lines. We played a six, which I thought helped us. It was a little different and they hadn't practiced against it too much.

Again, in Portsmouth and Detroit, Potsy had the men to make it work; in Brooklyn, he was gathering talent but not quickly enough to have a winning team.[46]

PIVOTAL GAMES

Two games highlight Clark's teams at their best: the Portsmouth Spartans 19–0 vanquishing of the hated Packers in 1932, and the 1935 title-game victory over the New York Giants.

Still angry about the Packers backing out of a tentatively scheduled showdown at the end of the 1931 season, Portsmouth was aching for revenge. The fact that the Packers whipped the Spartans, 15–10, in October in Green Bay only intensified those feelings. Potsy Clark frothed before the first match, "We'll take the Packers, Sunday, and get even for the raw deal of last December. My team is in the pink of condition, and we are tuned up for a battle royal. It is a grudge game if there ever was one. . . . We're out to show up the Packers."[47]

After that bitter loss, Clark upped the ante for the December 5, 1932, rematch. Glenn Presnell recalled,

> Before the game, Potsy Clark gave one of his most impassioned pep talks. Then he named the starting lineup and said, "You people, you 11 men, are going to stay in the game. The only way any one of you is going to come out is by being carried off on a stretcher." And sure enough, we played that game with 11 men, didn't make a single substitution all afternoon.[48]

On a windy day, Portsmouth dominated. The run-based Spartans completed five of 10 passes for 87 yards, while the aerial Packers completed just one of 17 passes for nine yards and had three passes picked off. Local broadcaster Grant P. Ward observed that the Packers made several unaccustomed tactical mistakes and seemed flat and tired all day.[49] The Spartans scored following a 60-yard drive in the first quarter, a drive aided by a 22-yard interference call on the Packers Clarke Hinkle and a 25-yard pass from Presnell to Father Lumpkin. Presnell ran the final four yards for the score.

In the second quarter, Arnie Herber's punt from his own 20 went straight up in the air and was buffeted down by the wind at the Green Bay

25. A five-play drive culminated in Dutch Clark's nine-yard touchdown burst off-tackle. Portsmouth tacked on one more score in the final period when Presnell returned a punt 27 yards to the Green Bay 28. After one running play, Presnell tossed to Clark at the five, and Dutch powered in to make the final 19–0.

Potsy flipped the script a bit three years later in the NFL championship game against New York. Dutch Clark remembered December 15, 193, as "cold and snowy, but Potsy was a type like Bud Grant in Minnesota. You couldn't holler about it. He'd run you around the track if you hollered. Nobody said anything. The game was played in a snowstorm."[50]

The big fear before the game was New York's top-rated passing game with Ed Danowski and Harry Newman, but the combination of the weather and the Lions hard-charging line negated that factor, allowing the Giants to complete just four of 13 passes. By contrast, Detroit's first score was aided by a 26-yard pass from Presnell to fullback Frank Christensen and then another 26-yarder from Ace Gutowsky to end Ed Klewicki to the New York seven. Two rushes later, Ace Gutowsky scored for Detroit. Christensen then halted a Giants drive with an interception of a Danowski pass that he returned to the New York 46. Two plays later, Dutch Clark broke two tackles and raced for a 42-yard touchdown to make the score 13–0 in the first quarter. The Giants drove to the Detroit 10 at the end of the second quarter but turned the ball over on downs.

In the third quarter, Danowski hit halfback Ken Strong for a 42-yard touchdown strike to tighten the game. Not for long. In the second quarter, Detroit had blocked a Giants punt, but nothing came of it. The Lions blocked a second punt in the fourth quarter and recovered at the New York 26. Five running plays took the ball to the one. On the next play, a fake to Gutowsky drew the defense's attention, while wing back Ernie Caddell took the handoff on the wide end sweep (described earlier) and scored. Minutes later, Buddy Parker picked off Harry Newman and returned the ball to the New York 10. Three plays later, Parker scored to make the final 26–7. Detroit had run the ball 65 times for 246 yards, with Clark gaining 80, Parker 70, and Caddell 62.

That was Potsy's lone championship, but throughout the 1930s his teams were consistent contenders who ran the ball and defended as well as any team in the league. His strong teams and colorful personality made him famous enough that he became the first coach to record his thoughts in print, a significant aid for researchers in trying to understand the game of yesteryear. The coach he bested in that 1935 title match would continue to enhance his own reputation in the very things that brought celebrity to Clark: tough defense, the running game, and a personable way with the press.

5

SMASH MOUTH

Steve Owen Wins with Defense and the Kicking Game

When Steve Owen died in 1964, George Halas eulogized his old rival:

> A fellow like Steve comes along so rarely. I knocked heads with him
> when we both were players, and I knocked heads with him when we
> both were coaches. Every time he gained my hearty respect. He wasn't
> afraid to try something new. He was an innovator, and he taught all of
> us a lot. He was the first to stress the importance of defense and the
> first to see the advantage of settling for field goals instead of gambling
> for touchdowns. Every team strives to do today what Steve was doing
> 20 years ago. [1]

Halas, who was still coaching at the time, accurately described
Owen's coaching style and was correct that the emphasis on defense and
the kicking game held wide sway in the NFL of the 1960s, but the point
he missed was that Owen wasn't so much a pioneer in this approach as a
throwback to the game of the 1920s. Owen was indeed an innovator in
strategy on both sides of the ball, but his kind of football was the type of
game that he played in his younger days. He opened his 1952 autobiography—the first memoir by a NFL coach—by saying, "Football started
tough for me, and it stayed tough. It's a game that can't be played with
diagrams on a tablecloth. You have to get down on the ground with the
other fellow and find out who is the best man." [2]

Later, in the opening chapter, he added, "In my time I have seen the rudimentary game of the early 20s, a smash-and-shove affair of brute force, grow into the streamlined, exciting, scientific, long-scoring football of today. But the fundamentals are unchanged—block, tackle, and practice."[3] Owen was a large man, a former lineman, and he favored a physical game. For 23 years as coach of the New York Giants, he was considered the premier defensive coach in the game. Only once did his Giants score the most points in the NFL. By contrast, his teams allowed the fewest points in the league five times and seven other times finished in the top three. Six times Owen's Giants allowed the fewest yards in the league. In the post-1930 period, only George Halas and Don Shula, with five apiece, and the astounding Paul Brown, with 10, have achieved as many seasons allowing the fewest points in the league.

Moreover, Steve's Giants recorded 48 shutouts in the 268 games he coached. Leaving aside the 1920s, since shutouts were so plentiful then and Owen's coaching career did not begin until 1931, he has no rival in this category. Only five other post-1930 coaches have attained at least 20 shutouts: Potsy Clark and Curly Lambeau with 34 each, Paul Brown with 25, George Halas with 24, and Don Shula with 22. Only Clark coached fewer games. In fact, Clark's record of 34 shutouts in 118 games from 1931 to 1940 is a bit better than Owen's 30 shutouts and 121 games in the same time span, but Steve kept on coaching for another 13 years after Potsy left pro football. Steve Owen kept the brutal origins of the pro game front and center, even as the sport evolved. He was the keeper of the primitive flame, but he stoked the fire with strategic and tactical brilliance.

LIFE AND CAREER

Befitting his old-school approach to football, Stephen Joseph Owen was not born in the United States proper. Steve came into this world on April 21, 1898, near Cleo Springs, in the Oklahoma Territory, nine years before the Sooner State attained statehood. In fact, both sides of his family participated in the northern Oklahoma land rush of 1893, staking out their claims along the Cherokee Outlet, which Owen confounds with the much narrower Cherokee Strip in his autobiography. His parents, James Rufus Owen and Isabella Doak, met some time after that rush.[4]

Steve's mother, Isabel, came from an Irish family that immigrated to Delaware before going west to Kinsley, Kansas. His father, James, was from Scotch-Irish stock. His family first settled in Virginia before moving to Tennessee and then to Troy, Missouri, where James was born. Steve's father worked on a Kansas ranch owned by the Rockefeller family before he staked out his claim to 160 acres near Cleo Springs. After James and Isabel married, Steve's father raised cattle, tamed horses, and grew corn and other vegetables on the family ranch, while also working on a neighboring ranch to make ends meet. Isabel formed the first school in the area, while tending to the homesteaders' two-room house.[5]

When Steve was six in 1904, the family moved to Kiowa, Kansas, where his father opened a livery stable. A few years later, the family moved again, this time to Valley Center, near Wichita, where James bought another livery. In 1911, Steve, his parents, and younger brothers Bill and Paul moved back to the Cherokee Strip, and James made his living raising horses, mules, and cattle. Steve had such an affinity for horses that, as a youngster, he aspired to be a jockey, but as he grew to be upward of 235 pounds that dream became impractical.[6]

Steve went to live with Isabel's sister in Aline, Oklahoma, to attend high school and graduated in three years by taking additional classes at the State Teachers College near Alva, Oklahoma, during the summer. In the summer, he worked on oil rigs, as well as on the ranch. When the United States entered World War I, Steve's mother encouraged him to enter the Student Army Training Corps at Phillips University in Enid, Oklahoma, to become an officer. One day in 1918, John Maulbetsch, head coach of the Phillips football team, spotted the oversized Owen lounging on campus and asked if he would be interested in playing football. Although Steve had done some semipro wrestling using the pseudonym Jack O'Brien to maintain his amateur status, he had never played organized football to that point. Maulbetsch, who was an All-America halfback for the University of Michigan from 1914 to 1916, gave Steve a half-hour rough-and-tumble tryout in which the coach pulled no punches and, duly satisfied, welcomed him to the team.[7]

Phillips had an abbreviated season in 1918, due to the war, but went undefeated in 1919, with the highlight being a 10–0 victory against the University of Texas, in which the "Iron Men" of Phillips upset the powerful Longhorns despite using just one substitute the entire game.[8] Maulbetsch coached just one more season in Enid before moving on to Oklahoma A&M in 1921. He was replaced by Monty "Tubby" McIntyre from West Virginia, and Steve credited McIntyre with providing a very different slant on the game than Maulbetsch's purely physical approach. McIntyre was more devoted to precision, timing, and strategy, and Owen soaked it up in his final two seasons at Phillips. After playing in a postseason barnstorming game against the visiting Toledo Maroons featuring the great Jim Thorpe, Steve received an offer to play professionally with Toledo in 1923; however, McIntyre interceded and talked Owen into finishing his degree work at Phillips, while helping out as Tubby's line coach.

With degree in hand, Owen again felt the lure of football drawing him and, in 1924, signed on with the new Kansas City Blues franchise of the NFL, coached by LeRoy Andrew. As a rookie, Owen started at guard but then shifted to tackle in 1925, on the rechristened Kansas City Cowboys, a traveling team that would arrive in town for a scheduled game decked out in cowboy regalia. In between the two seasons, Owen worked as a high school principal in a school where his predecessor had been knifed by a student, but Steve reached out to that student and so claimed to learn the efficacy of "human principles" in getting the best out of his belligerent charges. Kansas City struggled on the field and at the gate in those two seasons, finishing 2–7 in 1924 and 2–5–1 in 1925. After the Cowboys' 1925 season ended on Thanksgiving Day in Hartford, Connecticut, against the Cleveland Bulldogs, Owen appeared in one more league game that year as a member of the Bulldogs. He then played in a four-game series against the famed Notre Dame Four Horsemen that December and joined the New York Giants for a barnstorming tour of Florida in January. In the offseason, the Giants purchased Steve's contract from Andrew for $500, and his future path began to take shape.[9]

Owen joined the Giants as a tackle in 1926, and was named All-League that year, in 1927, and in 1929. He was named team captain in 1927, the year the Giants won the first NFL title in team history, with a rock-ribbed defense that allowed just 20 points in 13 games and posted 10 shutouts. Center Joe Alexander was the coach in 1926, but because his duties off the field as a medical doctor were too demanding, halfback Earl Potteiger took over in 1927. Owen claimed in his autobiography that the team's 13–7 victory against the Bears that year was the hardest game he ever played. He commented,

I played 60 minutes at tackle opposite Jim McMillen, later a world's championship wrestler. When the gun ended the exhausting game, both of us just sat on the ground. He smiled in a tired way, reached over to me, and we shook hands. We didn't say a word; we couldn't. It was fully five minutes before we got up to go to the dressing room. [10]

The Giants' fortunes took a big dip in 1928, causing Tim Mara to acquire the Detroit Wolverines franchise to restock the team, as described in chapter 2—the key elements being new passer Benny Friedman and the reappearance of Coach LeRoy Andrew in Steve's life. Also reappearing was his brother Bill, who had played under Andrew in Kansas City, Cleveland, and Detroit for the previous three years. Bill would play for the Giants for the next eight seasons, drawing some All-League notice in 1928 and again in 1930 and 1931.

Steve was an integral part of the second-best team in pro football for the next two seasons, as Friedman's high-flying passing offense made this team the original "Greatest Show on Turf"—real turf, that is, not the Astroturf on which the 1999 St. Louis Rams played. Even as a player, Owen took an interest in the strategy of the game. He told the story in his autobiography that in the 1929 showdown with the first place Packers, he implored Coach Andrew to switch from the omnipresent seven-man line to a six-man line to deal with the Packers' passing attack. Andrew relented, but after the first running play gained three yards, the Giants went back to the familiar seven-man line. The sudden and strange denouement of Andrew as head coach chronicled earlier led to Owen and Friedman being appointed cocoaches for the last game or two of the 1930 season, but the program for the season-ending benefit game against the Notre Dame All-Stars refers to Steve as Friedman's "first lieutenant and line coach." Benny was ultimately in charge. [11]

When Friedman retired in 1931, to take an assistant coaching position at Yale, Tim Mara asked Steve for coaching recommendations. Owen continually put forth Guy Chamberlin's name, even though the champion Nebraskan had been out of the NFL for three years. Mara kept calling Owen to talk for weeks until finally telling Steve he had decided on a new coach. When Steve asked, "Who?" Tim replied, "You." [12] No contract was signed then, and no contract would ever exist between the two men. Owen coached the Giants for the next 23 seasons on an annual handshake.

The initial results were not promising. The 1931 team fell from 1930's 13–4 record to 7–6–1. Friedman returned at midseason, moonlighting from his Yale job, and appeared in nine games. The announcement of his return was the first instance in which the *New York Times* referred to Owen as the Giants coach. Benny still led the team in both passing and rushing yards but threw just three touchdown passes in 1931. The team was middling on both sides of the ball, although rookie center Mel Hein showed great promise. The following season, Friedman moved on to play with Brooklyn, and the Giants dropped to 4–6–2. Jack McBride led the team in rushing and passing, but he was no Friedman. After the season, Owen undertook a trip through the South and West, interviewing prospective players in an effort to improve the team. Before he could see how successful his trip had been, however, Steve had to endure tragedy. During training camp, his first wife, Florence Carr Owen, died after a lengthy illness. He had originally met his wife, a Broadway actress, when he was a referee and she a performer during a 1929 trans-American foot race organized by promoter C. C. Pyle, and they married a year later. Steve left camp to attend the funeral.[13]

That infusion of talent to the Giants in 1933 brought big changes in the team's performance. Ken Strong finally joined the Giants four years after he had rebuffed them for the Staten Island Stapletons. Of even more importance, rookie passer Harry Newman arrived from Michigan to spearhead the offense. Newman had trained at Benny Friedman's football camp as a kid and followed Benny as a Wolverine All-America. At 5-foot-8, he was a couple inches shorter than Friedman and would not prove to be as durable, but he was a wizard directing the offense. In his first season in the league, he led the 11–3 Giants to the championship of the newly created Eastern Division of the NFL; however, the team would fall short to the winners of the West, the Bears, in the title game. Newman led the New Yorkers in rushing and passing, while Strong paced the team in scoring. This was the only Steve Owen–coached team to ever lead the league in scoring and one of only three that would finish in the top three in points.

It was also the end of Steve's playing career. Starting in 1934, Owen was no longer a player-coach. In his autobiography, Steve noted the significance of that:

When I sat down as a bench coach in '34, I began to study football for the first time. I realized that no matter how much I thought I had known up to that time, most of it was concerned with mechanics of play on the field. As a coach I began to develop the overall conception of the game, and to see it from the different points of view of 11 players on offense and 11 on defense. [14]

In the early 1930s, the pro game at last was starting to gain traction with the public. The rules changes of 1933 helped open things up. The division of the league into two conferences with a culminating championship game gave the football season a focus. The fact that the first such contest in 1933 (discussed in chapter 3) was such an exciting back-and-forth thriller gave the pro game another boost. The 1934 championship, discussed later in this chapter, had its own twist, with icy footing and bad weather that perhaps made it the first "named" game in league history—the "Sneakers Game."

Steve Owen, coaching a successful team in the media capital of New York, was in the middle of all that, and his profile began to rise. Sportswriter Bill Corum lauded Owen on the day of the 1934 championship as deserving of that acclaim from the low status of pro football coaches by noting, "I also know that if you should say to 55,000 of the 60,000 paying guests who will grace the Stoneham stockade [the Polo Grounds]: 'Quick now, no looking at your programs, who coaches these two football teams?' your reply would be, 'Er, ah, ummm, wait now until I think.'" [15]

Owen's Giants slipped to 8–5–1 in 1934, but the team still won the Eastern Conference. They went into the title game underdogs to the undefeated, two-time defending champion Bears with rookie signal caller Ed Danowski taking the place of injured starter Harry Newman and won the NFL championship. A year later, New York again won the East and returned to the title game to face the Detroit Lions. Despite losing that day, it also marked the third straight year that Owen had coached a team in the league's championship game. Steve had remarried that November to Miriam Sweeny, sister of the Giants team doctor, but their honeymoon had to wait until after another postseason appearance by Owen's team.

Steve was starting to get a lot of attention in the press, and he was quite adept at cultivating that coverage. For the rest of his career, Owen was regularly quoted in the papers and became a frequent topic of New York columnists, who referred to him admiringly as "Stout Steve." His weight was usually listed at 270 pounds in the days he prowled the New

York sidelines. It didn't hurt that he had a folksy manner and a curious Americana background of growing up on the frontier amid real Native Americans. It also didn't hurt that he and Columbia coach Lou Little struck up a friendship that seemed to involve conversing with the local college and pro coaches, as well as visiting coaches, in a social circle the press enjoyed covering.

Steve also liked to foster a close-knit environment with his team, similar to Potsy Clark. Mel Hein opined, "The closeness of the Giant team in the 1930s was one of the reasons we did so well. There was a lot of team spirit and togetherness. Most of the players lived in the same area—between 100th and 103rd Streets around Broadway. We stayed in about three different hotels up there."[16] Owen lived with his wife in one of the three, the Whitehall, and encouraged his players to stay there during the season. In Owen's opinion, the human factor was key in coaching: "There is no mystery to coaching. . . . All you need are the right players. Coaching is not primarily technical, as many believe. It is human. Understanding how to handle the individual player . . . is the most important function of a coach."[17]

In his first decade as a coach, Owen had that rapport. Hein recalled, "The players respected Steve. He usually made it pretty hard on the first-year men, the rookies, by driving them and making them realize that every game we were playing during the year that we've got to think about that Eastern Division championship." He may have been hardest on star back Hank Soar, who told author Robert Peterson, "We had a feud going on, but it wasn't really a feud. When we were alone, we'd talk a lot. We lived in the same hotel, and we'd often discuss things about a game or the team. But yet, I'd get on the field and he'd fight me like hell."[18]

After emerging star Ed Danowski led the team to a 9–3 mark in 1935, the Giants dropped to 5–6–1 in 1936, and the defense dipped from first to seventh in points allowed. Newman and Strong had jumped to the new American Football League, formed that year by former Giants president Harry March, but the problems were more extensive. Owen set about completely reimagining the team in 1937. Of the 30 players on the 1937 roster, 17 were rookies and another three were second-year men. Among the freshmen were such significant contributors as Hank Soar, Jim Lee Howell, Jim Poole, Kayo Lunday, Tarzan White, Ed Widseth, and Ward Cuff. Despite two-thirds of the team having no more than one year's experience, the Giants improved to third in points allowed and rebounded to a 6–3–2 record.

Moreover, Owen made a serious strategic change as well. Until this point, he had relied on the single wing to power his offense, as did most teams. In 1937, he unveiled his own creation, the A formation, which, in essence, was a balanced single wing. In the single wing, the line is unbalanced to one side, and the backfield slants to that side as well. In Owen's A, the line was unbalanced to one side and the backfield to the other. In addition, the line spacing was much wider than in any other formation of the time (see figure 5.1).

A year later, Owen added triple-threat back Len Barnum, blocking back Nello Falaschi, and All-Pro tackle Frank Cope. He tweaked his defense, converting to a 5–3–3 scheme (see figure 5.2), and made the best of the limited substitution rules of the time by introducing two-platoon football to a one-platoon game, but more about those items later. The 1938 Giants gave up the fewest points in the league and scored the second highest. They swept to the league title, and Owen was at the high point of his career. He would have many additional good years and introduce several new stratagems, but he would never win another league title after 1938.

Actually, what Steve considered his greatest thrill as a coach came the following August and illustrated the continuing struggle of pro football to gain the upper hand on the college game during this time. Starting in

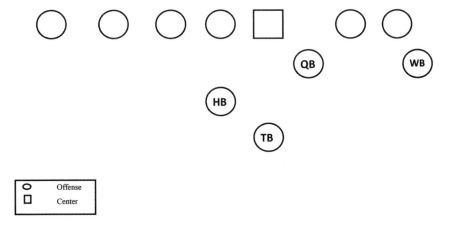

Figure 5.1. Steve Owen's A formation

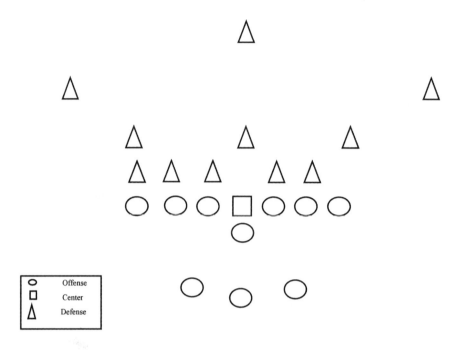

Figure 5.2.   The 5–3–3 defense

1934, Arch Ward of the *Chicago Tribune* devised a football companion piece to the Major League Baseball All-Star Game, which he had started a year earlier. Begun as a benefit game for Chicago-area charities, the College All-Star Game would pit the previous year's NFL champion against a team of college players who had graduated that June. While just an exhibition, it was also an arguing point for the debate of whether college or pro players were better. It seems absurd today, but at that early point of pro football history, the answer was not so clear. When the Giants took the field in August 1939, representing the NFL, the College All-Stars actually led the series, 2–1–2. Thus, when New York evened the series with a 9–0 victory, it prompted Owen to write, "When the New York Giants turned back the best 70 college football men from the 1938 season and won the first game the professionals have taken in the series in four years, it was my all-time thrill."[19] The All-Stars would never regain the lead in the series, but as late as 1947, they only trailed 7–5–2.

New York repeated as Eastern Conference champs in 1939 and again allowed the fewest points in the league, but the team was undone by

Green Bay in the title game. Owen, however, was not present for that game. Four days before the title game, Steve's 63-year-old mother was visiting him in New York when she died of heart failure. He turned over the coaching to his assistant, Bo Molenda, and travelled back to Kansas to bury Isabel.

With the start of the 1940s, the Giants continued to battle the Redskins for supremacy of the Eastern Conference. During the first 14 years of the conference, the Eastern crown was worn by the Giants eight times and the Redskins six, with four of the six 'Skins winners led by Ray Flaherty, Owen's one-time assistant in New York. In 1940, it was the Redskins' turn, and with that honor came the punishment of being gutted by the Bears, 73–0, in the title game. That game, perhaps the most significant in league history, began the transformation of the pro offense to the modern T formation. Owen would stick with his A formation, continuing to insist that it was the players who made the difference. He sneered, "Styles in football change like vogues in ladies' hats."[20]

Steve's 1941 Giants again allowed the fewest points in the league and won the East but were pummeled, 37–9, in the title game by those rampaging Bears. With the onset of the war, the challenges facing a pro football coach were insignificant in the greater scope of the world, but still the game went on, and Owen struggled to stay on top. In 1942, New York dropped to 5–5–1 but rose back to 6–3–1 the following season in what the *Washington Post* called a "beauty of a patch job."

"Eighteen rookies and 10 veterans make up the Giant squad," the *Post* continued,

> and of the holdovers center Mel Hein seldom sees practice because of his duties at Union College [as the football coach]; Ward Cuff spends most of his time coaching a high school 11; back Hank Soar is a private in the army and available only on Sundays; and Tuffy Leemans, who is both a back and an assistant coach, is a Washington businessman during the week.[21]

The patching was even more impressive in 1944, when Owen brought in 34-year-old Arnie Herber, four years out of football, as passer, and 38-year-old Ken Strong as a kicker, and posted an 8–1–1 record, and earned a return trip to the NFL title game against the Packers. The Giants also featured Bill Paschal, the league-leading ground gainer (who didn't play defense), and Howie Livingston, the leading interceptor (who didn't play offense). Those roles were made possible by the relaxed substitution rules during the war. The Packers won the championship in the last title game in which both teams eschewed the T formation.

The band-aids fell off in 1945, and the team dropped to 3–6–1. But the end of the war brought new optimism when New York acquired veteran signal caller Frankie Filchock from Washington. Filchock was equally adept at the single wing and the T, and gave the Giants offense a shot in the arm. Owen had the team come out in the T and then shift to either the A or the single wing, and New York won the East for the last time in his tenure. Owen said of the shifting offense, "I've been wanting to do it for several seasons, but we never had the personnel. Frankie was the difference."[22]

The title game, however, was an embarrassment. On the morning of the game it came out that Filchock and fullback Merle Hapes had been offered bribes to throw the game and had not reported their contact with gamblers. Hapes admitted that he had been approached and was immediately banned from the game. Filchock lied about knowing of the attempted bribe and was allowed to play. The game was tied at 14 after three quarters, but the Bears scored the winning touchdown on a surprise 19-yard bootleg run by Sid Luckman in the fourth quarter.

Filchock was suspended indefinitely after the bribery case was litigated, so the Giants acquired former Columbia quarterback Paul Governali in 1947; however, the team dropped to ninth in both offense and defense, and posted a dismal 2–8–2 record. The offense improved in 1948, with the addition of rookie Charlie Conerly, who was the passer in the A and a halfback behind Governali when the team shifted to the wing T. Owen finally introduced the regular T formation 1949, with Conerly at the controls, and the team rose to 6–6. Owen suffered a heart attack in the summer of 1949, and with the team's continuing lackluster performance, calls for his resignation were floated.

His brother Bill, who had served as one of Steve's assistants and head coach of the Giants Jersey City farm team since 1937, moved back to Kansas. But Steve still had his friends in the media and the coaching profession. Closest of all was Philadelphia coach Greasy Neale, who had known Steve for almost 30 years. Their friendship was so close that the two would travel to college Bowl games together and frequented horse races and baseball games together during the offseason.

Nonetheless, his relationship with his players began to deteriorate. Still, the worst the press might have said about Steve's manner might have been, "Owen's way with his players is simple, direct, and only occasionally explosive. He can be caustically bitter but seldom is."[23] William Hachten later recalled his time with the 1947 Giants as follows:

> Steve Owen cajoled and coerced his players with a mixture of gruffness, profanity, a sound knowledge of defensive football (although little real expertise of offense), and mostly plain bullying. When a player performed badly, on returning to the bench he would be often met with an outburst from Owen. The coaches spent little time teaching the players the finer points of the game; it was assumed players knew how to play. They just had to be motivated to play well.[24]

Years later, Giants owner Wellington Mara said, "His players really feared and respected him. He had a relationship with his players you don't have today. His word was absolutely the law."[25]

Even among the more modern players, Owen had his defenders. Emlen Tunnell, the first black player for the Giants, revered him.[26] By contrast, Frank Gifford demeaned Owen as a "fat, snarly Oklahoman who dipped snuff—the juice would dribble onto his dirty rubber jacket—and stuck rigidly to his old way of doing things."[27]

However, Steve had one more act to go in his NFL career. With the merger of the All-America Football Conference in 1950, the Giants absorbed Hall of Fame tackle Arnie Weinmeister and star defensive backs Tom Landry, Otto Schnellbacher, and Harmon Rowe from the defunct New York Yankees to shore up the defense. With talent like that at his disposal, Owen was able to ride his defense to the top of the standings once more—almost. His set of three games against the powerhouse Browns in 1950 are classics that deserve further analysis here, along with the umbrella defense he unveiled against Cleveland. The Giants were the first team to shut out the Browns and held Cleveland to just one touchdown in those three games. New York lost just two games in both 1950 and 1951, but the squad finished second to Cleveland both years. An offensive failure in 1952 led to a 7–5–2 mark. Steve tried to counter the decline by introducing the "swing T" in 1953, but the bottom fell out with a 3–9 record.

The Maras informed Steve before the season finale that he was done. It was announced that he had resigned due to health reasons, but Owen was crushed. He did some scouting for the team in 1954, leaving the team the following year to work as an assistant under George Sauer at Baylor. Next season, he took the job as the Philadelphia Eagles defensive coach and was there two seasons before the entire staff was let go. In 1959, he moved to the Canadian Football League as head coach of the Toronto Argonauts, the Calgary Stampeders in 1960, and the Saskatchewan Roughriders in 1961 and 1962. Overall, he compiled a less-than-stellar 21–27–3 record in the CFL but still won Coach of the Year honors in 1962, after lifting the Roughriders to an 8–7–1, third-place finish. He finished his coaching career in 1963, with the minor-league Syracuse Stormers, who he led to a 0–7 record as part of a 0–12 season. At that point, the Maras brought him back to New York as a scout, but it wouldn't last long. Steve Owen died of a cerebral hemorrhage on May 17, 1964; his wife Miriam would survive until 2001.

COACHING KEYS

On the eve of his election to the Pro Football Hall of Fame, Giants halfback Tuffy Leemans recalled a game against the Redskins from 1942 that provides a snapshot of Steve Owen's approach to the game. Leemans said New York was at midfield, and he called a pass play early in the game because he saw a rainstorm rolling in and felt the team needed to score quickly. Center Mel Hein cautioned him because Owen did not allow passes until the Giants were near the opposition's 40-yard line. Leemans went ahead with the call and threw a 50-yard touchdown to Will Walls, and the Giants went on to win, 14–7. Owen later fined Leemans for the call but then gave the money back at season's end.[28]

In a magazine article that appeared shortly after this game, Owen wrote, "My theory is that if we are behind by seven points, we will kick field goals right up to the middle of the third quarter before taking the bigger gamble of a try for a touchdown. If we are tied or ahead, we'll kick them all afternoon."[29] That article highlighted the Giants' affinity for three-pointers and outlines the stress Owen put on the kicking game in practices. It's no surprise that Steve's teams led the league in field goals five times in his 23 seasons and were in the top three eight more times.

Owen was a conservative coach who thrived on taking advantage of other teams' mistakes. His standard procedure, unorthodox for the time, was to kick off if he won the game-opening coin toss and put his defense on the field first. He traced the roots of his view to that game in his undergraduate days in which the undermanned Phillips squad upset the University of Texas by getting a quick lead and then having the defense sit on it for the rest of the game, while the offense concentrated on making no mistakes. He also attributed the birth of his own A formation to watching the movements of Bears tackle Link Lyman on defense.[30] Steve wrote,

> At that time defenses were set, but Lyman was a guy who was never set. When I played against him first, I wondered what he was up to. He would move, or drift away from his guard, and make it very difficult to block him. He moved here and there, sometimes coming in to jam up against his guard, rather than splitting.[31]

From this example, Owen saw the value of line splits in creating confusion in the opposition.

For his first six years as coach, however, Steve stuck mostly with the standard single wing attack—sometimes with a flanker—and a 6–2–3 defense. Both the tailback and the fullback would take snaps from the center in his offense. Pretty standard stuff, although the play he gave Dutch Bergman for *Fifty Football Plays* was a gimmick play, the hidden-ball trick, devised by Harry Newman in the 1933 championship game.[32] In 1937, Owen broke the mold and created the A formation, and later wrote,

> My theory behind the A was this: I wanted to spread without losing concentrated attacking power and yet keep the defense scattered along a wide front so that it could not jam in on us at any point. To do this I hit on the idea of deploying my line strong to one side and my backs strong to the other side.[33]

One key point that is often lost in discussing the A 70 years later is that Owen employed wide splits on both sides of his tackles, forcing the defensive line to spread out wide as well.

He liked to claim, "It's balanced. With the players to make it go, you can run equally well to the right or to the left, to the inside or outside."[34] Not everyone agreed with that assessment. Giants quarterback Charlie Conerly told historian Stan Grosshandler, "The A was a powerful formation up the middle, and fellows like Bill Paschal and Eddie Price won rushing titles going right up the middle. However, it was a little weak going over the ends."[35] Owen stuck with his A for most of the rest of his career and won his second title with it in 1938.

Owen did employ variations according to his personnel. In 1941, he added reverses, shovel passes, and laterals to take advantage of an influx of speedy backfield men on the team. When he had a pure passer like Emery Nix in 1943, he dusted off the double wing spread. With the trade for the multitalented Frankie Filchock in 1946, Steve had the offense shifting to the A, the single wing, the Notre Dame box, and the T at various times. In 1948, he tried the wing T, in which the quarterback uses the option play to hand off, toss, or keep the ball himself. In 1949, his friend Greasy Neale sent Owen his former backup quarterback, Allie Sherman, to install the regular T formation in New York at last. In the 1950s, Owen did his best to employ all these formations in an effort to confuse defenses, but he probably just confused his own players. In 1953, the new offense was heralded as the swing T because it could swing from one scheme to another, but the team scored the fewest points in the league.

Ultimately, Steve was prolific at drawing up formations, but his offenses often tended to be dull and ineffective. It was no accident that no other pro team followed him to the A like teams eventually flocked to Halas's T formation. In his 23 years as coach, the league average for points per game was 16.9; Owen's Giants scored just 16.7 in that period—although they only allowed 14 per game. His overall run/pass ratio of 67.4 rushing was 108 percent of the league average in running the ball. His teams ran the ball almost 10 percent more than the league average but scored slightly less than an average team. Steve liked to say, "I would rather win by 3–0 than lose by 38–36."[36] He saw the value of versatility in formations, but his passing game was often nonexistent. The Giants' best seasons were ones in which Owen had a credible passing threat—Harry Newman, Ed Danowski, Frankie Filchock, or Charlie Conerly—even if he employed it sparingly.

Versatility was a big element of Owen's approach to both offense and defense. Another innovation of his cultivated that quality as well. In single-platoon football, Steve saw the value of having fresh troops throughout the entire game, but the substitution rules of the time stipulated that once a player left the game, he could not return until the next quarter. Starting in 1937, however, Owen began substituting all 11 players, or a substantial subset, with each quarter break so that his players would have more energy as the game went on.

There were two keys to making this two-team approach work. First was having enough players of comparable ability on hand to create balance between team A and team B. If your second 11 is purely substandard, then this strategy is not going to yield a benefit. Second, thought must be given to how each unit will match up to this week's opponent. There were frequent pregame stories in the papers concerned with how Owen was mixing up his backfields so each would be able to cope with the opposition on defense—especially against a team like the Bears, which also substituted backfields wholesale—and mesh effectively on offense. Injuries, of course, would short-circuit this strategy at times, but it was another example of Owen staying one step ahead of his opponent.

But it was on defense that Owen had no peer in his time. He was a leader in the shift from the seven-man defensive line to the six-man in the early 1930s. Then, in 1937—that year again—Owen introduced the five-man line with three linebackers. There were, however, some growing pains with this alignment. The Giants lost twice that year to Ray Flaherty's Redskins, including a 49–14 beating in the season finale, but Owen stayed with the 5–3 in 1938, even as Flaherty told Shirley Povich, "That's great. If they use it, we'll murder 'em."[37] New York beat Washington twice that year and swept to the NFL title.

And yet Owen did not abandon the 6–2. He would shift between the two basic sets throughout each season and even during a game. With the advent of the Bears' T formation, Owen's five-man line was adopted throughout the league to counter it. On balance, the 5–3 was better in dealing with the incremental increase in passing offense throughout the league; however, there was more to it than the simple placement of players on a diagram. Owen wrote, "In addition, linemen began to slide and loop and drop out of the line, so as not to present stationary targets for blocking in the long-accustomed spots."[38] Halfback Hank Soar told Stan Grosshandler, "We had stunting linemen, rushing linebackers although we did not call it the blitz, and as the safety man I often performed what is now called the safety blitz."[39]

Football historian T. J. Troup stressed Owen's ability to take advantage of his best players and have his linemen and linebackers coordinate their movements. He also lauded Owen's skill at disguising his defenses as unique for his time.[40] Owen was noted for his special defenses. He regularly worked to make the opponent's best player—Sammy Baugh, Sid Luckman, Don Hutson—a nonfactor. Against Green Bay, for example, Owen would have linebacker Mel Hein reroute Hutson toward the sideline, where the defensive halfback would cover him. And if he got past the halfback, the Giants safety was on alert. Hutson caught just four touchdown passes in 12 games against the Giants in his career. The only team to allow him fewer touchdown catches was the Boston Yanks, who gave up three (but in just two games).[41]

What Owen is best remembered for today is his last big advance, the umbrella defense, which he sprung on the Cleveland Browns in 1950. Paul Brown's team came into the NFL that year as the four-time defending champion of the defunct All-America Football Conference, and they blasted their first two NFL opponents—one of whom was the two-time defending champion Eagles—66–10. Steve watched the film, read the scouting reports, and came up with a unique counter to the Browns' well-coached passing attack. He gathered his defense and told them they were going to align in a 6–1–4 defense and then left studious cornerback Tom Landry to work out the details on the chalkboard (see figure 5.3).

In essence, what Owen sprang on the Browns was the embryonic 4–3 defense, which would emerge later in the decade and has largely held sway ever since. Steve's defense was called the umbrella because the ends and halfbacks would fan back in what resembled an umbrella, with the middle linebacker looking like the stem in the alignment. Owen conceived it as a flexible formation that could slide into a 4–1–6, 5–1–5, or 5–2–4 as needed. In the *New York Times* game story the next day, there was no mention of Owen's tactics. Sportswriter Louis Effrat simply mentioned that quarterback Otto Graham was facing a heavy rush, not that his receivers were blanketed by seven defenders.[42] The second day after the game, Effrat reported on Owen's description of how his defense worked. Once again, Owen proved that when he had the talent on defense, he knew how to employ it. A year later against the Redskins, he devised a 5–3 in which the two ends dropped back in coverage, making it a precursor to the 3–4 defense. Steve retained his vitality for defense until the end of his career, but his lack of similar vibrancy on offense was his downfall.[43]

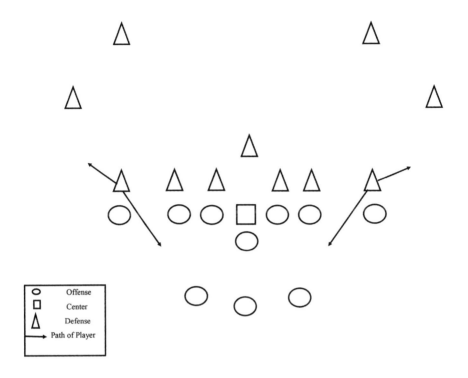

Figure 5.3.   The 6–1–4 umbrella defense

PIVOTAL GAMES

Both of Steve Owen's league championships reveal his penchant for cleverness and taking advantage of his opponent's mistakes. On December 9, 1934, Steve's 8–5–1 Giants met the undefeated, two-time defending champion Bears and upset the favored Chicagoans on an icy Polo Grounds field. The Giants prevailed despite missing two vital starters in passer Harry Newman and end Red Badgro. The Bears lacked rookie halfback Beattie Feathers, who was the league's first 1,000-yard rusher that season.

New York took an early 3–0 lead, but the Bears scored twice in the second quarter to go up 10–3. Chicago also lost two touchdowns on penalties. At the half, the Giants swapped their cleats for sneakers, which had been hastily acquired by an underling from the gym at Manhattan University while the game was being played. Even with the rubber soles,

New York continued to slip further behind and trailed, 13–3, after three quarters.

Everything changed in the final period. A short punt gave New York the ball on the Chicago 28. A deep pass by Ed Danowski seemingly was intercepted by the Bears Carl Brumbaugh, but the Giants Ike Frankian stole the ball away and landed in the end zone to close the gap to 13–10. The next time New York got the ball, Strong bolted free for a 42-yard touchdown run to give the Giants the lead. After the Bears turned over the ball on downs, New York drove right down the field with Strong barreling over from the 11. Now trailing by 10, Chicago tried a desperation pass that was intercepted and returned to the Bears 21. A few plays later, Danowski ended the scoring with a nine-yard touchdown run. New York prevailed, 30–13.

Four years later, the Packers were a 7–5 favorite with the bookies in the NFL title game, even though New York had whipped Green Bay, 15–3, just three weeks prior. The opportunistic Giants allowed the fewest points in the league and intercepted the most passes. The Packers were big and talented with an exciting passing game, but mistakes were their downfall. The subtitle to Rud Rennie's game story in the *New York Herald Tribune* was, "Brilliant Green Bay Passing Attack Futile as N.Y. Capitalizes on Blocked Kicks, Boners, Penalty."[44]

Statistically, Green Bay dominated—164 to 115 in rushing yards, 214 to 94 in passing yards, 378 to 209 in total yards—but Steve Owen's smart kicking teams blocked two punts deep in Packers territory, and both led to easy Giants touchdowns. The Packers fought back to take a 17–16 lead in the third quarter, but a Danowski-to-Soar touchdown pass of 23 yards later in the period was the final score of the game as the Giants defense held firm.

Owen's final triumph was the trio of games against Cleveland in 1950, despite losing the final match. On October 1, the two squads met for the first time, and Owen unveiled the umbrella. With both ends dropping off in coverage 68 times and the right end charging the passer to make a five-man rush just once, quarterback Otto Graham was thoroughly confused. He completed just 12 of 30 passes and tossed three interceptions as the Giants triumphed, 6–0. On offense, Charlie Conerly played in the T with a wide split end and usually a flanker, and sometimes a wingback as well.

For the rematch three weeks later, Owen varied the defense. Most accounts indicate that this time he had the ends "crash" or rush the passer with a six-man front. The film tells a different story, however. Owen mostly used a 5–2 variant and rushed five men 53 times. Three times, he rushed six men; six other times, he used a six-man line with both ends dropping off. It was a different look, and Graham again struggled, completing 10 of 18 passes for just 118 yards and tossing three more picks in a 17–13 loss. On offense, New York used Travis Tidwell at quarterback in the T but ran the ball 56 times. Conerly replaced an injured Tidwell and led the Giants to the winning score in the fourth quarter.

With the two teams tied for the Eastern Conference crown at season's end, they met a third time in a playoff game on a frozen field in Cleveland. Conerly led the offense in the A in the first half, but a penalty nullified his one touchdown pass. Tidwell was ineffective from the T in the second half. Hence, the two teams entered the final period tied at three. Graham managed to lead a late field goal drive, while a last-minute safety by the Browns made the final score 8–3. Each team completed just three passes on the day in a brutal slugfest, but Owen's luck ran out. Steve pulled out all the stops on defense. Mostly, he operated out of a 5–2, but it featured just three linemen in the middle with their hands in the dirt, while the ends and two linebackers were upright and spread out, and sliding all over; sometimes three would rush, sometimes four, sometimes five. Still, he came up short, and Paul Brown was the wave of the future. Three years later in the penultimate game of 1953, Cleveland destroyed New York, 62–14. Owen was fired that week.

Upon Steve's death, New York sports columnist Jimmy Cannon remembered him as a "trudging fat man in a rumpled brown suit which seemed creased in the wrong places." Expanding on that, he added,

> He was a cranky guy and his rages were violent. There was a big lineman he kicked in the rear after a dressing room harangue. He was savage with malingerers and wondered why guys played football if they couldn't take the beatings. He used sarcasm like a knife, and yet the guys who played for him respected Steve Owen, and most of them liked him when they got used to his furious ways. [45]

The 1930s were his high point as a coach, but he reached peaks in the 1940s and 1950s as well and never stopped trying new things; however, the 1920s were when he learned his kind of football, and everything flowed from that time. Jimmy Cannon's take is a good one and more honest than Owen's image in the press throughout most of his career. He was a good talker with writers and something of a media star in New York. Although not always 100 percent accurate, Owen's autobiography, *My Kind of Football*, is a delightful read, making it both a summation and metaphor of his lengthy career.

6

WING MAN

Ray Flaherty Masters the Tried and True

When Redskins owner George Preston Marshall went looking for a new coach following the 1935 season, he was ready for a new direction after going through three former college coaches in the team's first four years. Marshall took the advice of Steve Owen, coach of the rival New York Giants, who recommended his assistant coach, Ray Flaherty, for the job. While hiring a hot assistant coach from a team at the top of the standings is a common occurrence nowadays, Marshall choosing Flaherty as his new coach in 1936 was a first for the league. Marshall would hire 13 men as head coaches of the Redskins in his 34 years of ownership, but Ray Flaherty was, by far, the best coach he ever hired and had the longest tenure as well.

Marshall was a meddler who consistently made life difficult for his coaches, before and after Flaherty; however, Ray insisted on autonomy in running the team and got it. Of course, it's easier to keep a bothersome owner at bay when the coach wins 72 percent of his games, captures four Eastern Division crowns in seven years, and wins two NFL titles. After serving in World War II, Flaherty moved on to coach the New York Yankees of the All-America Football Conference and twice led that team to the league championship game before ending his career coaching the lowly Chicago Hornets, also of the AAFC.

Although Flaherty began his coaching career as an assistant under Steve Owen in New York, his offense was much more dynamic and pass-oriented than Owen's. Ray was devoted to the single wing formation, but he favored a wide-open offense. After his first season with the Redskins, he saw the need to improve his passing attack and drafted Sammy Baugh from Texas Christian University, the best passer in college football. Under Flaherty, the Redskins ran the ball 63.8 percent of the time, but that was just 95.4 percent of the league average. Those Redskins teams threw the ball 4.5 percent more than the rest of the league. Like LeRoy Andrew, for whom Ray played end on the Giants in 1929, Flaherty had the best passer in the game, and he took advantage of it.

As to the shape of his offense, however, Flaherty was not so flexible. The single wing was his base, with some double wing and short punt to augment it, and there was no changing that. He resisted the wholesale movement to the T formation that occurred during the 1940s right through the end of the decade. He and Jock Sutherland were the only two coaches in this book still coaching in the late 1940s who ran the single wing. Sutherland died in 1948, but Flaherty's career died in 1950, when there was no one left who wanted to run a wing-back offense.

LIFE AND CAREER

Raymond P. Flaherty was born on September 1, 1903, on a farm near Lamont, Washington, to Thomas J. and Alice M. Flaherty. Thomas was an Irishman, born in England in 1866, who immigrated to the United States as a boy in the 1870s and grew up in Pennsylvania before heading west. In 1899, he married Wisconsin native Alice Owens in Seattle, Washington. Eldest son Richard was born there in 1900, followed by Ray, three years later, on the opposite side of the state. Younger siblings Eugene, Rose, and Wilfrid would follow in the next 10 years.

In the 1910s, the family moved about 45 miles northeast to Seattle, where Ray met a lifetime pal in Harry "Bing" Crosby. Ray recalled his early friendship with Crosby to music writer Gary Giddins:

> We played on the Ideal Laundry team in the commercial or business league. We'd play at Mission Park, five blocks up the street from Gonzaga. Oh, we were the best of friends, used to chum around all the time, wrestled, played handball, though he didn't play too much handball. Bing was more into entertainment in the evening. [1]

Both Ray and Bing attended Gonzaga High School, which was affiliated with the local Jesuit university. In high school, Flaherty was a four-sport star in football, baseball, basketball, and track.

Ray enrolled first at Washington State University but then transferred to Gonzaga University in his hometown of Spokane after his freshman year. Gonzaga was where his older brother Dick started out before transferring to Marquette in Wisconsin. While at Gonzaga, Dick played end on the football team and was known as "Big Buck." Ray also played end on the Bulldogs football team and was known as "Buck" or "Red" for his hair color.

At Gonzaga, Flaherty again was a multisport star and a born leader, captaining the football, basketball, and baseball teams his senior year. Ray played football for three years at Gonzaga. The first two were under coach Gus Dorais, the man famous for throwing passes to Knute Rockne at Notre Dame a decade before. Dorais was an advocate of the passing game and taught the Notre Dame shift on offense. Gus guided the Bulldogs to a 4–3 season in 1923 and a 5–0–2 mark in 1924, before moving on to the University of Detroit, where he would coach for the next 18 years. He was succeeded at Gonzaga by Clipper Smith, another Notre Dame alumnus, who would go on to have a highly successful college coaching career. Both Dorais and Smith also would coach in the NFL in the 1940s.

In Ray's senior season, the Bulldogs had a powerful team that finished 7–2–2 and sent several players to the pros. Beefy linemen Ivan "Tiny" Cahoon, Roger Ashmore, and Hec Cyre joined Ray's brother Dick on the 1926 Green Bay Packers. Ray's most famous and accomplished teammate at Gonzaga was tailback Houston Stockton, the grandfather of future basketball hall of famer John Stockton. Hust left Gonzaga in 1925, for a successful pro career with the Frankford Yellow Jackets. Another back, Mal Bross, joined Ray and five other Gonzaga Bulldogs on the Los Angeles Wildcats of Red Grange's American Football League in 1926. The Wildcats were a traveling team of mostly West Coast stars, led by All-America halfback George "Wildcat" Wilson from the University of Washington. The team was owned by Grange's agent, C. C. Pyle, who also owned Grange's New York Yankees and had an interest in the league's Chicago Bulls franchise. The Wildcats posted a 6–6–2 record in the AFL's sole year of existence.

While the AFL flopped, Grange's Yankees were absorbed into the NFL in 1927, and Pyle signed Flaherty for one of its end posts. Fellow Gonzaga men Jim Lawson and Ray Stephens also joined the Yankees, while Bross signed with the Packers. Grange's Yankees got off to a 7–3 start, but after Red suffered a serious knee injury, the team limped to a 7–8–1 finish. Grange then sat out the 1928 season with his bad knee, and the Yankees fell to 4–8–1, although Flaherty was named All-Pro for the first time and acquired by the Giants at season's end.

In that offseason, the Giants also acquired Benny Friedman from Detroit and were remade as a passing team in 1929. Flaherty led the NFL with eight touchdown receptions and caught 18 passes for 449 yards (unofficially), an average of 24.9 yards per catch, on the second-place Giants. Once again, he was named All-Pro but then stepped away from the game in 1930. He spent the summer playing second base for the Providence Grays of the Eastern League, where he batted an impressive .302. The team's third baseman was future Reds pitching star Bucky Walters. In the fall, Ray took on his first coaching position at the age of 27—head football coach at his alma mater—while contemplating pursuing a medical degree. Unfortunately, success eluded him with the Bulldogs, as Gonzaga struggled to a 1–7–1 finish.

In 1931, Flaherty returned to the Giants, who were now coached by teammate Steve Owen. Ray did his team a major service by bringing center Mel Hein, another Washington player, with him. Flaherty told the Maras about the star Washington State center, and they authorized Ray to sign Hein for $150 per game. When he got in touch with Hein, however, Mel had just mailed a signed contract for $125 a game to the Providence Steam Roller. Flaherty urged Hein to contact the Providence postmaster and ask for the letter to be returned, and thus New York had a Hall of Fame center for the next 15 years.[2] Unofficially, Ray caught just nine passes in Friedman's last season in New York, but he averaged 31.2 yards per catch. Despite the loss of Friedman in 1932, Flaherty returned to All-Pro status by leading the league in catches, receiving yards, and touchdown catches, as well as being a demon blocker and defensive stud.

Ray took on a new role in August 1933, when he was named as Owen's assistant coach. The *New York Times* notice of that promotion stated that the new coach was "ordered to watch the East–West game in Chicago and was given authority to conclude negotiations with several former college stars."[3] There's no record of which college men Flaherty signed, but Owen's Giants won the championship of the new Eastern Conference that year and faced the Bears in the first-ever NFL championship game. New York lost that contest, but both teams returned to the title match a year later.

Flaherty had begun to decline a bit in 1934, at age 31, but he played a pivotal role in the championship game by recalling some advice of his college coach, Gus Dorais. When Flaherty saw the frozen field at the Polo Grounds on the day of the championship, he remembered a similar experience from 10 years earlier:

> I had a badly bruised heel. It was hard for me to run. So, we played the University of Detroit on Thanksgiving Day. We had a freeze, and the field was frozen. Gus said, "You better put on some basketball shoes and put a sponge in your heel so that you can run." So I did. These fellas were out on this frozen field. They were running with those cleats. They couldn't stop. They were skating all over the field. I could run out there and I could cut, just like running on a basketball court.[4]

Flaherty advised Owen and the Maras to get some sneakers for the team, and the Giants cruised to a victory once the rubber soles arrived in the second half.

Flaherty continued as the Giants assistant coach in 1935, but he appeared in just two games in his final season as a player. Once again, New York reached the title game, this time losing to the Lions, but Flaherty was attracting notice. The last-place Redskins were in need of a coach, and owner George Preston Marshall took the advice of Steve Owen and hired the Giants assistant on Christmas Eve 1935. In the next day's *Boston Herald*, sportswriter Arthur Sampson, the former football coach at Tufts, celebrated the hiring of a pro assistant rather than a college coach because "most of the good college coaches have better berths than any of the professional clubs could offer. None of these top-notchers would consider leaving their present jobs for a berth in the professional league."[5]

At this point, most NFL coaches were former NFL players. A team would usually have no more than one assistant coach, and often he would be a player as well—like Flaherty had been. There were occasions of a team's assistant moving up to become its head man, for example, Doc Alexander with the Giants in 1926 and George "Dim" Batterson with Buffalo in 1927, but not of an assistant on one team being hired as the head man by another team. Ray and the Redskins were breaking new ground, and it would be very successful.

Flaherty was hired without an assistant, however, so he brought in former player Roy "Bullet" Baker as his trainer because Baker could help out with the team's backfield as well. Ray, who extolled the virtue of practice, recalled,

> You'd have one of your good veteran linemen take charge of the line if you had to. Then you'd go down with your backs and work on your pass defense and your pass offense. . . . Then you would come up and have one of your backs take care of those others down there while you went up and worked with the line. [6]

He inherited a 2–8–1 team, but one that had several good players. This included backs Cliff Battles, Erny Pinckert, and Pug Rentner; linemen Turk Edwards, Jim Barber, and Frank Bausch; and end Charley Malone. Flaherty supplemented that base with 11 rookies. These included the likes of backs Riley Smith, Don Irwin, Eddie Britt, and Ed Justice; ends Wayne Milner and Bob McChesney; and guard Jim Karcher. When asked at a welcome luncheon whether he would be using the single wing, Flaherty replied,

> Yes, we'll use something like that, but I have a few ideas of my own which I hope to try out in the preseason practice. I never have felt that the pro teams took full advantage of the rule which permits them to throw forward passes from any point behind the line of scrimmage, and I have one or two ideas along that line which I hope to work out. [7]

Still, the team took time to gel, reaching midseason at 3–3. They then beat the Cardinals and lost badly to the Packers and Bears at home, before beating the Dodgers and Pirates—also at home—to set up the season finale against the 5–5–1 Giants for the Eastern crown. Flaherty had lost his first encounter with his mentor, Steve Owen, but in a defensive struggle at the Polo Grounds, the Redskins prevailed, 14–0, in the rematch to take the East and slide into the championship match against the Packers. The next day, George Marshall announced that the title game would also take place in New York because of Boston's lack of support for his team. *Boston Globe* writer Paul Craigue pointed out, "They gave their worst exhibition of the season before their largest crowd [versus the Bears] and lost three of their five home games before starting their title surge against the lowly Brooklyn Dodgers. Maybe, after all, Boston would turn out for a real attraction."[8]

It would be decades before that would be determined. The Redskins were done with Boston. They were not done with the season, however, having to meet Green Bay for a third time on December 13. The Packers had easily handled the Redskins in Green Bay, 31–2, in October and edged them 7–3 in Boston in November. In New York in December, the Packers completed the sweep with an easy 21–6 victory. In all three games the difference was the same—Green Bay's superior passing attack, which netted six touchdowns to zero for Boston. Flaherty, who, after all, had played with the best passer of his day in Benny Friedman, knew what he needed to take the Redskins to the next level: a great passer. He found the best one in football in Texas.

Flaherty drafted TCU tailback Sammy Baugh with his first-round selection in the 1937 NFL Draft, and Baugh made an immediate impact by leading the league in passes, completions, and passing yards. He also became an instant attraction in the Redskins' new Washington, D.C., home, where Marshall moved the team in the offseason. When Ray arrived in the city that August, he told the *Washington Post*, "When we get that passing attack clicking those Giants will have to step aplenty to stay ahead of us. We're going to work hard, train hard, and play hard to take the championship for Washington."[9]

Before the home opener against New York, Flaherty told his team, "I want 60 minutes of the best that's in you. I won't take anything less. Sixty minutes of 100 percent effort. Those Giants are going to be tough tonight. You know how they hate us. . . . You're as big as they are. And I think you're tougher, understand?"[10] In front of a crowd of more than 24,000, the Redskins prevailed, 13–3, but then lost two of three games before hitting their stride in mid-October. After that 2–2 start, Washington won five of six to head to the season finale at the Polo Grounds with a 7–3 record, trailing the 6–2–2 Giants.

That December 5 showdown against the Giants featured a dominant performance by the Redskins, who took the game, 49–14. Flaherty shook up his playbook, and the Giants were caught flat-footed. Cliff Battles ran for 165 yards and won the NFL rushing title. This season saw big changes for the Giants, with Coach Owen installing the A formation on offense and the five-man line on defense. In contrast, New York writer Stanley Woodward wrote,

> The Redskins used the old Giant attack, learned by Ray Flaherty, their coach, when he helped Steve Owen handle the Giants. They ran from a single wing formation right or left, with a big split between the strong side end and outside tackle, Pinckert and Justice alternated on the wing, with Riley Smith, the quarterback, in the blocking position and Baugh and Battles shifting around in the back positions. [11]

The championship game one week later on a frozen field in Chicago provided an apt culmination to the season, as Washington's dynamic passing attack overcame the powerful Bears, 28–21, in an exciting game that is described in more detail later in this chapter. Flaherty had beaten Steve Owen three times in a row, whipped Curly Lambeau during the regular season, and then knocked off George Halas in the postseason. He was on top of the pro coaching world. Years later, George Marshall would recall that he offered Ray stock in the Redskins instead of a raise in the aftermath of the 1937 championship; however, "Flaherty wasn't interested in the stock offer. He squawked that I spent too much money on the band," Marshall related. [12]

Washington added some talented rookies in 1938, including runner Andy Farkas, end Bob Masterson, and massive tackle Wee Willie Wilkin, but the best first-year man was Frank Filchock, who the Redskins purchased from the struggling Pittsburgh Pirates at midseason. The big loss was rushing champion Cliff Battles, who retired from football when Marshall lowballed him in contract negotiations. In the attempt to stay on top of the league that year, Flaherty continually lamented the lack of enthusiasm from his veterans and threatened to start the younger backups late in the season against the Pirates. "They had so much dash and pep that it was contagious, and my regular backs caught the spirit when I sent them into the game," he said. "Maybe that's the answer to some of the Redskins' troubles this season." [13]

At that point, Washington was coming off a 31–7 pasting by the Bears to drop to 5–2–2. The Redskins recovered against Pittsburgh to set up another season finale against the Giants with the Eastern crown in the balance. In a column in the *Washington Star*, Flaherty wrote that he was hoping for good weather conditions to prevail so that passing stars Baugh and Ed Danowski of the Giants would be at their best. [14] He got the weather he wanted but not the result as the Giants repaid the Redskins for the previous year's denouement by rolling to a 36–0 victory at the Polo Grounds in front of 58,000 fans (including 12,000 Redskins rooters who, on Sunday morning, arrived by train from Washington and marched up Fifth Avenue, led by the Redskins band). Washington actually outgained the Giants but turned over the ball *10* times on six interceptions and four fumbles to give the game away.

The 1939 season began on the West Coast, as Marshall moved the team's training camp to a cooler location. In the next few years, Flaherty's connection with singer and film star Bing Crosby would bring a side benefit: "He would have our players come out to the studio for lunch or something and have the whole team come out there. The next year when he had them back, he'd call them all by name."[15] The new season also brought another haul of skilled rookies to bolster the team, including backs Dick Todd and Wilbur Moore, and guards Clyde Shugart, Steve Slivinski, and Dick Farman. After finishing fifth in the league in both points scored and fewest allowed the previous season, the club improved to second in both categories in 1939.

Washington thundered through its schedule, pausing only for a 0–0 tie against the Giants in week two and a 24–14 loss to the Packers in week six. So the momentous annual Polo Grounds season finale matched two 8–1–1 teams and proved to be one of the most controversial games in league history. The ground-oriented Giants built up a 9–0 lead through three periods on three field goals. A 20-yard touchdown pass from Frank Filchock to Bob Masterson with 5:34 to play closed the gap to 9–7. A subsequent Redskin drive took Washington inside the Giants 10, where Bo Russell attempted a 15-yard field goal with 45 seconds to play. In the twilight, official Bill Halloran ruled the kick wide. Flaherty and several Redskins rushed the field to argue, to no avail. New York ran out the clock, and fistfights broke out between players and fans. Wingback Ed Justice went after Halloran but missed him. Flaherty said after the game,

> I know it was good. The players know it was good. The other three officials know it was good—Danowski and Widseth said so. The cops who were guarding the goalpost know it was good. If that fellow [Halloran] has any conscience, he'll never have another night's good sleep as long as he lives. He cheated these boys out of a thousand dollars apiece.[16]

The next year, the Redskins got off to a 7–0 start, averaging almost 29 points per game. Then they lost a close one, 16–14, to Jock Sutherland's Brooklyn Dodgers, before the offense started to sputter, scoring just 41 points in the last four games. Washington rallied to defeat the Bears, 7–3, the week after the Dodgers' loss, but Chicago players complained about the officiating and were labeled "crybabies" by Marshall after the game. The next game, against the Giants, featured a bit of foreshadowing on two fronts. First, New York's 21–7 victory was highly attributable to the Redskins throwing six interceptions, a problem that would reoccur in the title contest. Second, Arthur Daley described Steve Owen's defense for that game as an early precursor to his 1950 umbrella defense. Said Daley, "He floated his ends to protect against passes in the flat and had his tackles keeping on the pressure, surging in time after time to bounce Baugh off the turf."[17] Even the season finale against a wretched 1–9 Eagles squad produced a lackluster 13–7 win, in which Philadelphia's 5-foot-7 tailback, Davey O'Brien, completed 33 of 60 passes for 316 yards.

Flaherty called his players in the next day—their usual off day—to go over the Bears offense and try to rouse them from their torpor. He later commented, "As we prepared for the game, I got the distinct impression our players thought the Bears were going to show up and then beat themselves. Our whole approach to that game was entirely too relaxed."[18] The Bears were anything but relaxed, with the sour taste of the late-season loss to Washington and the taunts of George Preston Marshall still fresh.

That title game is perhaps the most famous in league history with its unfathomable 73–0 final score. While that game receives more extensive analysis in chapter 8, it merits some summary comments here. Chicago threw just ten passes, rolling up that large score mostly on the ground and on defense. Washington's three passers (Baugh, Filchock, and rookie Leroy Zimmerman) threw 49 passes and had eight intercepted, in addition to losing a fumble at the Redskins two-yard line. Chicago returned three interceptions for touchdowns and had two other turnovers lead directly to short scores. The Bears scored on the second play of the game and took a 21–0 lead into the second quarter. They extended that lead to 28–0 right before the half, and essentially the game was over. A desperate Washington team gave up four touchdowns in the third quarter and three more in the fourth. Historically, that game marks the beginning of the ascent of the T formation as the dominant approach in pro football and the descent of Ray Flaherty's preferred single wing. That doesn't entirely comport with what actually happened, but it became the perception of the day in hindsight.

The 1941 season began as if the Redskins had shaken off the effects of the title-game beating, with the team sprinting to a 5–1 start, marred only by an opening day 17–10 loss to the Giants, propelled again by eight Redskins turnovers; however, that 5–1 start was followed by a four-game losing streak. A three-game road trip produced losses to the Dodgers, Bears, and Giants, and then a loss at home to the Packers, to drop the Redskins from contention and into third place in the East. The loss to the Bears was by a convincing 35–21 score, but at least it wasn't a complete embarrassment. A victory over the Eagles in the season finale gave Flaherty another winning season, at 6–5, but it was hardly a satisfying one as the nation went to war.

The 1942 Redskins were probably Flaherty's most consistent team, going 10–1, with the only loss coming in week two at the expense of the Giants. In that 14–7 loss on a rainy day in Washington, New York scored on a 50-yard pass play and a 66-yard interception return. There were no other letdowns for the rest of the season. The reward for winning the East, however, was the privilege of meeting the two-time defending champion Bears, who were 11–0 on the year, having scored the most points and allowed the fewest in the NFL—a per game average margin of 34.2 to 7.6. The Redskins were third in points scored and second in fewest allowed, but they were nowhere near this level of supremacy. But the title game demonstrated why they play the games. The 'Skins overcame their history with the Bears and Chicago's overwhelming talent to produce a remarkable 14–6 upset in Flaherty's last game as the team's coach. The game validated his belief that the "T may be all right, but I'll get along all right without it. There's nothing magic about the T formation, and it's not so new either."[19]

By the day of the game, Ray had already enlisted in the U.S. Navy and would serve for almost three years as a lieutenant commander in charge of physical training, mostly at a naval base in northern Idaho, before returning to coaching pro football in 1946. That return would not be with the Redskins nor in the NFL. On this day, however, he poignantly told his players in the locker room after the game, "Half of us are going into the service in a couple weeks. Hit the enemy just half as hard as you hit the

Bears today. Do that and this war won't take long to finish, and we can get back here pretty quick."[20]

Despite Flaherty's patriotic optimism, World War II dragged on. In September 1944, former boxer Gene Tunney was reported to be in negotiations with Flaherty to coach a new Baltimore franchise in the fledgling All-America Football Conference, which was being organized that summer, but nothing came of it. The following August, Ray signed instead to coach the NFL's Brooklyn Tigers (formerly the Dodgers); however, Tigers owner Dan Topping, who had just joined with construction magnate Del Webb and baseball executive Larry MacPhail to purchase the New York Yankees baseball team, aimed to move his Brooklyn football franchise into Yankee Stadium. Tim Mara, owner of the Giants, who played nearby in the Polo Grounds, objected strenuously to the infringement upon his turf. When negotiations concerning scheduling broke down in December 1945, Topping jumped leagues and took his team to the AAFC for its inaugural season of 1946.

As to why the newly married Flaherty did not return to Washington after the war, there are at least two reasons. First and foremost, Topping offered Ray more money. "I was getting more money than Mr. Marshall offered me," he said. "And he was in kind of a bind because his [current] coach had two years left on his contract."[21] Second, the Redskins had shifted to the T formation during the war—by 1946, half the NFL was using the T—and Flaherty ran the wingback formations instead. Five of the initial AAFC teams were running the single wing as their base offense in 1946, but for the remaining three years of the league's existence that number would drop to two or three per season.

The 1946 Yankees were primarily a mix of holdovers from the Dodgers/Tigers franchise (linemen Bruiser and George Kinard, end Perry Schwartz, and backs Ace Parker and Pug Manders); a few players once the property of the Redskins (end Bob Masterson, fullback Ray Hare, and drafted tailback Spec Sanders); and rookies who were first drafted by the NFL during the war (ends Bruce Alford, Jack Russell, and Derrell Palmer, and backs Lloyd Cheatham, Dewey Proctor, and Eddie Prokop). Flaherty had seen many of these players play service ball during the war and formed a strong team that came together in training camp, held that summer at Gonzaga University.

The Yankees raced through their initial season with a 10–3–1 record, leading the East. The only setbacks in the season were losing and tying the mediocre Chicago Rockets and losing twice to the powerful Cleveland Browns. The losses to Cleveland were made worse by a reported slur uttered by Flaherty that the Browns were a "bunch of podunks coached by a high school coach."[22] That bunch of podunks then upended the Yankees for a third time in the championship game, 14–9, with a late touchdown pass from Otto Graham to Dante Lavelli proving the difference.

After the game, Flaherty was berated by some of his own players. The *Washington Post* indicated that Perry Schwartz was the spokesman for the disgruntled group. Schwartz claimed, "Flaherty had no consideration for the players at any time, and we were mentally burned out before we met the Browns. This is the first successful but unhappy season I have ever had."[23] The *New York Herald Tribune* anonymously quoted players, said to be veterans from the NFL, who were unhappy with the game plan: "We were overcautious in the first half. We did not pass enough." Furthermore, one added, "We were using the same stuff that we'd been using all year. And boy those Browns really had us scouted. They knew our plays better than we did."[24]

It is interesting to note that the only former Brooklyn Dodger remaining on the 1947 Yankees was Bruiser Kinard. Parker, Schwartz, Manders, and George Kinard were all gone. Whether due to age, ability, or dissension is not certain. Flaherty brought in several talented rookies for his second season, most notably guard Dick Barwegen and halfback Buddy Young. The fast and elusive Young was a player he never would have been able to sign in Washington because George Preston Marshall would not use black players. Young's speed helped transform the offense. With Spec Sanders rushing for a pro football record 1,432 yards and Young gaining another 1,015 on the ground and through the air, the Yankees produced the second most points in the league. Ray enthused about Sanders to writer Shirley Povich, saying, "I waited 10 years for another Cliff Battles, and I got him. They run alike. They act alike, and they think alike." He added, "He's a great back without Buddy Young. With Young, he's super."[25]

New York improved to 11–2–1 in 1947, but the team still could not beat the Browns. The Browns triumphed, 26–17, in Cleveland in October. Six weeks later in New York, the Yankees bolted to a 28–0 lead in the second quarter but ended up with a disheartening 28–28 tie by game's end. Once again, the league championship game featured these two powerhouse clubs, and, once again, Cleveland prevailed, 14–3. It was ironic that the game was played on an icy field, but Flaherty and Paul Brown reached an agreement for the teams not to wear sneakers. Afterward, Flaherty—the man who suggested the Giants wear sneakers in an icy NFL title game 13 years earlier—conceded the decision was probably detrimental to his club, commenting, "We rely more on a running game, and the runners were handicapped more than the Browns with their passing."[26]

While the dominance of the Browns was frustrating for Flaherty, it was also causing problems with the league in that there was such a disparity between the weak and strong teams. The league sought to rectify that by having the strong teams transfer some players to the bottom-dwellers. The Yankees gave up tailback Eddie Prokop and tackle Nate Johnson to the Chicago Rockets, and guard Dick Barwegen to the Baltimore Colts. The Yankees beat the lowly Dodgers on opening day but then lost twice to the rebuilding Colts and were trounced, 41–0, by the 49ers to drop to 1–3. At that point, Topping had seen enough, and the team announced on September 18 that Ray had "resigned under pressure from the club," which seems an odd way to say he was relieved of his duties. Flaherty disagreed with ownership regarding which players the team gave away. He commented, "You can't give away players like Eddie Prokop, Nate Johnson, and Dick Barwegen and expect to have a winning team."[27]

Four months later, Flaherty was reunited with Prokop and Johnson when he was named head coach of the Chicago Hornets (formerly the Rockets) in January 1949. As the Rockets, Chicago had posted back-to-back 1–13 seasons in 1947 and 1948. To help Flaherty make the Hornets competitive, the league transferred 23 players from the folded Brooklyn Dodgers franchise—most notably tailback Bob Hoernschemeyer—and one (wingback Bob Sweiger) from the Yankees. Paul Brown joked, "It looks like the championship will be played in Cleveland or Chicago next fall. I'm glad to have Red back to butt heads again."[28] For his part, Flaherty opened training camp by saying, "When we have wound up our training chores, we'll have the toughest and roughest batch of players it is possible to put on a football field." Chicago did start the season in top shape and won three of its first four games, but then the reality of the talent pool set in and the Hornets stung just one more opponent the rest of the year.[29]

The AAFC died in December, when three clubs (the Browns, 49ers, and Colts) were accepted into the expanding NFL. With the Hornets defunct, Ray was out of a job. His name was floated in connection to three openings in the NFL: the New York Bulldogs, Chicago Cardinals, and Colts. The problem was that each of those clubs used the T formation and wanted to stick with it; however, Flaherty was strictly a single wing coach. In 1950, the only pro team still running the single wing was the Pittsburgh Steelers, and that job was not open. In February, Ray was listed as a contender for the coaching job at St. Mary's College in California, but he lost out on that as well. He was done coaching at age 46, the same age as Vince Lombardi when he was hired by the Green Bay Packers in 1959.

Flaherty's wife had tired of the coaching life anyway and urged him to move on, so that's exactly what Ray did. He was a fan of the outdoors and returned to the rural West. He ran a beer distributorship in Idaho for the next 14 years and then sold that to concentrate on real estate investments. Ray and his wife, Jackie, and son, Ray Jr., lived comfortably in western Idaho for the next three decades. He continued to keep tabs on local college football and stayed abreast of the pro game as well but was never again involved in the sport to which he was so instrumental in the first half of the century. He was elected to the Pro Football Hall of Fame in 1976. Flaherty passed away on July 19, 1994. Jackie died in 2007.

COACHING KEYS

Ray Flaherty had similar traits and values of many of the coaches in this book. In later years, he maintained, "If I were still coaching, I'd still be stressing fundamentals. You've got to block and tackle and play defense. It's a specialist's game now, but it's still a game of fundamentals. That's how you win."[30] Tackle Jim Barber, who spent seven years playing under Ray in Washington and then coached under him after the war, once summarized his coach by stating, "He had a brilliant football mind. He developed the screen pass. He could handle players. He knew when to kick you in the fanny and pat you on the back. Everyone respected him."[31]

Flaherty's approach began with conditioning and practice. He was noted for driving his players relentlessly in two-a-day practice sessions in training camp, with each session lasting two hours. A big reason that the Redskins moved their training camps to the West Coast was for the cooler weather so the players could better endure the intense summer practices. There was a point to the practice for Ray, and it was precision. He recalled,

> I'd be out there for an hour and run the same play for an hour till they got the thing timed right. One play. We'd just run it and run it till they got it timed right. That pulling guard's working with a blocking back. They've got to be there at the same time, and the ballcarrier's got to be right behind them just as they block. [32]

Flaherty also prided himself on his motivational ability. "I started working on those pep talks three or four days before the game," he said. "We would try to pick up some angle or some way of getting those fellows a little more enthusiastic or try to get them in a better frame of mind."[33] Shirley Povich wrote that before one game, Ray wasn't convinced his team was focused. "He made every last one of them lie on their backs in front of their lockers and say nothing to each other," wrote Povich. "They could do little but look at the ceiling, and ceiling-gazing, Flaherty deduced, would make them ought but reflective. He was never more correct. That day the Redskins tore the opposition apart to win the ballgame."[34]

In terms of strategy, Flaherty was known for his devotion to the single wing. Halfback Cliff Battles remembers that Ray's alignment was a little different, however. Said Battles, "Flaherty put in the box formation, and we did well with it. In the box formation, the tailback and fullback would switch off throughout the game. The idea of that was to disguise intent. This meant I was often in the fullback spot."[35] Film study of Redskins games reveals that Flaherty's offense usually lined up in the single wing—sometimes with a flanker but also used the short punt formation and a double wing spread often. From the single wing, with the tailback and fullback lined up deep, the team would either pass or run the ball. Many running plays resulted from direct snaps to the fullback, who would charge straight ahead. Short punt or double wing usually meant a pass play. The primary thrust of the passing attack was flips to the backs in the flat and short, intermediate passes to receivers over the middle, along with screen and shuttle passes. There were some deeper passes, but those weren't as frequent. With New York, Ray didn't have a passer as talented as Sammy Baugh or Frankie Filchock, so he ran the ball more (see figures 6.1 and 6.2).

The screen pass is frequently given as Flaherty's contribution to the game, but that needs a little explanation because terminology evolves throughout time. The term "screen pass" goes back to the early years of the 20th century, and Bob Zuppke is often given credit for the play. When Zuppke wrote of the "screened pass," he claimed it went back to 1906, when the forward pass was first legalized, and he noted that the high school team he coached from 1910 to 1912 (Oak Park) "used the screened pass almost entirely and quite often from a double pass, one of which was a lateral."[36]

The thing about the original screened pass was that it was not thrown to a back or behind the line of scrimmage. Instead, the line would charge straight forward, and one of the ends would go downfield a few steps and cut behind the blockers, who were screening him from the pass defenders. A rule change that kept downfield blockers from interfering with pass defenders made the play illegal in 1928. Flaherty recalled, "I'd been working for all of 1937 and in 1936 on this screen pass. We'd use a screen pass in college, then they outlawed it. You couldn't use it because you couldn't screen across the line of scrimmage. So I got to thinking, 'Why the hell don't we screen back of the line of scrimmage?'" He devised a behind-the-line screen pass for his single wing attack before the championship game in 1937, to combat the heavy rush his rookie passer,

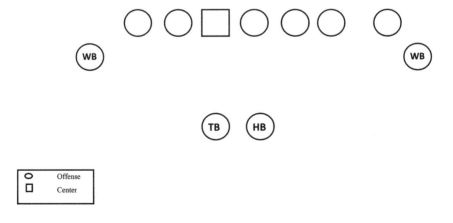

Figure 6.1. Ray Flaherty's double wing

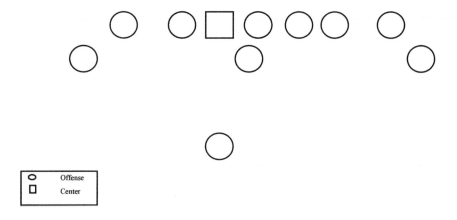

Figure 6.2.   Ray Flaherty's spread

Sammy Baugh, was encountering. "They were breaking their necks trying to rack up Baugh," he continued. "That's what made the screen pass go. It had been nullified downfield, but we put it behind the line of scrimmage, and the Bears didn't know how to stop it."[37]

The other innovation that Flaherty often is given credit for is his use of two platoons in the era of two-way players. As is discussed in the previous chapter, however, Steve Owen originated the wholesale use of this tactic in 1937. Flaherty followed a year or two later. Frankie Filchock made the two-platoon system possible for Washington because he was a talented alternative to Baugh as the team's tailback. Filchock was acquired from Pittsburgh in the middle of his rookie season of 1938, so the practice was likely fully operational in 1939. Even before Filchock, Flaherty liked to keep his players fresh and substituted liberally. Depending on the opponent, Baugh did not always start; sometimes he was saved for later in the game.

Flaherty remembered,

> We made the defense change. They'd get all set for Baugh's passing, and they'd have to change when we put the running combination in. Filchock was a great ball handler. [Wilbur] Moore was great on reverses, so we put a lot of spin plays in with this unit. Filchock could also throw, so it made a pretty effective combination both ways.

He further elaborated on another occasion:

When I would put Sammy Baugh in there, I would put [Andy] Farkas and Ed Justice, who was a very good pass receiver—a big fella about 6-foot-3 or three-and-a-half and weighed about 215 pounds . . . could run like hell. He was a good pass receiver. I had Farkas in that backfield. He was a good runner. He would do practically all the running, and Baugh wouldn't have to run the ball much. I had a good blocker in there in Max Krause. He was a good pass receiver. We had Millner and Malone and those fellas in there at that time. They were good receivers, so we would throw the ball 50 percent of the time or more when Baugh was in there.[38]

On the other side of the ball, Flaherty consistently had solid defenses. He recalled, "We had pretty much the same defenses they have today. We had zone defenses. We had man-to-man defenses. We had combination defenses." He added, "We used to have them red dog and things of that kind in our day. Just like they do today. Once in a while, we would send a safety on a blitz, but not as often as they do today. But we would put pressure on that passer all the time with our linebackers."[39]

New York World-Telegram football writer Joe King declared, "The writer would say Flaherty's dominant defensive trait is a complete mastery of end and tackle play, to contain a foe's offense in the middle and automatically restrict his gains."[40] Ray used both six- and five-man lines, and would sometimes curl his ends next to the tackles so they looked like linebackers. His defense was the primary reason for one of his two NFL titles, but his offense led the way in the first championship.

PIVOTAL GAMES

Those two championship games provide a good look at Flaherty's approach to football. After losing the 1936 championship game to the Packers, Flaherty sought to upgrade his passing attack and drafted Sammy Baugh, who had an excellent rookie year in leading the 8–3 Redskins back to the 1937 title game against the rugged 9–1–1 Bears. The Bears primarily relied on the T formation with the man-in-motion but still used the single wing and short punt formations at times as well. That season Chicago scored the second most points in the league and allowed the fewest. The *Chicago Tribune* pointed out that the favorite play of league-leading rusher Cliff Battles was the weak-side reverse but that the Bears had experience defensing this tactic against the Lions. [41]

For his part, Flaherty presciently commented, "If anything is being underestimated, I believe it is the Redskins' defense. We are vastly improved there. And I think we can shake Cliff Battles loose or manage some passes from Sammy Baugh that will win the game for us." On game day, it was 15 degrees with the wind blowing 12 miles per hour at Wrigley Field with a frozen field. End Wayne Millner recalled, "Afterwards it took us an hour and a half to take care of all the bruises and cuts we'd picked up." [42]

As noted earlier in this chapter, Flaherty planned on unveiling his screen pass during this game. "We just kept throwing the screen pass all day. They didn't know what the hell we were doing," he said. "I had got the officials before the game and warned them." [43] The first time Washington ran the screen the team was pinned at its own eight following a Bears punt in the first quarter. Baugh screened to Battles, and the play carried to the Bears 49; however, Chicago's defense stiffened. An exchange of punts gave the Redskins the ball back at their own 47. An early nine-play drive resulted in Battles scoring from seven yards out on the weak side reverse.

Chicago evened the score in four plays, including a 51-yard pass, and then intercepted Baugh to set up a 37-yard touchdown pass from Bernie Masterson to Jack Manders. Baugh was knocked out of the game on a hard tackle early in the second quarter and did not return until the next period with the score still 14–7 Bears. On the fifth play of the third quarter, Baugh hit Millner on a 55-yard crossing pattern to tie the score. The Bears answered by driving to a four-yard touchdown pass to Eggs Manske for a 21–14 advantage.

From his own 22, Baugh hit Millner at midfield, and the Redskins end raced for a spectacular 78-yard touchdown to tie the game again. The next time Washington got the ball, the offense converted a fourth-and-three at the Bears 45. Two plays later, Baugh pumped to Charley Malone short and then fired deep to wingback Ed Justice for a 37-yard touchdown pass. The fourth quarter was scoreless, although it did feature a bench-clearing brawl, and the Redskins triumphed, 28–21. Despite the Arctic playing conditions, Flaherty encouraged Baugh to pass for a record-setting 358 yards and three dazzling deep-strike touchdowns. Five years later, the approach would be radically different.

In 1942, the undefeated Bears, who led the league in both offense and defense, and were just two years removed from beating Washington 73–0, met the Redskins again for the title. Not surprisingly, the two-time defending champion Bears were favored by 20 points. The 10–1 Redskins, however, were an excellent team, second in defense and third in offense, and it was that defense that was most responsible for Washington's upset victory. The Redskins line shut down the Bears quick opening rushing attack and held quarterback Sid Luckman to two yards passing.

Chicago scored first in the second quarter when Redskins center Ki Aldrich forgot that speedy Dick Todd was in the game rather than the more plodding Andy Farkas and snapped the ball behind Todd. Bears tackle Lee Artoe scooped up the loose ball and rumbled 50 yards for the score. Artoe then missed the extra point. Halfway through the quarter, Wilbur Moore intercepted a Luckman pass at the Bears 42. Two plays later, Baugh hit Moore for a 38-yard scoring strike. Midway through the third quarter, Washington received a Chicago punt at the Bears 43. Baugh then guided the team on an 11-play drive on the ground that culminated with an Andy Farkas one-yard touchdown plunge and a 14–6 lead.

Bears backup quarterback Charley O'Rourke replaced Luckman in the fourth quarter and led Chicago on two long drives to the Washington red zone, but the first drive ended with a Baugh interception in the end zone and the second with a fourth-down incompletion from the three. Redskins scout Dutch Bergman outlined the plan to control the Chicago attack: "We used five- and six-man line under- and overshifted—covered their man-in-motion three different ways and used four different defenses in secondary against quick opening plays, as well as our defending against their passing attack."[44] Even nine months later, Bears cocoach Luke Johnsos moaned, "The Washington defense was guessing and happened to guess right."[45] But the shifting was planned. Cardinals coach Jimmy Conzelman credited Baugh's quick kicks and punts (Sammy had a 10-yard advantage over Sid Luckman, 52.5 to 42.2 yards per kick) as the key in keeping Chicago bottled up.[46] Flaherty praised Bergman's scouting report and later commented, "There may have been better teams, but never one with more determination."[47]

That game was the capstone to Flaherty's relatively brief career. "T formation didn't do a damn thing that day. We had some good football players. . . . Never let them get it going at all. We just completely shut them down," he related. Flaherty was correct that players ultimately determine success on the field, but he was too stubborn to change to the T, even when everyone else in the pro game, save the Steelers, had done so. It cost him his livelihood and cost the NFL one of its best coaches.

7

BIG MAN OFF CAMPUS

Jock Sutherland Finds a New Challenge

When the Brooklyn Dodgers football team hired Jock Sutherland as their new coach in January 1940, he arguably was more renowned than any other pro coach covered in this book. Sutherland had coached five teams with claims to the national championship in his 19 years as a college coach. Within the brotherhood of helmsmen of major college programs who had won more than 100 games, only three had outperformed Jock's .812 winning percentage: Notre Dame's Knute Rockne, at .881; Penn's George Woodruff, at .846; and Michigan's Fielding Yost, at .833. Today, 78 years after coaching his last college game, he still ranks 11th on that list. It is no wonder National Football League officials reacted with joy at the news of the hiring of the "Dour Scot," as Sutherland was sometimes called.

Although the college game still reigned supreme in 1940, Sutherland's signing heightened the NFL's prestige and was a clear indication that the pros were making headway. He was the first national championship coach to join the pro ranks. Paul Brown would be the next in 1946, followed by John McKay in 1976 and 13 accomplished college coaches since then. In the two decades before Jock switched to the pros, 24 college head men and seven assistants had taken a turn in the early NFL. Just four of those men belonged to the elite fraternity described here—100 wins at major college programs: Robert Folwell, Eddie Robinson, Hugo Bezdek, and Gus Henderson. While none of the four had led a team to a national title, each had led his team to the leading bowl game of the time, the Rose Bowl. In the pros, none of the four coached more than 14 games.

Only two coaches had gone the other way—switching from the NFL to a major college team. Arnold Horween, who played for the Chicago Cardinals from 1921 to 1924, and coached the team in the latter two seasons, was so worried that his mother would find out that her son was wasting his Harvard education by playing pro football that he and his brother, Ralph, a Cardinals teammate, used the alias "McMahon" while playing the "Sunday game." When Arnie was hired to oversee his alma mater's football squad, he reverted to his real name and coached the Crimson for five years before returning to the family leather business in Chicago. Similarly, Jimmy Conzelman, who won a NFL title with Providence in 1928, returned to his alma mater, Washington University in St. Louis, to coach the Bears from 1932 to 1939.

NFL chronicler Harry March foresaw the dawning of a new era in 1934:

> Colleges and professionals should work in harmony, the boys who have the stability and the sturdiness to be recommended by their mentors to the pro team which seems best suited to their abilities, to be matured by experience and come back to their alma mater or to another school well trained for the uplift which is their duty and their heritage.[1]

Sutherland's move reflected that greater harmony between the two camps.

After Sutherland moved to the NFL, 19 prominent college coaches would follow his lead during the 1940s, and seven were part of the 100-win group: Bill Edwards in 1941, Gus Dorais in 1943, Dud DeGroot in 1944, Clark Shaughnessy and Clipper Smith in 1947, and Jimmy Phelan and Bo McMillin in 1948. But Greasy Neale and Paul Brown, neither of whom won 100 games in the college ranks, were the most successful of the 19.

With Jock, however, it wasn't just the five titles, four Rose Bowl appearances, and .812 winning percentage that established an aura to his persona, it was the way he did it. He was an immigrant who learned the single wing offense from the man who invented it, Pop Warner, and then went about perfecting it. He was taciturn to the extreme and inspired a string of mocking monikers—the Dour Scot as noted earlier, as well as the "Silent Scot," the "Sour Scotsman," the "Sphinx of Football," and the "Great Stone Face." Although trained by the genial Warner, Sutherland was his emotional opposite. His teams won with relentless precision—the "Sutherland Scythe"—obtained through hours of stern, repetitive practice. His players did things entirely his way, so the question when he came to the NFL was, Could he get the same results from men that he drew from boys?

LIFE AND CAREER

John Bain Sutherland was born on March 21, 1889, in Coupar Angus, a town in the Strathmere valley of Scotland. He was the fifth child of Archibald Sutherland, a molder by trade, and Mary Burns Sutherland, a descendant of poet Robert Burns. John was named after an uncle and had three older sisters, Margaret, Jessie, and Marion, and an older brother, Archie. His younger siblings were Louisa and William.[2]

When Jock was very young, his father died in a work-related accident, leaving his 32-year-old mother to raise a brood of seven on her own. Everyone had to pitch in. At eight, Jock was sent to a local farm to earn money by doing farm chores while living on the property in a one-room hut with a stone floor. School was a four-and-a-half-mile walk. At 11, he left school and continued working to earn money for the family by caddying at the nearby golf links. At 15, he began working as a boy porter at the railway station and worked his way into the parcel room.[3]

When Jock was 16, his adored older brother Archie left home to work on a farm in Canada before moving on to Pittsburgh six months later. Two years after that, Archie and Jock had saved up enough money for the younger brother's passage to the United States to reunite with Archie in Pittsburgh in 1907. At first, both worked at the Dixmont Mental Hospital, until Jock had his throat slit by a patient with a makeshift shiv. After recovering, the 6-foot-1, 200-pound Sutherland took up work as a policeman in the neighboring community of Sewickley, Pennsylvania, while sister Marion rejoined the new-world clan in Pittsburgh.[4]

In 1911, Sutherland began competing in track and field events for the Sewickley YMCA, and a younger friend who had enrolled at the University of Pittsburgh to attend dental school and play football recommended the same course of action for Jock. Sutherland spent one year at Oberlin

Prep Academy in Ohio before enrolling at the Pitt Dental School in 1913. Although he had never played football, he made the team as a tackle in 1914, under Coach Joe Duff, who taught him the basics of line play. He recalled his initial rapture with the nature of the game years later in a letter: "This is football—or football as it should be played. Unless there is fierce determination such as I marveled at in my first days at camp— flaming competitive spirit—there can't be successful football. Faint hearts neither win fair ladies nor football games."[5]

The Panthers finished 8–1 that season but changed coaches, as Duff graduated from Pitt's law school that spring and began working as an attorney. Sadly, Duff would lose his life three years later in World War I. To replace Duff, the university hired Glenn "Pop" Warner, the inventor of the wing-back offense and one of the greatest coaches in the game's history. Pitt would not lose another football game until the final game of the 1918 season, compiling undefeated seasons in 1915, 1916, and 1917. Warner shifted Sutherland to guard, and Jock was named All-America in 1917. Sutherland later wrote of Warner, "My first impression as I met him was his big, powerful, beaming countenance, his quiet, slow, soft-spoken voice—always reassuring and encouraging."[6]

Sutherland also lettered in wrestling and track while completing his dental studies at Pitt. He became a U.S. citizen on September 10, 1917, and two months later enlisted in the U.S. Army Reserve. After graduation in June 1918, he was called into active service and assigned to the Dental Corps. Jock's military service provided his entrée into coaching, as he was given command of the football team at Fort Greenleaf in Georgia, and he led it to the championship of its division. With the ending of hostilities, Sutherland was mustered out of the service and hired by La-fayette College in 1919 to run its football program. That same fall, he would appear in a couple of games for the Massillon Tigers professional team and play against Jim Thorpe's Canton Bulldogs.

His coaching career got off to a slowish start, with a 6–2 season in 1919 and 5–3 campaign in 1920. One of the losses in 1920 was to Pitt and Warner; however, 1921 brought a 9–0 finish, featuring a 6–0 triumph over Warner's Pitt Panthers, and generated claims of the national cham-pionship for the small Pennsylvania school. Lafayette All-America Char-lie Berry later stated, "Dr. Sutherland was the one and only perfectionist of the famous single wing back formation. His thoroughness and individual efforts for the exactness of each minute detail were without a doubt the secret of its success."[7]

Records of 7–2 and 6–1–2 in 1922 and 1923, respectively, brought his five-year mark at Lafayette to 33–8–2, but 1924 delivered a major change. Warner left Pitt in 1924, after nine years and three national titles, to go west to Stanford, and Sutherland's alma mater called him home to his beloved Pittsburgh and his dream job as coach of the Panthers.[8] Following Warner's glorious reign was a tall order, even though Pitt was just 5–4 in 1923, so Sutherland's initial 5–3 season drew criticism. An 8–1 season in 1925 quickly quieted the doubters, and the 5–2–2 1926 season earned Sutherland a contract renewal. That 1926 team featured a halfback named Jimmy Rooney, the younger brother of Art Rooney, who would establish the NFL's Pittsburgh franchise six years later. After graduation, the younger Rooney played on a local semipro team owned by Art and later served two terms in the Pennsylvania legislature.

Sutherland produced his first undefeated team at Pitt in 1927. As the best team in the East, the 8–0–1 Panthers were invited to the Rose Bowl to face Pop Warner's 7–2–1 Stanford Indians. Warner prevailed, 7–6, in a game in which both touchdowns were scored on fumble recoveries, with the difference being a blocked extra point by Stanford. Sutherland would never have much success in Rose Bowl games, but at least this one was closely contested. The 1928 squad featured two future NFL coaches— Mike Getto of Brooklyn and Luby DiMeolo of Pittsburgh—and finished 6–2–1. Sutherland won his first national championship in 1929, with a 9–0 team that again was invited to the Rose Bowl. Pitted against Southern California, the champion Panthers were trounced, 47–14, by the Trojans.

Following a 6–2–1 season in 1930, Sutherland notched another national title in 1931, with an 8–1 season. The University of Southern California and Purdue also claimed the championship that year. In 1932, an undefeated 8–0–2 Pitt team was invited back to the Rose Bowl, where they again were whipped soundly by USC, 35–0. The undefeated Trojans claimed the national championship. That Panthers team included future pros Warren Heller, Joe Skladany, Frank Walton, and Mike Nixon, and the latter three would serve later as Jock's assistants in the pros. The 1933 and 1934 teams both finished 8–1, and both lost to Minnesota, with the Golden Gophers winning the national title in 1934.

The next two seasons also were one-loss seasons for Sutherland and brought him back to the pinnacle of the college game. In 1935, the highlight of the season was a brutally fought 0–0 stalemate with Fordham that began a three-year string of 0–0 games between the two Eastern powers from 1935 to 1937. All three Panthers teams were quarterbacked by John Michelosen, who later coached under Sutherland at both his NFL stops and succeeded his mentor with the Steelers in 1948. Michelosen eventually returned to his alma mater to coach the Panthers from 1955 to 1965. Fordham's team was led by its famed Seven Blocks of Granite line that included guard Vince Lombardi in 1935 and 1936. Lombardi would find a lot to like in Sutherland's power running attack. The 1936 Pitt team also featured star backs Marshall Goldberg and Harold Stebbins, and the squad returned to the Rose Bowl, where they upended the Washington Huskies, 21–0, and claimed the national championship. The 1937 team went undefeated with a 9–0–1 record, won the national title, and shocked everyone by voting down (reportedly a 16–15 tally) an invitation to the Rose Bowl to spend the holidays at home.[9]

The university's administration had been tightening academic regulations on the football program in recent years, but the refusal of the bid was not viewed well by the school. Sutherland was willing to comply with the strictures put on his program but wanted to play a lighter schedule because with football deemphasized he would not be able to compete with national gridiron powers. After an 8–2 season in 1938, Sutherland tendered his resignation to the university. His 15-year tenure resulted in a stellar 111–20–12 mark, a winning percentage of .818. While the celebrated coach was in immediate demand, he decided to take a year off, spending 1939 making speeches, conducting coaching clinics, and charting a new path for his life.

In addition to being courted by college football programs, he was pursued by two pro teams: Pittsburgh and Brooklyn. It may have been Sutherland, however, who reached out to the Pirates. According to Art Rooney biographer Rob Ruck, Sutherland sent an emissary to Rooney in the fall of 1939 and offered to buy controlling interest in the Pirates and become its general manager and coach. But Rooney wanted to maintain ownership of the club. He offered Jock a salary of $7,500 plus 20 percent of the profit.[10] When it was reported in the *New York Herald Tribune*, Rooney said he offered "somewhat less than $15,000 a year" to Sutherland, who had drawn $12,000 at Pitt,[11] all of which is a bit ironic in that Sutherland had advised his Pitt star, Marshall Goldberg, to avoid the pros. "Coach Sutherland didn't want me to play professional football," said

Goldberg. "Like many of the college coaches of that time, he didn't like the pro game. He wanted me to take a coaching job he'd obtained for me at a small college in Pennsylvania."[12]

On January 29, 1940, Brooklyn owner Dan Topping signed Sutherland to coach the Dodgers for $15,000 per year. League owners applauded. Bears owner/coach George Halas commented, "Dr. Sutherland's record shows he is undoubtedly one of the greatest coaches of all time, and the National Football League is greatly benefitted by his coming into our game." Eagles owner/coach Bert Bell added, "I feel sure that Jock will not only be a great asset to the Brooklyn Dodgers, but also to the National Football League." Redskins general manager Jack Espy continued, "Pro football welcomes the addition of such a keen football mind as Jock Sutherland." Packers coach Curly Lambeau held, "Without a doubt he will be a great addition to our league." League president Carl Storck said, "It brings a fine man and the number-one football coach in the country into the league."[13]

Sutherland declared, "I don't see any vast difference between college ball and professional ball. The league is well organized, and an increasing amount of interest is being shown in professional football." The 50-year-old coach added, "I never coached a loser, and I hope to continue that record. If I did not believe I could make a go of pro football I certainly would not have assumed my new position. No one likes to win more than I do, and I will try my utmost to give Brooklyn fans a winner."[14]

Jock was inheriting a 4–6–1 team, but it was one that predecessor Potsy Clark had begun building with several young studs, including tailback Ace Parker, fullback Pug Manders, end Perry Schwartz, and linemen Bruiser Kinard and Jim Sivell. Sutherland augmented that base with 17 rookies so that the only men older than 26 on the roster aside from Parker and Manders were 29-year-old back Ralph Kercheval and 27-year-old back Sam Francis. Despite starting four interior linemen weighing less than 200 pounds, the Dodgers had an improved offense and allowed the fewest points in the league in 1940.

Parker was the key. He was a multithreat back who could pass, run, catch, punt, and kick the ball with skill. While Parker had reservations about Clark, he was a Sutherland fan. "He changed the whole works. Everything you did, you had to do right, and everybody had to do it the same way," Parker related. "In other words, if your linemen were pulling, they had to cross over instead of up. Everybody had to do it the same. In the backfield, when you crossed over, everybody had to do it. It was a unity that he got out of it."[15] Parker contrasted his two Brooklyn coaches, saying, "Potsy would let you do fundamentally what you'd learned in college. Now when Sutherland came in you had to adapt and do everything his way, which brought us all together, and that's when we started to produce and win."[16]

Brooklyn had not had a winning season in seven years, so Sutherland opened training camp earlier than most teams—the first of August. Rookie halfback Banks McFadden recalled the need for training: "He was a very demanding coach. If he told you to take three steps and cut, you did exactly that or practiced until you did."[17] All eyes were on the Dodgers when they opened their 1940 schedule in Washington, D.C. They lost to the Redskins, 24–17, but trailed 17–0 at the half. Sportswriter Stanley Woodward's first impression was, "Only once in a while, however, did they show real flashes of Sutherland football. Obviously, the 'Doctor' needs more time to work on the detailed position play and speed which makes his attack move."[18]

The Dodgers also lost to the Bears, 16–7, in week five and the Giants, 10–7, in week seven. Week eight brought the rematch with the Redskins and provoked a bit of gamesmanship out of Sutherland when he took the home team's prerogative to insist Washington wear its white jerseys for the game. Brooklyn's resultant 16–14 victory kicked off a four-game winning streak to close the season with an 8–3 record, good enough for second place in the East, behind the 10–1 Redskins. In the process, the Dodgers beat the Giants for the first time in 10 years in the season finale. Ace Parker, coming off a broken left ankle from a sliding accident in a minor league baseball game, was named the league MVP. In November, Jock uncharacteristically praised Ace effusively, stating, "Parker is the greatest competitor that I have ever seen. He is the best football player in the National Football League."[19]

The Doctor's first year in the NFL allowed him to observe that while college spirit is great, there is more to football. "Pro ball is a continuation of college ball," he said.

> The players average to be bigger and stronger and faster. The pros kick better—not only for distance, but also for accuracy. The pros throw and receive forward passes better. The pros have better physical balance, they protect themselves better, they have better poise defensively. The pros are more cagey. A pro team has about twice as many plays

in its repertoire as a college team. The pros have less regard for conventional football; any pro club is likely to go 80 yards in three or four plays.[20]

In the offseason, Ace Parker broke his right ankle, again while sliding in a minor league baseball game; however, he was ready in time for Sutherland's second season in Brooklyn. In 1941, Jock brought in 15 more rookies and resumed his pursuit of the Eastern crown. Again, Brooklyn finished in second place but just one game behind the Giants, who they beat twice. A three-game losing streak in the first half of the year almost torpedoed their chances, but three straight wins brought them to a 5–3 record and just one game behind the leading Giants. The killer to the season came the following week with a 14–7 loss to the Pirates, in which three Dodgers turnovers allowed Pittsburgh to win its only game of the year. Once again, Brooklyn beat New York in the finale, and once again it only made them runner-up.

That finale was played on December 7, 1941, as word came of the Japanese attack on Pearl Harbor. The Doctor was a proud immigrant and staunch patriot. At the age of 53, and with mediocre eyesight, he pulled strings to get back into the military. In July 1942, he was commissioned a lieutenant commander in the U.S. Navy Reserve and assigned to the training department. During the war, Jock set up and ran rest and rehabilitation centers for battle-fatigued soldiers. He set up the first one in Asheville, North Carolina; the second in the Pocono Mountains in Pennsylvania; and the third in Deland, Florida.

When the war ended in September 1945, Jock wrote his former player and assistant John Michelosen, saying, "Soon we'll be having a job back in football coaching again. Offers have been coming in from all over the country, and I don't just know yet where that job will be, but in any event I am counting on you to be in harness with me."[21]

Michelosen did stay in harness with Sutherland, and the Doctor's next move brought them both home to Pittsburgh. The 1945 Steelers were an awful team that finished 2–8 and were coached by Jim Leonard, formerly an assistant coach with the team. Reportedly, co-owner Bert Bell told Leonard when he hired him that Jock Sutherland was the man he really wanted. At season's end in December, Leonard returned home to New Jersey and telephoned the *Pittsburgh Press* to tell the newspaper that he was resigning.[22] Later that month, Rooney and Bell struck a five-year deal with Sutherland for $15,000 per annum to take over the sad-sack Steelers.

From the weak 1945 squad, the only returning starters were center Chuck Cherundolo and tailback Bill Dudley. Sutherland brought in 19 rookies and whatever waiver-wire players he could find to improve the talent base. Rookie guard and future NFL coach Nick Skorich recalled,

> Jock Sutherland took over as coach, and we became a respectable team that first year I was there. Sutherland was a disciple of Pop Warner. He was probably the one man I hated most to play for. At the same time, he was the coach I respected the most and learned the most from. He was a strong disciplinarian, the Prussian general type, and made you pay the price. [23]

Training camp was particularly difficult. A two-hour workout in pads in the morning was followed by three hours of scrimmaging in the afternoon, with oatmeal dumped in the water bucket to discourage its use by fatigued players. The day's practices were supplemented by chalkboard lectures in the evening and lights out by 10:00 p.m. Once again, Sutherland's interior line was extremely lean, with two linemen weighing less than 200 pounds and Chuck Cherundolo the heavyweight at 215 pounds. [24]

The Steelers improved to 5–5–1 in 1946, and gave up the fewest points in the league. They also scored the fewest, although Bill Dudley was essentially a one-man team. The multitalented tailback also had his problems with the Doctor, although in 1946 Dudley was named league MVP by leading the loop in rushing on offense and interceptions and fumble recoveries on defense. But a series of incidents drove a wedge between the two men. Dudley felt he was being overused, particularly when he was forced to play while injured late in the year.

After the season, Dudley took a job as an assistant coach at his alma mater, the University of Virginia, and retired because he could not face another season under Sutherland. Eventually, the Doctor traded him to Detroit for three players and moved on with Johnny Clement taking over many of Dudley's duties. Fifteen rookies joined the team in 1947, including two linemen, Red Moore and Frank Wydo, who were both more than 225 pounds. The offense improved to seventh in points scored, but the defense dropped to seventh in points allowed, and the Steelers actually surrendered 19 more points than they scored despite finishing 8–4. The team lost to the Rams, 48–7, the Bears, 49–7, and the Eagles, 21–0, to account for the drop on defense; however, the fourth loss was the toughest, 27–26, to the Redskins on October 5. Washington scored the winning touchdown with five minutes to play, while Steelers kicker Joe Glamp missed his fourth field goal of the day in the final minute. A 9–3 record would have given Pittsburgh the Eastern Conference title outright. Instead, they and Philadelphia tied with 8–4 records, and then the Eagles breezed to a 21–0 win in a playoff. That would be the last game Jock would ever coach.

The ensuing spring, Sutherland undertook a scouting trip of Southern colleges to talk to coaches about players. He even stopped to visit with Ace Parker in North Carolina. In April, he was found wandering in a field in Kentucky, only able to mutter, "I am Jock Sutherland." He was rushed back to Pittsburgh and operated on for a brain tumor but did not survive. He died on April 11, 1948, at the age of 59. Encomiums poured in from throughout the football world. Sportswriter Bill Cunningham remembered Jock this way:

> A bachelor of generous tastes, he lived in the Pittsburgh Athletic Club, and he lived well. He dressed tastefully and quietly, but expensively. He owned a flashy-looking automobile, but he almost never drove it. He lived quietly and studiously. His favorite hobby was reading, especially biographics [sic]. He was an extensively read and extremely well-educated man. [25]

COACHING KEYS

Few positions offer more of a sense of authority than pro football coach. Ramrod-straight Doctor Sutherland fully embodied that persona and demanded total adherence to his strictures. He viewed the gridiron as a place of Manichean dualities—there was the right way to play and the wrong way. His coaching tenets were simple and unalterable.

Sutherland believed in the single wing almost religiously as the one true way. While Jock's teams sometimes switched into the double wing, most plays were run out of the single wing, just as the Doctor had learned it from Pop Warner decades earlier. He maintained,

No offense has hit its peak. There is no stagnation in any football offense. Defense makes you do things you don't want to do. The Warner system at one time had six or seven unstoppable plays. But the defense finally caught up. So you've got to make little adjustments here and there to keep a step ahead. [26]

Sutherland always dismissed talk of switching to the T with the explanation that he did not have the right kind of players to run it, namely, he didn't have the speed.

To run the delayed deceptive maneuvers of the single wing required the utmost in exactness, so Sutherland's practice sessions were frequent and lengthy. He needed his players to master the fundamentals, summarized by his biographer as follows:

He learned the proper stance—how to balance his weigh correctly, what to do with his hands and feet and head so as to give him the maximum advantage and at the same time not to reveal the direction of the next play. He learned how to get away fast as soon as the ball was snapped. He learned how to pivot, to spin, to cut, to carry the ball, to fake, to tackle, to throw all kinds of blocks, such as the body block, the shoulder block, the cross-check block, the crab block, among others. [27]

Some veterans, like Ralph Kercheval in Brooklyn, did not buy into the constant scrimmaging. "Getting back to the fundamental basics that we had in high school and continuing that day after day I thought was a little bit on the absurd side," Kercheval reflected. "Tackling and blocking and all of that, if you couldn't do it by that time, you shouldn't have been up there."[28]

Film study reveals that the Sutherland offense was overly reliant on a multitalented tailback—Ace Parker, Bill Dudley, or Johnny Clement—to call the plays, throw the passes, run the ball, and sometimes catch and punt the ball. Highly choreographed plays usually massed blockers to one side with the ballcarrier going that way, with occasional counteraction. At times, the man-in-motion was employed, and on some pass plays, the tailback would start dropping back before the snap. Dudley's favorite plays were the off-tackle play and the trap. He commented,

The off-tackle play from the balanced and unbalanced line and the trap were all basic plays in the single wing. We ran it 60 percent of the time. The first two steps were always identical. You always looked to the sideline before making a cut to go off tackle, off guard, or to the weak side on the trap. [29]

Sutherland once wrote of the importance of play sequencing to his offense:

> Once a thrust has been made at a certain spot, the quarterback must remember what the defensive man at that spot did. Then, a few plays later, he directs the attack at the same spot again but chooses a play that appears identical with the previous formation but which actually is different, designed to take advantage of the lineman's expected location. [30]

Precision was one key for Sutherland's single wing. A second was power. Pop Warner once said of his celebrated pupil, "Jock put more power and punch into single wing than any other coach." [31] That matched the Doctor's broader philosophy that the "only permanent satisfaction is to attain your objective by facing difficulty squarely and overpowering it." [32]

Opponents noticed. One anonymous Cardinals player said, "Teams using and playing against the T formation look for brush blocks. But those sock-it-to-'em blocks and tackles we got from the Steelers didn't do us any good. I can still feel 'em. Sixty minutes of that kind of football wears a man down." [33] George Halas pointed out to Art Rooney that there was a downside to that kind of play: "The other team takes that beating once. Your team takes it every week." [34]

The third "P" to describe Sutherland's system was possession. Jock operated from the view that nothing bad can happen to you as long as you hang on to the ball. Unlike most teams from the time, his teams tended to punt less on early downs even if bottled up in their own territory. Time of possession was an important factor to him. A fourth "P," passing, was not. When the Doctor was hired by the Dodgers, Pop Warner assumed, "Well, Jock will have to open up in that league, lots of passes. He was very conservative at Pitt, but he knows enough about football to meet any emergencies." [35]

At his first press conference in Brooklyn, Sutherland was asked about his feelings toward the passing game and replied, "If you'll look over the record of my Pitt teams for the last few years, you'll see that while they were supposed to be power teams, the figures show we completed more passes and gained more ground with them than most of the teams we played against."[36]

However, an anonymous former Pitt player had a different take:

> If we had mixed a good sprinkling of passes with our running attack, we would never have had a close game. . . . We were forced to run against what amounted to a nine-man line most of the time. No one will ever know what out running attack would have amassed in yardage had it been varied with a few passes to loosen up the defense.[37]

While in the military, Sutherland recalled that he considered switching to the short punt formation in the pros but decided to go with what he knew best instead. Looking at the numbers, the Doctor's pro teams were heavily run-oriented, but there is a difference between his time in Brooklyn and that in Pittsburgh. With the Dodgers, Jock's offense ran the ball 68.6 percent of the time, 4 percent more than the league average of 64.8 percent. When he returned to the game in 1946, Sutherland went further in the opposite direction of the passing trend. His Steelers ran the ball 71.1 percent of the time, 16 percent more than the declining league average of 61.3 percent.

The Doctor seems to have gotten a bit crustier in his second pro stop, not only in play selection, but also player relations. In particular, his relationship with Steelers star tailback Bill Dudley was disastrous. Dudley told of a series of incidents during the 1946 season that drove player and coach apart: Dudley was late for his first practice; in another practice, Sutherland confronted him after an interception, and Dudley replied that it would be helpful if the offense and defense wore different colors; in midseason, the slightly built Dudley was banged up but got no reprieve from the Doctor in practices or games; in one game, guard Nick Skorich signaled Dudley to take a different hole than the one specified by the play, and Sutherland reprimanded Bill despite the fact that he scored; finally, there was another practice incident when Jock demanded to know who had told him to run a play the way he did, and Dudley, supported by assistant coach Mike Nixon, said, "You did, Doctor." Jock viewed these episodes as evidence of insolence and disrespect.

The result was that Dudley retired at the end of the year, so Sutherland traded him to Detroit. When he was interviewed in later years by Myron Cope, Richard Whittingham, and NFL Films, however, Bill would recount the incidents but essentially say that Sutherland was the best coach he had played for and his coaching made Dudley NFL MVP. In interviews conducted by his son-in-law shortly before he died, however, Dudley was more frank: "I respected Jock, but I didn't like him. I thought he was arrogant. Looking back on it, I think Jock was a real SOB when it came to trying to get along with everybody. If he hadn't been the head coach, I think some of the ballplayers would have kicked the living shit out of him."[38]

Ultimately, the entire episode was curious and best summed up by a comment Dudley had made years before to Cope: "If you're a football coach and you can't get along with a good football player, something's wrong."[39]

PIVOTAL GAMES

In Sutherland's brief four-year tenure in the NFL, he never got to play for a championship, but there were other important games that illustrate his approach to football. The November 10, 1940, rematch with the undefeated Washington Redskins is one good example. As noted earlier in this chapter, Washington beat the Dodgers in Sutherland's NFL debut that year, and the Doctor pulled out all the stops to even the score two months later. He discovered that Brooklyn's official colors were red and white, as chosen by the previous coach, Potsy Clark, even though the Dodgers were wearing blue again in 1940. Because of the league rule that the opposing team must wear a contrasting jersey, Jock pulled out the Brooklyn red jerseys and forced the Redskins to put away their regular burgundy shirts for white ones. Since they almost never wore whites, several Redskins, including Frank Filchock, Ray Hare, and Bob Seymour, had to switch numbers for the game. Washington coach Ray Flaherty bristled, "I don't give a [three words censored here] what he does. We're going out there to play football."[40]

Perhaps the jersey flap had nothing to do with it, but Brooklyn got off to a 16–0 lead through the first three quarters before the Redskins mounted a desperate late comeback. The three Brooklyn scores were set up by long punts that buried the 'Skins inside their own 10-yard line. In the exchanges of punts, Brooklyn twice got short fields and the third time trapped a fumbling Dick Todd in the end zone for a safety. As a novelty, both touchdowns were scored on pass plays. In the first quarter, Ace

Parker threw 14 yards to end Waddy Young, who lateraled back to quarterback Rhoten Shetley at the six, and Shetley scored from there. In the third quarter, Brooklyn ran a sequence of plays off the deep reverse where wing back George Cafego took a handoff from fullback Pug Manders and ran with the ball. On the scoring play, tailback Ace Parker slipped out of the backfield and Cafego fooled the defense by hitting him in stride at the 20, and the uncovered tailback raced in for the score.

The Redskins rushed for a mere 19 yards during the game, but Sammy Baugh completed 25 of 47 passes for 312 yards and drove Washington to two late, albeit insufficient, scores. Brooklyn ran for 73 yards and threw for 94, and posted just seven first downs to Washington's 20. The game was the first time Sutherland bested a team with a winning record and set the Dodgers on a four-game winning streak to end the campaign. It was Washington's first loss of the regular season.

Seven years later, the Doctor was in his second year as the Steelers head coach and led the team to a tie for the Eastern crown with the Philadelphia Eagles. While Pittsburgh beat Philadelphia in October in the Steel City, the Eagles won the November 30 rematch in the City of Brotherly Love. In that rematch, Pittsburgh's top two passers were hurt, so Philly put as many as 10 men on the defensive front and dared the Steelers to pass. The Eagles won easily, 21–0.

The playoff was played in Pittsburgh on December 21. The Steelers had their injured players back, but they were ineffectual against the Eagles defense, with the Philadelphia linemen outweighing their Pittsburgh counterparts by 20 pounds per man and the ends by 15. The Steelers managed to hold the vaunted Eagles rushing attack to 124 yards, but T formation quarterback Tommy Thompson completed 11 of 17 passes for 131 yards and two touchdowns. Steelers tailback Johnny Clement was four of 16 for 52 yards passing, and the team eked out a paltry 102 yards on the ground.

Philadelphia won the title on big plays. End Pete Pihos blocked a punt in the first quarter, which led to a Thompson-to-Steve Van Buren scoring toss of 15 yards. End Jack Ferrante caught a 28-yard touchdown strike from Thompson in the second quarter, and scatback Bosh Pritchard returned a punt 79 yards for the final score in the third quarter. Sutherland's single wing could get nothing going all day. Jock admitted afterward, "The better team won. They're a great aggregation. But I don't think they're better than us without Van Buren."[41]

The point the Doctor was missing was that Van Buren was held to 45 yards rushing for the game. It was the passing of the T formation quarterback that really did them in that day. By 1948, Sutherland was dead and replaced as the Pittsburgh coach by his longtime assistant, John Michelosen. While that may have seemed the logical thing to do since they had tied for the Eastern pennant using Jock's single wing, it actually set the franchise back. Pittsburgh was the only NFL team running the single wing as its base offense from 1948 to 1951. When Michelosen was fired in 1952, Pittsburgh became the last NFL team to move to the T.

When Sutherland arrived in Brooklyn, the single wing was still the dominant offense both in the pros and college football, and the Doctor was the master practitioner. Seven years later, everything had changed in the pros, where the T was ascendant, while colleges were moving in that direction, too, but a bit slower. In fact, both teams that Sutherland coached showed marked improvement under his whip and tutelage, but there is no proof that the success would have continued had not war and death intervened. His teams lacked the talent and flexibility of their competitors and struggled against the best ones. It's likely that Jock went out as close to the top as he was likely to get using an outmoded attack.

8

T-MEN II

Halas, Jones, and Clark Shaughnessy Go All In

In 1939, the Chicago Bears set a new NFL season record for most points per game with 27.1, besting the previous high of 25.4 by the 1924 Cleveland Bulldogs. The top three teams in the league averaged more than 20 points per game in 1939, and each used a different offensive strategy. The Bears used the T formation, the Redskins scored 22 points per game with the single wing, and the Packers averaged 21.2 via the Notre Dame box. The following season, those same three teams again each topped 20 points per game, but by the end of 1940, the T had established itself as a superior system. In 1941, Chicago became the first team to average better than 30 points per game, and its per-game average of 36 that year still ranks fifth in league history. Curly Lambeau's Packers set the standard for a non-T formation offense in 1942, by averaging 27.3 points a game, but that paled next to the revealed power of the T.

George Halas's Bears had a pivotal year in 1939. The team had moved to the T formation exclusively and handpicked the man to run the offense in rookie Sid Luckman, a single wing tailback from Columbia. Halas made a strange deal with Pittsburgh owner Art Rooney to select Luckman with the second overall pick in the 1939 NFL Draft and then transfer his rights to Chicago. Prior to the 1938 season, Chicago had sent end Ed Manske to Pittsburgh. The Bears then reclaimed Manske in October. At the draft, newspaper reports indicated that Rooney was sending Luckman to Chicago because Halas agreed to take over the contract of Manske.

What likely happened is that cash-strapped Rooney was covering the tracks of a purely financial deal.

Luckman was originally slotted at left halfback in Chicago as he learned the intricacies of the T from former Bears quarterback Carl Brumbaugh, and he was ready to take the reins from starting signal caller Bernie Masterson by the end of 1939. In his hands, Chicago would demonstrate the unbridled firepower of the T throughout the 1940s, a decade dominated by Halas's team. Halas had been using the T since the inception of the league, but it had evolved. Chapter 3 details the modifications that Ralph Jones made to the system in the early 1930s to open it up, and the Bears were a continual contender throughout that decade; however, Chicago dominated the 1940s with an offense that often seemed unstoppable. Who or what brought on this overwhelming power? Primarily, the tinkering of an obsessed, eccentric, teetotaling Halas advisor named Clark Shaughnessy. Shaughnessy was a mad scientist of the gridiron, a grave, difficult football mastermind who caused Bob Zuppke to deadpan, "The world lost its greatest undertaker when Clark Shaughnessy decided on football coaching."[1]

LIVES AND CAREERS

Clark Daniel Shaughnessy was born March 6, 1892, in St. Cloud, Minnesota. His father, Edward, was from Pennsylvania and his mother, Lucy Ann Foster, was born in Canada. Edward worked as a farmer and school teacher, and he and Lucy had three sons: Percy, Clark, and Edward Jr. The family moved to the Saint Paul area when Clark was small, and he graduated from North Saint Paul High School without ever playing any sports. Hardworking and studious, he saved money from delivering newspapers and many odd jobs, and enrolled at the University of Minnesota before he was 18. He continued to work his way through college waiting on tables and washing dishes.[2]

Shaughnessy claimed the first football game he ever saw was Minnesota defeating Jim Thorpe's Carlisle Indians, 11–6, on November 21, 1908. The next season, Clark tried out for the Gophers but did not make the team. A year later, Shaughnessy made the squad as an end. He later switched to tackle, where he was named All-America in 1912. That year, against Iowa, he recovered three Hawkeyes fumbles. In the offseason, he diligently practiced his passing and punting, and performed at fullback as a senior in 1913. He also lettered in track and basketball.[3]

The Gophers were coached by Dr. Henry L. Williams, a former teammate of Amos Alonzo Stagg at Yale, who, in 1893, coauthored with Stagg one of the seminal early texts on football: *A Scientific and Practical Treatise on American Football for Schools and Colleges*. Williams did his medical training at the University of Pennsylvania and Harvard but put that aside in 1900 to take the head coaching job at Minnesota. He coached the Gophers through 1921, posting an impressive 136–33–11 record before retiring to return to medicine at age 52. Williams was known for running a shift offense, sometimes called the "Minnesota shift" and sometimes the "Williams shift." There seems to have been different versions of the shift throughout time, but the gist of it was that the tackles and either the ends or the guards would be in a row behind the line of scrimmage with the backs in a T formation behind that second row. On a three-count, the linemen would jump into the line on either side to set up strong and weak sides, while the backs would usually shift into a wingback look. The ball would be snapped almost immediately upon the shift, so the players were in almost continuous movement.[4]

Williams brought Clark on board as an assistant coach upon his graduation in 1914, and one year later Shaughnessy was one of several applicants (including Notre Dame assistant Knute Rockne) for the head coaching job at Tulane. Clark travelled to New Orleans for the interview and was offered the job as athletic director and coach of the football, basketball, and track teams for $1,875 a year. Tulane's football field was overgrown with weeds and surrounded by a fence in bad disrepair. The team had just one game scheduled for the following season, so Shaughnessy got right to work, writing to more than 60 schools to fill out the schedule. That first season the Green Wave went 4–4 before improving slowly to 4–3–1 in 1916, and 5–3 in 1917. That year, Clark married a local girl, Louvania Mae Hamilton, and took an approved three-month break from Tulane to work as the athletic director at the Vedado Tennis Club in Havana, Cuba. Clark Jr. was born in 1918, as Tulane posted a 4–1–1 record in the war-shortened season. Shaughnessy followed that with 6–2–1 seasons in 1919 and 1920, before stepping away from the game in 1921.

He returned to the sidelines in 1922, and brought home a 4–4 season. Then, led by a talented backfield of quarterback Lester Lautenschlager, tailback Brother Brown, and fullback Peggy Flournoy, Tulane went on a three-year run of 6–3–1, 8–1, and 9–0–1, respectively. The undefeated 1925 team was invited to play in the Rose Bowl, but school administrators declined the bid because they felt their players were too small. Despite that, the team's success initiated a $300,000 building drive that resulted in a new Tulane Stadium for 1926, a concrete-and-steel edifice that later became known as the Sugar Bowl. Shaughnessy was not happy with the decision about the Rose Bowl and resigned after finishing 3–5–1 in his first and only season in the new stadium.[5]

He did not have to go far to find work. The story has been told in several places that an unnamed millionaire offered Shaughnessy $175,000 for 10 years to coach Loyola of New Orleans. Clark accepted and convinced school administrators to refer to the institution as Loyola of the South for the next few years. The odd thing was that Loyola was coming off a 10–0 season coached by Eddie Reed, a former Tulane star under Shaughnessy. Yet, Clark was hired as head coach and Reed was made his assistant. Loyola slipped to 6–2–2 in 1927, and then posted a 7–3 record in 1928, during which time the highlight was a last-minute 12–6 loss to Notre Dame. Knute Rockne's possibly apocryphal comment after this game was, "Never get me another warm-up game with a team coached by that guy."[6] It should be noted, however, that the Fighting Irish finished just 5–4 that year, the worst record of Rockne's career.

Loyola dropped to 4–5–2 in 1929, but the team bounced back to 9–1 in 1930, and Shaughnessy was drawing notice for his own formation, known simply as the "Shaughnessy shift." The Shaughnessy shift was similar to the Williams shift, with both linemen and backs shifting, sometimes multiple times. Clark emphasized speed and brains over brawn, stating,

> Split-second timing, perfect rhythm are so vital to that type of play that in practice at Loyola we chant the count—one, two, three, four—just as the metronome music teachers used to place on top of a piano ticked out the beat for the student of music. With the split-second timing and perfect rhythm like this you can use deception combined with speed that advances the ball much faster than a ton of beef can crash it through.[7]

However, following 5–4 and 6–4–1 seasons in 1931 and 1932, respectively, the deal with the millionaire was terminated after just six years.

Shaughnessy's next move was back to the Midwest in what seemed at the time a colossal mistake on his part. The University of Chicago forced out the 70-year-old Stagg—who took a position at the University of the Pacific—and began to deemphasize football as Shaughnessy came in. Stagg had left Clark with one star recruit, halfback Jay Berwanger, and the Iowa schoolboy star managed to keep the Maroons at .500 from 1933 to 1935. Once Berwanger won the first Heisman Trophy and became the first-ever NFL Draft pick following the 1935 season, the bottom fell out in Chicago. Shaughnessy's teams not only went 6–23–2 from 1936 to 1939, but also they were regularly getting pummeled: 61–0 to Harvard, 61–0 to Ohio State, 85–0 to Michigan, and so on. It was a blessing when the administration did away with football entirely following the 1939 season.

Nonetheless, Chicago turned out to be Shaughnessy's smartest move. It was while coaching at the university that he met George Halas, and that would be the turning point of his career. Clark began to go to Bears games and then met Halas at a civic dinner in the mid-1930s. According to Halas, the two coaches immediately hit it off and started exploring T formation possibilities right there at dinner. Shaughnessy had shown an interest in the pro game as far back as 1930, when he attended the New York Giants postseason exhibition game against a team of Notre Dame All-Stars. At that time, Clark singled out three things that impressed him about the pros: the simplicity of their plays; how their blockers did not leave their feet when blocking; and, most of all, the passing game. "They passed and received passes with a cool confidence and effectiveness that few college teams ever show," he said. "The pass was used as a regular part of the attack and not haphazardly. The successful use of the pass saves wear and tear on a team that is another prominent factor in the professional game."[8]

Shaughnessy began to attend Bears practices and was added to the payroll as an advisor for $2,000 per year starting in 1937. Halas said that Shaughnessy assisted him with "terminology and analyzing game scout reports."[9] Clark did not use the T at the university because he did not have players good enough or fast enough to run it; however, he did get to see his ideas come to life when he watched the Bears play and became quite expert at this evolving system.

When Halas obtained Sid Luckman from the 1939 draft, Shaughnessy played a big role in training the former single-wing tailback in the T. Luckman told sportswriter Paul Zimmerman, "I'd be up in Shaughnessy's room every night in training camp going over every aspect of the thing. The whole idea was to spread the field and give the defense more areas to cover."[10] Luckman was a quick study, but the T was so radically different that he did not move into the quarterback slot until late in his rookie year. The Bears finished a game behind the Packers in the West in 1939, while the University of Chicago went 2–6. In its two victories (against Wabash and Oberlin), the Maroons scored 37 points and allowed two; in the six losses, Chicago allowed 306 points and did not score at all. Mercifully, the administration closed down the football program entirely at season's end.

Shaughnessy was tenured as a physical education instructor, so he had a secure future on campus, but he was driven to be a football coach. Throughout the years, Clark had reportedly turned down numerous high-profile coaching jobs, including Indiana, Northwestern, Wisconsin, and Harvard. His reputation as a top-tier coach remained intact within the fraternity but had taken a beating with the public at large. Thus, the announcement in January 1940 that Stanford had signed Shaughnessy to a five-year contract was greeted with disapproval by the school's alumni.

Stanford was coming off a 1–7–1 record. The previous coach, Tiny Thornhill, who played and coached under Pop Warner, had taken the Indians to consecutive Rose Bowls in his first three years as head coach. Those teams were known as the "Vow Boys" because they had vowed never to lose to USC, and they didn't; however, Thornhill had no subsequent success and was fired. The favorites for the job were Stanford alumnus Dudley DeGroot, coaching at San Jose State, and Santa Clara coach Buck Shaw. But Shaughnessy dazzled the interviewers by demonstrating the principles of the upgraded T formation offense on the blackboard and got the job.[11]

Key for Shaughnessy was that a perfect T formation backfield was already in place, although those same players were mismatched to the single wing. Frankie Albert was not much of a blocker or runner, but he was an excellent faker, passer, and field general as a T quarterback. Fullback Norm Standlee worked best when not having to wait for a deep snap from center. Slightly built Pete Kmetovic was ideal as the man-in-motion halfback. Hugh Gallerneau was not a skilled passer or punter but could block well and run off-tackle plays perfectly. Shaughnessy's coaching staff included line coach Phil Bengtson, backfield coach Marchy Schwartz, and end coach Jim Lawson. In addition, former Bears quarterback Bernie Masterson was hired to tutor Albert in the intricacies of quarterback play. These coaches bore the brunt of Shaughnessy's odd work habits. Clark would usually get up between two to three in the morning and go to work. Predawn meetings were not unusual. Shaughnessy would return home for breakfast and then return to work, taking the occasional catnap during the day. [12]

Stanford stormed through a magical turnaround season so momentous that it has been the subject of two books that go game-by-game, analyzing what Stanford's "Wow Boys" did and how each opponent tried to stop the souped-up T. Among the defenses Stanford encountered in 1940 were the 6-2, the 5-3, a 5-2-2-1-1, a 5-1-2-2-1, a 7-2-1-1, and even a 4-3. Only Santa Clara, UCLA, and California kept Stanford's margin of victory to seven points or less, as the Indians swept to a 9-0 season and were invited to play 7-1 Nebraska in the Rose Bowl. The Cornhuskers' only loss came in their opener against top-ranked Minnesota. [13]

At that time, there was no other major college team in the nation employing the T, so its features of speed and deception, for example, the quarterback taking the hand-to-hand exchange from center, the man-in-motion, and brush blocking by the line, were surprising and fresh to college football fans. Meanwhile, in Chicago, the Bears weren't running quite as smoothly. The Bears did finish the season on top of the West with an 8–3 record, but their attack was a bit inconsistent. In three games, two of them losses, Chicago scored just seven points or fewer. That included a late season 7–3 loss to the Redskins, the top team in the East, which set the stage for arguably the most significant game in NFL history, the championship played on December 8, 1940.

With Stanford off for a month until the Rose Bowl on New Year's Day, Shaughnessy headed east to huddle with Halas about the Bears offense. "I drew up the entire offense," he reflected. "Threw out all the junk that wasn't working. Then I looked at the pictures [of the loss to Washington]. It was obvious that Washington was going to use a certain defense and wasn't going to change it." As a test, Shaughnessy had the Bears open the game with two particular counterplays off the man-in-motion and confirmed that the Redskins defense was the same as three weeks before. The onslaught began with a 68-yard touchdown run by Bill Osmanski on the second play from scrimmage. Shaughnessy left to fly back to Palo Alto before the 73–0 game concluded, but it was essentially over after the second play. Bears press box coach Luke Johnsos returned the favor in the Rose Bowl, phoning down an early key defensive adjustment after Nebraska scored first. George Halas watched the game from the Stanford bench, so that both coaches were present for one another's greatest triumph.[14]

Even Pop Warner, inventor of the wing-back offense, praised Clark:

> Shaughnessy is entitled to the fullest credit for the phenomenal way he is making use of the T formation. The formation is almost as old as football itself. We used it when I played at Cornell from 1892–1894, and when I started coaching the next year at Iowa State and Georgia. The methods by which Shaughnessy gets so much deception from the formation is a tribute to his coaching strategy. He has given football out this way a tremendous lift. It is something new and a tonic for the game.[15]

By itself, a 73-point margin in a game between the two best teams in the league would have a big impact. Coupled with Stanford whipping Nebraska, 21–13, in the Rose Bowl three weeks later, however, this innovative formation forever changed the game in both the pros and the college ranks. The fact that Shaughnessy had taken the same players who had won just one game and led them to 10 victories one season later was a winning argument for the efficacy of the T. That spring, Shaughnessy, Ralph Jones, and Halas published an instructional guide to the T, *The Modern "T" Formation with Man-in-Motion*, which they would distribute at scores of coaching clinics they conducted during the decade. Halas did not try to keep the T a proprietary system but was its leading proselytizer, spreading the word far and wide. Jones remained an important consultant with Halas and was a popular speaker at coaching clinics.

The transition to the T occurred throughout the decade of the 1940s. The Eagles switched in 1941; the Redskins in '44; the Cardinals and Rams in '45; the Packers, Lions, and Yankees in '47; and the Giants in '48. Only the Steelers held out with the single wing until 1952. In the All-America Football Conference, only Chicago and Los Angeles still eschewed the T in 1949. In the college ranks, Boston College was an early adaptor, but within a few years major programs like Notre Dame and Army were making the switch. A *Football Digest* poll of the top 350 college programs at the end of the decade indicated that 250 used the T. In 1940, that number was just two—Stanford and Lake Forest, where T innovator Jones coached.[16] Halas, Jones, and Shaughnessy were alone on the launch pad as the T rocketed skyward.

Shaughnessy could not stay on top in 1941. Standlee and Gallerneau both graduated (and were drafted by the Bears), and the team had some injury problems that caused Stanford to slip to a 6–3 mark following the Rose Bowl season. Halas's Bears, however, fully hit their stride with a 10–1 record, which tied the Packers for the top spot in the West. The Bears averaged 36 points per game and easily vanquished the Packers, 33–14, in a playoff and the Giants, 37–9, in the title game. After winning their last seven games in 1941, the Bears went 11–0 in 1942, racking up 18 straight victories before being upset, 14–6, by Washington in the title game. Halas had left in midseason to accept a commission with the U.S. Navy as lieutenant commander and turned the team over to his chief assistants, Luke Johnsos and Hunk Anderson.

Halas was a skilled manager who had a propensity for delegating duties to talented assistants. As such, he was a leader in the evolution of the NFL coaching staff. In the early years of the league, when most head men were playing coaches, most assistants were as well. There were a few exceptions in the 1920s, but it wasn't until the 1930s that former players began to serve as assistant coaches on a regular basis. Halas had cocoached the Bears with co-owner Dutch Sternaman throughout the 1920s. When he returned to coaching in 1933, after a three-year hiatus, he hired halfback Red Grange as his first assistant. Grange would retire from playing in 1935, but he continued as Halas's assistant for the remainder of the decade.

The Bears went to two assistants in 1935, when end Luke Johnsos assumed coaching duties in his last two years as a player. Chicago was the first team to go with three assistants in 1939, when former quarterback Carl Brumbaugh was hired to tutor Sid Luckman in the intricacies of T formation quarterbacking. Halas also had several consultants on staff. Former Cardinals tackle Fred Gillies was a so-called $1-a-year man who helped out with the line at times. Former coach Ralph Jones continued to advise Halas, as did Clark Shaughnessy, but they weren't official members of the coaching staff.

Brumbaugh left in 1940, and line coach Hunk Anderson joined the staff. A year later, Paddy Driscoll replaced Red Grange as the backfield coach. Chicago went to a four-man staff in 1947, when Gene Ronzani was added, but Pittsburgh was actually the first team to go with four assistants in 1946, when Jock Sutherland took over the reins. At the end of the 1940s, only the Bears and Packers continued with four assistant coaches in the NFL, although Paul Brown employed anywhere from four to six assistants during his team's years in the AAFC.

Anderson and Johnsos were widely hailed as the best in the business and had a modern demarcation of duties, with Hunk running the defense and Luke the offense. That was clear in 1942, when the two became cocoaches of the best team in the league and kept things humming until the manpower drain of the war weakened the team and dropped it from contention. When Halas returned after the war, Anderson and Johnsos continued to demonstrate the effectiveness of a quality coaching staff.

The Halas-less Bears won the West for the fourth straight time in 1943; averaged more than 30 points per game for the third straight year; and won the championship against the Redskins, 41–21. The war's drain on talent finally began to kick in for Chicago in 1944, when the Bears slipped to 6–3–1, and then 3–7 in 1945. With the war over in 1946, Halas and many Bears stars returned for one last hurrah. Once again, Chicago won the West and then defeated the Giants, 24–14, in a title game marred by gambling allegations against Giants Frank Filchock and Merle Hapes. It was their fourth NFL title in seven years, but Halas would have a long wait for his next championship.

Shaughnessy opted out of his Stanford contract in 1942, when it appeared the school would drop football during the war. Hired to coach Maryland, Clark switched the team's colors from yellow and black to red and white, brought in Bears tackle Joe Stydahar to help with the line in spring practice, and hired George Halas's brother Walter and former Bear Jack Manders as his assistants. The Terrapins fashioned a 6–3 record in Shaughnessy's first year. In August, he penned an article for *Esquire* on how football helps in the war effort, stressing the aspects of not only fitness, but also teamwork and strategy. In particular, he averred that the T formation offered the best option because of its "emphasis on feinting and deceptions and quickness and speed." He added,

> You can find more boys who will become adept at using the T formation of the principles that have made the T formation, and that's exactly why it fits so exceptionally well into the present situation when the military requires as many men as possible to be groomed and tempered in the hot crucible of competitive football. [17]

Halas asked him to work with Anderson and Johnsos to help with their preparations for the championship game, but the two cocoaches so disliked Clark that they locked him out of practice.

One thing the two had in common was a dislike and distrust of consultant Clark Shaughnessy. Anderson went to great lengths in his book to accuse Shaughnessy of claiming to Halas that plays designed by Johnsos and Driscoll or blocking schemes devised by Anderson had, in fact, been drawn up by him. Anderson said that, at first, "The staff's attitude toward Shaughnessy was charitable, realizing that professional football was seeking a status of equality with college football." He continued,

> We knew that writers assigned to cover the pro game tried to assist the game in attaining at least par with the college game. Mentioning a successful college coach as an abettor in a pro game was similar to the street cleaner escorting a bank president's daughter to social functions—prestigious. [18]

A year later, Shaughnessy jumped to the University of Pittsburgh for more money and teamed with *Esquire* on a book stressing the connection of football to the war effort. Shaughnessy was an amateur military historian and used that knowledge in designing plays. In the book, British general Bernard Montgomery's El Alamein campaign is compared to a fullback counterplay with its feints and deceptive movements, while a Penn–Princeton game is said to evoke the siege of Stalingrad. [19] At Pitt, he again switched the team's colors to red and white but encountered much resistance in that strong redoubt of the single wing. Records of 3–5, 4–5, and 3–7 did not endear him to Panthers followers, and the administration took a dim view of Shaughnessy taking a side job as advisor to the Redskins beginning in 1944, to guide their transition to the T. Returning to Maryland in 1946, Shaughnessy could not repeat his success with the Terps and left after a 3–6 season. He maintained his advisory position with the Redskins for one more year, despite being a source of friction that reportedly contributed to the resignation of Dud DeGroot as head coach in 1946, and undermined DeGroot's replacement, Turk Edwards.

Halas had the Bears averaging more than 30 points a game again in 1947 and 1948, but both squads finished second in the West by one game behind Jimmy Conzelman's T formation Cardinals with the "Dream Backfield" of quarterback Paul Christman, halfbacks Charlie Trippi and Elmer Angsman, and fullback Pat Harder. Shaughnessy was let go by the

Redskins at the end of the 1947 season but was hired as an advisor by Rams coach Bob Snyder on December 30. Snyder, a former Bears quarterback, remarked, "Everything I know about the T formation, I owe to Clark. I consider this a great break for the Rams."[20]

Bob had led the Rams to a 6–6 record in his first season as coach. He would not get a second chance. After dropping a preseason game to Washington in September, the Rams were boarding a plane to play two exhibition games in Hawaii. Snyder was barred from the plane and Shaughnessy promoted to head coach. It was announced that Snyder was stepping down due to health reasons, but it later came out that owner Dan Reeves had fired him. The mercurial Reeves was entranced by Bears coaches in his attempt to field a winner. From 1947 through 1954, all four of his head men had come from Chicago, but none lasted longer than three years in Los Angeles.

Shaughnessy managed a marginal improvement in the Rams in 1948, leading them to a 6–5–1 record. The following year, the team won its first six games before limping to an 8–2–2 finish, one game better than the Bears. The 1949 Rams, decked out in red jerseys, as per Shaughnessy, featured hall of famers Bob Waterfield and rookie Norm Van Brocklin at quarterback, and hall of famers Elroy Hirsch and Tom Fears catching passes. It is no surprise that Los Angeles averaged 30 points per game that season and then did so for three of the next four years. Waterfield said of his coach, "Clark Shaughnessy has given the Rams about five times as much offense as we had under Adam Walsh at Cleveland."[21]

Fears recalled, "He was dedicated and worked long, hard hours. If he had a fault, it was a tendency to work his players too long. He'd have these long meetings and long practices, and a lot of guys would lose interest."[22]

Los Angeles headed to the NFL championship game against the Eagles, which was a rematch of a midseason contest that Philadelphia had won, 38–14. Philly coach Greasy Neale openly remarked, "I think we can beat the Rams much easier than we can take the Bears."[23] Game-day weather made that statement even truer. Playing in the rain on a muddy field, the conditions favored the run-oriented Eagles over the pass-friendly Rams, and Philadelphia repeated as NFL champs with a 14–0 victory. It was the last game Shaughnessy coached in the pros. Two months later, Reeves fired him and promoted line coach Joe Stydahar to head coach. Clark's high-toned written statement concluded, "Inasmuch as this was the first time in my two years as head coach that any expression of dissatisfaction relative to my services was made to me by any official of the Ram organization, it leaves me at a loss for words." Unfortunately, he could not maintain the high road when meeting with the press, bitterly sniping, "When Stydahar gets through coaching the Rams I can take any high school team in the country and beat them."[24]

Stydahar had requested permission to become the line coach for the Packers that month because, he said, "Mr. Shaughnessy ran the Rams like a one-man show. He wouldn't let anybody do anything. I didn't learn a thing, and I wanted to move. But I never dreamed it would end like this."[25]

Rams GM Tex Schramm remembered, "Shaughnessy was so brilliant, so obsessed with new things that he couldn't make a balance. He should have been an assistant as he was later with the Bears . . . feed all the material in and then have somebody use what they want."[26]

Ironically, the Packers, whose new coach was former Bears assistant Gene Ronzani, brought in Shaughnessy for training camp to help install the offense. He did not stay for the entire year, as he was rehired by Halas before the Rams–Bears playoff game for the West crown at season's end, won by Los Angeles, 24–14. In 1951, while Stydahar was leading the Rams to the NFL title, Shaughnessy's presence in Chicago caused the direct, practical Hunk Anderson to quit the Bears after a dozen years as their line coach. Halfback Chuck Hunsinger, who played for the Bears from 1950 through 1952, remembers seeing little of the anointed advisor, saying, "Shaughnessy was a drawing board coach. You'd never see him on the field. He'd spend all his time in the Blue Room devising the plays and the defenses."[27]

The Bears began to decline in the early 1950s, but the team returned to contender status in 1954 and 1955, at which point Halas decided to step aside. The dissension on the Chicago staff did not make the choice of his successor easy. Reportedly, neither Shaughnessy nor Johnsos was willing to work under the other man, so loyal soldier Paddy Driscoll was given the reins for two seasons before Halas returned as head coach in 1958. Shaughnessy was given full control of the defense, and Johnsos ran the offense. Shaughnessy threw himself into working on the other side of the ball, commenting, "To my great surprise, I thoroughly enjoyed coaching defense. . . . We started from scratch, trying to develop new strategies and mechanics that might be tailor-made to stop these modern offenses."[28]

Sid Gillman added, "Halas and Shaughnessy were among the first in the history of the game to give you more looks in one game than you saw all season."[29] A 1959 article by Packers beat man Chuck Johnson asserted, "Most pro teams use three or four defenses and variations thereof in a game. The Bears use 15 or more."[30]

Once again, however, Shaughnessy ran amok when given too much freedom. Halas allowed Clark free reign over the defense, and Shaughnessy would not even tell Halas what his plans were each week. It was said that the only person aside from Shaughnessy to understand the defensive game plans was middle linebacker Bill George, and the performance of the Chicago defense was extremely erratic in the years Shaughnessy was in charge. When the Bears shut out the 49ers new shotgun offense in 1961, Shaughnessy was lauded in the press and milked the attention, although others claimed that the reason the Bears dominated that day is that San Francisco center Frank Morze simply could not block Bill George because he had his head down to concentrate on his shotgun snaps. A month later, the two teams met again, and the 49ers now-conventional attack compiled more than 500 yards of offense in a 41–31 thrashing of Chicago.

Halas assigned young coach George Allen to assist Shaughnessy, and Allen recalled, "Clark and I used to ride on the train to Green Bay, ride on planes, eat our meals together. After the evening meeting at training camp, we would take rides in the countryside to relax. I learned a great deal from him. He was a great man with a very fertile mind."[31]

Sportswriter Bill Gleason anonymously quoted a prominent coach (later identified as Vince Lombardi) telling him, "Some of the Bears, particularly the defensive backs, have been asked to do things that are impossible to do. We put some of those Chicago defenses on the blackboard, and they just won't work."[32]

Late in the 1962 season, Halas attempted to assert some control over a Shaughnessy defensive game plan that was unfeasible. When Halas refused the defense, Shaughnessy resigned from the Bears and complained publicly, "There's a lot of satisfaction in cooking up things and seeing them work, but it's no fun copying things or just doing things that you are told to do." He added, "I love to try things. In fact, I have a tendency to try too much. I usually throw out about two-thirds of everything I work out."[33]

Halas would win one last title in 1963, on the strength of a simplified defense set loose by George Allen. It would have been a perfect exit for the 68-year-old Halas and a chance to promote a popular assistant to usher in a new era for the Bears. Instead, Halas hung on and gave no indication to the ambitious Allen that he would ever advance in the Windy City. Allen subsequently signed with the Rams and then was sued for breach of contract by Halas. The elder George won the suit and then released Allen once the principle had been established.

Halas coached his team for four more seasons, losing one more game than he won, before retiring from coaching at age 73. The organization continued on its downward path until Halas hired Jim Finks as general manager and vice president in 1974. Finks rebuilt the team but then resigned in 1982, after Halas hired former Bears great Mike Ditka as head coach without consulting Finks. Still active with his team, Halas died a year later, and Chicago won its last NFL title to date two years after that.

Shaughnessy patched things up with his greatest benefactor a few months after he quit and was paid for West Coast scouting reports for the rest of his life. Clark worked on a book that was never completed; started a business designed to supply teams with playbooks that never got off the ground; and spent one last year as a head coach with the University of Hawaii, where he produced a 1–8–1 record. He died in 1970, at the age of 78, survived by his wife, three children, and several grandchildren, one of whom is Bill Kreutzmann, drummer of the rock band the Grateful Dead.

COACHING KEYS

Former Lions single wing fullback Ace Gutowsky made an important point in 1941: "It's about time somebody is giving the players some credit. T formation, my eye. Those Bears George Halas has gathered together could win, and win just as handily, with any kind of formation or system!" He added, "These fellows are all good, sound football players, and they're three deep at nearly every position. I think the first 11 men on the 1934 Bears were just as good as the first outfit Halas had this year, but they didn't have the reserves."[34]

Halas did not disagree with the basic point, having earlier commented, "It is not the formation but the men who make the touchdowns. It takes years to school even a talented key man in the T."[35] The counterargument was provided by Stanford's leap from one win to 10 in one season using the same players but switching to the T. The key point is that the coach's job is to put his players in the best position for them to succeed and not ask them to do things they are not able to do. Shaughnessy took players who struggled in the single wing and made stars of them in the T. The point he made in his previously cited *Esquire* article is that the specialized nature of backfield players' roles in the T formation—as opposed to the more complete set of skills required by single wing backs—makes it easier to find players to make the T go, assuming you can fill the key position of quarterback.[36]

Throughout the 1940s, discussion of the merits of the revamped T continued. Shaughnessy often engaged in semiformal debates about the T at various football gatherings. At a meeting of the New York Football Writers Association in 1944, Clark faced off with Cornell's Carl Snavely and Andy Kerr of Colgate, with Kerr quoting his mentor Pop Warner in stating, "The T formation is ruining football. It is a fad, and it won't last. This new style of game makes the players forget to knock the opposition down."[37]

An opinion poll of college coaches conducted by the Associated Press in 1945, reported a majority agreeing that the T had hit its peak. Virginia Military Institute coach Pooley Hubert contended a year later,

> I could write a book on the merits of the single wing as opposed to the T. We figure we get better passing, first because our tailback has a better view of the field than the T quarterback up under the center. Our passer always has three receivers—the ends and the wingback—going down and a fourth man who is only one yard back; the T passer's fourth man is four yards back."[38]

Even as most of the country had shifted to the T in one form or another, Shaughnessy still was debating Snavely over the T at a football clinic for high school and college coaches in Atlantic City, New Jersey, in the spring of 1948.[39] At this time, Shaughnessy had taken an advisory position with the Rams that would allow him to continue to open up and modernize the T well beyond any wingback attack. By that point, graduate students had begun to write master's theses on the T formation, according to a search of ProQuest's Dissertations and Theses database.

As the T evolved in the 1940s, sportswriter Stanley Woodward pointed out,

> The T as the Bears play it actually isn't a T because they employ one or more men-in-motion, varied with or combined with widespread ends to destroy the symmetry of the formation before the ball is put into play. Halas and Clark Shaughnessy, the Stanford maestro, feel that it is easier to decoy a defensive man out of the play than to block him.[40]

George Halas agreed with this assessment, saying,

> Consequently, when the Bears talk T formation football, we aren't referring to any alphabetical pattern which the players fall into for an instant as they come out of the huddle. Instead, we're talking about the myriad attacking combinations our players can shift into before the play actually starts.[41]

Watching game film from the time, one can see that the Bears line splits widened from the 1930s and that most of their plays employ a man-in-motion. Sometimes one end would spread wide, and sometimes the spread end was used in conjunction with the man-in-motion.

Football historian Paul Zimmerman summed up the Bears offense in the 1940s as follows: "Quick traps, counters, passes to the flat, look-ins, and the occasional seam pass off a quick drop to keep the defense honest—that was the Bears' package. A relentless series of thrusts that left defenses breathless."[42]

In the playbook published by Shaughnessy, Jones, and Halas, they wrote, "The modern T formation affords a boxing type of offense. The quick opening plays can be compared to the left jab of a boxer, the man-in-motion and the faking of the backs to the feints, and the fullback plays to the real punch. The pass plays should be used as the unexpected sock."[43]

Shaughnessy told fellow coach Jimmy Conzelman at the time, "I've always liked spread formations, too, and the man-in-motion brings about the same result. It draws players from their normal defensive positions."[44]

That playbook covers the basic principles of the offense, the mechanics of the quarterback, the maneuvers of the other backs, the linemen's assignments, the signal system, and overall strategy. Of highest interest, it includes 70 plays of the Bears offense, including such oddities as the quarterback acting as the man-in-motion with the ball snapped deep to a halfback or the quarterback lined up to the right of the center, again with the snap going deep to a halfback. These plays occasionally show up on film but generally run without success. On film, one can also come across gadget plays, for instance, in the Packers game on November 15, 1942. Each side of the Bears line shifts wide away from the center. The center then laterals the ball to left halfback Harry Clarke, who, in turn, laterals back to Sid Luckman, who passes to right halfback Scooter McLean in a round robin.

However, the main thrust of the offense was in basic plays run quickly with speed and deception. In the 1940s, Halas's T offense was primarily a running attack. In the 73–0 triumph against Washington in the 1940 title game, Chicago threw just 10 passes, one of which was a halfback option. Before the 1941 College All-Star Game, Halas issued a challenge to the All-Stars by printing in the *Chicago Tribune* three of the plays the Bears would run in the game: a quick opener, a fullback end run, and a favorite passing play.[45] He was confident that there were so many options off each play that the defense likely would be confused long enough for the play to succeed.

Watching game film of that Bears team is like viewing a machine drive down the field. They moved quicker, hit harder, and pursued faster than their opponents. In 1947, Halas noted that the Bears ran a play every 19.5 seconds: "We believe in swift execution. Each play is a potential touchdown. The more plays you execute, the more touchdown chances you have. We hope to cut our average down to 19 seconds this year."[46]

The key man, Halas asserted, was the quarterback:

> The T formation places a heavy burden on the quarterback, who handles the ball on every play. After you've spread your halfbacks and ends over a wide attacking front, it's the quarterback's responsibility to put the ball in the hands of the man who's in the best position to penetrate the defense.[47]

That quarterback had to master one-half, one-quarter, and three-quarter reverse pivots to the right and left, lateraling right and left, feeding and faking the ball to backs quickly and accurately, and passing the ball downfield according to the playbook. Left unsaid was that the quarterback was calling the plays as well, prompting the term "field general."[48]

Bears quarterback Sid Luckman maintained, "The whole secret is to fool your opponent by feinting in one direction and then hitting him hard from another. Get him off balance, get him moving in the wrong way, fake him with your head, your eyes, your hips, your knees, then follow up fast while you have the advantage."[49] That Luckman was so skilled and mastered the intricacies of quarterback play in the T contributed to its rapid success and spread throughout the decade. Sid, and Frankie Albert on Shaughnessy's Stanford team, allowed the possibilities of the system to quickly flower and present themselves plainly for the football world to appreciate.

One of the initial reactions of coaches was to try to merge aspects of the T with their own systems. Cardinals coach Jimmy Conzelman and Auburn's Jack Meagher got together following the 1940 season to try to figure out how to incorporate the T with the Notre Dame box offense they used. Boston Yanks coach Herb Kopf developed the Q-T, in which the quarterback lined up under center with two backs behind him and one on the wing; sometimes the quarterback took the snap and sometimes it went through his legs to one of the deep backs. Kopf stressed, "The T's strength is on the inside; the single wing's on the outside. With the Q-T . . . I can run a quick opening play to the inside, the man-in-motion flanker sweeps, and pass." Curly Lambeau would also experiment with the center snap through the quarterback's legs in 1947. It was not successful.[50]

A more effective spinoff was the split T, devised by Don Faurot of Missouri in 1941, in which the line splits are very wide and the quarterback slides down the line after taking the snap, with a triple option to run, hand off, or pass the ball. Another popular variation was the wing T, developed by Columbia's Lou Little and others in the 1940s, which had two backs behind the quarterback and a third on the wing. These variations were more commonly used in the college ranks but signaled more support for the flexibility of the T. As late as 1947, 78-year-old Pop Warner was still advocating his own wing-back offenses. The T, he said, "is the poorest setup for the passing game," and he added that it "is inferior as a running attack because it lacks power."[51] But columnist Bob Wills countered, "The T is more amenable to changes in offensive tactics than any other system."[52]

With the T formation still providing the underpinning of the motley, myriad offensive systems in pro and college football three-quarters of a century later, Wills has been proven correct. In fact, Clark Shaughnessy pushed the T offense forward later in the decade when he coached the Los Angeles Rams for two seasons and began a serious move to the passing game. When working with the Bears, Shaughnessy was credited by George Halas with helping invent ways to run wide in the T, an inherent weakness in the original formation. "He worked out many new blocking assignments, which helped in the development of end runs," said Halas. "He also developed counterplays, which prevented opponents from playing a tight defense. For instance, he worked out a counter running play for every pass play and vice versa."[53]

Shaughnessy was a man of imagination. In 1943, he claimed that in a few years the "offense will have so far outreached the defense by that time that it may be necessary to make teams travel 12 or 15 yards for a first down."[54] Going into his second season as head coach of the Rams, he toyed with the idea of using two quarterbacks simultaneously with four ends for some plays. He often is credited with establishing the pro set offense of two running backs and three wide receivers (two ends and a flanker), but that is not the case. Clark did use that alignment on occasion in 1949, with Elroy Hirsch as his flanker, but Hirsch often lined up as a halfback and ran the ball 68 times, the second highest total on the team. Moreover, Paul Brown often employed three-receiver sets in Cleveland at the time as well. It appears the 1952 Rams, coached by former Bears end Hampton Pool, was the first pro team to go to the pro set offense on a full-time basis (see figure 8.1).[55]

Shaughnessy was a leader in that direction, however. His short stewardship of the Rams set the stage for Stydahar and Pool, who followed him in Los Angeles. Clark's Rams ran the ball just 53 percent of the time

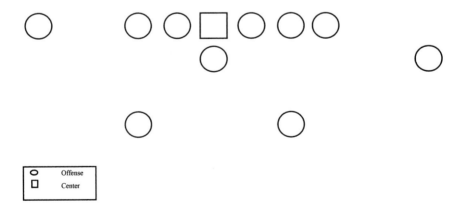

Figure 8.1. Standard pro set

and presented a spectacular, fast strike offense that passed the ball almost 10 percent more than the league average. He based his tactics on his understanding of military strategy. Shaughnessy wrote,

> Football is the closest approach to war that we have in sports. All the basic strategy of the two competitions are related. You mass men for a quick thrust here; you feint the enemy out of position. It's quickness, precision, co-operation, determination. They all work together—in both football and war. [56]

Forty years later, journalist William Furlong wrote an article for *Smithsonian* detailing Shaughnessy's military mind-set, as when he drew an analogy between the repetitive trench warfare of World War I and the football played in the 1920s and 1930s. [57] Furthermore, Clark found his greatest strategic inspiration from World War II German general Heinz Guderian, a proponent of blitzkrieg operations using tanks. Similarly, Shaughnessy's football offense was based on speed, deception, and concentrated power.

When Shaughnessy was put in charge of the Bears defense in the 1950s, more of his military interests came to the fore. He established a chain of command for his defense with middle linebacker Bill George, the general; safety Richie Petitbon, the colonel; and so forth. His defensive style mirrored that of his offense—attack! Shaughnessy favored man-to-man coverage in the secondary, constant blitzing from the linebackers, and a boundless series of loops and stunts on the line. Defensive end Doug Atkins recalled, "Shaughnessy had one scheme where I lined up at defensive end; then I had five different places to go. It was slam, slide, slue, smooch, and all that. You were supposed to react. You just can't do that. We were struggling all the time." [58]

Despite having top talent, the Bears defense was wildly inconsistent under Shaughnessy. The schemes were not only too complex and convoluted to perform, but also masked in an unintelligible 1,700-word vocabulary that most players struggled to comprehend. In the Hall of Fame archives, there is an unfinished manuscript for a book Shaughnessy was writing that included the "Clark Shaughnessy Glossary, A–Z." Most of the terms were based on a pneumonic, but one that made sense only to the originator.

Richie Petitbon marveled in 1959, "Football genius is the only way to describe Clark Shaughnessy. I believe he knows more football than anyone in the world. He is the absolute boss of our defensive unit, and no one tells him what to do—not even George Halas."[59] Halas put George Allen in charge once Shaughnessy quit, and the simplified Chicago defense allowed the fewest points in the league in driving the Bears to the 1963 NFL championship. Petitbon recalled in 1984, "George took Clark's good stuff and threw out the bad. As with most geniuses, some of Clark's stuff was off the wall."[60]

What Allen did to the Bears defensive scheme was similar to what Herman Ball did to the Redskins offense in 1948, and Joe Stydahar to the Rams in 1950: simplify and streamline or jettison the impractical and overly complicated parts of Shaughnessy's schemes. That and Clark's inability to get along with his fellow coaches were what ultimately kept him from success as a head coach in the pro game.

PIVOTAL GAMES

George Halas coached the Bears to three NFL championships in the 1940s. Each is worth a look, but the first is as dominant a performance as there has ever been in a title match. Arthur Daley's lede in the *New York Times* said it best: "The weather was perfect. So were the Bears."[61]

In 1940, Washington had the best record in the league, had scored the most points, had allowed 10 fewer points than the Bears, and had beaten Chicago, 7–3, just three weeks prior to their title game rematch. Still, Chicago was a 7–5 favorite. Redskins coach Ray Flaherty's plan was to unleash his offense and outscore Chicago, and he was pleased the day before the game, commenting, "When you see them begin to snarl and snap at each other, you can pretty well be sure they're at a fine mental edge for the game."[62]

Halas and Shaughnessy had watched the film of Chicago's regular-season loss and constructed a plan to attack the defense Washington had played that day. To make sure that Flaherty hadn't switched up the Redskins defense, the Bears ran two test plays at the outset to confirm how Washington would cover the man-in-motion. On the first play, left halfback Ray Nolting motioned to the right, and right halfback George McAfee ran a quick opener up the middle for seven yards. On play two, McAfee went in motion to the left and fullback Bill Osmanski took a pitchout around the left end for a 68-yard touchdown run. The play was designed to go off tackle, but Osmanski read the blocking and bounced around end instead. Bears center Bulldog Turner recalled, "We got so much publicity from the game that later all Bill Osmanski wanted to do was run up into the line and then slide out and go around end. I got so I was disgusted with him because he wouldn't run Clark Shaughnessy's play the way it was supposed to be run."[63]

The Redskins answered by driving right down the field, with Sammy Baugh finding end Charley Malone open at the Chicago five. But Malone dropped the pass, and Washington missed on the subsequent 32-yard field goal attempt, giving Chicago possession on its own 20. T master Sid Luckman led the Bears on a relentless 16-play, 80-yard drive that culminated in a one-yard scoring plunge by Sid with four minutes left in the first quarter. The drive included just one pass play and established the unstoppable power of the Bears offense. After a Redskins punt, the Bears took over on the Washington 42, and second-string fullback Joe Maniaci dashed around left end for a touchdown to put Chicago up, 21–0, with two and a half minutes to go in the first quarter.

Filchock replaced Baugh in the second quarter, threw two interceptions, and turned over the ball on downs at the Chicago 18. After the second interception, Luckman hit Ken Kavanaugh with a 30-yard touchdown strike to make the score 28–0 at the half. The third quarter was a complete disaster even though Chicago ran just seven offensive plays. Fifty seconds into the period, Hamp Pool picked off a swing pass and returned it 15 yards for a touchdown, 35–0. Beyond desperate, Sammy Baugh went for a fourth-and-20 play at his own 34 and failed. Two plays later, Nolting hit a quick opener for a 23-yard touchdown, 41–0.

Third quarterback Leroy Zimmerman came in for Washington. George McAfee intercepted him at the 35 and ran it in for another touchdown, making it 48–0. Then, Bulldog Turner completed the third pick six of the third quarter from 30 yards, 54–0. In the final period. Harry Clarke scored twice on runs, and third fullback Gary Famiglietti scored after a Filchock fumble at the Redskins two. Final score: 73 to zero.

Sid Luckman only played in the first half and completed three of four passes for 88 yards. His backups were four of five for 50 yards, and George McAfee misfired on one halfback option pass. On the ground, the Bears ran 53 times for 381 yards, with Osmanski the high man, at 109. On defense, Chicago picked off eight passes and recovered a fumble. Five of Chicago's 11 touchdowns came from turnovers. Four of their touchdowns were from 30 yards or more, displaying the quick-strike capability of the refitted T formation.

From the film, one can see that the Bears used the man-in-motion 36 times—19 to the left and 17 to the right—and no motion on 31 plays. On 16 plays, they used a spread end and once deployed two spread ends. They ran the ball up the middle 23 times, to the left 18, and to the right 16. Overall, they were balanced in their attack and continually mixed it up to keep the Redskins off balance.

After the game, Washington owner George Preston Marshall angrily accused his players of quitting.[64] It wasn't that. The Bears were so good that they were capable of rolling over any team at any time with that offense leading the way. Watching the film almost 80 years later, it's still shocking to see holes open that quickly—381 yards rushing! With that big lead, the Bears dropped back into coverage on defense and smothered the Redskins receivers—eight interceptions! In retrospect, Halas summarized it as the "greatest game ever played." He added, "Since then football hasn't been the same. That one made us major league. It showed the country the potential in professional football. It made us accepted as professionals."[65]

It was a game without precedent, and the Bears continued to dominate the league. In 1941, the Packers and Bears both were undefeated except for one loss apiece to one another. In the Western Division playoff game, however—the first game in league history in which "sudden death" overtime procedures were in play—Chicago spotted the Packers a 7–0 lead before rolling to 30 unanswered points in the first half to win easily, 33–14. A week later, in the title game against the Giants, the Bears got off to a slow start and allowed New York to tie them at nine in the third quarter. Thence, the onslaught of two Chicago touchdowns in both the third and fourth quarters enabled the Bears to win going away, 37–9. Chicago rang up 389 yards of offense to 157 for New York and provoked five turnovers from the normally stingy Giants. Before 1940, the Packers held the record for widest margin in a championship game with their 27–0 triumph in 1939. The Bears not only trampled that in 1940, but also exceeded it again in 1941.

Had it not been for World War II, it's easy to imagine the Bears appearing in seven consecutive championship games, but the last one the team actually did appear in for the decade was 1946, the first postwar year. Chicago still had great talent, but the gap had shrunk between them and the top contenders. Besides, Luckman and his crew were starting to age a bit. Still, they were the most powerful team in the league and met the Giants again in a championship match that has been overshadowed by the fact that two New Yorkers, one of whom was signal caller Frank Filchock, had been approached by gamblers in the week before the game.

The opportunistic Giants lived off turnovers, but against the Bears, once again, they died by them. Filchock threw six interceptions and New York fumbled twice, but the game was still tied at 14 in the fourth quarter before Luckman called his own number on a 19-yard bootleg run away from the flow of the play for the winning score. It was a play suggested by offensive coach Luke Johnsos from his perch in the press box and the final moment of triumph for the team of the decade. Chicago continued to contend, but eventually they were outstripped by their T formation imitators—the Eagles, Cardinals, and Rams.

The 1948 and 1949 Rams were Shaughnessy's shot at establishing himself as more than the man behind the throne in pro ball. In his second season, he got the Rams to the championship game, but the slogging rain and mud that day worked against the open offense he had developed, and his team lost to Philadelphia, 14–0. A better game to examine to see what Clark was up to at decade's end is the 1949 season finale against Washington, which clinched the Western Division for Los Angeles. The Rams had begun the season 6–0, but then the team won one, lost two, and tied two in the next five games to allow the Bears to stay on their heels. Prior to the West Coast start of the Rams game, the Bears obliterated the Cardinals—their crosstown rivals and two-time defending Western Division champs—52–21, with Johnny Lujack throwing for 468 yards and six touchdowns. The Rams knew they needed to win.

Los Angeles got off to a fast start with Bob Waterfield hitting Tom Fears on a 29-yard touchdown strike early, which was followed by two from Norm Van Brocklin to Bob Shaw (of nine and 48 yards, respectively) to give the Rams a commanding 20–7 lead after one quarter. Two rushing touchdowns in the second quarter made the game a blowout, 34–7, at the half. Waterfield connected with Shaw in the third quarter for a 45-yard score, and Van Brocklin hit scoring tosses to Shaw for 25 yards and Fears for 51 in the fourth quarter to widen the lead to 53–14, before Washington managed two late touchdowns to make the 53–27 final a bit more presentable.

On film, the game is a fascinating display of offensive firepower and strategy. Again, it's a big-strike offense. Shaughnessy had his team operating out of three sets, usually featuring a spread end and a closed one. One set was a straight full-house T with three backs, the second was the full-house T with a man-in-motion, and the third was the pro set with two running backs and one flanker. Sometimes he had the flanker and spread end lined up on the same side, and sometimes he used the man-in-motion from the pro set so that only one back remained behind the quarterback. Both Waterfield and Van Brocklin got substantial playing time, and even third stringer Bobby Thomason had one series of downs in the fourth quarter.

The overall breakdown shows 31 plays in the pro set, including five with a man-in-motion, 22 T plays with the man-in-motion, and 19 without. Waterfield directed the pro set 24 times, Van Brocklin five, and Thomason two. Waterfield used the T with motion 11 times, Van Brocklin six, and Thomason five. Waterfield aligned in the pure T eight times, Van Brocklin seven, and Thomason four. Four touchdowns—two by air and two by ground—resulted from the pro set, three by motion, and one from the pure T. Waterfield directed 10 drives and completed 11 of 17 passes for 235 yards and two scores, while Van Brocklin led seven drives and completed six of 10 passes for 152 yards and four scores. Thomason was three for five for 18 yards in his one drive. Los Angeles generated 405 passing yards and 179 rushing. On defense, they allowed Sammy Baugh 308 yards and three touchdowns but did pick off four passes as well. The Rams' eight touchdowns on offense matched what the 1940 Bears did to a more talented Washington squad, but there was a big swing in how those yards and scores were attained. The passing game was in bloom, and the Rams were leaders in its promulgation in the next decade. Unfortunately, Shaughnessy was not part of that triumph.

Halas drew a distinction between the skills of a head coach and the most talented of assistants:

> I would say that Clark Shaughnessy comes very close to being the pure football scientist. Not all his ideas were included in the Bears' T formation. They would be discussed at staff meetings, just as those advanced by Johnsos, Anderson, and Paddy Driscoll. The important thing to remember is that the final decision was mine. [66]

Despite Shaughnessy's major contribution to the advancement of the game, it is Halas who is best remembered and with some justification.

Halas was the first coach to make use of an extended staff, and he knew how to hire good people. Paul Brown would develop that into an art form and produce a coaching tree of assistants who learned from the best and went on to create their own legacies as head coaches. Halas stunted his own tree by keeping men like Hunk Anderson and Luke Johnsos from taking opportunities elsewhere.

The United Press harshly noted,

> Until his Chicago Bears beat the Washington Redskins 73–0 for the professional football title, Halas's reputation best was described as "just another pro football coach." Now Halas is a national football figure as a result not only of the Bears' astounding professional triumph but of the success of Clark Shaughnessy at Stanford, using the Bears' famed T formation, man-in-motion offense, a brain-child of the Chicago owner-coach.[67]

What Halas, Shaughnessy, and Jones did with the T ultimately changed the game and its hierarchy. For the first time, the college game was following the lead of the professional one with the spread of the T formation offense. It wouldn't be long before the NFL would be seen as the top tier of football—and its coaches as the vanguard of their profession.

9

PLAYERS' COACH

Jimmy Conzelman's Championship Charm

Having originated in 1898, the Cardinals are the oldest continuing professional football team in the country, as well as charter members of the NFL. They shared Chicago with the Bears for almost 40 years but rarely as equals. The one exception was a brief period following World War II when a multitalented, personable, peripatetic pied pianist beat Halas's Bears four of six games and led the Cards to the league title in 1947. Aside from a disputed league championship in 1925, that title is still the only one in the team's nomadic history—from Chicago to St. Louis to Phoenix to Tempe, Arizona.

That creative piano player was Jimmy Conzelman, and he had the gift of gab and the gift of imagination. In his vibrant life, he was a writer, songwriter, musician, actor, boxer, football player, football coach, team owner, baseball manager, newspaper owner, after-dinner speaker, and advertising executive. He had a self-effacing waggishness that drew players and others to him. As he told columnist Bob Considine,

> It's just like a fellow said to me. He said, "Jim, you're in a tough spot. You can't coach well enough to coach and can't write well enough to write. You should write sports books for boys. They won't know you don't know enough football, and they'll be too dumb to know you can't write."[1]

Cardinals halfback Marshall Goldberg once claimed that Conzelman's "mere presence gave everyone a lift."[2] Indeed, Jimmy lifted a perennial NFL doormat to a championship and, in the process, pushed aside George Halas's T formation advantage.

Unlike most coaches, he was slow to anger but quick with a smile, a story, and a joke. Moreover, he struck a distinctive demonstrative figure on the sidelines, standing out from the crowd with his overgrown white thicket of hair, chain smoking cigarettes as he gestured wildly. Conzelman hated losing but generally didn't take it out on his players. His son recalled, "If they lost, he'd go to the locker room and be so mad he'd pound and punch the lockers. The players would just let him burn it off."[3] Football is a serious business, and most coaches stress the negative as they harshly criticize their players to goad improvement. Jimmy's lighter approach would not work for most—every coach has to be true to himself—but any coach who can provide joy in the hard work of mastering football has a special talent. And that was Conzelman, the merry Irishman with the Dutch name.

LIFE AND CAREER

He was born James Gleason Dunn on March 6, 1898, in St. Louis, Missouri. Sadly, his father, the original James Gleason Dunn, died just 11 months later. When Jimmy was four and a half years old, his mother, Margaret Ryan Dunn, married dentist Oscar Conzelman, and young Jimmy took his stepfather's name. The family grew in the coming years as Jimmy welcomed a stepsister and later two stepbrothers into the house.

Conzelman proved himself to be a talented athlete always on the move. In 1912, he played quarterback for Loyola High School in St. Louis and then moved on to play halfback at Central High in 1914 and quarterback at McKinley High in 1915. As a college freshman, he stayed in his hometown and played halfback for Washington University in the fall of 1916. The next semester, he looked into dental school but did not find that course of study to his liking.

By the fall of 1917, Conzelman had enlisted in the U.S. Navy and was sent to the Great Lakes Training Station, where he played football and also won the base's middleweight boxing championship. He continued on the football team in 1918, when the squad added such notables as George

Halas and Paddy Driscoll, and swept to an undefeated season and a Rose Bowl triumph on January 1, 1919. Returning to Washington University after the war, he again starred for the Bears that autumn.

His family life had changed drastically, however, from the smallest bit of misfortune. In the spring of 1918, Oscar Conzelman cut his thumb while operating on a patient. The cut became infected and eventually necessitated the amputation of Oscar's right forearm. In May 1919, he contracted another infection in the area, and it killed him.

With Jimmy's mother struggling to support herself and her three younger children, a teenage daughter and two preschool sons, Conzelman left Washington University before completing the requirements for his degree and worked to support his family. He relied on his most obvious skills, playing football and music, to earn money. Jimmy joined the Decatur Staleys in 1920 and played quarterback for the team but also ran a dance band on the side. His lack of football focus disturbed the Staleys' cocoach, Dutch Sternaman, who left handwritten notes about Conzelman in his files. Sternaman was upset that Jimmy would miss practices and could not remember the plays, and compared him to another well-known free spirit—Johnny Blood. Dutch fumed, "He once told me he had to play banjo or piano in [his] band at Milwaukee and could not practice." Sternaman also derided Conzelman as a player, saying he was a "scrambler, not a quarterback" and that he "ran all over the field."[4]

No doubt, Sternaman was pleased that Conzelman signed with the Rock Island Independents in 1921 as a player, because Rock Island owner Walter Flanigan was impressed by Conzelman's 43-yard touchdown run that beat the Independents the prior year. Soon Jimmy began his coaching career there as well. The story he told author Bob Curran was that during the game with the Staleys on October 10, Flanigan sent tackle Ed Healey into the game for player-coach Frank Coughlin. Healey then informed Conzelman that he was the new head coach of the team.[5]

It's a great story, one that a raconteur like Conzelman would tell with relish but not likely to be wholly accurate. Coughlin played the entire game without substitution against the Staleys that day. The next week against the Chicago Cardinals, Coughlin was substituted out, but it wasn't until two days after that, on October 18, that Flanigan announced that Coughlin and two other players had been cut and Conzelman was the new coach.[6]

Jimmy, the team's star back, took over a 1–1–1 team and led it to a 5–2–1 finish. He stuck around Rock Island after the season and was hired as the catcher and manager for the Class D minor-league Rock Island Islanders baseball team. He batted just .244 that season and then exited baseball for two decades. Returning to the Independents in 1922, Conzelman again led the squad to a winning season, but after a 3–0 loss to the Bears on November 19, the next week's season finale against Minneapolis was cancelled, and Flanigan dropped out of the league. Conzelman quickly signed as player-coach with the Milwaukee Badgers for the last three games of their season, all losses as it turned out. Prior to the Badgers next game against the Green Bay Packers, the *Green Bay Press-Gazette* noted that two other former Rock Island players, Dewey Lyle and Dutch Lauer, were excited to settle the score with Conzelman, who they felt had "ruled with an iron hand."[7]

Conzelman stayed with the Badgers as player-coach in 1923 and led the team to a fourth-place 7–2–4 record, receiving some All-League notice as well. The following season, with a fledgling real estate business on the side, he stepped down as coach but remained in the Badgers backfield. He also got married in 1924, to Peggy Udell, a former Ziegfeld Follies chorus girl from Milwaukee. She would begin divorce proceedings in 1925, but the couple remained married. It was also in this period that Jimmy worked as a business agent for a sculptor in Greenwich Village and modeled the fallen French soldier for sculptor Frederick MacMonnies's monument for the World War I Battle of the Marne, which was given to the French people and now sits in Meaux, France.

Fully exploring his artistic side, Conzelman also wrote a half-dozen songs that were published during this time, notably "What a Baby" and "Fools in Paradise." It's not surprising that he tried to organize a summer vaudeville tour in 1925 with Notre Dame's famed "Four Horsemen" backfield. He wanted to tie that into his purchase of a NFL franchise in Detroit and hoped to bring the Horsemen to the Motor City. Neither the tour nor the backfield worked out, but Conzelman's Panthers were an on-the-field success in 1925, finishing third in the league with an 8–2–2 record. Financially, they were in the red, and Jimmy hoped a late-season match on the Red Grange tour would bail him out. Unfortunately, Grange was hurt and unable to play, so Conzelman had to refund most of his gate receipts. After a 4–6–2 season in 1926, Jimmy threw in the towel and gave the franchise back to the league.

He moved on to Providence, where the Steam Roller played their games in a bicycle racetrack called the Cycledrome. Conzelman was named the team's player-coach in 1927, and he brought over star tackle Gus Sonnenberg and four other key Panthers who helped improve the Steam Roller from a 5–7–1 team in 1926 to an 8–5–1 club in Jimmy's first season. The key acquisition, however, was George "Wildcat" Wilson, a moody All-America halfback from the University of Washington who had spent the previous season in Red Grange's American Football League. Wilson was the Roller's single-wing tailback who directed the attack, although Conzelman, the quarterback, called the plays.

In Jimmy's second season in Rhode Island, the team again won eight games but this time lost just one and tied two to win the NFL title. Providence had the best defense in the league, shutting out five opponents and only allowing one team, Frankford, to score as many as 10 points against them, and that came in the Roller's only loss. Conzelman tore knee ligaments in the fourth game, so he paced the sidelines on crutches for the rest of the season.

Despite playing in just four games, Conzelman was unanimously voted the team's "Most Valuable Man" by the Providence players at the end of the championship season and awarded a silver loving cup by the city, along with a collapsible cane by his teammates. Quarterback Curly Oden remarked, "His spirit kept us going through the season." Wilson added, "Never have I played on a team, either in or out of college, that has shown the spirit, the desire to win, and the friendship for one another that the Roller has. Neither college or high school football has given me half as much enjoyment as playing under Jimmy Conzelman."[8]

That good feeling would not last, however. The Roller dipped to 4–6–2 in 1929. Conzelman got married for a second time that September, to Lillian Granzon, having divorced his first wife in July on grounds of desertion. Oddly, his first wife sued Jimmy for divorce in January 1930, before she found out their marriage already had been dissolved. He returned to the Providence backfield but never recovered from his knee injury. Sonnenberg left football to concentrate on his wrestling career, and Wilson seemed to lose interest. The team rebounded to 6–4–1 in 1930, but Jimmy decided it was time to return to his native St. Louis and be closer to his family. The Steam Roller would go out of business after the 1931 season.

He began publishing a weekly newspaper in the St. Louis suburb of Maplewood and took on a new coaching position. The local National Guard armory formed an independent football team, and Conzelman was hired as its first coach. He led the St. Louis Gunners to a 5–2–1 record in 1931, before taking the head coaching position at his alma mater in January 1932. During his tenure as coach at Washington University, he put both his younger brothers, John and Robert, through school there. Jimmy would coach the Washington Bears for the next eight years to a cumulative 40–35–2 record and win three Missouri Valley Conference championships. By far, it was the longest he ever stayed at one football job.

Upon taking the job, he asserted, "I'm going to teach the Warner system, using a double wing-back formation for deception and the single wing back for my power plays."[9] But he was more than just a gridiron strategist. He raised money for the struggling program with an annual party for the well-heeled of St. Louis and charmed his players by flying kites with them and serving them ice cream. He also ran a summer sports camp for kids in Richland, Missouri.

He and his second wife separated in 1934, and divorced in October 1936, and he married for a third and final time, to Anne Forrestal, that December. That marriage would last the rest of his life and produce a beloved son, James Jr. His horizons continued to expand in many ways. He began writing pieces for the *Saturday Evening Post* in the late 1930s and started a syndicated column for the *St. Louis Post-Dispatch* in 1939. One summer, he played the role of the coach in a local revival of the musical *Good News*. In the 1950s, he would tackle a second stage role, as the baseball manager in a local production of *Damn Yankees*. He also came to be in high demand nationally as an after-dinner speaker, averaging 60 talks a year, as his self-deprecating humor and entertaining manner with sportswriters became known.

In January 1940, some in the school's administration pushed for his resignation, and he gave it to them. When it was announced that he was stepping down, 500 students staged a demonstration to protest, and the faculty athletic committee refused to accept his resignation. Conzelman had already arranged for a sponsored radio post to start in February and declined to reconsider his resignation. The school unsuccessfully pursued Jock Sutherland as its new coach before settling on Frank Loebs.

Conzelman returned to pro football in April when the Chicago Cardinals hired him to replace Ernie Nevers. Coming off a 1–10 season, the

Cards had enjoyed just one winning record in the 14 years since they won the NFL title in 1925. Jimmy invited just 15 incumbent players to training camp and brought in 36 newcomers.[10] The 1940 Cardinals included 22 rookies and eight men in their second year.

Jimmy also switched up his offense, converting from the Warner system to the Notre Dame method. To help in the transition, he hired Fighting Irish alumnus Chile Walsh as his assistant coach and traded for two rookie linemen from South Bend—Ed Beinor and Joe Kuharich. Halfback Marshall Goldberg loved playing for Conzelman, saying, "He had a temper, and once in a while, he let it go, but he also was always planning some sort of joke or innovation to keep things going." He added, "Everyone tried to do their best for him because he was such a likable person. You'd break your neck for him!"[11]

The Cardinals did improve to a 2–7–2 mark in 1940, with the season's highlight being a 21–7 victory against the Bears in week three. More slight progress continued in 1941, as the team edged up to 3–7–1. Jimmy even announced he had written a team fight song, "It's in the Cards to Win," on December 5, two days before Pearl Harbor and the season finale against the Bears. The Cards dipped slightly to 3–8 in 1942, while basing their offense largely on rookie passer Bud Schwenk from Washington University. Schwenk led the league in pass attempts but tossed just six touchdowns against 27 interceptions.

The year was more interesting for what happened off the field. Conzelman was invited to give the commencement speech at the University of Dayton—a first for a NFL coach according to author Joe Ziemba—and veered completely away from his usual witty commentary. In light of the war raging throughout the world, Jimmy addressed the usefulness of football training for boys headed for the conflict. Speaking of naval trainees, he explained,

> He plays football and participates in other sports for coordination, accustoming himself mentally and physically to violence, learning how to take it and give it. Here again is an excellent example of the use of body contact sports as an agency to develop mental poise in the face of physical shock. Correct mental attitude, as much or more than physical condition, is the objective of the Naval Reserve Aviation program.[12]

Conzelman told columnist Harry Grayson,

Football coaches have always been apologists for their profession. For years we've been on the defensive from the attacks of reformers and long-hair intellectuals, who regard us as muscle-bound mentalities, exploiting kids to make a soft living. That's all over now. The bleeding hearts haven't the courtesy to apologize to us, but they're coming round and asking our help in this tremendous national emergency. We don't want their apologies. The chance to help is all we want. That's our vindication. [13]

The address was twice read into the *Congressional Record*, and the National Football League distributed 35,000 copies of it as a pamphlet. A year later, it also earned him a honorary master's degree from Dayton. Jimmy later quipped,

That's Conzelman for you. He has to do things differently. When I broke into baseball, did I start as a player? Not me. I began as a manager. When I sold my first magazine article, did I sell it to a pulp? No, siree. I started with the *Saturday Evening Post*. When I went on stage, my first part was a lead. Now the first degree I ever had is that of a master. [14]

Jimmy then surprised everyone by quitting the Cardinals in June 1943, to work for Don Barnes, owner of the St. Louis Browns baseball team. The Browns, who had represented St. Louis in the American League since 1902, were the only major-league team to never win a pennant and residing familiarly in last place when Conzelman came on board. Jimmy was hired to direct public relations for both the Browns and Barnes's American Investment Company. A month later, however, he said to columnist Shirley Povich, "But it's not fair to the Browns to say that I have anything to do with the business affairs of the club. My job is to round up baseball talent." [15] The nature of his relationship with general manager Bill DeWitt is unclear. But one year later, the Browns won their first and only pennant and then lost the World Series to the Cardinals, with all six games played in Sportsman's Park.

Conzelman remained with the Browns through August 1945, when Barnes sold the team, and Jimmy resigned. He was still a vice president of the Chicago Cardinals, and owner Charley Bidwill announced in November 1945 that Jimmy would be returning as the team's coach the following season. Negotiations dragged on until March, but Conzelman signed on and was back in pro football and nearing his time of greatest triumph. He even wrote an article for the *Saturday Evening Post* that year entitled "I'd Rather Coach the Pros."[16] After Jimmy left in 1943, the undermanned Cards experienced an unmatched three-year period with just one victory, a record of 1–29 under Conzelman's once and future line coach, Phil Handler.

The good news was that with the war over, a lot of talented players, including several originally acquired by Conzelman (Paul Christman, Ray Mallouf, Vince Banonis, Billy Dewell, Chet Bulger, Pop Ivy, and Walt Rankin) were back. Add to them players drafted during the war who had yet to report (Stan Mauldin, Buster Ramsey, Pat Harder, and Red Cochran) and rookies Mal Kutner and Elmer Angsman, and the Cardinals suddenly had an abundance of talent. Marshall Goldberg recalled, "It wasn't a big team, but it was very fast and very creative."[17]

The Cardinals started to run the T in 1945, but management brought in ace coach Carl Brumbaugh to train quarterbacks Christman and Mallouf in the intricacies of the position in 1946. The Cards hovered around .500 for the entire season, ending up at 6–5, but it was still a major step forward for the team. They were missing just one piece, and they got it in January 1947, when Bidwill outbid the Yankees of the All-America Football Conference to sign Georgia halfback Charley Trippi to a four-year, $100,000 contract. Three months later, however, Bidwill passed away suddenly at the age of 51.

With the so-called Dream Backfield of quarterback Christman, halfbacks Trippi and Angsman, and fullback Harder, the Cardinals were picked by some to win the West in 1947, although Conzelman tried to play down those expectations. The Cards bolted to a 7–1 start before dropping two in a row to the Redskins and Giants, two clubs with losing records, to fall behind the Bears in the West. In addition, a second tragedy befell the team in October, when halfback/punter Jeff Burkett died in a plane crash while attempting to rejoin the team from a hospital stay on the West Coast. Vince Banonis remembered the humane, understated response from Conzelman to the loss of Burkett, saying, "Jimmy did a good job telling us about how life goes, all the ups and downs."[18]

In week 11, the Cardinals whipped the Eagles, while the Bears were losing to the Rams to set up the season finale Bears–Cardinals match as the determinant of the pennant. Conzelman had bested Halas two times in a row, and on December 14, 1947, he made it three. The Cards jumped on top on the first play of the game when halfback Babe Dimancheff slipped by Bears linebacker Mike Holovak to catch an 80-yard touchdown pass from Christman. It was a play especially designed by Conzelman for the Bears. The Cardinals led, 27–7, at the half and won easily, 30–21. Two weeks later, Chicago played host to the Eagles for the NFL championship.

On a chilly day with a frozen field at Comiskey Park, the Cards outgunned the Eagles with four big plays: runs of 70, 70, and 44 yards, and a 75-yard punt return. Conzelman was voted Coach of the Year, and George Halas commented, "Jimmy hasn't gotten the credit he deserves for his judicious handling, which brought the team home a winner."[19] Eagles coach Greasy Neale agreed, stating, "He always had a bold, imaginative attack, solid blocking, and tackling. Jimmy was as good as they came."[20]

The next year, the Cardinals were even better. The season began with a victory against the Eagles, which was offset by the death of star tackle Stan Mauldin due to a heart attack in the locker room after the game. Jim Conzelman Jr., who was in the locker room that sad day, remembered players sobbing and his father going out of the clubhouse to inform and console Mauldin's widow.[21] Despite the pall that placed over the season, Chicago averaged a league-leading 33 points per game and compiled an 11–1 record. Once again the pennant came down to the season finale with the Bears, and once again Jimmy prevailed. This time, the Cardinals traveled to Philadelphia for the title game, and it was played on a snow-covered field in a blizzard. The only touchdown of the game came four plays after a botched snap by Cardinals quarterback Ray Mallouf at his own 17-yard line.

Neale congratulated Conzelman after the game and told him, "I never beat you, Jim, when you had Mauldin. He was the greatest tackle I ever saw."[22]

Three weeks later, Jimmy surprised everyone again by stepping down as the Cardinals coach to accept a job as an account executive with D'Arcy Advertising in St. Louis. He had worked for the firm in the offseason but now had the opportunity to work on a full-time basis. The idea appealed to him for several reasons. First, it would be better for his family to stay put in St. Louis rather than divide his time between there and Chicago, particularly for his 11-year-old son. Jim Jr. recalled, "He wanted to get back to St. Louis, and I am probably responsible for that because he wanted me to get situated back then and lead a normal life—

my life was sitting on the bench or on the field."[23] Second, he was looking for a position with more security and more to offer in terms of a pension. Third, as he commented at the end of the 1948 season, "I am very tired—this is a helluva grind."[24]

Conzelman was rumored to have been offered two coaching jobs in 1949, with the Redskins and Giants, but nothing came of either one, and Jimmy never coached again. He had coached five NFL teams—four of them defunct—for 15 years altogether and won two league titles. He continued to work at D'Arcy until retirement and continued to be a favorite with sportswriters and audiences for his humorous tales and expert delivery. In 1964, he was elected to the second class of the Pro Football Hall of Fame under protest. Conzelman was part of the 10-man selection committee and was blocking his own nomination until the other nine members invoked a parliamentary procedure to link his name to that of Art Rooney and elected both by voice vote.[25] His presenter was Supreme Court justice William O. Douglas. Jimmy passed away on July 31, 1970. His wife survived him by five years.

COACHING KEYS

The key to Jimmy Conzelman as a coach was his personality and innate feel for motivational psychology. His son, Jim Jr., remembered those Cardinals as a "pretty happy little family." Junior traveled with the team, sat on the bench during games, and worked as a gofer for the players in the locker room. He laughingly recalled one time the players taped his ankles and wrists and dropped him in the whirlpool, "Because I was a pain in the ass." The clubhouse, however, said Jim Jr., "was my favorite place because I got all of the information and saw all the screwing around. It was a very fun-oriented team."[26]

Star back Marshall Goldberg said, "Jimmy was not a fundamentalist, but he was a creative coach, a personality who could stimulate a team to do unusual things to win a ballgame."[27] Cardinals defensive back and longtime NFL coach and scout Red Cochran concurred: "I thought he was extremely smart. He was a great guy, a fine motivator, and was laid back as far as his coaching. Most importantly, he knew football and how to handle people." Halfback Babe Dimancheff added, "Plus, he knew how to use the talents of his assistants."[28]

One of those assistants, backfield coach Buddy Parker, would go on to have a successful career as a NFL head coach. Although Parker had a dramatically different personality than Conzelman, he was grateful to his former mentor, relating, "I learned a lot of things from Jimmy. He knew how to handle ballplayers, get the best out of them. When you're an assistant, there's always something to learn from a head coach."[29]

The thing about Conzelman is that he was a free-spirited player, and as a coach he appreciated the talents of fellow free spirits. As mentioned earlier, Dutch Sternaman compared him to Johnny Blood and complained about him skipping football practice for a band performance; however, there was a seriousness at Jimmy's core, and he was a much more successful coach than Blood. Conzelman likely set a high priority on his band in 1920, because that money helped him support his widowed mother and three younger siblings. While he exuded a life-of-the-party persona, there was a practical side to him. Ultimately, he left football because it was the practical thing to do.

That practicality drove his strategic approach as well. As a player-coach with four teams in the 1920s, he ran the single wing. His championship Providence team "was strong defensively and controlled the ball on offense with strong power running and an occasional pass by Wildcat Wilson to backs Conzelman and Simmons. Conzelman's single wing used the ends primarily for blocking and only infrequently for pass receiving."[30]

Jimmy stuck to the Warner system coaching his alma mater in the 1930s, but when he took the helm of the Cardinals in 1940, he switched to the Notre Dame box. He had no experience with that system and made some changes. On film, it appears he doesn't always have the team using the system's' celebrated shift, and with those teams undermanned, tailbacks Johnny Clement and Bud Schwenk hoisted a lot of passes into the air. On defense, his early Cardinals aligned in a 6–2 scheme.

With a shortage of talent, Conzelman attempted to substitute ingenuity. In 1940, Redskins coach Ray Flaherty claimed that the Cards were using a varied attack of five different offensive formations. Giants coach Steve Owen devised a special defense in 1942 for Conzelman's spread passing formation.[31]

Nonetheless, even in 1941, Jimmy gave indications that he would like to move to the T formation. Reporter George Kirksey wrote that Conzelman had scribbled down for him several ways to defense the T and commented, "Because of the fact that there's not much pulling out of the line by their linemen, that's why the Bears can play those big 235- and 250-pound linemen. They don't have to move around. They can stand still and do their job." He added, "There are no super men in football and no super systems. Power will prevail most of the time. It's harder to prepare a defense for the T than it is actually to stop it. That's because there are so many variations of a single play."[32]

Jimmy made the switch to the T when he returned to the Cardinals in 1946. Finally, he had the horses. "We've got some football players this time," he declared. "We never had anything like this squad when I was with the Cardinals before. We've got a new type of boy—studious, serious kids who want to play winning football."[33]

On film, Conzelman's Cards line up in a tight T, sometimes with a split end and sometimes with two split ends. Prior to the 1947 season, he told columnist Hugh Fullerton Jr., "Look for the T formation to employ the use of the flanker back set out from the huddle this year on many formations. While the man in motion still will be the basic way of putting a backfield man out on the flank, the wide flanker will be used much more than . . . in the past."[34]

Paul Christman's book *Tricks in Passing* provides more clues to Conzelman's attack. Christman advocates passing the ball on first down and describes double moves by receivers, quarterbacks going through their progressions in looking for the open receiver, and the effectiveness of having passing sequences—having one pass play set up a defense for a different one.[35]

Film of the Cardinals defense shows them generally in a 5–3–3 alignment and unafraid to blitz a linebacker. Conzelman's substitution patterns were another key to the defense's efficiency. Secondary members Red Cochran and Marshall Goldberg played only defense, while the third member of the deep pass defense was speedy end Mal Kutner, rather than a quarterback or halfback. The defensive line also employed some players who rarely appeared on offense, like Pop Ivy and Bob Dove. Vince Banonis, however, was a two-way standout, playing center on offense and middle linebacker on defense.

PIVOTAL GAMES

Conzelman liked to call George Halas the best of all coaches, but when Jimmy had equivalent talent he did well against both Halas and Greasy Neale, beating Halas four of six times and Neale three of four from 1946 through 1948. In both cases, he attacked boldly with big plays. For the 1947 season finale, the 8–3 Cardinals and Bears were tied for first in the West, although the Cards had beaten the Bears the last two times they had played.

For this game, Conzelman devised a knockout blow for the Cards' first offensive play. On film, he noticed that the Bears tended to double cover swift right end Mal Kutner with left linebacker Mike Holovak, so he planned to attack the area vacated by Holovak. He inserted speedy reserve left halfback Babe Dimancheff into the starting lineup at right halfback and had him race down field while Kutner went to the outside and took two Bears with him. The concern was that Dimancheff was with his wife at the hospital all week awaiting the birth of their daughter and never did get a chance to practice the play.

The Cards won the toss and received the kickoff in the end zone, so they started the game at their own 20. Christman called the special play, and it went just as drawn up, with Dimancheff running freely downfield. Christman hit him at the Cardinals 45, and Babe ran the rest of the way untouched for a 7–0 lead. Later in the first quarter, linebacker Vince Banonis picked off Sid Luckman at the Cardinals 45 and lumbered 41 yards to the Bears 14. Three plays later, Elmer Angsman made the score 14–0 with a touchdown plunge.

The Bears got one back with an 81-yard strike from Luckman to Ken Kavanuagh, but then tackle Stan Mauldin picked off Luckman and returned it to the Bears 29. A few plays later, another Angsman plunge upped the lead to 20–7. The Cards closed out the second quarter with a lightning drive powered by a 34-yard pass to Billy Dewell and a touchdown toss to Kutner for 33 yards to extend the halftime lead to 27–7. Bears backup quarterback Nick Sacrinty threw two fourth-quarter touchdown passes to close the gap, but Pat Harder booted a field goal following a blocked punt to make the final score 30–21. The Bears outgained the Cards 502 yards to 329, but their six turnovers and 101 yards in penalties defused that advantage.

Two weeks later, the Cards hosted the Eagles for the championship. Chicago had manhandled Philadelphia, 45–21, just one week before disposing of the Bears. Chicago was listed as a 12-point favorite for the title tilt, but the teams were a closer match than that. This contest marked just the second time the championship game paired two T formation teams; that trend has continued unbroken to this day.

The Eagles claimed to be concerned chiefly with Kutner, just as the Bears had been. Instead, the Cards attacked Philadelphia's eight-man line on the ground on an icy field that caused its own bit of controversy. In the first five minutes of the game, the Cards twice had the officials check the cleats of an opposing Eagles player. On each occasion, the fingered Bird was sent to the sidelines to remove his sharpened spikes, and the Eagles were penalized five yards. Philadelphia lost quarterback Tommy Thompson for four plays while he adjusted his footwear. The Eagles howled that their cleats had been approved by the officials prior to kickoff.

The slick surface did create problems. The first indication came six minutes into the game, when Charley Trippi burst through the Eagles' eight-man front and zipped 44 yards for the game's first touchdown. Conzelman later noted, "That eight-man line was hell on passing," as Christman had a terrible day, completing just three of 14 passes. Pitchin' Paul took a beating, however, particularly from Bucko Kilroy: "Yeah that dumb so-and-so. Even his teammates were telling him to cut it out. He hit me once, knocked me down, then brought both his fists down on the back of my head."[36]

Big plays on the ground would make the difference. Midway through the second quarter, Chicago struck again on a play called "42 double trap." This time Angsman exploded through the middle of the line from his own 30 and bolted free until halfback Pat McHugh managed to catch up to him on the five, but Elmer continued into the end zone for a 14–0 lead.[37] Thompson managed to keep the Eagles in the game by finding McHugh for a 53-yard touchdown with two minutes to go in the half.

Philadelphia opened the second half with a drive to the Cardinals 27, but Thompson was picked off by Buster Ramsey to end the threat. Later in the period, the Eagles punted the ball to the Chicago 25, where Charley Trippi grabbed it on the bounce. Trippi careened off a couple of Eagles and even slipped down once but got up and eluded all tacklers for a 75-yard punt return touchdown that pushed the Chicago advantage to 21–7. At this point, the Eagles rolled out their Z-wide spread formation, akin to a shotgun-style formation, in the attempt to stage a comeback. The Cardinals employed a special 6–1–4 defense for this game that nullified the Eagle rush. For the game, the vaunted Philly running game would be limited to 60 yards on 37 carries, but Thompson completed 27 of 44 passes for 297 yards.

A 15-play, 73-yard Eagle drive resulted in a Steve Van Buren one-yard touchdown smash to make the score 21–14 at the close of the third quarter. The teams continued to trade possessions in the final period until Chicago received a punt at their own 10. A rare Christmas completion to Trippi netted 20 yards, and then Angsman struck again. On the same play as his first touchdown, Elmer shot through a gap in the front wall and sprinted 70 yards untouched to give the Cards a 28–14 lead with seven minutes to play.

Once more the Eagles responded with a 73-yard touchdown march to draw within one score with four minutes remaining. They would never get the ball back, as the Cardinals ran out the clock with a 12-play drive to secure the title. Conzelman explained after the game, "They were delayed smashes that caught Philadelphia entirely off guard and left their secondary badly faked out of position."[38]

Greasy Neale complained, "We had our defensive men all set, but they couldn't recover on the slippery field when Angsman and Trippi set sail." Chicago line coach Phil Handler crowed, "How did you like what we did to that line? We put in special blocking last week. Just wanted to show those guys we could run through their eight-man line."[39]

In contrast, Neale said, "We did everything but beat them." He added a prescient challenge: "I hope they win the Western title next year so that we can have the pleasure of knocking them off in Philadelphia."[40]

The Cardinals did their part for Neale in 1948 by arriving at the season finale tied with the Bears for the West lead with identical 10–1 records. The Cards' only loss was to the Bears early in the year, and the Bears were six-and-a-half-point favorites in this rematch. Led by rookie quarterback Johnny Lujack, the Bears leapt out to a 14–3 halftime lead on his two touchdown passes. Meanwhile, the Cardinals gained just 21 yards on the ground and 43 in the air against the stout Bears defense.

Conzelman responded calmly during the intermission: "I told our fellows not to worry too much about that 14–3 score at the time, that they were overanxious, and if they relaxed in the second half, the Bears would start making mistakes. Thank goodness, they did."[41] In fact, the Bears opened the second half with a daring move that backfired. They tried an onside kick to start the third quarter, but the Cards Pat Harder alertly recovered the ball at the Bears 46. A mix of passes and runs got the Cards to the three, and then Harder carried the ball over the goal line for the touchdown to narrow the score to 14–10. Another Bears drive late in the third quarter resulted in a George Gulyanics one-yard touchdown just four seconds into the fourth period.

Down 21–10, the Cards replaced a banged-up Christman with Ray Mallouf, who led the team on an 85-yard drive that culminated with a two-yard marker by Charley Trippi. With the score now 21–17, the Bears took possession, but not for long. Vince Banonis intercepted a Lujack pass at the Bears 45 and returned it to the 18. It was the second year in a row Banonis picked off a pass against the Bears in the season-ender. Three plays later, Angsman ran in a score from the seven, and the Cards led, 24–21. With eight minutes to play, Sid Luckman replaced Lujack and started to lead the Bears downfield. At the Cardinals 15, however, the drive ended when Red Cochran nabbed Luckman's pass into the end zone. The Cards then erased the last four minutes from the clock with a four-minute drive to the Bears' 10-yard line when the gun sounded to end the game. Once again, the Bears outgained the Cardinals 462 yards to 312, but the team turned over the ball five times, lost an onside kick, and were penalized 91 yards.

A week later, the Cardinals and Eagles met again in Philadelphia for the rematch wished for by Greasy Neale. While the Eagles prevailed, 7–0, that snowy day with Christman unavailable, it's unclear whether they were actually the best team. Conzelman had built an 11–1 team that had beaten Neale's Eagles five consecutive times including preseason contests. They were no longer champions, however, and the return to Cardinals ineptitude would be remarkably swift. Charley Bidwill was dead, and Conzelman stepped down as coach shortly after this title game loss. Under an odd cocoaching arrangement with Phil Handler and Buddy Parker, the team posted a 6–5–1 record in 1949. Parker fled the dysfunctional organization in 1950. He would coach the Detroit Lions to two NFL titles in that decade, while the Cardinals posted just one winning season in that same period.

The 1948 blizzard bowl was a tough game to go out on, but it was Jimmy's last game on the sidelines. Nevertheless, he turned over the

championship to a coach with similar player-friendly characteristics—
Greasy Neale.

10

COUNTERPUNCH

Greasy Neale Defenses the T

Perhaps the most famous story told about Greasy Neale is that after the Eagles hired him as head coach in 1941, he paid $156 for a print of the 1940 Bears–Redskins championship game film. He then spent months screening the film for hours each day to appropriate the Bears T formation offense. Neale was the first pro coach to convert to the Bears T; however, his greatest contribution to the game may have been the "Eagle defense," which he devised a few years later to counter that attack.

Neale took over the worst team in the league, a team that had never had a .500 season, and led the Eagles to a winning record in year three of his tenure. In fact, he led Philadelphia to seven winning seasons, three division titles, and two league championships in his last eight seasons coaching. While his powerful T formation offense led the league in points scored three times, his defense finished first or second in fewest yards or points allowed seven times and was the true basis for his success.

Greasy lived a unique life in the realm of sports and triumphed in a remarkably disparate range of situations. Before coming to the Eagles, Neale led a pre-NFL team to a pro football championship, won a World Series as a player, and coached a small Pennsylvania college to the Rose Bowl. He played and managed in baseball's minor leagues and played and coached in the big leagues, too. He coached football at small colleges, as well as at major universities, and achieved success almost everywhere he went. He was profane, combative, and hard on his players. Yet, he became intimately involved in their lives and was loved and revered by them. Neale was supremely confident in his ability to chart his own path in the world and was never wedded to any particular system but the one he thought would work at the present. Among pro coaches, he was sui generis.

LIFE AND CAREER

Alfred Earle Neale was born in Parkersburg, West Virginia, on November 5, 1891. The Neale family had deep roots in Parkersburg, with Earle's great-great-grandfather Tom having moved to the area from Virginia in 1792. Earle's great-aunt, Julia Anne, was the mother of Confederate general Stonewall Jackson, but there was nothing high-toned about Earle's upbringing. His father, William, worked in the produce business, and his mother, Irene, was a homemaker raising their six children—four boys and two girls. Earle summarized his childhood by saying, "We weren't poor and we never went hungry, but we certainly weren't rich."[1]

Earle became "Greasy" at a young age due to a neighbor boy named Homer Stanton. "Because his mother worked," Neale remembered, "Homer roamed as free as Huckleberry Finn, much to the envy of the Neales. He didn't have to wash nearly as often as we did. In resentment over his privileges, I called him 'Dirty,' and he retaliated by calling me 'Greasy.'"[2] Neale began working at the age of seven, selling newspapers, and moved up at age 11 to setting pins at the local bowling alley. In his freshman year of high school, he found he was failing Latin and dropped out of school to work in the local steel mill. Two years of hard mill work built him up physically and taught him that he needed to do better in school.

Neale returned to the classroom in 1909, excelling on the sports teams. A year later, as a junior, he took over the coaching of his high school football team since he was older than the rest of his teammates. The team won just one game, and the school hired a paid coach the next year. As a senior in 1911, Greasy attracted the notice of West Virginia Wesleyan and was recruited by Wesleyan student Harry Stansbury. He enrolled there in 1912, but Neale spent that summer playing minor league baseball for London of the Canadian League, where he batted .250. He subsequently starred at end on the gridiron for two years and also played baseball and basketball at Wesleyan, while continuing to play minor league baseball through 1915. That year, Greasy married his college sweetheart, Genevieve Horner, and also began his college football coaching career at Muskingum College in Ohio, where he led the team to a 2–4–1 season.

The following year, Neale made the major leagues as a starting outfielder with the Cincinnati Reds, although his career almost ended abruptly before it started. In spring training, he got into an altercation with star pitcher Fred Toney that resulted in a fight in which Toney cracked a bone in his hand. Fortunately, manager Buck Herzog overlooked the scuffle.[3] Neale batted .262 in his rookie year, three points higher than his ultimate career average, and proved himself to be a heady clutch player, fine fielder, and swift base stealer in his eight-year major-league career.

After the 1916 baseball season, Stansbury, now athletic director at Wesleyan, signed Greasy to coach football and basketball. Neale signed another former WVW teammate, John Kellison, to coach the line. "Honest John" would subsequently coach alongside Greasy at five different institutions in the next three decades. In one year, Neale lifted Wesleyan to the point where they upset their chief gridiron rival, West Virginia, in 1917. That year, Kellison also brought Greasy into the pro game, inviting him to play with Jim Thorpe's Canton Bulldogs. Playing under the assumed name "Foster," Neale started at end. A year later, with football curtailed at many sites due to the war, Neale worked for the Dayton Wright Airplane Company and was player-coach of the Dayton Triangles, guiding them to an 8–0 record and claiming the Ohio League championship.

After compiling a 10–8 record in two seasons at Wesleyan, Greasy was hired to coach at Marietta College in Ohio in 1919; however, he missed the first game of the season because he was playing in the World Series. That Series, although tainted by the Black Sox Scandal, in which eight Chicago White Sox players were implicated in a gambling scheme to throw games, was Neale's finest hour on the diamond. He batted .357 and always maintained that the Sox only threw the first game. The Reds won the title, and Greasy took over Marietta, leading them to seven straight wins that year and then a 7–1 record in 1920. He also coached the basketball team.

Philadelphia received a foreshadowing of Neale's aggressive nature during the 1920 baseball season. The Reds defeated the Phillies at the

Baker Bowl on June 24 and were leaving the field. Tradition dictated that the winners would toss the game ball to the stands as they went to the locker room; however, Reds pitcher Slim Sallee refused and was confronted on the field by an angry Philadelphia teenager. At this point, Greasy interceded by knocking the fan down and kicking him. Neale was then attacked by scores of Philly fans. "Hundreds of spectators joined in the fracas and dozens of blows were rained on Neale," wrote the *Philadelphia Inquirer*. "He was staggered with a couple punches to the jaw but fought his way through the crowd. Meanwhile, his teammates climbed the bleacher walls and slipped him into the clubhouse that way."[4] He had proved himself to be a Philly kind of guy.

In the offseason, Greasy was traded to the Phillies and negotiated a large raise, to $6,000, for the 1921 season. After 22 games, however, Philadelphia waived Neale, as he was batting just .211. The Reds reclaimed him and were forced to pay his salary increase despite him being just a sometime-starter now. That fall, he attracted national attention by coaching the football team at tiny Washington & Jefferson College, near Pittsburgh, to an undefeated season, highlighted by a 7–0 victory against Pop Warner's Pitt Panthers. Neale's squad included Herb Kopf, the brother of onetime Reds teammate Larry Kopf, at end and African American Charlie West at quarterback. One prominent player that Neale unsuccessfully recruited was future Giants coach Steve Owen. Greasy spotted Big Steve when the Reds were coming north from spring training. Although Owen remained at Phillips University in Oklahoma, he and Neale began a lifelong friendship.[5]

The team's success earned them an invitation to play undefeated California in the Rose Bowl. Cal was heavily favored, but the Presidents held the Golden Bears to a scoreless tie, with Greasy's bruising defensive stratagems at the fore. He later wrote, "The Rose Bowl game proved there is no substitute for physical condition."[6]

That W&J team was the last Rose Bowl team to play just 11 men for the entire game, and that squad was said to have emulated its coach:

> He is confident, aggressive, a fighter every inch of him, and a philosopher when he does not sniff the scent of battle, which is as incense in his nostrils. He conducts himself as a true gentleman off the battleground and like a panther thirsting for blood when the heat of the fray is in his blood.[7]

The Presidents slipped a bit to 6–3–1 in 1922, and Neale was wooed by the University of Virginia in 1923.

Neale did not play baseball in 1923, but he returned to the Reds briefly in 1924, when he appeared in just three games. At Virginia, Neale sandwiched two losing seasons around four winning ones and left in 1929 to take a coaching job for baseball's St. Louis Cardinals and their new manager, Billy Southworth. Neale had done some managing in the minor leagues with Clarksburg in 1927 and 1928, and had played against Southworth in the National League. Unfortunately, halfway through the season, the Cardinals determined that Southworth needed seasoning as a manager and sent him down to the minors, leaving Greasy out of work, but not for long.

Neale returned to Clarksburg in 1930 as manager, and then was hired to coach the semipro Ironton Tanks football squad in the fall. Ironton was a strong independent Ohio team that featured future NFL star halfback Glenn Presnell and future Boston College coach Denny Myers. It defeated three NFL teams that season. The Tanks lost to the Portsmouth Spartans in their opener on September 28, and in their Thanksgiving finale on November 27, but in between the team beat Portsmouth, the New York Giants, and the Chicago Bears. With the Tanks shorthanded for the October match with Portsmouth, 39-year-old Greasy Neale suited up to play his last football game at end. In fact, it was his 30-yard reception that set up the winning field goal. [8]

That season put him back on the radar in the football-coaching market, and West Virginia hired him as head coach in 1931. Neale's three years at WVU were not successful, producing no winning seasons and an overall 12–16–3 mark, but he did coach future Hall of Fame tackle Joe Stydahar for one year, as well as future Syracuse coach Ben Schwartzwalder. In 1934, Yale University approached Neale about coaching its football team, and the University of Virginia was said to be interested in bringing him back as well.

Greasy's brother, William "Widdy" Neale, had attended Yale in the 1920s and returned to the school in 1933 as an athletic administrator. He arranged a meeting with Yale's athletic director, who wanted to hire Greasy as head football coach. Greasy was interested and planned to bring along his West Virginia assistant, Denny Myers, and his old friend, John Kellison, as assistants. When the alumni got wind of the arrangement, however, objections were raised because the Elis had always hired

Yale alumni as head men. A compromise was worked out, with Yale alumnus Ducky Pond hired as head coach and Neale and Myers as his assistants. It didn't take long, however, for observers to see that Neale was the squad's strategist and inspirational leader.[9]

Neale coached two Heisman Trophy winners—Clint Frank and Larry Kelley—at Yale, and Kelley played a key role in a pivotal upset win in 1934, against undefeated Princeton. In an echo of the 1922 Rose Bowl, that game was the last in which one team—Yale—made no substitutions, and all 11 starters played all 60 minutes. Yale swimming coach Bob Kipkuth wrote, "[Neale] had a great impact on Yale football. In addition to his great skill as a coach, his homespun philosophy and humor gave him a unique attachment to the students and his fellow coaches."[10]

Neale enjoyed his time at Yale, where the team compiled a 30–25–2 record in seven years under Pond. Another Yale man, Alexis Thompson, was responsible for his next move, which would lead to his greatest enduring legacy as the head coach of the NFL's Philadelphia Eagles. But it's a complicated story.

In anticipation of Pennsylvania rescinding its Blue Laws, which, among other things, prevented football from being played on Sundays, the NFL granted two new franchises for the Keystone State in 1933: Bert Bell founded the Philadelphia Eagles and Art Rooney the Pittsburgh Pirates. Indeed, those Sunday restrictions were rescinded, but Bell and Rooney had a tough go of it throughout the decade. In their first eight seasons, the Eagles compiled a 19–65–3 record, while Pittsburgh recorded a 24–62–5 mark. Neither team had a single winning season, and both were in financial trouble from the continual flood of red ink.

Bell and Rooney became quite friendly through time and considered pooling their resources into one team that would represent both cities. In December 1940, they struck a deal with the aforementioned 26-year-old millionaire Alexis "Lex" Thompson, in which Thompson would purchase Rooney's renamed Steelers, and Rooney would buy half of the Eagles from Bell. Thompson, a Yale graduate who played on the 1936 U.S. Olympic field hockey team, had inherited his wealth from his father's steel holdings. His father died when Lex was just 16. At this point, Thompson hired Neale as the new coach of the renamed Pittsburgh Ironmen to start in March, and Greasy hired John Kellison as his line coach.

The players of the two franchises were divided so that Thompson got seven Eagles and 16 Steelers, while Bell and Rooney kept 16 Eagles and

11 Steelers. The ultimate plan was for Thompson to move the Pittsburgh franchise to Boston a year later to be closer to his New York business interests and for Bell and Rooney to unveil their dual-city Pennsylvania Keystoners; however, the other NFL owners neither were keen on returning to Boston nor on one franchise representing two cities. In addition, Rooney missed his native Pittsburgh, so Bell and Rooney convinced Thompson he'd be better off in Philadelphia, where he'd be closer to New York, and the franchises were swapped in April. Greasy was now the coach of the Philadelphia Eagles, owned by Lex Thompson.

All that player swapping could not mask the fact that neither team had many players of passable quality. Of the 23 players allotted to the new Eagles, only four (Tommy Thompson, Phil Ragazzo, Lou Tomasetti, and Foster Watkins) ever played for Neale, and Thompson was the only one who was still with the team after Greasy's first two losing seasons. Neale told Bob Curran, "When I took over the club, we had two real ballplayers, Tommy Thompson, a quarterback, and Phil Ragazzo, an end. I didn't know anything about drafting, but we did all right that year."[11] Neale would learn quickly about the NFL Draft. He and general manager Harry Thayer instituted an extensive scouting system involving contacts with college coaches nationwide to produce an abundance of data, which they brought to the 1942 draft. "We had 64 books with files on the college players, each book a couple of inches thick and about 15 inches by eight," said Neale. "It took two bellhops and a baggage truck to get our information into the room. The general inclination was to snicker, but our dope, which cost about $3,000 to assemble, paid off handsomely."[12]

As noted at the beginning of this chapter, Neale's first move was to obtain a copy of the game film of the 1940 championship game so he could install the T formation. He had always used the single wing or short punt formations, but he was open-minded and practical about what offense would give him the best chance to succeed. While Greasy always freely admitted that he "stole" the Bears' offense, he also pointed out that he made changes to it. "I found a way to improve on the Bears' offense," he told Curran.

> They used quick openers that relied on brush blocking. This made them strong to the inside. But they weren't too powerful to the outside. So I decided I would work out an offense that would use some single-wing type blocking. I also figured that I would use my fullback more

for blocking than for carrying the ball. Later the Bears used this idea too.[13]

Neale acquired Len Barnum from the Giants to play quarterback, but Barnum was one of just eight NFL veterans on the 1941 Eagles. Of the 40 who played for the Eagles that year, 32 were rookies, and four of the veterans were just second-year men. On the eve of the season, Greasy reflected,

> We can't be sure of course, but I have great faith in the T and also great faith in my boys to execute it correctly. You see, we have a young team, and it is much easier to teach young players new stuff than to instill the same methods into veterans who have become wedded to more orthodox styles.[14]

Four days before the season started, Neale transported his team to Brooklyn to watch a preseason night game between Chicago and Brooklyn so his young squad could see how the Bears executed their offense. Incidentally, this game was the one in which Chicago assistant Luke Johnsos first called Chicago's plays from the press box. Nine of Greasy's starting 11 were rookies even though he actually preferred veterans. Halfback Jack Hinkle once commented, "The only players who didn't get along with Greasy were the first-year men. Greasy loved the veterans. He'd say, 'Give me a team of veterans, and I'll win the title.'"[15] In 1941, however, Neale didn't have that luxury, as he cleared the decks of substandard veterans. Among those rookies were several who would be contributors to the championship clubs at the end of the decade, including tackle Vic Sears and ends Jack Ferrante, Larry Cabrelli, and Dick Humbert.

By week four, Neale had moved Barnum to halfback and installed the unsung Tommy Thompson at the key quarterback position. Thompson had a rough start to his career. A passing star at Tulsa, he lost his eligibility after he got married as an undergraduate. Since his class would not graduate for a year, he played semipro ball before landing in Pittsburgh as a single wing tailback, although possessing little skill at rushing the ball. He was ideally suited as a T quarterback. Thompson spent two years with the Eagles and then was inducted into the service despite the fact that he was blind in one eye. With the onset of World War II, Neale's building job got tougher still, but he persisted. His first club finished 2–8–1, so in

1942 he brought in 25 more rookies, although only two made the starting lineup. The two best rookies were halfbacks Bosh Pritchard, who came on waivers from the Rams, and Ernie Steele, acquired from the Steelers, but the team only managed a paltry 2–9 season.

The following year brought new challenges. To deal with manpower shortages, the Eagles and Steelers merged to form the Steagles. The head coaches of the two teams were made cocoaches, but the alliance was so uneasy that Neale was given charge of the offense, while Steelers coach Walt Kiesling handled the defense. John Kellison was let go. Al Wistert, who was a rookie that year, along with Bucko Kilroy and Allie Sherman, later said, "When Greasy Neale is the head coach, there is nobody else gonna be the head coach. He was a very domineering person."[16]

But then, so was Kiesling. Ernie Steele added, "Both coaches wanted to be the head honcho. The ballplayers, they were listening to their coach and not listening to the other coach."[17] Vic Sears described the coaches' relationship succinctly, saying, "They hated each other."[18]

Despite animosity between the coaches and turf wars between the merged players, the team posted a 5–4–1 record, the first winning season for the Philadelphia half of the squad. Greasy had traded with Washington for quarterback Leroy Zimmerman to replace Thompson, who was off to the military, but it took Zimmerman a year to get used to the T. In 1944, the Eagles were again a solo entry, while the Steelers merged with the Cardinals, and John Kellison returned to coach the line. Greasy brought in 15 rookies, including halfback Steve Van Buren and center Vic Lindskog, but at the outset of the season he cut his own salary from $12,000 to $3,000 because, according to Philadelphia's Thayer, "He said he couldn't produce an improved team with the material on hand, because good college players are unobtainable these days."[19]

Greasy protested too much. That year his Eagles flew to a 7–1–2 record, just a half game behind the Eastern champion Giants. Neale had developed several fine running backs in his first three years, but drafting Steve Van Buren gave Greasy probably the most important piece in assembling a championship team. Van Buren was destined to be the best runner in the league for the rest of the decade and the bulwark of the Eagle offense. Philadelphia, using just nine rookies, won seven and lost three in the last year of the war and finished one game behind Washington in the East.

Thompson had returned in 1945, but he played little. He got more playing time in 1946, as he rounded back into shape, but the team slipped to a 6–5 record despite the addition of such key rookies as fullback Joe Muha, defensive back Russ Craft, and guard/kicker Cliff Patton. They also toughened their defense by adding veteran linebacker Alex Wojcie-chowicz from the Lions in a cash deal; however, Steve Van Buren missed three games due to a chest injury and was hampered in several others. But Neale's team building was nearly complete, as the Eagles' third straight second-place finish proved them a worthy contender about to ascend to the throne.

In 1947, they took the next step and won their division, although not without some inconsistent play that forced them into a playoff game against Jock Sutherland's resurgent Steelers. The Eagles added three roo-kie ends—Pete Pihos, Neill Armstrong, and Johnny Green—who would be key performers throughout their championship run. Van Buren stayed healthy throughout the year and became the second NFL player to rush for more than 1,000 yards in a season. Furthermore, with Leroy Zimmer-man traded to Detroit, Tommy Thompson blossomed into one of the top quarterbacks in the league. Still, there were down games. In week three, for example, the Bears beat Philadelphia, 40–7, and then the Eagles tum-bled, 35–24, to the Steelers a week later, despite taking a 10-point lead into the fourth quarter. Later in the year, the Birds dropped a shocker to the lowly Boston Yanks and were pounded by the Cardinals, 45–21. Greasy had introduced the Eagle defense, a 5–2–4 alignment this year, but the team was still working out the kinks. Philadelphia ended the regular season tied with Pittsburgh at the top of the East with 8–4 records. The playoff the next week was noncompetitive, with the Eagles winning handily, 21–0, against a team that gave up more points than it scored during the regular season.

The championship game was held on an icy field at Chicago's Comis-key Park and was a disappointment to Neale, who complained afterward that the Eagles were not able to use some cutback plays he had installed for the game. As a result, the Eagles were undone by big play-scoring runs up the middle by halfbacks Charley Trippi and Elmer Angsman of 44, 70, and 70 yards, as well as a 75-yard punt return touchdown by Trippi. With that weakness in the middle of the line exposed, Neale sought to plug it in 1948 by importing sizeable rookie linemen Mario Gianelli, Piggy Barnes, George Savitsky, and John Magee.

Philadelphia's points allowed per game improved from 20 to 13 in 1948, and their offense produced more than 30 points per contest as well. The Eagles recorded four shutouts and won three games by the identical imposing score of 45–0. They even topped the Bears for the first time in franchise history, 12–7. Their only losses were an opening-day 21–14 heartbreaker to the Cardinals on a 64-yard touchdown pass in the fourth quarter and another inexplicable loss to the Boston Yanks. Philadelphia was also tied by the Los Angeles Rams early in the season and finished 9–2–1, to win the East and impel a rematch with the West winners, the 11–1 Cardinals, who had beaten them the last three matches. This time the title game was played in a blizzard in Philadelphia's Shibe Park, but the Eagles toughed out a 7–0 victory, described later in this chapter. Neale had taken the worst franchise in the league and slowly but steadily upgraded it until Philadelphia had a football champion at last. But because of the money-draining war with the rival All-America Football Conference, Lex Thompson had dealt with enough red ink and sold the team to the "100 Brothers," a group of local investors headed by James Clark, a trucking magnate.

Since 1947, the NFL had instituted a drawing for the bonus first pick of the NFL Draft, and the Eagles won that honor in 1949. They made excellent use of the pick by selecting Penn center/linebacker Chuck Bednarik, who would become the belligerent face of the franchise for the next 14 years. Neale broke in Bednarik by having him spell Wojciechowicz at linebacker and developed a strong rapport with a rookie for a change. The Eagles defense grew even stingier, allowing just 11 points per game, while maintaining an average of 30 points per game on offense. The 1949 Eagles compiled an 11–1 record, with a 38–14 loss to the Bears the only blemish. In the championship game, they faced the high-flying Rams and whipped them, 14–0, on a muddy field in the rain.

Neale's Eagles had accomplished something that no team had ever done or has done since: consecutive NFL championships won by shutout. He was proud of his team. "Everyone is giving me credit for keeping them 'up' for so long," he told Arthur Daley of the *New York Times*. "But I had nothing to do with it. They play with such spirit that they've done it all themselves. I coached college football for 20-odd years, and I never saw collegians with more flaming spirit than my professionals."[20] They were the greatest team in the league, and Greasy was confident about the future. "I don't see why our boys can't do it again," he remarked. But big changes were just ahead.[21]

The NFL had instituted free substitution on a trial basis in 1949, making it permanent in 1950. Neale, the man who had led the Washington & Jefferson iron men in the 1922 Rose Bowl and the Yale iron men in 1934, was dead-set against it, saying, "The free substitution rule has made specialists out of a lot of players. Any man should be able to play 60 minutes, and I wouldn't give a dime for a football player who is only an offensive specialist."[22] Greasy made his peace with that, however, and took full advantage of it. What he could not adapt to was the merger with the AAFC.

The four-time AAFC champion Browns entered the NFL in 1950, but Neale did not take the threat seriously. Commissioner Bert Bell smartly scheduled the league opener to pit the reigning NFL champion Eagles against the Browns in Philadelphia. On his own, tackle Al Wistert scouted the Browns and tried to prepare his coach, but Greasy sloughed it off. According to Wistert, Neale commented, "'Well they can't do that against us. They'll never do that against us. They can't do that,' because he was very proud of his football team."[23]

When the Browns took apart the Eagles 35–10 with a precision passing attack, Neale was left in shock. He said of the Cleveland quarterback, "Graham is the ideal passer because he just hangs the ball up there and lets the receivers go get it." Of the Brown receivers, he added, "We would be on top of their receivers, but they caught the ball anyway because it was so well timed. It was like trying to cover three Don Hutsons . . . impossible . . . impossible."[24]

Philadelphia righted itself and had a 6–2 record two-thirds of the way into the season but then dropped its last four games—two to his old friend Steve Owen—to finish 6–6, but with five of the losses by a total of 18 points. Following a 7–3 loss to the Giants, an angry James Clark stormed into the locker room and began to berate Neale, who was restrained from going after the owner and shouted, "If you want my resignation, you can have it right now!"[25] The two patched up their differences to finish the season at least, after which Greasy and his wife went on vacation in Florida. On February 7, 1950, he received a telegram from Clark firing him. Neale forlornly commented, "The Eagles were my life work. My life work was wiped out by one telegram."[26] Two months later Greasy's wife of 36 years, Genevieve, died, and Neale turned to his close friend Kellison for consolation.[27]

Neale was mentioned as a possibility for the coaching job at Indiana University in 1951, and for the Washington Redskins in 1952, but he never coached again. He remarried in 1953, to Adelaide Bray Donahoe, and the two lived in an apartment in New York. She died in 1961, and in 1968 Greasy married for a third time, at age 77, to Ola Maurice. He was inducted into the College Football Hall of Fame in 1967, and the Pro Football Hall of Fame in 1969, where Chuck Bednarik was his presenter. Greasy died three days shy of his 82nd birthday in Lake Worth, Florida, on November 2, 1973, and was buried back home in Parkersburg, West Virginia.

COACHING KEYS

Greasy was a players' coach, but not in the same way that Jimmy Conzelman was. At practice, Neale was tough on his players. He cursed them and berated them. When he first joined the team, tackle Al Wistert was taken aback by the volume of the profanity, but ultimately he was amused by the creativity of such phrases as, "You couldn't knock a sick whore off a shit pot" or "You stand around like a bear cub playing with his prick."[28]

End Neill Armstrong also was a bit shocked at first. "He had a few words for everyone," he said. "And yet I always believed he was a fair coach. One of his assistants told me when I joined the team, 'You have to pay attention to what he says, not how he says it.' Some of the players would even argue back with him. I remember thinking, 'Gee, those fellows are going to get cut.'"[29]

The thing was that Neale was happy when his players fought back. He wanted a proud, combative, intelligent team. He told reporter Stan Baumgartner, "I have 32 coaches, not just 32 football players. With one or two exceptions, they are all college men. Why shouldn't I listen to what they have to say? They may have better ideas than I have."[30] On another occasion, Greasy asserted, "If a player doesn't think he's the best man on the field, I don't want him on my team."[31]

Linebacker Alex Wojciechowicz also looked back fondly on Neale, relating, "On the football field, he was tough as hell, stern, he was almighty God out there. But off the field, he was one of us. He'd gamble with us, beer up with us, go to the racetrack with us, play golf, anything we'd do he'd be part of it."[32] End Dick Humbert agreed, reflecting, "He'd come to your house and have dinner with you and your family, but the next day on the field, why, you wouldn't even think he knew you."[33]

That blend of familiarity and authority is a tough one to maintain, but the record of his team and warm reminiscences of his players years later attest to Greasy's success in attaining the atmosphere he wanted. "I am a firm believer in the theory that a coach should know his players off the field as well as on," he asserted. "The once moody [Tommy] Thompson, for instance, became a frequent golfing opponent of mine. With the assistance of [John] Kellison, who rejoined me with the Eagles, and my wife, we managed to make the squad pretty much of a family affair."[34] On some occasions, the other players would implore Thompson, the quarterback, to convince Neale to call off practice and go golfing with him.

Neale's first strategic decision as Eagles coach was to install the T formation as his offense, although he had never used it before. He later recalled, "I saw the Bears score four touchdowns against the Giants in the first half and beat the Redskins 73–0 in the championship game. If that wouldn't convince you, you'd be a very stubborn man." He elaborated, "It's the fastest starting offense there is. In pro football the linemen are all too good to be held in check long by a block, and the T formation takes advantage of momentary openings instead of weak spots in the line."[35]

The Bears T also fit Neale's propensity for the running game. His Eagles ran the ball 67.3 percent of the time from 1941 to 1950, which was 11 percent more than the league average. Because they ran the ball so effectively, those Eagles also had a potent passing attack. Quarterback Tommy Thompson became just the third quarterback in history to throw for 25 touchdowns (in 1948) and led the NFL in highest touchdown pass percentage from 1947 through 1949. Dick Humbert reasoned, "Greasy Neale's attitude was we're going to have an offensive team that can run the ball first, pass the ball second, but our passing attack had to be near as good as anybody else's. That way, if they tried to load up and stop our football running attack, we'd throw."[36]

Neale did not simply run the Bears offense, however. He added his own touches. On film, one can see that the Eagles liked to run wide, while the Bears ran more inside. In Neale's attack, delays are mixed with deception and crisscrossing backs. Greasy favored sweeps and end runs with pulling linemen, and his fullback was primarily a blocker. He recalled one play of his that George Halas later borrowed for the Bears: "You send a man out in motion and then pitch out wide to the same side. You thus outflank the defense, and you don't even have to block out the tackle on that side. You just outrun him."[37] He told columnist Shirley Povich, "Speed makes it go. You can do wonders with backs who can run like Van Buren and Steele and Bleeker. There are a lot of plays on which we don't even bother with the end or defensive back playing on one side. We can fake them out of position and then run around them."[38]

Cardinals coach Jimmy Conzelman remarked at the time, "In recent years I've always thought that the Eagles were the most interesting club to watch in the National League. Neale not only adopted the T formation, but he made it more spectacular, at least on plays to the outside, than did George Halas with the Bears."[39] Those wide plays were often toss plays, but the Eagles' laterals from quarterback to halfback were deeper than those of the Bears and thus faster developing to the outside.

Neale himself was particularly proud of the "stutter series" he developed for Steve Owen's five-man line, in which one halfback faked one way while the ball would go to the second halfback going the other direction or the fullback up the middle. As defensive back Russ Craft put it, "Cagey is the word I would use to describe Greasy. He always seemed to come up with a new wrinkle here and there."[40]

The Eagles had a split T series of plays and switched to the short punt formation or a spread formation when trailing late or at the end of a half. In a game against the Redskins in 1946, the Eagles fell behind, 24–0, at the half, so Greasy had Philadelphia come out in the single wing in the second to spark a 28–24 victory.

That caginess extended even further to the defensive side of the ball. Tackle Vic Sears remembers Neale saying, "I'll spend my time on defense." And it is his Eagle defense for which he is most recalled today.[41]

Glenn Presnell remembered Greasy being a defensive innovator going back to his time coaching the Ironton Tanks:

> Instead of charging straight ahead, Neale had us looping around to try and fool the blockers on offense. I remember playing Portsmouth in 1930, and they had a strong running game with Willis Glassgow from Iowa, Chief McLain, and Chuck Bennett from Indiana. They had some good football players for Portsmouth, but we looped our linemen and beat them.[42]

In the early 1940s, film shows Neale's Eagles usually in a 6–2 alignment, but he moved to a 5–3 in the mid-1940s. What's most noticeable is
the amount of movement along the line and strong pursuit to the ball.
Greasy would put his linebackers over the ends and spread his defensive
ends wide. Confronting the T formation, most teams would shadow the
man-in-motion with a linebacker or defensive halfback. Against the Rams
in 1945, however, Neale pulled 200-pound guard Enio Conti out of the
line to follow the motion man, while the other guard slid to the middle of
the line.

Greasy was well attuned to the particular skills of his players. At the
end of the 1946 season, he tried dropping agile end Dick Humbert back as
a fourth member of the secondary to better thwart the passing game, and
thus was born the Eagle defense in 1947. The other two key elements to
that defense were getting a strong pass rush from the five-man line and
having the two linebackers line up on the offensive ends to chuck them
and delay them from getting off the line of scrimmage. Even if an end
flexed out wide, the linebacker followed him. If the offensive ends were
in tight, the linebackers played inside the defensive ends. Greasy stuck to
this basic defense for the rest of his career, except when he played the
single-wing Steelers and reverted to a 6–2 alignment (see figure 10.1).

Neale recalled, "We practically used a seven-man line. It put pressure
on the passer, and as I have said before, the best defense against the pass
is the rush." Greasy added that he didn't like the later move to the 4–3
defense, relating, "The five-man pressure was steadier. Why we used to
offer a $10 bonus each time a man knocked down the passer. One after-
noon, Johnny Green collected $80."[43]

Linebacker Wojciechowicz also was unimpressed by the changes in
pass defense in the 1960s: "The most remarkable thing to me is that you
see these fast receivers coming off the line without even being touched,"
he stated. "Greasy Neale would have hit the ceiling if we were not on top
of them and slugging away at them while they were going out."[44] It also
should be noted that despite his railing against the specialization that
came with free substitution, Greasy took full advantage of it with players
like Wojciechowicz, Johnny Green, Mario Gianelli, and the entire defensive secondary. It was the first regular four-man secondary in the NFL.
Neale clearly saw how the game was developing. In 1946, there were
42.6 passes per game for an average of 288 yards, almost identical to the
numbers for the three previous years. Those two figures jumped to 49.9

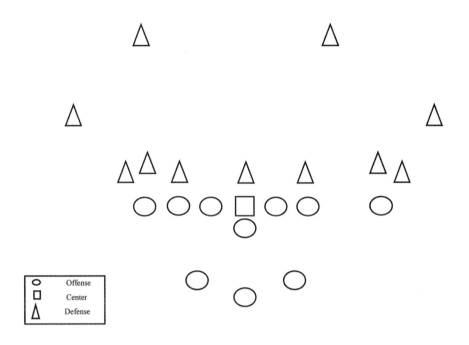

Figure 10.1.   The 5–2 Eagles defense

and 361 in 1947, 51.9 and 348 in 1948, 54.6 and 357 in 1949, and 55.2 and 372 in 1950, respectively. Greasy kept his defense ahead of the curve, and that was instrumental to the Eagles' championship run.

The hole in the defense was in the middle of the field. The Cardinals demonstrated that on the ground in the 1947 title game, so Neale added bulky Mario Gianelli and Piggy Barnes to shore up the middle guard slot. A few years later, however, Paul Brown would exploit that hole via the pass and spur the eventual movement to the 4–3 defense. But beyond the stratagems was a commitment to toughness and the value of intimidation. Neale stressed hard hitting and pursuit—get there first with a bad attitude. Guard Bucko Kilroy recalled in the 1980s, "The Eagles in those days were like the Raiders are today. We were tough, and we intimidated teams. When people accused us of playing dirty football, our answer was, 'That's how losers talk.'"[45]

PIVOTAL GAMES

Neale won back-to-back championships with Philadelphia, but both were played in extreme weather conditions, so a look at a couple of regular-season games will broaden our view of Greasy's style. Through the start of 1948, Philadelphia struggled with both Chicago teams. The Eagles had never beaten the Bears and lost to the Cardinals in the 1947 title game, as well as in the regular season in 1947 and 1948. To become champions, Neale had to overcome those demons.

To make matters worse, when the 2–1–1 Eagles prepared to host the 4–0 Bears on October 24, 1948, quarterback Tommy Thompson had a bad shoulder and could not start. Instead, untested second-year man Bill Mackrides made his first career start. The Eagles defense rose to the challenge in a brutally hard-hitting game. The Bears outgained the Eagles a bit in yardage, but Philadelphia made the big plays to win. End Pete Pihos partially blocked a punt, allowing the Eagles to take over on the Chicago 38. Van Buren took a pitchout and raced to the 23. Pihos caught a deflected pass at the four, and after a loss of four, Van Buren ran wide again for a touchdown in the first quarter.

Johnny Lujack tied the game in the third quarter with a 42-yard scoring strike to Ken Kavanaugh. Then Tommy Thompson came in following a Bears fumble and willed the team on a short drive for a field goal. An end zone sack of Sid Luckman by Piggy Barnes in the final minute made the final score 12–7 and marked a coming of age for the Eagles.

Two months later, the Eagles met the Cardinals in Philadelphia for the championship. The game was played in a blizzard, and the Cards were forced to rely on backup quarterback Ray Mallouf. Neale had the Eagles go for the jugular on their first offensive play and Thompson hit Jack Ferrante for a 65-yard touchdown, but the score was nullified because Ferrante was offside.

Despite the field being covered by snow, the Eagles continually moved the ball on the ground, outgaining Chicago, 225–96. Thompson would complete just two of 12 passes for seven yards through the air, while Mallouf passed for 35 yards. Eagles guard Cliff Patton missed field goal attempts from 12, 37, and 39 yards, while Cardinals fullback Pat Harder missed one from the 37. Finally, at the end of the third quarter, Mallouf fumbled at the Chicago 17, and Bucko Kilroy recovered for Philadelphia. Four running plays—one by each member of the backfield—culminated with Steve Van Buren's seven-yard touchdown burst for the game's only score.

As a side note, after the game Neale praised Thompson, saying, "His signal calling was just about perfect."[46] Even when coaching from the sidelines was against the rules, Neale had been widely known for signaling the plays with his rolled-up program; however, Thompson had changed that practice the previous season, demonstrating both Greasy's adaptability and faith in his players.

Defending the title a year later, the main challenge was Clark Shaughnessy's high-powered Los Angeles Rams. The 6–0 Rams visited the 5–1 Eagles on November 6, and were taken apart, with the Eagles showing complete domination. The Rams scored first in the opening quarter on a pass from Bob Waterfield to Tom Fears, but then Philadelphia scored 38 straight points until Los Angeles scored a late touchdown to make the final score 38–14. On the first scoring drive, the Eagles were rushing seven men on every play, but then they switched back to the five-man rush for the remainder of the game and shut down the Rams.

Philadelphia gained 264 yards on 64 rushes and 208 yards on 16 passes, while Los Angeles eked out 27 yards rushing and threw for 237 yards on 36 passes. The Rams also turned over the ball five times. The most glaring turnover came in the third quarter, when Elroy Hirsch caught a short pass and then had the ball stolen out of his hands by Russ Craft, who raced 21 yards for the score. Hirsch was benched in Shaughnessy's doghouse for the rest of the season.

A jubilant Neale commented, "This is a great team. I never said it before, but I'll say it after how they fought their hearts out today. No team ever assembled could have beaten them today."[47]

Six weeks later, the teams met again in the muddy Los Angeles Coliseum on a rare rainy day in Southern California. While the final 14–0 score was much closer, the actual game wasn't. Again, Philadelphia dominated on the ground, rushing 61 times for 274 yards and completing five of nine passes for 68 more. Los Angeles was held to 21 yards rushing in 24 carries and completed just 10 of 27 passes for 98 yards. The smothering Philadelphia defense, combined with Steve Van Buren's 194 yards rushing, was much too much for the Rams.

With back-to-back NFL championships—both won by shutout—Neale was on top of the football world, but things change quickly in the pro game. A year later, he ran head on into the future—the Cleveland

Browns, led by the game's first modern pro coach, Paul Brown. Greasy was noted for his adaptability, but after a 6–6 season, he was tossed aside and never coached again. The 1950 Eagles had two big problems: Steve Van Buren was hurt and, in fact, would never really recover, and Tommy Thompson was done. Could Neale have reloaded and gotten the Eagles back to the top? Probably not, but he deserved the opportunity to try.

EPILOGUE

Paul Brown: Modern Pro Football Coach

The warring National Football League and All-America Football Conference struck a deal in December 1949 and agreed to merge, with the AAFC's Cleveland Browns, San Francisco 49ers, and the original Baltimore Colts joining the established league. Commissioner Bert Bell wisely recognized the publicity opportunity the merger created and scheduled the Browns to meet the Eagles in Philadelphia's massive Municipal Stadium to open the 1950 NFL season. This showdown between the four-time AAFC champion Browns and the two-time NFL champion Eagles was essentially the first Super Bowl, pitting the titlists of the rival leagues against one another, as well as the symbolic passing of the coaching torch from the past to the future.

Greasy Neale's Eagles were six-point favorites on game day, despite lacking injured feature back Steve Van Buren. Neale was so confident that he made no special effort to scout the Browns. By contrast, Paul Brown was thoroughly prepared. The Browns had been scouting Eagle games for a year, and they drew motivation from four years of quotes from NFL players, coaches, and executives, mocking the strength of their league and team. Before they took the field in front of more than 71,000 people, Browns coach Paul Brown told his revenge-minded team, "We're new, and they don't like us. It may get rough out there. But remember just this—the worst thing you can do to an opponent is defeat him. Nothing hurts as bad as losing."[1]

Cleveland kicked off and quickly forced a punt that Browns halfback Don Phelps returned for a touchdown. The score, however, was nullified by a clipping penalty. Browns quarterback Otto Graham threw three straight incompletions in the first series, but those plays provided clues to the Eagles defensive game plan. On each play, left halfback Dub Jones, flanked to the other side, ran an out pattern to the sidelines, while right halfback Rex Bumgardner went in motion right and took a linebacker with him, clearing out the middle of the field for the Browns ends.

Cleveland punted on fourth down, and the Eagles put together a successful drive completed by a 15-yard field goal for the first score. Toward the end of the first quarter, Philadelphia defensive back Russ Craft wearied of Dub Jones running short out patterns in front of him and began to creep closer to the line, hoping to jump the route. That's what Jones and Graham were waiting for. Jones faked the out and blew by Craft to catch a 59-yard touchdown pass from Graham to take a 7–3 lead they never relinquished.

In the second quarter, the Eagles had two drives end without points deep in Browns territory due to an unsuccessful fourth-down conversion at the two and a lost fumble. Graham then put together a 71-yard drive that culminated with a 26-yard touchdown strike to Dante Lavelli, and the Browns led, 14–3, at the half.

The Browns received the third-quarter kickoff, and Graham completed five of six passes for 80 yards, with Mac Speedie catching a 12-yard touchdown toss to make the score 21–3. Philadelphia then went into its z wide shotgun spread formation, with Bill Mackrides briefly replacing Tommy Thompson at quarterback, and closed the gap to 21–10 on a 17-yard scoring pass to Pete Pihos at the end of the third quarter. Although the Browns had only run the ball 10 times in the first three quarters, they spent the fourth quarter grinding out the clock and scored two more touchdowns on the ground to make the final score a thoroughly convincing 35–10.

Paul Brown later wrote that the first phase of his attack that night was forcing single coverage by the use of Bumgardner in motion and Jones flanked. The second phase was "spreading the Eagles' defensive line by imperceptibly widening our guards and tackles on each successive play." He continued,

With no middle linebacker in the Eagle defense, the center of the line was the weak area, even though their defensive tackles tried to compensate by charging to the inside shoulder of our offensive tackles. We knew their tackles were taught to line up opposite our tackles, and we reasoned that if we moved ours wider with each play, theirs would follow and the middle guard would be isolated.[2]

During the game, Brown was surprised by the Eagles' strategy. "We had noticed that the Eagles seemed so fearful of our traps and draws that their pass rush suffered," he explained. "We had expected just the opposite—that their pass rush would be so furious that we would need our traps and draws to cool it off—but their strategy just invited us to stay with our deep passing game."[3]

Graham ended up completing 21 of 38 passes for 346 yards and three touchdowns, and Cleveland rushed 24 times for 141 yards. Philadelphia ran the ball 44 times for 148 yards and completed just 11 of 32 passes for 118 yards. In his first NFL game, Paul Brown served notice that there was a new king of the jungle, and the Browns began a six-year string of NFL title game appearances. Brown established himself as the first modern pro football coach. Five-time Super Bowl champion Bill Belichick recently commented:

There's nobody in the game that I have more respect for than Paul Brown. His contributions to the game, from the way it's played to protective equipment, the playbook, every film breakdown, every meeting, everything that he did when he was a coach—50 years later, everybody's still basically doing the same thing. I really think of him as the father of professional football.[4]

Brown never worked directly with any of the coaches in this book and was influenced more by Dave Stewart, his unheralded high school coach in Massillon, Ohio. Paul Brown was born on September 7, 1908, in Norwalk, Ohio, and was the 145-pound starting quarterback for Washington High School in Massillon in 1924 and 1925, leading the team to a 15–3 record under Stewart, with whom he began a lifelong friendship. Brown enrolled in Ohio State University in 1926, but once he discovered the Buckeyes had no interest in such a slightly built quarterback, he transferred to Miami of Ohio. There, he started at quarterback in 1928 and 1929 under Coach Chester Pittser and went 14–3 as a starter.

Upon Brown's graduation, Stewart recommended him for a coaching position at Severn Prep in Maryland. Paul led Severn to a 16–1–1 record in 1930 and 1931 before the coaching position opened up at his high school alma mater. Brown took over at Massillon and, in nine years, achieved a fearsome 80–8–2 record. In his last six seasons there from 1935 through 1940, Paul came as close to perfect as possible. Massillon finished 58–1–1 and won six straight state titles.[5]

Brown liked his players "lean and fast." The main qualities he sought of every prospect were encapsulated by three questions: "Is he brave enough? Is he smart enough? Can he run?" His offense was primarily single wing, but he also ran plays from the double wing and the short punt formation. His major influences were Jimmy DeHart from Duke, whose offense was based on speed and deception, and Purdue's Noble Kizer, whose blocking schemes allowed Brown to update those of Jock Sutherland.[6]

When Francis Schmidt was forced out as the Ohio State coach in 1940, there was a statewide clamor for the Buckeyes to hire the high school wunderkind. Brown was tapped by OSU in 1941, and won a national championship in 1942, before enlisting in the U.S. Navy in 1943. He was assigned to coach the Great Lakes Naval Station team in 1944, and led them to a 9–2–1 season and a national ranking of 17th. The Bluejackets already were running the T formation, so Paul mastered that offense in his two years at Great Lakes, although he had seen it run the year before when OSU met Pittsburgh, coached by Clark Shaughnessy. Altogether, Brown had an 18–8–1 record at OSU and 15–5–2 at Great Lakes.

Offered the head coaching job with the new Cleveland team of the fledgling AAFC in 1945, Brown moved up to pro football, while remaining in his home state. Since the team would not begin playing for a year, Precision Paul had a golden opportunity to use his singular organizing skills to create a truly great team that would overwhelm its league. And that's what he did.

Brown may not have been directly influenced by the coaches in this book, but he drew on the spadework they had done in shaping the profession and the game. Guy Chamberlin established a standard of professionalism by holding regular practices and demanding perfect execution. Curly Lambeau, LeRoy Andrew, and Ray Flaherty cultivated the aerial attack and opened up the game. George Halas, Dutch Sternaman, Ralph

Jones, and Clark Shaughnessy steadily modernized the T formation, enabling one of the sport's earliest schemes to become the basis for the modern game of the past 75 years. Steve Owen and Greasy Neale nurtured and refined defenses to balance the game's progress. Jock Sutherland fostered the bridge between the college and pro games. Potsy Clark and Jimmy Conzelman opened the lines of communication with media and the fans.

Brown took that base to another level, as his 25–5–1 record in games in which he matched up with these pioneer coaches indicates. The sheer range of his innovations to professional football is astounding. At the fundamental level for the sport as a whole, he reintegrated the game. He had used black players at Massillon, Ohio State, and Great Lakes, and Cleveland was no different, with Marion Motley and Bill Willis smashing the pro football color bar in 1946 (along with Kenny Washington and Woody Strode with the Los Angeles Rams in the NFL). He also invented the taxi—or practice—squad and made his assistant coaches full-time year-round employees, saying, "There was no dignity, I felt, in having a man coach our offensive line for six months and then sell automobiles for six months."[7]

On the field, he was in the forefront in developing the pass pocket, the draw play, flare passes to the backs, and timing patterns to the ends, as well as calling plays via messenger guards. As for equipment, he popularized the helmet face guard and invented the radio helmet for the quarterback. Behind the scenes, he led the way in instituting playbooks, grading players on their playbook maintenance, evaluating his players' performances and scouting opponents via game films, charting his teams' tendencies and those of his opponents, testing his players on game plans, performing intelligence and personality tests on players, and timing them in the 40-yard dash.

Brown's son Mike felt that his father's biggest effect on the game was on the practice field. "It was very organized, scripted, every play was prepared before they went out on the field, and very short," the younger Brown recalled. "No one was allowed to stand around and talk or play catch, they had to be intent on what was going on. There was a time in pro football when they just milled around. He believed in classroom discipline, so he incorporated that into everything."[8] Brown made everything businesslike and professional.

Paul himself modestly said, "There's no great mysteries attached to our success. We were meticulous in all our preparations, and we even practiced how to practice."[9] He considered himself a teacher and cited Dave Stewart for that view of coaching, commenting, "He, first of all, put great emphasis on teaching, on stressing fundamentals. Our high school practices more than 50 years ago were nothing more than extensions of our classroom work. Only the subject matter was different."[10]

Brown was looking for only the best: "We wanted our players to be intelligent, fast, coachable, to have good size and good character—in other words, to be solid citizens and solid football players."[11] And he found them. From 1946 to 1955, the Browns were the early version of the "Greatest Show on Turf." They won the championship of the AAFC four straight years, and Brown bested Ray Flaherty, his main coaching rival in that league, seven times in eight games, with one game ending in a tie.

Moving into the NFL in 1950, Cleveland won the Eastern title six years in a row and the league championship three of those years. Brown went 2–0 against Greasy Neale, 8–0 against Curly Lambeau, 3–1 against George Halas, and 5–4 against Steve Owen. Paul's offense gets most of the glory. Led by Otto Graham, it featured six hall of famers and, in those first 10 years, finished first or second in points scored six times and four times in yards.

The defense was even better, despite featuring just two Canton-bound players. The Browns defense led the league or finished second in fewest points allowed his first 10 seasons and eight times for fewest yards allowed. That defense included an outstanding pass rushing front line, able and versatile linebackers, and a smart secondary that ran a combination zone/man-to-man coverage scheme devised by ace assistant Blanton Collier. Collier spoke highly of his boss's confidence in his staff, relating, "That's the way Paul is. He gives you a job to do, assumes that you know how to do it, and leaves you alone. If you don't produce, he finds somebody who will."[12]

Maintaining that level of dominance in pro football, however, is next to impossible. Once Graham retired in 1956, Brown never coached another champion, and, in fact, he never won another postseason game. He was still an excellent coach but won 55 percent of his games rather than the 85 percent that Cleveland won in its first decade. Many other coaches had borrowed and adapted Brown's practices and strategies, and leveled the gridiron.

Brown died in August 1991, but his influence lives on through the coaching forest that he seeded. Among his former players who went into coaching were Super Bowl champions Chuck Noll and Don Shula, league champion Lou Saban, and collegiate national champion Ara Parseghian. From his staff, Blanton Collier and Weeb Ewbank won NFL titles, and Ewbank and Bill Walsh won Super Bowls. In turn, these and other followers of Paul Brown taught others the basics learned from the master, and his inspiration continues to enrich the contemporary game of pro football. In a more hidden way, so too does the yeoman work of the pro football coaching pioneers covered in this book.

AFTERWORD

Fritz Pollard's Dream Deferred

The coaches in this book differ in many respects, but the one thing they have in common is that they were all white. The Pro Football Hall of Fame lists 13 African American players from the league's outset until the color ban arrived in 1934. Just one of those 13 trailblazers is a member of the Hall—Fritz Pollard—and he also served as a coach. Pollard was, in fact, the only black head coach in NFL history until the Raiders hired Art Shell in 1984.

Frederick Douglass Pollard was born on January 27, 1894, in Chicago, and named after the renowned 19th-century abolitionist. Pollard's father was a barber and his mother a seamstress, and both stressed the value of education to their children, who grew up in an integrated neighborhood.

A wispy and elusive 5-foot-9, 165-pound tailback, Pollard was one of the best players of his era. He was a high school track champion, as well as a football star, and enrolled at Brown University, where he was a two-time All-American, leading the Bears to the 1916 Rose Bowl as a freshman. While in Rhode Island, he also coached the backfield for the independent Providence Steam Roller on the side. Fritz was declared ineligible for football at Brown in 1918 because he had grade problems, so he entered the U.S. Army. During World War I, he was in the Student Army Training Corps near Philadelphia and coached the football team at Lincoln University, a historically black college.

Akron Pros owners Frank Nied and Art Ranney signed Fritz in 1920 to play for their franchise in the newly formed American Professional Football Association. Officially, Elge Tobin was the coach, but years later Pollard claimed that he had instituted the Brown University system of offensive plays in Akron and actually was the Pros coach. Although there is no proof of that, Tobin and Pollard were listed as cocoaches in 1921. That season, the Pros lost three of their last four games, and Pollard was released.

In 1922, Fritz signed on with the new Milwaukee Badgers franchise to be close to his Chicago home, where he had begun his own brokerage firm. Teammate Budge Garrett is listed as the Badgers coach that year, but Pollard later claimed that he was Garrett's cocoach.

Pollard signed with Hammond in 1923, and maintained in later years that he was the team's coach from 1923 to 1925. In this same busy period, Fritz was coaching Wendell Phillips High School in Chicago and playing for the independent Gilberton Cadamounts in the Pennsylvania coal regions through 1924. Local halfback Wally Hess is credited as the Hammond coach in 1923 and 1924, although Pollard was undoubtedly involved to some extent. Fritz is recognized as the team's coach for one game in 1925, before he moved on to play for the Providence Steam Roller, owned by Pearce Johnson, whom he had known since his days at Brown. Fritz finished 1925 back with Akron and then played one last season with the Pros.

After leaving the NFL, Pollard ran his brokerage firm, as well as a black newspaper, a black movie studio, a theatrical agency, and a tax consultancy. In addition, he coached two independent all-black football teams—the Chicago Black Hawks from 1929 to 1932, and the Harlem Brown Bombers from 1935 to 1938—showcasing the abilities of several prominent African American players not permitted to play in the NFL at the time.

Fritz lived to be 92 and eventually began to receive some attention for his varied and accomplished life before he died on May 11, 1986. After Pollard, there would not be another black coach in the league until 1957, when Art Rooney added Lowell Perry to the Steelers' staff as an assistant. Perry had starred at end for the team as a rookie in 1956, until a brutal tackle by the Giants' Rosey Grier fractured his pelvis and dislocated his hip in midseason. Perry coached the Pittsburgh ends for one year and then scouted for another before earning his law degree and launching a successful career in business and government service. Perry also became the first African American national TV broadcaster for the NFL in 1966, although he stayed for just one season.

The next black assistant coach in the league was Hall of Fame safety Emlen Tunnell, who coached the Giants defensive secondary from 1963 to 1974, when health concerns forced him to step down. In 1966, Tunnell was joined on the Giants staff by fellow hall of famer Rosey Brown, who coached the team's offensive line for five seasons. Three other black former players worked as assistant coaches in the late 1960s: Joe Perry, Ernie Green, and Irv Cross (although Cross was initially a player-coach). Based on the Pro Football Researchers Association's all-time list of NFL assistant coaches, it appears 16 black coaches got their start in the 1970s: Lionel Taylor in 1970; Lamar Lundy and Earnell Durden in 1971; Willie Wood in 1972; Garland Boyette in 1973; Elijah Pitts, Johnny Roland, Ralph Goldston, and Allan Webb in 1974; Al Lavan in 1975; Buck Buchanan in 1976; Jimmy Raye and Bob Ledbetter in 1977; Ernie McMillan in 1978; and Billie Matthews and Dennis Green in 1979.

Dennis Green would be the only one of that group of pioneers to become a head coach in the league, but prospects for black coaches were beginning to improve. The first four black NFL head coaches after Fritz Pollard began their professional coaching careers as assistants between 1979 and 1984, with Green in 1979, Tony Dungy in 1981, Ray Rhodes in 1982, and Art Shell in 1984. One other coach from the 1970s group also broke new ground as the first black pro head coach in the modern era, as Willie Wood was named head coach of the Philadelphia Bell of the World Football League in 1974, and later for the Toronto Argonauts of the Canadian Football League in 1981.

The best route to a NFL head-coaching position remains via a coordinator slot, either offensive or defensive, and African Americans began to assume those roles slowly starting in the 1980s. Lionel Taylor was the first black offensive coordinator in 1980 and 1981, with the Rams, while Tony Dungy became the first black defensive coordinator in 1984, with Pittsburgh. The offensive route has proven much rarer for black coaches. Just two of the nine black offensive coordinators through 2015—Hue Jackson and Anthony Lynn—have become head coaches. On the other side of the ball, 10 of 22 black defensive coordinators from the same period have moved up to the head job: Tony Dungy, Ray Rhodes, Marvin Lewis, Lovie Smith, Romeo Crennel, Mike Tomlin, Leslie Frazier, Todd

Bowles, Vance Joseph, and Steve Wilks. This count does not include such coordinators as Mel Tucker, Perry Fewell, and Emmitt Thomas, who only served as interim head coaches.

Because of the sluggish progress made by black head coaches in the 1990s, the NFL instituted the so-called Rooney Rule in 2003, mandating that a minority candidate be interviewed whenever a team was filling a head coaching or senior management position. The rule seems to have had a positive effect in that for more than a decade and a half, there generally has been between six to eight black head coaches in the NFL each season. Moreover, since Ozzie Newsome became the first black general manager in NFL history in 2002, the league has made progress at that level as well, with several black GMs getting hired.

Fritz Pollard was elected to the Hall of Fame in 2005, 19 years after his death. One would suppose that he would be pleased that his dream, once deferred, has become reality in the much more equitable 21st century, 100 years after the founding of the NFL.

POSTSCRIPT

Equivalencies

In closing, a fun, shorthand way to understand who these pioneer coaches were is to draw comparisons to more modern coaches with whom we are familiar. Some of these equivalencies are a stretch, but they do encapsulate key characteristics of those who came earlier.

Guy Chamberlin: Player-coach only; emphasis on few plays thoroughly practiced; training, conditioning, teamwork, organization, compressed period of extreme success. *Think Vince Lombardi.*

Curly Lambeau: Early emphasis on passing game and wide-open attack; belligerent, bellicose, and ultimately outdated. *Think Allie Sherman, Mike Shanahan, and Hank Stram.*

LeRoy Andrew: Defensive/running game–oriented coach who switched to passing game after hooking his star to the best passer in game. *Think Tony Dungy, Weeb Ewbank, and Dick Vermeil.*

George Halas: Head of the firm who hired smart men and delegated. *Think Al Davis, Joe Gibbs, and Jim Lee Howell.*

Ralph Jones: Professorial former small college coach who revitalized an offensive scheme. *Think Blanton Collier, Jim Harbaugh, and Marv Levy.*

Potsy Clark: Defensive-oriented coach who loved to talk to the press and was the first pro coach to write an instructional football book; moved around a lot. *Think Brian Billick, Marty Schottenheimer, and Lou Saban.*

Steve Owen: Smashmouth football; most sophisticated defensive coach of his time; designed his own offense, too, but it was generally dull and ineffective; Stout Steve revered by the press. *Think George Allen; Jim Mora, John Harbaugh, and Chuck Knox.*

Ray Flaherty: Solid defensive coach; enamored of the passing game; known for platooning; so devoted to single wing that he was no longer able to find a position at age 47 because he wouldn't coach the T. *Think Jon Gruden, Dan Reeves, Mike Holmgren, and Andy Reid.*

Jock Sutherland: Celebrated national championship college coach; intense and dour; scrimmaged his teams relentlessly to the point of exhaustion; power running game. *Think Jimmy Johnson, Tom Coughlin, and John McKay.*

Clark Shaughnessy: Innovative mad scientist intent on outscheming the opposition despite whether his players understood their assignments; aloof and most comfortable at a blackboard; professorial and foulmouthed. *Think Buddy Ryan, Mike Martz, Don Coryell, and Sid Gillman.*

Jimmy Conzelman: Players' coach; promoted a fun locker room, with players and coaches as family; solid on x and o but not an innovator; flexible and adaptable; good judge of talent. *Think John Madden, Pete Carroll, Bum and Wade Phillips, and John Fox.*

Greasy Neale: Run-oriented but adapted to the offense of the time; innovative defensive schemer; foulmouthed and vocal but players felt free to yell back; close with players off the field. *Think Bill Parcells, Bill Cowher, and Don Shula.*

Paul Brown: First modern-day pro football coach; teacher; organizer; not a yeller but clearly registered his displeasure with team's poor execution; scientific approach and devotion to film study; lessened scrimmaging to keep players fresh. *Think Chuck Noll, Bill Belichick, Bill Walsh, Tom Landry, and Bud Grant.*

NOTES

INTRODUCTION

1. Michael Oriard, *King Football: Sport and Spectacle in the Golden Age of Radio and Newsreels, Movies and Magazines, the Weekly, and the Daily Press* (Chapel Hill: University of North Carolina Press, 2001), 6–7.

2. Chris Willis, *The Man Who Built the National Football League: Joe Carr* (Lanham, Md.: Scarecrow, 2010).

3. Knute Rockne, *The Autobiography of Knute K. Rockne*. Ed. Bonnie Skiles Rockne (Indianapolis, Ind.: Bobbs-Merrill, 1931), 158.

4. Glenn S. Warner, *Football for Coaches and Players* (Palo Alto, Calif.: Stanford University, 1927), 1.

5. Knute K. Rockne, "Rockne, Notre Dame Coach, in Bitter Attack against 'Pro' Football, Calls It Menace," *Green Bay Press-Gazette*, 19 January 1922, 10.

6. Amos Alonzo Stagg and Wesley Winans Stout, *Touchdown!* (New York: Longmans, Green, 1927), 293.

7. Stagg, *Touchdown!*, 295.

8. John Kryk, *Stagg vs. Yost: The Birth of Cutthroat Football* (Lanham, Md.: Rowman & Littlefield, 2015), 264.

9. Stagg, *Touchdown!*, 301–2.

10. Jim Campbell, "John Alexander: Pro Football Pioneer," *Coffin Corner* 16, no. 2 (1995): 4.

11. Campbell, "John Alexander," 3.

12. Campbell, "John Alexander," 5.

13. Campbell, "John Alexander," 5.

14. Campbell, "John Alexander," 8.

15. Willis, *The Man Who Built the National Football League*, 289.

16. Dan Daly and Bob O'Donnell, *The Pro Football Chronicle: The Complete (Well, Almost) Record of the Best Players, the Greatest Photos, the Hardest Hits, the Biggest Scandals, and the Funniest Stories in Pro Football* (New York: Collier, 1990), 9.

17. Ed Pollock, *Philadelphia Public Ledger*, 1 March 1933, quoted in Chris Willis, *The Man Who Built the National Football League*, 307.

I. PLAYER-COACH

1. Wally Provost, "Camp Earns Vote of Halas," *Omaha World-Herald*, 21 November 1957, 33.

2. Wally Provost, "From Farm in Gage County Came an N.U. and Pro Giant," *Omaha World-Herald*, 23 August 1964.

3. Dorothy Chamberlin Savener interview with E. A. Kral, 23 May 1996, Guy Chamberlin file, Gage County Historical Society.

4. Wally Provost, "Young Chamberlin's Plans Didn't List College Football," *Omaha World-Herald*, 24 August 1964, 19.

5. Wally Provost, "Dazzling Crete Performance Charmed Chamberlin's Dad," *Omaha World-Herald*, 25 August 1964.

6. "Ewald O. (Jumbo) Stiehm," *Nebraska Huskers*, www.huskers.com/ViewArticle.dbml?ATCLID=920443 (16 January 2018); Wally Provost, "Bone-Breaking Tackle Ends 'Star from Wesleyan' Taunt," *Omaha World-Herald*, 27 August 1964.

7. Knute Rockne, *The Autobiography of Knute K. Rockne*. Ed. Bonnie Skiles Rockne (Indianapolis, Ind.: Bobbs-Merrill, 1931), 181–82; RSM, "The Upper Room," *Beatrice Daily Sun*, 11 July 1954, 8.

8. Patrick McCaskey, *Pillars of the NFL: Coaches Who Have Won Three or More Championships* (Crystal Lake, Ill.: Sporting Chance Press, 2014).

9. "Scholarship Goes to Girl," *Omaha World-Herald*, 4 October 1945.

10. PFRA Research, *A War Year: 1918*, *Pro Football Researchers Association*, www.profootballresearchers.org/articles/A_War_Year.pdf (1 January 2018); "Other Teams Bid against Bulldogs for Chamberlin," *Canton Repository*, 28 September 1919; Wally Provost, "Chamberlin Rates Thorpe the Greatest—in Everything," *Omaha World-Herald*, 4 September 1964, 35.

11. Wally Provost, "Chamberlin Never Dreamed of Stature Pro Football Would Achieve after WWI," *Omaha World-Herald*, 5 September 1964, 9.

12. Provost, "Chamberlin Never Dreamed of Stature Pro Football Would Achieve after WWI," 9; "Sports in a Sentence or Two," *Akron Beacon Journal*, 27 July 1922, 15; Wally Provost, "An Old-Timer Looks Up, Down the Trail," *Omaha World-Herald*, 21 January 1965, 6.

13. Wally Provost, "Canton Crowns Emphasize Halas's Biggest Grid Error," *Omaha World-Herald*, 7 September 1964, 36–37.

14. "We've Had Our Day Off," *Canton Repository*, 7 November 1922, 16.

15. David S. Neft, Richard M. Cohen, and Rick Korch, *The Football Encyclopedia: The Complete Year-by-Year History of Professional Football from 1892 to the Present* (New York: St. Martin's, 1994).

16. Provost, "Canton Crowns Emphasize Halas's Biggest Grid Error," 38.

17. PFRA Research, *Goodbye, Bulldogs, Hello: 1924, Pro Football Researchers Association*, www.profootballresearchers.org/articles/Goodbye_ Bulldogs,_Hello.pdf (1 January 2018).

18. PFRA Research, *The Third Time Is Charmed: 1924, Pro Football Researchers Association*, www.profootballresearchers.org/articles/Goodbye_ Bulldogs,_Hello.pdf (1 January 2018).

19. Wally Provost, "Fears of Robbery Prove Unfounded," *Omaha World-Herald*, 8 September 1964, 17.

20. RIG, "Yellow Jackets Will Start Work Monday," *Philadelphia Inquirer*, 13 September 1925, 27.

21. "Yellow Jackets Coach Suspends Capt. Behman on Eve of Red's Visit Here," *Philadelphia Inquirer*, 2 December 1925.

22. Lawrence Perry, "For the Game's Sake," *Canton Daily News*, 21 December 1925, 14.

23. "Bulldog Tackle and Guy Chamberlin Head South to Play Winter Football," *Canton Repository*, 22 December 1925.

24. RIG, "Chamberlin to Quit Jackets Is Rumor at Hornets Feast," *Philadelphia Inquirer*, 19 December 1926.

25. Directors, "What Price Championship," *Frankford Yellow Jacket News*, April 1927, 3–4.

26. Joe Ziemba, *When Football Was Football* (Chicago: Triumph, 1999).

27. "Champ Through Now," *Canton Repository*, 19 November 1928, 10.

28. Charlie Powell, "Chamberlin Enjoyed Fabled Career, Thought Pro Ball Wouldn't Progress," *Canton Repository*, 13 April 1965, 22.

29. Dorothy Chamberlin Savener interview with E. A. Kral; "Betrothal Announced," *Beatrice Daily Sun*, 18 May 1941.

30. "Guy Chamberlin Trophy," *Nebraska Huskers*, www.huskers.com/ ViewArticle.dbml?DB_OEM_ID=100&ATCLID=204967320 (27 January 2018).

31. Guy Chamberlin, *Radio Interview*. NFL Films, 1965.

32. Provost, "Canton Crowns Emphasize Halas's Biggest Grid Errors," 36.

33. "Grid Pioneer Dies," *Cleveland Plain Dealer*, 6 April 1967, 54; "Guy Chamberlain: All-American Gridder from Nebraska, Will Come about Sept. 15th to Take Control," *Canton Repository*, 11 August 1922, 26.

34. "Bulldogs Rip Open Practice on Field Here," *Canton Daily News*, 21 September 1922, 14.

35. "Giant Line Smasher with Hoosier School Last Fall; Bowe Also Here Wednesday," *Canton Repository*, 25 September 1922.

36. "Frankford's New Grid Coach Here," *Philadelphia Evening Bulletin*, 3 September 1925, 16.

37. "Blackboard Drill for Yellow Jackets," *Philadelphia Inquirer*, 13 November 1925.

38. Wally Provost, "Hall of Fame Inductee Guy's Life Is Rated 'Most Victorious,'" *Omaha World-Herald*, 13 September 1965, 9; Ray Didinger, "Elevating Frankford," *Philadelphia Daily News*, 29 August 1991, F8.

39. John Bentley, "I May Be Wrong," *Nebraska State Journal*, 15 December 1938, 11.

40. Didinger, "Elevating Frankford," F8; Provost, "Canton Crowns Emphasize Halas's Biggest Grid Errors," 36.

41. Chris Willis, *Old Leather: An Oral History of Early Pro Football in Ohio, 1920–1935* (Lanham, Md: Scarecrow, 2005), 58.

42. Neft, Cohen, and Korch, *The Football Encyclopedia*.

43. "Frankford Points for 1924 Champions," *Philadelphia Inquirer*, 18 November 1925, 27.

44. "Two Great Teams Clash at Chicago Today as Bulldogs Tackle Bears in Own Lair," *Canton Repository*, 29 October 1922, 40.

45. "Bulldogs Dispose of Bears," *Canton Repository*, 30 October 1922, 12.

46. "Champion Bulldogs Expect Tough Combat with Bears but Also Predict They Win," *Canton Repository*, 21 October 1923, 39.

47. Wally Provost, "Chamberlin: Today's Football 'Interesting,'" *Omaha World-Herald*, 11 September 1964, 35.

48. "Grid Pioneer Dies," 54.

49. Steve Owen and Joe King, *My Kind of Football* (New York: David McKay, 1952), 214.

50. Sam Walker, *The Captain Class: The Hidden Force That Creates the World's Greatest Teams* (New York: Random House, 2017).

51. Provost, "From Farm in Gage County Came an N.U. and Pro Giant," 35.

2. TAKING FLIGHT

1. David S. Neft, Richard M. Cohen, and Rick Korch, *The Football Encyclopedia: The Complete Year-by-Year History of Professional Football from 1892 to the Present* (New York: St. Martin's, 1994).

2. Lee Remmel, "Curly Lambeau, 1898–1965," *Green Bay Packer Yearbook 1965* (1965): 24.

3. Dal Andrew, author interview, 10 August 2017.

4. Andrew, author interview.

5. Andrew, author interview.

6. Bob Carroll, "Ollie's All-Stars," *Coffin Corner* 5, no. 7 (July 1983).

7. Cliff Christl, *Packers Heritage Trail: The Town, the Team, the Fans from Lambeau to Lombardi* (Stevens Point, Wisc.: KCI Sports Publishing, 2017).

8. Christl, *Packers Heritage Trail.*

9. Christl, *Packers Heritage Trail.*

10. Cliff Christl, "A Leap in Lambeau's History," *Milwaukee Journal Sentinel*, 28 October 2001.

11. Steve Owen and Joe King. *My Kind of Football* (New York: David McKay, 1952).

12. Owen and King, *My Kind of Football*, 59.

13. Andrew, author interview.

14. Andrew, author interview.

15. Andrew, author interview.

16. Andrew, author interview.

17. "Bulletin," *Green Bay Press-Gazette*, 20 September 1927.

18. Andrew, author interview.

19. Arthur J. Daley, "Pro Giants Defeat Stapletons, 19–9," *New York Times*, 14 October 1929.

20. "Benny Friedman and Other Stars in the Lineup," *Honolulu Star-Advertiser*, 23 November 1929.

21. Barry Gottehrer, *The Giants of New York: The History of Professional Football's Most Fabulous Dynasty* (New York: Putnam, 1963); Arthur Daley, "The Unforgettable Rockne," *New York Times*, 1 December 1963; "Andrews Let Out as Coach of Giants," *Portsmouth Times*, 8 December 1930.

22. Gottehrer, *The Giants of New York*, 79.

23. Andrew, author interview.

24. W. P. Minego, "Sparks from the Sports Anvil," *Portsmouth Times*, 10 February 1931; "Pro Coach," *Arizona Daily Star*, 27 August 1931.

25. Green Bay Football Corporation, "Andrews Critical of Bays' Defense," *Green Bay Packers Bulletin* 4, no. 4 (4 October 1931): 1.

26. "Andrews Resigns as Card Coach; Reasons Differ," *Chicago Tribune*, 6 October 1931, 25.

27. Andrew, author interview.

28. Lou Little letter to Bert Bell, dated 4 April 1932, in Chris Willis, *The Man Who Built the National Football League: Joe Carr* (Lanham, Md.: Scarecrow, 2010); "Cincinnati Represented," *Green Bay Press-Gazette*, 7 July 1933.

29. "Lambeau Quits as Card Coach; Club Head Flays Him for Alibis," *New York Herald Tribune*, 8 December 1951, 12.

30. Michael Richman, *The Redskins Encyclopedia* (Philadelphia, Pa.: Temple University Press, 2008).

31. Bud Furillo, "Lambeau Green Bay Legend and Palm Springs Twister," *Los Angeles Herald-Examiner*, 8 March 1963.

32. George Halas, "Thank the Likes of Curly—Halas," *Green Bay Press-Gazette*, 2 June 1965, 19.

33. John Walter, "Looking Up in the Realm of Sports," *Green Bay Press-Gazette*, 14 October 1937.

34. Dutch Sternaman handwritten note, undated, Dutch Sternaman Collection, Pro Football Hall of Fame.

35. George Halas, "Halas Calls Friedman Pioneer Passer—Rest Came by Design," *Chicago Daily News*, 4 February 1967, 4.

36. Sternaman handwritten note.

37. Benny Friedman, "The Professional Touch," *Collier's* 90 (15 October 1932): 46.

38. Ray Flaherty, *NFL Films Interview*, NFL Films, 1985.

39. Andrew, author interview.

40. "Nevers, Rose, Holmer Play Here with Cards," *Madison Capital Times*, 10 September 1931, 13.

41. Freddy Mendell, "From the Press Box," *Hutchinson News*, 5 June 1938, 2.

42. Halas, "Halas Calls Friedman Pioneer Passer—Rest Came by Design."

43. This paragraph is a synthesis of several sources: 1) A 1929 scouting report prepared by Dutch Sternaman from the Dutch Sternaman Collection at the Pro Football Hall of Fame; 2) A letter from Clarke Hinkle to Stan Grosshandler at the Pro Football Hall of Fame; 3) Curly Lambeau, "These Great Plays Will Win for Grammar and High School Teams," *True Sport Picture Stories* 3, no. 5 (January/February 1946); 4) Ralph Hickok, *Vagabond Halfback: The Saga of Johnny Blood McNally* ([United States]: CreateSpace, 2017); and 5) Cliff Christl, "Lambeau's 'Notre Dame Box Offense' Not a Simple Scheme," *Cliff's Notes*, 17 March 2016, http://www.packers.com/news-and-events/article-cliffs-notes/article-1/Lambeaus-Notre-Dame-Box-offense-not-a-simple-scheme/7de53247-6024-4104-b572-82582d8a1660 (12 February 2018).

44. Shirley Povich, "This Morning," *Washington Post*, 9 November 1942, 10.

45. John Dietrich, "Rams Lose, 35–10," *Cleveland Plain Dealer*, 17 October 1937, 7.

46. Murray Olderman, *The Running Backs* (Englewood Cliffs, N.J.: Prentice Hall, 1969), 18.

47. "Lambeau Sees Great Season," *Green Bay Press-Gazette*, 14 February 1936.

48. Hickok, *Vagabond Halfback*, 84–85.

49. Richard Whittingham, *What a Game They Played: Stories of the Early Days of Pro Football by Those Who Were There* (New York: Harper & Row, 1984), 125.

50. Pat Gannon, "Curley Spouts Advice; Nobody Pays Attention," *Milwaukee Journal*, 14 December 1936.

51. Gary D'Amato and Cliff Christl, *Mudbaths and Bloodbaths: The Inside Story of the Bears–Packers Rivalry* (Madison, Wisc.: Prairie Oak Press, 1997), 31.

52. Whittingham, *What a Game They Played*, 96.

53. Myron Cope, *The Game That Was: The Early Days of Pro Football* (New York: World Publishing, 1970), 86.

54. "Former Packer Stars Laud Lambeau as 'Great Leader,'" *Milwaukee Sentinel*, 2 June 1965, 6.

55. Cliff Christl, "Lambeau: More than a Name," *Voyageur* 17, no. 2 (June 2001): 13.

56. Oliver E. Keuchle, "Lambeau's Most Satisfying Game Recalled," *Milwaukee Journal*, 30 June 1969, 3.

57. Lee Remmel, "Greatest Packer Games: No. 9," *Pro* (9 August 1975): 54.

58. Andrew, author interview.

3. T MEN

1. Walter Camp and Lorin F. Deland, *Football* (New York: Houghton Mifflin, 1896); Susan Reyburn, *Football Nation: Four Hundred Years of America's Game, from the Library of Congress* (New York: Abrams, 2013); Tom Bennett, *The Pro Style: The Complete Guide to Understanding National Football League Strategy* (Englewood Cliffs, N.J.: Prentice Hall, 1976).

2. Jeffrey J. Miller, *Pop Warner: A Life on the Gridiron* (Jefferson, N.C.: McFarland, 2015).

3. Robert C. Zuppke, *Football Technique and Tactics* (Champaign, Ill.: Bailey and Himes, 1924).

4. George Halas, with Gwen Morgan and Arthur Veysey, *Halas by Halas: The Autobiography of George Halas* (New York: McGraw-Hill, 1979).

5. Halas, with Morgan and Veysey, *Halas by Halas*.

6. Mark W. Sorensen, "Dutch Sternaman," *Staley Museum*, https://staleymuseum.com/staleys-bears-20-21/dutch-sternaman/ (28 February 2018).

7. Dutch Sternaman handwritten letter, 9 September 1969, Dutch Sternaman Collection, Pro Football Hall of Fame.

8. Francis J. Powers and Ed Prell, "George Halas: The Papa Bear," *Sport* 5 (December 1948).

9. Halas, with Morgan and Veysey, *Halas by Halas*, 35.

10. Sorensen, "Dutch Sternaman."

11. George Halas, "My 40 Years in Pro Football," *Saturday Evening Post* 230 (23 November 1957): 34.

12. George Halas, "The Era of Red Grange," *Saturday Evening Post* 230 (30 November 1957).

13. Halas with Morgan and Veysey, *Halas by Halas*, 132.

14. Halas with Morgan and Veysey, *Halas by Halas*, 136; Halas, "The Era of Red Grange," 108.

15. Ralph Jones, *Basketball from a Coaching Standpoint* (Champaign: University of Illinois Press, 1916).

16. "School to Pick New Grid Coach," *Winston-Salem Journal*, 16 January 1927, 16.

17. Joe Cermak, "T Formation Born in 1911—When Halas Played as a Boy," *Washington Post*, 7 December 1942, 17.

18. Halas, "The Era of Red Grange," 108.

19. Halas, "The Era of Red Grange," 110.

20. Halas, "The Era of Red Grange," 110; Red Grange, *CBS Interview*, NFL Films, 1978.

21. Gregg McBride, "T-Doctor Avoids His Own Medicine," *Omaha World-Herald*, 19 August 1941, 10.

22. Harry Grayson, "Scoreboard," *Daily Herald*, 26 October 1945, 5.

23. Chauncey Durden, "The Sportview," *Richmond Times-Dispatch*, 16 December 1945; Chauncey Durden, "The Sportview," *Richmond Times-Dispatch*, 11 January 1947; Chauncey Durden, "The Sportview," *Richmond Times-Dispatch*, 19 February 1950; Chauncey Durden, "The Sportview," *Richmond Times-Dispatch*, 22 October 1950; Chauncey Durden, "The Sportview," *Richmond Times-Dispatch*, 3 February 1963; Chauncey Durden, "The Sportview," *Richmond Times-Dispatch*, 9 February 1967; Chauncey Durden, "The Sportview," *Richmond Times-Dispatch*, 11 September 1977; Halas, with Morgan and Veysey, *Halas by Halas*; Halas, "My 40 Years in Pro Football."

24. "Zuppke the Opportunist," *Philadelphia Inquirer*, 30 August 1942, 3.

25. "Staleys to Use Open Game against Tigers Sunday," *Chicago Tribune*, 4 November 1921, 17.

26. George Halas, "Lessons in Football," *Chicago Daily Journal*, 2 October to 13 November 1922.

27. Dutch Sternaman handwritten notes, undated, Dutch Sternaman Collection, Pro Football Hall of Fame.

28. Sternaman handwritten notes.

29. Halas, with Morgan and Veysey, *Halas by Halas*, 129.

30. Harry Grayson, "The Payoff," *Muncie Evening Press*, 14 October 1937, 14; George Halas, "New Coach, Change in Tactics, and a Fresh Idea Bring Bears Championship," *Chicago Tribune*, 14 October 1937, 31.

31. Sol Metzger, "Man in Motion," *Colliers* 88 (12 December 1931): 22; Allison Danzig, *The History of American Football: Its Great Teams, Players, and Coaches* (Englewood Cliffs, N.J.: Prentice Hall, 1956), 77.

32. George Halas and George Dunscomb, "Hold What Line?" *Saturday Evening Post* 212 (2 December 1939): 69.

33. Arthur J. "Dutch" Bergman, ed., *Fifty Football Plays* (New York: Barnes, 1936), 84–85.

34. Halas, with Morgan and Veysey, *Halas by Halas*, 171–72.

35. "Bears Defeat Giants for Pro Football Title, 23 to 21, on Lateral Pass in Closing Minutes," *New York Herald Tribune*, 18 December 1933, 21.

4. ALMOST FAMOUS

1. Stanley Woodward, "Potsy Clark to Govern Dodgers on and off Field via Committees," *New York Herald Tribune*, 8 January 1937, 23.

2. Robert C. Zuppke, *Football Technique and Tactics* (Champaign, Ill.: Bailey and Himes, 1924); Percy D. Haughton, *Football and How to Watch It* (Boston: Marshall Jones, 1922); George "Potsy" Clark, *Football: A Book for Players and Football Fans* (New York: Rand McNally, 1935).

3. Clark, *Football*, 25.

4. "100 Landmarks in the Life of George (Potsy) Clark," Potsy Clark File, Pro Football Hall of Fame.

5. Leo Macdonnell, "Sports," *Detroit Times*, 8 February 1940, 21.

6. Bob Carroll, "Potsy Clark: A Success Story," *Coffin Corner* 7 (March–April 1985): 5.

7. Kyle Crichton, "For Love and Money," *Colliers* 22 (1 December 1934).

8. Major John L. Griffith and George "Potsy" Clark, titles in Wilson Athletic Library: *Football Offense, Football Defense, Fundamentals of Football Training, Football Forward Passing, How to Play Quarterback and Other Football Positions, Fundamentals of Basketball Defense, Training the Basketball Team, Basketball Plays and Attack, Fundamentals of Boxing,* and *The Field Events and Analysis of Correct Form* (Chicago: T. E. Wilson, 1923).

9. "Bell to Take Up Butler Duties," *Muncie Evening Press*, 12 August 1930.

10. "Potsy Clark Writes Times," *Portsmouth Times*, 8 May 1931, 20.

11. "Spartan Coach Makes His Bow," *Portsmouth Times*, 29 July 1931, 10.

12. Bob Curran, *Pro Football's Rag Days* (New York: Bonanza Books, 1969).

13. Carroll, "Potsy Clark."

14. "And It Worked," *Portsmouth Times*, 14 September 1931, 15.

15. "Christensen Sings Praises of Spartans," *Portsmouth Times*, 21 February 1932, 12.

16. "Tackle Douds Is Suspended," *Portsmouth Times*, 24 November 1931, 1.

17. "Green Bay Pikers Cheese Champs," *Portsmouth Times*, 8 December 1931, 14; "Potsy Clark Insists Joe Carr Has No Right to Award Green Bay Packers National Loop Rag," *Portsmouth Times*, 13 December 1931, 14.

18. "Potsy Clark Used Only 11 Players to Avenge Old Grudge against Lambeau," *Portsmouth Times*, 12 December 1932, 8.

19. "Potsy Clark Turns Writer to Describe Sunday Game," *Portsmouth Times*, 19 October 1932, 8.

20. Curran, *Pro Football's Rag Days*, 92.

21. "Potsy Clark Predicts Team Will Be among League's Best," *Detroit Times*, 9 September 1934, 60.

22. Lloyd Northard, "Clark Predicts National Title for Lions," *Detroit News*, 18 November 1935, 6.

23. "Potsy Clark to Lose Detroit Coach Post, Says Frisco Report," *Portsmouth Times*, 28 January 1936, 25; Jerry Green, *Detroit Lions* (New York: Macmillan, 1973), 114.

24. "Potsy Clark Says He Prefers Pro to College Game," *Portsmouth Times*, 23 July 1936, 34.

25. Tod Rockwell, "Dispute Over Long-Term Contract Causes Action," *Detroit Free Press*, 5 January 1937, 15.

26. Allison Danzig, "Sports of the Times," *New York Times*, 18 December 1937.

27. Harold Parrott, "Potsy Clark Provides Football Dodgers with College Atmosphere," *Brooklyn Daily Eagle*, 18 August 1937; Harold Parrott, "I'll Say," *Brooklyn Daily Eagle*, 18 July 1937.

28. Roger A. Godin, *The Brooklyn Football Dodgers: The Other "Bums"* (Haworth, N.J.: St. Johann Press, 2003), 78.

29. Green, *Detroit Lions*, 112.

30. Kingsley Childs, "Shellogg, Old Notre Dame Tackle, Reports for Action with Dodgers," *New York Times*, 2 November 1939, 35.

31. "Potsy Clark Leaves Position as Coach of Detroit Lion Eleven," *Portsmouth Times*, 29 November 1940, 68.

32. Crichton, "For Love and Money," 48.

33. Woodward, "Potsy Clark to Govern Dodgers on and off Field via Committees," 23.

34. Woodward, "Potsy Clark to Govern Dodgers on and off Field via Committees," 23.

35. Major John L. Griffith and George "Potsy" Clark, *Football Offense* (Chicago: T. E. Wilson, 1923).

36. Glenn Presnell, *NFL Films Interview*, NFL Films, 1998.

37. Woodward, "Potsy Clark to Govern Dodgers on and off Field via Committees," 23.

38. Dick Friedman, *The Coach Who Strangled the Bulldog: How Harvard's Percy Haughton Beat Yale and Reinvented Football* (Lanham, Md.: Rowman & Littlefield, 2018).

39. Clark, *Football*, 1.

40. Clark, *Football*, 5.

41. Green, *Detroit Lions*, 113.

42. Arthur J. "Dutch" Bergman, *Fifty Football Plays* (New York: Barnes, 1936).

43. Clark, *Football*; Zuppke, *Football Technique and Tactics*.

44. Presnell, *NFL Films Interview*.

45. Tod Rockwell, "Lions Ground Game Clicks Nicely, But Aerials, Well—," *Detroit Free Press*, 24 August 1936, 12.

46. Green, *Detroit Lions*, 113.

47. "Portsmouth Coach Is Confident of Victory over Packers," unidentified clipping, 8 October 1932, Potsy Clark File, Pro Football Hall of Fame.

48. Richard Whittingham, *What a Game They Played: Stories of the Early Days of Pro Football by Those Who Were There* (New York: Harper & Row, 1984), 75.

49. Grant P. Ward, "Packers Disappoint Ohio Pro Followers in Spartan Contest," *Ohio State Journal*, 5 December 1932.

50. Green, *Detroit Lions*, 112.

5. SMASH MOUTH

1. Arthur Daley, "A Legacy of Friendship," *New York Times*, 22 May 1964, 25.

2. Steve Owen and Joe King, *My Kind of Football* (New York: David McKay, 1952), 3.

3. Owen and King, *My Kind of Football*, 4.

4. Owen and King, *My Kind of Football*.

5. Owen and King, *My Kind of Football*.

6. Owen and King, *My Kind of Football*.

7. Owen and King, *My Kind of Football*.

8. Jim Strain, "The Iron Men of Phillips Used Just 12 Players in Upsetting Mighty Texas," *Sports Illustrated* 55 (19 October 1981).

9. Owen and King, *My Kind of Football*; Mike Moran, "Steve Owen," *Hap Moran*, http://hapmoran.org/images/Steve Owen.pdf (12 March 2018).

10. Owen and King, *My Kind of Football*, 65.

11. "Notre Dame All Stars vs. New York Giants" (game program), *Hap Moran*, http://hapmoran.org/giantsnd/Giants_vs_Notre_Dame_page1.htm (12 March 2018).

12. Frank Graham, "Steve Owen: The Man Behind the Giants," *Sport* 3 (December 1947): 48.

13. "Friedman, Assistant Coach at Yale, Rejoins Football Giants," *New York Times*, 27 October 1931, 32; "Football Giants Coach Back," *New York Times*, 6 January 1933, 26.

14. Owen and King, *My Kind of Football*, 109.

15. Bill Corum, "Wherein a New York Scribe Lauds Smiling Steve from Oklahoma," *New York Evening Journal*, 8 December 1934, 12.

16. Richard Whittingham, *What a Game They Played: Stories of the Early Days of Pro Football by Those Who Were There* (New York: Harper & Row, 1984), 58.

17. James P. Terzian, *New York Giants* (New York: Macmillan, 1973), 162.

18. Mel Hein, *NFL Films Interview*, NFL Films, 1983; Robert Peterson, *Pigskin: The Early Years of Pro Football* (New York: Oxford University Press, 1997), 121.

19. Steve Owen, "Receives All-Time Thrill When Giants Beat College All-Stars," *Green Bay Press-Gazette*, 24 July 1940, 13.

20. Owen and King, *My Kind of Football*, 131.

21. "Giants a Beauty of Patch Job by Owen," *Washington Post*, 17 December 1943, 18.

22. Barry Gottehrer, *The Giants of New York: The History of Professional Football's Most Fabulous Dynasty* (New York: Putnam, 1963), 204.

23. Graham, "Steve Owen," 48.

24. William A. Hachten, "A Superior Season: A New York Giant Remembers His Rookie Year," *Wisconsin Magazine of History* 86, no. 1 (Autumn 2002): 30–31.

25. Michael Eisner, "Giant of the Decade—1940s: Steve Owen," *Gameday* (23 October 1994): 10.

26. Emlen Tunnell and William Gleason, *Footsteps of a Giant* (Garden City, N.Y.: Doubleday, 1966).

27. Frank Gifford and Harry Waters, *The Whole Ten Yards* (New York: Random House, 1993), 88.

28. Dave Brady, "Leemans Lives Another Day," *Washington Post*, 29 July 1978.

29. Steve Owen and Arthur Daley, "Keeping the Foot in Football," *Collier's* 110 (31 October 1942): 24.

30. Red Smith, "Owen Knew Defense for Good Reason," *Washington Post*, 12 December 1953, 14.

31. Owen and King, *My Kind of Football*, 46–47.

32. Arthur J. "Dutch" Bergman, *Fifty Football Plays* (New York: Barnes, 1936), 66–67.

33. Owen and King, *My Kind of Football*, 156–57.

34. "Owen's Alphabet Soup; 'A' Over 'T,'" *Green Bay Press-Gazette*, 24 November 1950, 16.

35. Stanley Grosshandler, "Coach Steve Owen: The Great Innovator," *Football Digest* 2 (March 1973): 98.

36. Owen and King, *My Kind of Football*, 94.

37. Maury Povich, "This Morning," *Washington Post*, 2 December 1938, 23.

38. Owen and King, *My Kind of Football*, 139–40.

39. Grosshandler, "Coach Steve Owen," 96.

40. T. J. Troup, conversation with the author, 2017.

41. Owen and King, *My Kind of Football*.

42. Louis Effrat, "Giant 11 Hands Browns First Shut-Out for Upset Victory at Cleveland," *New York Times*, 2 October 1950, 38.

43. Louis Effrat, "Owen Outlines Defensive Pattern Used by Football Giants in Upset," *New York Times*, 3 October 1950, 49.

44. Rud Rennie, "Giants Rout Packers 23–17 and Win Football Title Before 48,120," *New York Herald Tribune*, 12 December 1938, 19.

45. Jimmy Cannon, "Sports Today," *New York Journal-American*, 19 May 1964, 24.

6. WING MAN

1. Gary Giddins, *Bing Crosby: A Pocketful of Dreams* (Boston: Little, Brown, 2001), 64.

2. Ray Flaherty, *NFL Films Interview*, NFL Films, 1985.

3. "Flaherty Assistant Coach," *New York Times*, 11 August 1933, 20.

4. Flaherty, *NFL Films Interview*.

5. Arthur Sampson, "Success of Flaherty with the Redskins Hinges on His Ability to Handle Men," *Boston Herald*, 25 December 1935, 7.

6. Flaherty, *NFL Films Interview*.

7. Arthur Sampson, "Flaherty Says Much about Redskins between Bites of Beef and Cabbage," *Boston Herald*, undated clipping from Ray Flaherty file, Pro Football Hall of Fame.

8. Paul Craigue, "Redskins Transfer Game to New York," *Boston Globe*, 8 December 1936, 24.

9. Bob Garrison, "Ray Flaherty, Redskins' Coach, Arrives; Promises Washington Great Pro Eleven," *Washington Post*, 17 August 1937, 17.

10. Shirley Povich, "This Morning," *Washington Post*, 19 September 1937, 16.

11. Stanley Woodward, "Giants Could Have Held 'Em by Using 12–7–5–4 Defense," *New York Herald Tribune*, 6 December 1937, 19.

12. Jack Walsh, "Flaherty Once Rejected Redskins' Stock," *Washington Post*, 23 January 1961, A12.

13. "Redskin Reserves May Start against Pirates Here Sunday," *Washington Post*, 24 November 1938, X19.

14. Ray Flaherty, "Flaherty Hopes for Fast Field Sunday," *Washington Star*, 2 December 1938.

15. Flaherty, *NFL Films Interview*.

16. William H. Taylor, "Yes, Says Flaherty, No, Says Halloran, as Strong Men Flee," *New York Herald Tribune*, 4 December 1939, 24.

17. Arthur J. Daley, "Bears 5–7 Choices to Beat Redskins in Play-Off Today," *New York Times*, 8 December 1940, 99.

18. Jack Clary, *Washington Redskins* (New York: Macmillan, 1974), 25.

19. Shirley Povich, "This Morning," *Washington Post*, 5 September 1942, 13.

20. Al Costello, "Confusion Reigns in Locker Room," *Washington Post*, 14 December 1942, 11.

21. Rick Snider, "Redskins' First Coach Returned to Town," *Washington Post*, 8 September 1986, 28.

22. Jack Clary, *Cleveland Browns* (New York: Macmillan, 1973), 25.

23. Shirley Povich, "This Morning," *Washington Post*, 25 December 1946, 8.

24. Rud Rennie, "Yankees Declare Overcaution Cost 11 All-American Title," *New York Herald Tribune*, 24 December 1946, 18.

25. Shirley Povich, "This Morning," *Washington Post*, 17 November 1947, 13.

26. Jesse Abramson, "Yankees–Browns Ban Sneakers on Field Well-Suited for Skating," *New York Herald Tribune*, 15 December 1947, 25.

27. "Flaherty Says Loss of Three Men Cost Him Job," *New York Herald Tribune*, 19 September 1948, B5.

28. "Flaherty New Coach of Rockets, Replacing McKeever in Pro Post," *New York Times*, 30 January 1949, S1.

29. "Hornets Will Buzz: Flaherty," *Chicago Tribune*, 14 July 1949, 35.

30. Don Smith, "Ray Flaherty," *Coffin Corner* 6, no. 5–6 (1984): 2.

31. Joe Holley, *Slingin' Sam: The Life and Times of the Greatest Quarterback Ever to Play the Game* (Austin: University of Texas Press, 2012), 186–87.

32. Flaherty, *NFL Films Interview.*

33. Flaherty, *NFL Films Interview.*

34. Shirley Povich, "This Morning," *Washington Post*, 12 October 1940, 17.

35. Bob Curran, *Pro Football's Rag Days* (New York: Bonanza Books, 1969), 134.

36. Robert C. Zuppke, *Football Technique and Tactics* (Champaign, Ill.: Bailey and Himes, 1924), 169.

37. Flaherty, *NFL Films Interview*; Smith, "Ray Flaherty," 1.

38. Steve Guback, "Ray Flaherty Knows They Remember Him," *Washington Star*, 27 January 1976, 30; Flaherty, *NFL Films Interview.*

39. Flaherty, *NFL Films Interview.*

40. Joe King, "Playing for Pro Grid Championships Is Old Story to Flaherty, Yankee Coach," Cleveland Browns vs. New York Yankees Game Program, 19 December 1946, 14.

41. George Strickler, "Chances Good If They Have Firm Footing," *Chicago Tribune*, 11 December 1937, 21.

42. "Ray Flaherty Sees Victory for Redskins," *Washington Post*, 12 December 1937, SP1; Curran, *Pro Football's Rag Days*, 151.

43. Flaherty, *NFL Films Interview.*

44. William F. Fox, "A Corner in Pigskin," *Indianapolis News*, 20 October 1943, 2.

45. Burton Hawkins, "Win, Lose, or Draw," *Washington Star*, 12 September 1943, 26.

46. Jim Conzelman, "Quick Kicks Put Crimp in Bears, Says Conzelman," *Chicago Tribune*, 14 December 1942, 25.

47. George Solomon, "Redskins of '42 Recall That Championship Season," *Washington Post*, 29 November 1972, C1.

7. BIG MAN OFF CAMPUS

1. Harry March, *Pro Football, Its Ups and Downs: A Lighthearted History of the Post Graduate Game* (Albany, N.Y.: J. B. Lyon, 1934), 144.

2. Harry G. Scott, *Jock Sutherland: Architect of Men* (New York: Exposition, 1954), 17.

3. Scott, *Jock Sutherland.*

4. Scott, *Jock Sutherland.*

5. Scott, *Jock Sutherland*, 51.

6. Scott, *Jock Sutherland*, 53.

7. Scott, *Jock Sutherland*, 102.

8. Gordon McKay "Jock Sutherland to Succeed Pop Warner," *Philadelphia Inquirer*, 3 February 1922, 16.

9. Edwin Pope, *Football's Greatest Coaches* (Atlanta, Ga.: Tupper and Love, 1955).

10. Rob Ruck, *Rooney: A Sporting Life* (Lincoln: University of Nebraska Press, 2010).

11. "Sutherland Offered Job as Pirate Coach," *New York Herald Tribune*, 5 January 1940, 22.

12. Bob Curran, *Pro Football's Rag Days* (New York: Bonanza Books, 1969), 170.

13. "Pros Laud Sutherland," *Pittsburgh Press*, 30 January 1940, 20.

14. "Jock Sutherland Accepts Three-Year Coaching Job with Brooklyn Dodgers," *Daily Press* (Newport News, Va.), 30 January 1940, 6; "Sutherland's Decision Surprises Grid Fans," *Brooklyn Daily Eagle*, 30 January 1940, 10.

15. Ace Parker, *NFL Films Interview*, NFL Films, 2000.

16. Richard Whittingham, *What a Game They Played: Stories of the Early Days of Pro Football by Those Who Were There* (New York: Harper & Row, 1984), 150.

17. Stan Grosshandler, "The Brooklyn Dodgers," *Coffin Corner* 12, no. 3 (1990): 4.

18. Stanley Woodward, "Views of Sport," *New York Herald Tribune*, 16 September 1940, 21.

19. "Topping Invites Parker's Family to Attend Ace's Celebration," *Brooklyn Daily Eagle*, 20 November 1940, 13.

20. John B. Sutherland and William S. Maulsey, "Those Pro's Can Point," *American Legion Magazine* 29 (November 1940): 65.

21. Scott, *Jock Sutherland*, 241.

22. Robert Lyons, *On Any Given Sunday: A Life of Bert Bell* (Philadelphia, Pa.: Temple University Press, 2010), 109.

23. Stuart Leuthner, *Iron Men: Bucko, Crazylegs, and the Boys Recall the Golden Days of Professional Football* (Garden City, N.Y.: Doubleday, 1988), 58.

24. Dan Daly and Bob O'Donnell, *The Pro Football Chronicle: The Complete (Well, Almost) Record of the Best Players, the Greatest Photos, the Hardest Hits, the Biggest Scandals, and the Funniest Stories in Pro Football* (New York: Collier, 1990).

25. Bill Cunningham, "'Jock' Wasn't Happy as a Pro," *Boston Herald*, 12 April 1948, 14.

26. Eddie Beachler, "Sphinx of Football," *Huddle* (September 1947): 3.

27. Scott, *Jock Sutherland*, 126.

28. Roger A. Godin, *The Brooklyn Football Dodgers: The Other "Bums"* (Haworth, N.J.: St. Johann Press, 2003), 138–39.

29. Murray Olderman, *The Running Backs* (Englewood Cliffs, N.J.: Prentice Hall, 1969), 231.

30. Jock Sutherland, "Good Grid Teams Make One Play Set Stage for Next One," *Altoona Tribune*, 15 October 1940, 9.

31. Pope, *Football's Greatest Coaches*, 249.

32. Pope, *Football's Greatest Coaches*, 253.

33. Les Biederman, "Hard Hitting Features Play of Steelers," *Pittsburgh Press*, 27 September 1946, 7.

34. Steve Stinson, *"Bullet" Bill Dudley: The Greatest 60-Minute Man in Football* (Lanham, Md.: Taylor Trade, 2016), 125.

35. Les Biederman, "The Score-Board," *Pittsburgh Press*, 26 March 1940, 25.

36. William H. Taylor, "Dodgers Will Give Sutherland All He Wants, Topping Promises," *New York Herald Tribune*, 1 February 1940, 25.

37. Arthur Sampson, "Sutherland Has Major Problem," *Boston Herald*, 30 January 1940, 20.

38. Stinson, *"Bullet" Bill Dudley*, 123.

39. Myron Cope, *The Game That Was: The Early Days of Pro Football* (New York: World Publishing, 1970), 197.

40. Al Hailey, "'Skins Forced to Don White Jerseys Today," *Washington Post*, 10 November 1940, SP8.

41. Frank O'Gara, "Eagles Beat Steelers for Title," *Philadelphia Inquirer*, 22 December 1947, 33.

8. T-MEN II

1. Ron Fimrite, "A Melding of Men All Suited to a T," *Sports Illustrated* 47 (5 September 1977): 93.

2. "Clark Shaughnessy, Green Kid Who Began at Minnesota," *Star Tribune*, 2 November 1924, 28.

3. Edwin Pope, *Football's Greatest Coaches* (Atlanta, Ga.: Tupper & Love, 1955), 225.

4. Allison Danzig, *The History of American Football: Its Great Teams, Players, and Coaches* (Englewood Cliffs, N.J.: Prentice Hall, 1956).

5. Clark Shaughnessy, *Football in War and Peace* (Clinton, S.C.: Jacobs Press, 1943), 28.

6. Pope, *Football's Greatest Coaches*, 228.

7. "Southern Grid Coach, Star Pianist, Now Works Out His Football Plays to Music," *Montana Standard*, 4 October 1931, 17.

8. Alan Gould, "Sports Slants," *St. Cloud (Minnesota) Times*, 30 December 1930, 12.

9. George Halas, with Gwen Morgan and Arthur Veysey, *Halas by Halas: The Autobiography of George Halas* (New York: McGraw-Hill, 1979), 157.

10. Paul Zimmerman and Peter King, *Dr. Z: The Lost Memoirs of an Irreverent Football Writer* (Chicago: Triumph, 2017), 194.

11. Tom Bennett, "By Football Possessed," *Pro! Magazine* (1973): 3C.

12. Shaughnessy, *Football in War and Peace*; Bennett, "By Football Possessed."

13. Cyclone Covey, *The Wow Boys: The Story of Stanford's Historic 1940 Football Season, Game by Game* (New York: Exposition, 1957); James W. Johnson, *The Wow Boys: A Coach, a Team, and a Turning Point in College Football* (Lincoln: University of Nebraska Press, 2006).

14. Jeff Davis, *Papa Bear: The Life and Legacy of George Halas* (New York: McGraw-Hill, 2005), 168.

15. Russell Newland, "Pop Warner Hops on Shaughnessy Bandwagon," *Los Angeles Times*, 31 October 1940, 30.

16. Fimrite, "A Melding of Men All Suited to a T," 92.

17. Clark Shaughnessy, "Football for Morale," *Esquire* (August 1942): 159.

18. Heartley "Hunk" Anderson and Emil Klosinski, *Notre Dame, Chicago Bears, and "Hunk"* (Los Angeles, Calif.: Panoply Publications, 2014), 163.

19. Shaughnessy, *Football in War and Peace*.

20. Paul Zimmerman, "Shaughnessy Signs as Rams Advisory Coach," *Los Angeles Times*, 30 December 1947, 11.

21. Frank Finch, "Rams Surpass Former Titlists," *Los Angeles Times*, 14 December 1959, C1.

22. Steve Bisheff, *The Los Angeles Rams* (New York: Macmillan, 1973), 106.

23. Ralph Bernstein, "Cockiness May Hurt Eagles," *Des Moines Tribune*, 12 December 1949, 14.

24. Frank Finch, "Shaughnessy Ousted as Ram Coach," *Los Angeles Times*, 19 February 1950, 1.

25. Art Daley, "Packers without No. 1 Line Coach Prospect—Stydahar," *Green Bay Press-Gazette*, 20 February 1950, 13.

26. Bennett, "By Football Possessed," 5C.

27. Bill Schrader, "Basic Football Rallied Bears," *Evansville Courier and Press*, 22 December 1963, 49.

28. Arthur Daley, "Sports of the Times," *New York Times*, 23 April 1958, 44.

29. Kevin Lamb, "Fatherly Advice," *Pro* IV (January 1985): 102.

30. Chuck Johnson, "It's the Defense That Decides Games," *Milwaukee Journal*, 27 September 1959, 59.

31. Bennett, "By Football Possessed," 6C.

32. Bill Gleason, "Shaughnessy Both Aloof Mystic, Practicing Genius," *Chicago American*, 8 December 1962, 19.

33. "End of an Era? Shaughnessy Quits Chicago Bears," *New York Herald Tribune*, 4 December 1962, 12.

34. Edgar Munzel, "'Bears Could Win with Any Kind of System,'" *Chicago Herald American*, 23 December 1941, 14.

35. Harold Parrott, "Both Sides," *Brooklyn Daily Eagle*, 8 September 1941, 15.

36. Shaughnessy, "Football for Morale," 159.

37. Harry Cross, "Coaches Brew Tempest of T at Writers Lunch," *New York Herald Tribune*, 31 October 1944, 25.

38. "T Hit Peak in '45 Football Men Say," *New York Times*, 4 December 1945, 35; "Defense Catching Up with T Claims Single Wing Advocate," *Washington Post*, 14 May 1946, 14.

39. "Football Coaches Debate T Formation," *New York Times*, 23 March 1948, 35.

40. Stanley Woodward, "Football Here and There," *New York Herald Tribune*, 8 October 1941, 26.

41. Allison Danzig, *Oh, How They Played the Game: The Early Days of Football and the Heroes Who Made It Great* (New York: Macmillan, 1971), 399.

42. Paul Zimmerman, "T Time for the NFL," in Will McDonough and Peter King, eds., *75 Seasons: The Complete Story of the National Football League, 1920–1995* (Atlanta, Ga.: Turner Publications, 1994), 70.

43. Clark Shaughnessy, Ralph Jones, and George Halas, *The Modern "T" Formation with Man-in-Motion* (Chicago: Shaughnessy, Jones, and Halas, 1941), iii.

44. Jimmy Conzelman, "Jimmy Conzelman, in First Article for Star-Times, Passes on Some Advice from Stanford Grid Coach," *St Louis Star and Times*, 10 March 1941, 13.

45. George Halas, "All-Stars! Here Is a Challenge from the Bears," *Chicago Tribune*, 3 August 1941, 23.

46. William Fay, "Anderson Puts Heat on Bears but Cools Pups," *Chicago Tribune*, 5 August 1947, 23.

47. George Halas, "Halas Tells What Modern Football's Basic Formation—the T—Is All About," *Chicago Tribune*, 4 February 1967, 39.

48. Shaughnessy, Jones, and Halas, *The Modern "T" Formation with Man-in-Motion*.

49. Sid Luckman, *The "T" Formation* (Chicago: Montgomery Ward, 1944), 3.

50. Eddie Brietz, "Trying to Get Bowl Teams for Contest against Bears," *Green Bay Press-Gazette*, 12 December 1940, 25; Harry Grayson, "Herb Kopf Caught Passes to Win Key Games for Little W. and J. on Unbeaten Team as Freshman," *Brownsville Herald*, 7 January 1944, 13.

51. "Football Hard Work for Fans, Too," *New York Times*, 2 October 1955, S8; "Warner Believes T Inferior to Other Grid Systems," *Democrat and Chronicle*, 30 November 1947, 50.

52. Bob Wills, "Sports an' Stuff," *Raleigh Register*, 3 November 1946, 11.

53. Warren Brown, "What's Happening at Halas U.?" *Sport* (November 1954): 87.

54. "Fifteen-Yard First Downs Seen as Trend in Wide Open Game," *Washington Post*, 28 October 1943, 16.

55. Frank Finch, "Shaughnessy to Use Four Ends, Two Quarterbacks on Offense," *Los Angeles Times*, 21 June 1949.

56. Shaughnessy, "Football for Morale," 22.

57. William Furlong, "How the War in France Changed Football Forever," *Smithsonian* 16 (February 1986).

58. Davis, *Papa Bear*, 369.

59. Buddy Diliberto, "Shaughnessy: A Football Genius," *Times-Picayune*, 18 December 1959, 33.

60. Gary Pomerantz, "Petitbon Drills," *Washington Post*, 19 October 1984, C1.

61. Arthur Daley, "Bears Overwhelm Redskins by Record Score to Capture World Football Title," *New York Times*, 9 December 1940, 28.

62. "Redskins Surliness Pleases Ray Flaherty," *Washington Post*, 8 December 1940, X1.

63. Myron Cope, *The Game That Was: The Early Days of Pro Football* (New York: World Publishing, 1970), 179.

64. Merrell W. Whittlesey, "Team Quit Is Charge of Marshall," *Washington Post*, 9 December 1940, 17.

65. Bob Oates, "Halas Traces Rise of Pro Football," *Los Angeles Times*, 30 April 1970, 71.

66. Brown, "What's Happening at Halas U.?" 87.

67. George Kirksey, "George Halas, Once 'Just a Pro Coach,' Now National Figure as Result of Bear Victory," *Washington Post*, 13 December 1940, 27.

9. PLAYERS' COACH

1. Bob Considine, "On the Line with Considine," *Washington Post*, 25 November 1942, 17.

2. Bob Curran, *Pro Football's Rag Days* (New York: Bonanza Books, 1969), 177.

3. Jim Conzelman Jr., author interview, 18 July 2018.

4. Dutch Sternaman, Jimmy Conzelman file, undated, Dutch Sternaman Collection, Pro Football Hall of Fame.

5. Rocky Wolfe, "Coach of the Year," *Pro Football Illustrated* (1947); Curran, *Pro Football's Rag Days*.

6. "Flanigan Fires Coach Coughlin," *Moline Dispatch*, 19 October 1921, 15.

7. "Lauer and Lyle, Pair of Rock Island Stars, Play with Green Bay on Sunday," *Green Bay Press-Gazette*, 24 November 1922, 11.

8. "Jimmy Conzelman 'Most Valuable Man' on Greatest Team in Pro Football," *St. Louis Post-Dispatch*, 9 December 1928, 21.

9. Walter W. Smith, "Dr. Sharpe, Bullman, and Davis to Remain on Staff at Hilltop," *St. Louis Star and Times*, 22 January 1932, 20.

10. Joe Ziemba, *When Football Was Football* (Chicago: Triumph, 1999), 210.

11. Ziemba, *When Football Was Football*, 211, 207.

12. Ziemba, *When Football Was Football*, 242; James G. Conzelman, "The Young Man's Mental and Physical Approach to War," *Pro Football Hall of Fame*, 10 May 1942, www.profootballhof.com/news/the-young-man-s-mental-and-physical-approach-to-war/ (1 January 2018).

13. Harry Grayson, "Grayson's Scoreboard," *Columbus Telegram*, 3 April 1942, 7.

14. Arthur Daley, "Sports of the Times," *New York Times*, 27 January 1943, 28.

15. Shirley Povich, "This Morning," *Washington Post*, 6 July 1943, 16.

16. Jimmy Conzelman, "I'd Rather Coach the Pros," *Saturday Evening Post* 219 (19 October 1946): 21.

17. Kent Somers, "Cardinals Glory," *Arizona Republic*, 10 August 1997, 43.

18. John Branch, "The One and Only," *St. Louis Post-Dispatch*, 18 January 2009, D1.

19. "Jimmy Conzelman Nominated by Halas as 'Coach of the Year,'" *St. Louis Post-Dispatch*, 21 December 1947, 60.

20. Ziemba, *When Football Was Football*, 282.

21. Conzelman Jr., author interview.

22. Ziemba, *When Football Was Football*, 364.

23. Conzelman Jr., author interview.

24. "Conzelman Quits as Card Pilot," *Detroit Free Press*, 8 January 1949, 14.

25. "Seven Are Elected to Football Hall of Fame," *Cambridge Daily Jeffersonian*, 28 February 1964, 11.

26. Conzelman Jr., author interview.

27. Kent Somers, "Renaissance-Man Coach Coaxed Great Effort from Players," *Arizona Republic*, 10 August 1997, 53.

28. Ziemba, *When Football Was Football*, 275.

29. Jerry Green, *Detroit Lions* (New York: Macmillan, 1973), 132.

30. John Hogrogian, "The Steamroller," *Coffin Corner* 2 (March 1980): 2.

31. Al Hailey, "Flaherty Fears Birds' Varied Attack," *Washington Post*, 9 October 1940, 23; "Football Giants Face Cards Today," *New York Times*, 29 November 1942, S4.

32. George Kirksey, "Grid's Famed T Studied," *Arizona Republic*, 5 September 1941, 14.

33. Untitled and undated newspaper clipping, Jimmy Conzelman file, Pro Football Hall of Fame.

34. Hugh Fullerton Jr., "Sports Roundup," *Freeport Journal-Standard*, 15 September 1947, 10.

35. Paul Christman, *Tricks in Passing* (Chicago: Ziff-Davis, 1948).

36. Harry Warren, "Trippi Zips 44, 75 Yds. to Scores," *Chicago Tribune*, 29 December 1947, 25.

37. Ziemba, *When Football Was Football*.

38. "Delayed Smashes at Eight-Man Line Brought Victory, Conzelman Says," *New York Times*, 29 December 1947, 25.

39. Warren, "Trippi Zips 44, 75 Yds. to Scores," 25.

40. Jerry Liska, "Eagles Did Everything but Beat Cards—Neale," *Philadelphia Inquirer*, 29 December 1947, 20; Frank O'Gara, "Angsman, Trippi Score Two Each; Thompson Completes 27 Passes," *Philadelphia Inquirer*, 29 December 1947, 21.

41. Harry Warren, "Cards Hear a Halftime Tune: 'It's Magic'?" *Chicago Tribune*, 13 December 1948, 54.

10. COUNTERPUNCH

1. Greasy Neale and Tom Meany, "Football Is My Life," *Collier's* 128 (3 November 1951): 29.

2. Neale and Meany, "Football Is My Life," 29.

3. Tom Swope, "Neale Fought Mound Ace While a Rookie," unmarked clipping, 31 December 1949, Greasy Neale file, Pro Football Hall of Fame.

4. "Angry Phil Fans Beat Red Player Who Struck Youth," *Philadelphia Inquirer*, 25 June 1920, 14.

5. Frank Graham, "One for the Book," *Sport* 10 (January 1951): 74.

6. Greasy Neale and Tom Meany, "Coaching from Muskingum to Yale," *Collier's* 128 (10 November 1951): 71.

7. Gordon Mackay, "Presidents' 11 Typical of Coach," *Philadelphia Inquirer*, 8 January 1922, 19.

8. Lynn A. Wittenburg, "Oh, My, Oh, My, What a Headache!" *Portsmouth Times*, 16 October 1930, 8.

9. Neale and Meany, "Coaching from Muskingum to Yale."

10. Allison Danzig, "Neale Gains a Niche in Football," *New York Times*, 3 March 1967, 39.

11. Bob Curran, *Pro Football's Rag Days* (New York: Bonanza Books, 1969), 42.

12. Greasy Neale and Tom Meany, "The Best Pros I Ever Saw," *Collier's* 128 (17 November 1951): 58.

13. Curran, *Pro Football's Rag Days*, 43.

14. Perry Lewis, "Eagles Drill on Stopping Frankie Reagan, Then Go to Brooklyn and See Grid Game," *Philadelphia Inquirer*, 10 September 1941, 39.

15. Matthew Algeo, *Last Team Standing: How the Eagles and the Steelers—the Steagles—Saved Pro Football during World War II* (Cambridge, Mass: Da Capo, 2006), 80.

16. David Cohen, *Rugged and Enduring: The Eagles, the Browns, and Five Years of Football* (Philadelphia, Pa.: Xlibris, 2001), 27.

17. Cohen, *Rugged and Enduring*, 27.

18. Algeo, *Last Team Standing*, 81.

19. "Neale Cuts His Salary," *New York Times*, 9 September 1944, 19.

20. Arthur Daley, "Friendly Rivals and Unfriendly Rivalry," *New York Times*, 4 December 1949, S2.

21. Stan Baumgartner, "Life Story of Earle (Greasy) Neale: Coach of Champions," in *Official National Football League Pro Record and Rule Book* (St. Louis, Mo.: Charles C. Spink & Son, 1950), 47.

22. Louis Effrat, "Football Coaches Cannot Agree on Unlimited Substitution Rule," *New York Times*, 2 November 1948, 37.

23. Cohen, *Rugged and Enduring*, 11.

24. Jack Clary, *Cleveland Browns* (New York: Macmillan, 1973), 63.

25. Al Buck, "Eagles' Owner, Neale Battle Following Giants' Victory," *New York Post*, 27 November 1950, 56.

26. "Wire Wiped Out Life's Work—Neale," *Washington Post*, 6 March 1951, 17.

27. Neale and Meany, "Football Is My Life."

28. Algeo, *Last Team Standing*, 80.

29. Mark Kram, "Players Relate Stories about Winningest Eagles Coach," *Philadelphia Daily News*, 12 October 2004, 72.

30. Baumgartner, "Life Story of Earle (Greasy) Neale," 48.

31. Philadelphia Eagles Media Guide, 1949, 22.

32. Richard Whittingham, *What a Game They Played: Stories of the Early Days of Pro Football by Those Who Were There* (New York: Harper & Row, 1984), 163.

33. Cohen, *Rugged and Enduring*, 26.

34. Neale and Meany, "The Best Pros I Ever Saw," 25.

35. Harry Grayson, "Neale Switched to T after Studying Films for Five Months," *Franklin News-Herald*, 3 November 1948, 8; Bob French, "'We've Got an Offense,' Eagles' Coach Asserts," *Philadelphia Inquirer*, 11 September 1941, 27.

36. Cohen, *Rugged and Enduring*, 45.

37. Arthur Daley, "Something Borrowed," *New York Times*, 21 December 1956, 30.

38. Shirley Povich, "This Morning," *Washington Post*, 22 November 1944, 10.

39. Shirley Povich, "This Morning," *Washington Post*, 25 December 1947, 14.

40. Neale and Meany, "The Best Pros I Ever Saw," 58; Kram, "Players Relate Stories about Winningest Eagles Coach," 72.

41. Vic Sears, *NFL Films Interview*, NFL Films, 1999.

42. Glenn Presnell, *NFL Films Interview*, NFL Films, 1998.

43. Hugh Brown, "Neale Reveals Giant Mistakes," *Philadelphia Bulletin*, 22 October 1963, 70.

44. Myron Cope, *The Game That Was: The Early Days of Pro Football* (New York: World Publishing, 1970), 160.

45. Stuart Leuthner, *Iron Men: Bucko, Crazylegs, and the Boys Recall the Golden Days of Professional Football* (Garden City, N.Y.: Doubleday, 1988), 145.

46. "Victory Due to Fine Team-Work Says Coach Neale of the Eagles," *New York Times*, 22 December 1947, 31.

47. Frank O'Gara, "Record 38,230 Watch Eagles Top Rams, 38–14," *Philadelphia Inquirer*, 7 November 1949, 32.

EPILOGUE

1. Shelby Strother, *NFL's Top 40: The Greatest Pro Football Games Ever Played* (New York: Viking, 1988), 37.

2. Paul Brown, with Jack Clary, *PB: The Paul Brown Story* (New York: Atheneum, 1979), 199.

3. Brown, with Clary, *PB*, 202.

4. NFL Films, *A Football Life: Paul Brown*, NFL Films, 2015.

5. Bob Yonkers, "Brown Maintains Winning Pace in Professional Football Ranks," New York Yankees at Cleveland Browns Game Program, 22 December 1946; Don Sanders, "Too Light to Play Football at Ohio State, Paul Brown Now Returns as Its Head Coach," *Muncie Evening Press*, 15 January 1941.

6. George Cantor, *Paul Brown: The Man Who Invented Modern Football* (Chicago: Triumph, 2008), 21.

7. Brown, with Clary, *PB*, 143.

8. Marla Ridenour, "Paul Brown . . . a Contradiction," *Akron Beacon Journal*, 11 September 1999, D5.

9. David Cohen, *Rugged and Enduring: The Eagles, the Browns, and Five Years of Football* (Philadelphia, Pa.: Xlibris, 2001), 104.

10. Jack Clary, *The Gamemakers* (Chicago: Follett, 1976), 22.

11. Brown, with Clary, *PB*, 7.

12. Gordon Cobbledick, "12th Man in the Huddle," *Collier's* 124 (12 November 1949): 20–21.

BIBLIOGRAPHY

Algeo, Matthew. *Last Team Standing: How the Eagles and the Steelers—the Steagles—Saved Pro Football during World War II*. Cambridge, Mass.: Da Capo, 2006.

Anderson, Heartley "Hunk," and Emil Klosinski. *Notre Dame, Chicago Bears, and "Hunk."* Los Angeles, Calif.: Panoply Publications, 2014.

Baker, Jim, and Bernard M. Corbett. *The Most Memorable Games in Giants History: The Oral History of a Legendary Team*. New York: Bloomsbury, 2010.

Barnes, Howard L. *A Documentary Scrapbook of Football in Frankford*. Philadelphia, Pa.: Historical Society of Frankford, 1985.

Barry, Jay. "A Rose Bowl Star—56 Years Ago." *Ebony* (January 1972): 106+.

Baumgartner, Stan. "Life Story of Earle (Greasy) Neale: Coach of Champions." In *Official National Football League Pro Record and Rule Book*, 1–48. St. Louis, Mo.: Charles C. Spink & Son, 1950.

Beachler, Eddie. "Jock Sutherland—'T' Buster!" *Huddle* (December 1946): 2–3.

———. "Sphinx of Football." *Huddle* (September 1947): 2+.

Becker, Carl M. "Carl Brumbaugh: A Darned Good Quarterback." *Coffin Corner* 17, no. 5 (1995): 1–11.

———. *Home and Away: The Rise and Fall of Professional Football on the Banks of the Ohio, 1919–1934*. Athens: Ohio University Press, 1998.

Bennett, Tom. "By Football Possessed." *Pro! Magazine* (1973): C–6C.

———. *The Pro Style: The Complete Guide to Understanding National Football League Strategy*. Englewood Cliffs, N.J.: Prentice Hall, 1976.

Bergman, Arthur J. "Dutch," ed. *Fifty Football Plays*. New York: Barnes, 1936.

Bisheff, Steve. *The Los Angeles Rams*. New York: Macmillan, 1973.

Brichford, Maynard J. *Bob Zuppke: The Life and Football Legacy of the Illinois Coach*. Jefferson, N.C.: McFarland, 2009.

Brown, Paul, and Bill Fay. "I Watch the Quarterbacks." *Collier's* 136 (28 October 1955): 66–71.

Brown, Paul, and Harry T. Paxton. "I Call the Plays for the Browns." *Saturday Evening Post* 226 (12 December 1953): 30+.

Brown, Paul, with Jack Clary. *PB: The Paul Brown Story*. New York: Atheneum, 1979.

Brown, Warren. "What's Happening at Halas U.?" *Sport* (November 1954): 87.

Camp, Walter, and Lorin F. Deland. *Football*. Boston: Houghton Mifflin, 1896.

Campbell, Jim. "John Alexander: Pro Football Pioneer." *Coffin Corner* 16, no. 2 (1995): 1–9.

———. "Oh, Those X's and O's! Or the Evolution of Pro Football Strategy." *Coffin Corner* 19, no. 4 (1997): 1–8.

Cantor, George. *Paul Brown: The Man Who Invented Modern Football.* Chicago: Triumph, 2008.

Carroll, Bob. *The 60-Yard Circus.* Pro Football Researchers Association, www. profootballresearchers.org/articles/1932 Season.pdf (1 January 2018).

———. *Giants on the Gridiron.* Pro Football Researchers Association, www. profootballresearchers.org/articles/Giants_On_The_Gridiron.pdf (1 January 2018).

———. *The Grange War: 1926.* Pro Football Researchers Association, www. profootballresearchers.org/articles/The_Grange_War.pdf (1 January 2018).

———. "Ollie's All-Stars." *Coffin Corner* 5, no. 7 (July 1983): 7–8.

———. *The Packers Crash Through.* Pro Football Researchers Association, www. profootballresearchers.org/articles/The_Packers_Crash_Through.pdf (1 January 2018).

———. "Potsy Clark: A Success Story." *Coffin Corner* 7, no. 2 (March–April 1985): 5–8.

———. *Triumph of the T: 1940.* Pro Football Researchers Association, www. profootballresearchers.org/articles/Triumph_Of_The_T.pdf (1 January 2018).

Carroll, Bob, Michael Gershman, David Neft, and John Thorn. *Total Football: The Official Encyclopedia of the National Football League.* New York: HarperCollins, 1997.

Carroll, John M. *Fritz Pollard: Pioneer in Racial Advancement.* Urbana: University of Illinois Press, 1992.

———. "Fritz Pollard and the Brown Bombers." *Coffin Corner* 12, no. 1 (1990): 14–17.

———. "Two American Heroes: Red Grange and Fritz Pollard." *Coffin Corner* 10, no. 4 (1988): 1–5.

Chamberlin, Guy. *Radio Interview.* NFL Films, 1965.

Christl, Cliff. "Lambeau: More than a Name." *Voyageur* 17, no. 2 (June 2001): 10+.

———. "Lambeau's 'Notre Dame Box Offense' Not a Simple Scheme." *Cliff's Notes,* 17 March 2016, http://www.packers.com/news-and-events/article-cliffs-notes/article-1/ Lambeaus-Notre-Dame-Box-offense-not-a-simple-scheme/7de53247-6024-4104-b572-82582d8a1660 (12 February 2018).

———. *Packers Heritage Trail: The Town, the Team, the Fans from Lambeau to Lombardi.* Stevens Point, Wisc.: KCI Sports Publishing, 2017.

Christman, Paul. *Tricks in Passing.* Chicago: Ziff-Davis, 1948.

Clark, George "Potsy." *Football: A Book for Players and Football Fans.* New York: Rand McNally, 1935.

Clary, Jack. *Cleveland Browns.* New York: Macmillan, 1973.

———. *The Gamemakers.* Chicago: Follett, 1976.

———. *Washington Redskins.* New York: Macmillan, 1974.

Cobbledick, Gordon. "12th Man in the Huddle." *Collier's* 124 (12 November 1949): 20+.

Cohen, David. *Rugged and Enduring: The Eagles, the Browns, and Five Years of Football.* Philadelphia, Pa.: Xlibris, 2001.

Conzelman, James G. "The Young Man's Mental and Physical Approach to War." *Pro Football Hall of Fame,* May 10, 1942, www.profootballhof.com/news/the-young-man-s-mental-and-physical-approach-to-war/ (1 January 2018).

Conzelman, Jimmy. "I'd Rather Coach the Pros." *Saturday Evening Post* 219 (19 October 1946): 21+.

———. "That's Football for You." *Saturday Evening Post* 210 (30 October 1937): 16+.

———. "To the Backs, Bless 'Em." *Saturday Evening Post* 211 (5 November 1938): 18+.

———. "Who's Yellow?" *Cosmopolitan* (November 1948): 64+.

Cope, Myron. *The Game That Was: The Early Days of Pro Football.* New York: World Publishing, 1970.

Covey, Cyclone. *The Wow Boys: The Story of Stanford's Historic 1940 Football Season, Game by Game.* New York: Exposition, 1957.

Crichton, Kyle. "For Love and Money." *Colliers* 22 (1 December 1934): 24, 48.

Curran, Bob. *Pro Football's Rag Days.* New York: Bonanza Books, 1969.

Daly, Dan. *The National Forgotten League: Entertaining Stories and Observations for Pro Football's First Fifty Years.* Lincoln: University of Nebraska Press, 2012.

Daly, Dan, and Bob O'Donnell. *The Pro Football Chronicle: The Complete (Well, Almost) Record of the Best Players, the Greatest Photos, the Hardest Hits, the Biggest Scandals, and the Funniest Stories in Pro Football*. New York: Collier, 1990.

D'Amato, Gary, and Cliff Christl. *Mudbaths and Bloodbaths: The Inside Story of the Bears–Packers Rivalry*. Madison, Wisc.: Prairie Oak Press, 1997.

Danzig, Allison. *The History of American Football: Its Great Teams, Players, and Coaches*. Englewood Cliffs, N.J.: Prentice Hall, 1956.

———. *Oh, How They Played the Game: The Early Days of Football and the Heroes Who Made It Great*. New York: Macmillan, 1971.

Davis, Jeff. *Papa Bear: The Life and Legacy of George Halas*. New York: McGraw-Hill, 2005.

Davis, Russ. "Little Town That Leads 'Em." *Saturday Evening Post* 213 (30 November 1940): 34+.

Deford, Frank. "I Don't Date Any Women under 48." *Sports Illustrated* 47 (5 December 1977): 47+.

Des Jardins, Julie. *Walter Camp: Football and the Modern Man*. New York: Oxford University Press, 2015.

Devine, Tommy. "The Man of Many Jobs." *Sportfolio* (December 1947): 74–84.

Dexter, Charles. "Steve Owen 'In the Giants' Locker Room.'" *Sport* 14 (January 1953): 16–19.

Didinger, Ray. *The Eagles Encyclopedia*. Philadelphia, Pa.: Temple University Press, 2005.

———. *The Pittsburgh Steelers*. New York: Macmillan, 1974.

Dooley, Eddie. "Football Systems Are the Bunk." *Liberty* 18 (18 October 1941): 16–17.

Dudley, Bill. *NFL Films Interview*. NFL Films, 2000.

———. *TNT Interview*. NFL Films, 1994.

Dunscomb, George. "Shaughnessy behind the Eight Ball." *Saturday Evening Post* 214 (1 November 1941): 18+.

Eisner, Michael. "Giant of the Decade—1940s: Steve Owen." *Gameday* (23 October 1994): 10.

Fay, William Cullen. "Press Box Quarterback." *Saturday Evening Post* 219 (23 November 1946): 28+.

Fimrite, Ron. "A Melding of Men All Suited to a T." Sports *Illustrated* 47 (5 September 1977): 90–100.

Finder, Chuck. *The Steelers Encyclopedia*. Philadelphia, Pa.: Temple University Press, 2012.

Finoli, David. *When Pitt Ruled the Gridiron: Jock Sutherland's Five-Time National Champions, 1929–1937*. Jefferson, N.C.: McFarland, 2015.

Flaherty, Ray. *NFL Films Interview*. NFL Films, 1985.

Frank, Stanley. "The Man Who Hates to Lose." *True* (1949): 58+.

Friedman, Benny. *The Passing Game*. New York: Steinfeld, 1931.

———. "The Professional Touch." *Collier's* 90 (15 October 1932): 16+.

Friedman, Benny, and Burton Benjamin. "You Can Beat the System." *Collier's* 110 (10 October 1942): 21–22.

Friedman, Benny, and Bill Davidson. "The Pros Have It." *Collier's* 106 (19 October 1940): 23+.

———. "Rational Defense." *Collier's* 108 (1 November 1941): 24+.

Friedman, Benny, and John B. Kennedy. "Pro and Coin." *Collier's* 92 (25 November 1933): 24+.

Friedman, Dick. *The Coach Who Strangled the Bulldog: How Harvard's Percy Haughton Beat Yale and Reinvented Football*. Lanham, Md.: Rowman & Littlefield, 2018.

Furlong, William. "How the War in France Changed Football Forever." *Smithsonian* 16 (February 1986): 125+.

———. "Last Puritan." *Sports Illustrated* 24 (31 January 1966): 12–17.

Giddins, Gary. *Bing Crosby: A Pocketful of Dreams*. Boston: Little, Brown, 2001.

Gifford, Frank, and Harry Waters. *The Whole Ten Yards*. New York: Random House, 1993.

Godin, Roger A. *The Brooklyn Football Dodgers: The Other "Bums."* Haworth, N.J.: St. Johann Press, 2003.

Gottehrer, Barry. *The Giants of New York: The History of Professional Football's Most Fabulous Dynasty*. New York: Putnam, 1963.

Graham, Frank. "One for the Book." *Sport* 10 (January 1951): 36+.

―――. "Steve Owen: The Man Behind the Giants." *Sport* 3 (December 1947): 46–49.

Grange, Red. *CBS Interview*. NFL Films, 1978.

Green, Jerry. *Detroit Lions*. New York: Macmillan, 1973.

Green Bay Football Corporation. "Andrews Critical of Bays' Defense." *Green Bay Packers Bulletin* 4, no. 4 (4 October 1931): 1.

Greenberg, Murray. *Passing Game: Benny Friedman and the Transformation of Football*. New York: PublicAffairs, 2008.

Griffith, Corrine. *My Life with the Redskins*. New York: Barnes, 1947.

Griffith, Major John L., and George "Potsy" Clark. *Football Defense* (Wilson Athletic Library). Chicago: T. E. Wilson, 1923.

―――. *Football Forward Passing* (Wilson Athletic Library). Chicago: T. E. Wilson, 1923.

―――. *Football Offense* (Wilson Athletic Library). Chicago: T. E. Wilson, 1923.

―――. *Fundamentals of Football Training* (Wilson Athletic Library). Chicago: T. E. Wilson, 1923.

―――. *How to Play Quarterback and Other Football Positions* (Wilson Athletic Library). Chicago: T. E. Wilson, 1923.

Grosshandler, Stanley. "The Brooklyn Dodgers." *Coffin Corner* 12, no. 3 (1990): 3–11.

―――. "Coach Steve Owen: The Great Innovator." *Football Digest* 2 (March 1973): 96–100.

―――. "Conversations about the A." *Coffin Corner* 5, no. 6 (June 1983): 8+.

Hachten, William A. "A Superior Season: A New York Giant Remembers His Rookie Year." *Wisconsin Magazine of History* 86, no. 1 (Autumn 2002): 24–39.

Haggerty, Michael. "Johnsos Was More Than Just Halas's Assistant." *Chicago Bear Report* (10 January 1985): 15.

Halas, George. "73–0." *Saturday Evening Post* 214 (6 December 1941): 24+.

―――. "The Era of Red Grange." *Saturday Evening Post* 230 (30 November 1957): 30.

―――. "Lessons in Football." 21-part series. *Chicago Daily Journal*. 30 September–13 November 1922.

―――. "My 40 Years in Pro Football." *Saturday Evening Post* 230 (23 November 1957): 34.

―――. "Quarterbacking a New Industry." *Nation's Business* (December 1966): 53+.

―――. "T―for Total Offense Football." In *1953 Yearbook of the National Football League*. New York: Don Spencer Company, 1953.

Halas, George, and George Dunscomb. "Hold What Line?" *Saturday Evening Post* 212 (2 December 1939): 18+

Halas, George, with Gwen Morgan and Arthur Veysey. *Halas by Halas: The Autobiography of George Halas*. New York: McGraw-Hill, 1979.

Haughton, Percy D. *Football and How to Watch It*. Boston: Marshall Jones, 1922.

Hein, Mel. *NFL Films Interview*. NFL Films, 1983.

Hewitt, Bill, and Red Smith. "Don't Send My Boy to Halas." *Saturday Evening Post* 217 (21 October 1944): 22+.

Hickok, Ralph. *Vagabond Halfback: The Saga of Johnny Blood McNally*. [United States]: CreateSpace, 2017.

Hogrogian, John. "The Steamroller." *Coffin Corner* 2, no. 3 (March 1980): 1–8.

Holland, Gerald. "Greasy Neale: Nothing to Prove, Nothing to Ask." *Sports Illustrated* 21 (24 August 1964): 32–39.

―――. "How to Take a Biscuit Apart and Put It Back Just Like It Was." *Sports Illustrated* 15 (18 September 1961): 94–110.

Hollander, Zander, and Phyllis Hollander. *They Dared to Lead: America's Black Athletes*. New York: Grosset & Dunlap, 1972.

Holley, Joe. *Slingin' Sam: The Life and Times of the Greatest Quarterback Ever to Play the Game*. Austin: University of Texas Press, 2012.

"Jimmy Conzelman." *Look* (6 October 1942).

Johnson, James W. *The Wow Boys: A Coach, a Team, and a Turning Point in College Football*. Lincoln: University of Nebraska Press, 2006.

Jones, Ralph. *Basketball from a Coaching Standpoint*. Champaign: University of Illinois Press, 1916.

Kiely, Ed. "Steelers Have Perfect Parlay." *Huddle* (July 1947): 5+.

King, Peter. *Football: A History of the Professional Game*. New York: Bishop Books, 1997.

Klosinski, Emil. "A Hunk of History: Hunk Anderson." *Coffin Corner* 3, no. 2 (1981): 1–5.

Kryk, John. *Natural Enemies: Major College Football's Oldest, Fiercest Rivaly—Michigan vs. Notre Dame*. Lanham, Md.: Taylor Trade, 2004.

———. *Stagg vs. Yost: The Birth of Cutthroat Football*. Lanham, Md.: Rowman & Littlefield, 2015.

Lamb, Kevin. "Fatherly Advice." *Pro* IV (January 1985): 102.

Lambeau, Curly. "These Great Plays Will Win for Grammar and High School Teams." *True Sport Picture Stories* 3, no. 5 (January/February 1946): 3–8.

Leuthner, Stuart. *Iron Men: Bucko, Crazylegs, and the Boys Recall the Golden Days of Professional Football*. Garden City, N.Y.: Doubleday, 1988.

Luckman, Sid. *Luckman at Quarterback: Football as a Sport and Career*. Chicago: Ziff-Davis, 1949.

———. *Passing for Touchdowns*. Chicago: Ziff-Davis, 1948.

———. *The "T" Formation*. Chicago: Montgomery Ward, 1944.

———. *TNT Interview*. NFL Films, 1994.

Lyons, Robert. *On Any Given Sunday: A Life of Bert Bell*. Philadelphia, Pa.: Temple University Press, 2010.

MacCambridge, Michael. *America's Game: The Epic Story of How Pro Football Captured a Nation*. New York: Random House, 2004.

March, Harry. *Pro Football, Its Ups and Downs: A Lighthearted History of the Post Graduate Game*. Albany, N.Y.: J. B. Lyon, 1934.

McCaskey, Patrick. *Pillars of the NFL: Coaches Who Have Won Three or More Championships*. Crystal Lake, Ill.: Sporting Chance Press, 2014.

McClellan, Keith. *The Sunday Game: At the Dawn of Professional Football*. Akron, Ohio: University of Akron Press, 1998.

McDonough, Will, and Peter King. *75 Seasons: The Complete Story of the National Football League, 1920–1995*. Atlanta, Ga.: Turner Publications, 1994.

Metzger, Sol. "Man in Motion." *Colliers* 88 (12 December 1931): 22.

Miller, Jeffrey J. *Pop Warner: A Life on the Gridiron*. Jefferson, N.C.: McFarland, 2015.

Moseley, Seth H., II. "Coach of a Different Color." *Gameday* 14, no. 11 (1983): 2A+.

Murdock, Gene. "The Year 'Greasy' Neale Was Fired." *Pro Football Digest* (April–May 1968): 35–38.

Neale, Greasy, and Tom Meany. "The Best Pros I Ever Saw." *Collier's* 128 (17 November 1951): 24+.

———. "Coaching from Muskingum to Yale." *Collier's* 128 (10 November 1951): 71–101.

———. "Football Is My Life." *Collier's* 128 (3 November 1951): 28–29.

Neft, David S., Richard M. Cohen, and Rick Korch. *The Football Encyclopedia: The Complete Year-by-Year History of Professional Football from 1892 to the Present*. New York: St. Martin's, 1994.

Newell, Mark. "100 Years of Football Development." *American Football Coach* 5 (December 1999): 23–25.

Newman, Harry. *NFL Films Interview*. NFL Films, 1999.

NFL Films. *A Football Life: Paul Brown*. NFL Films, 2015.

Oates, Bob. *Football in America: Game of the Century*. Coal Valley, Ill.: Quality Sports Publications, 1999.

Olderman, Murray. *The Defenders*. Englewood Cliffs, N.J.: Prentice Hall, 1973.

———. *The Pro Quarterback*. Englewood Cliffs, N.J.: Prentice Hall, 1966.

———. *The Running Backs*. Englewood Cliffs, N.J.: Prentice Hall, 1969.

Oriard, Michael. *King Football: Sport and Spectacle in the Golden Age of Radio and Newsreels, Movies and Magazines, the Weekly, and the Daily Press*. Chapel Hill: University of North Carolina Press, 2001.

O'Toole, Andrew. *Paul Brown: The Rise and Fall and Rise again of Football's Most Innovative Coach*. Cincinnati, Ohio: Clerisy Press, 2008.

Owen, Steve. "Pro Football." *Sport* (November 1950): 18+.

Owen, Steve, and Arthur Daley. "Keeping the Foot in Football." *Collier's* 110 (31 October 1942): 22–24.

———. "We Play for Pay—but We Want to Win!" *Liberty* 14 (30 October 1937): 53–54.

Owen, Steve, and Joe King. *My Kind of Football*. New York: David McKay, 1952.

Parker, Ace. *NFL Films Interview*. NFL Films, 2000.

Patty, Tom. "Winners (Splish!) and Still (Splash!) Champions." *Pro* (22 December 1974): 3C+.

Peterson, Robert. *Pigskin: The Early Years of Pro Football*. New York: Oxford University Press, 1997.

PFRA Research. *Ditto: 1923. Pro Football Researchers Association*, www.profootballresearchers.org/articles/Ditto.pdf (1 January 2018).

———. *A Few More Loose Ends: 1922. Pro Football Researchers Association*, www.profootballresearchers.org/articles/A_Few_More_Loose_Ends.pdf (1 January 2018).

———. *Goodbye, Bulldogs, Hello: 1924. Pro Football Researchers Association*, www.profootballresearchers.org/articles/Goodbye_Bulldogs,_Hello.pdf (1 January 2018).

———. *Nagurski's Debut and Rockne's Lesson. Pro Football Researchers Association*, www.profootballresearchers.org/articles/1930 Season.pdf (1 January 2018).

———. *The Third Time Is Charmed: 1924. Pro Football Researchers Association*, www.profootballresearchers.org/articles/Goodbye_Bulldogs,_Hello.pdf (1 January 2018).

———. *Three-Peat! Pro Football Researchers Association*, www.profootballresearchers.org/articles/1931 Season.pdf (1 January 2018).

———. *A War Year: 1918. Pro Football Researchers Association*, www.profootballresearchers.org/articles/A_War_Year.pdf (1 January 2018).

Piascik, Andy. *The Best Show in Football: The 1946–1955 Cleveland Browns*. Lanham, Md.: Taylor Trade, 2007.

———. *Gridiron Gauntlet: The Story of the Men Who Integrated Pro Football, in Their Own Words*. Lanham, Md.: Taylor Trade, 2009.

Pollard, Fritz. *NFL Films Interview*. NFL Films, 1976,

Pope, Edwin. *Football's Greatest Coaches*. Atlanta, Ga.: Tupper & Love, 1955.

Powers, Francis J. "Conzelman Is a Card." *Sport* 5 (October 1948): 52+.

Powers, Francis J., and Ed Prell. "George Halas: The Papa Bear." *Sport* 5 (December 1948): 56–109.

Presnell, Glenn. *NFL Films Interview*. NFL Films, 1998.

Provost, Wally. "Nebraska's Greatest Guy." 21-part series. *Omaha World-Herald*, 23 August–13 September 1964.

Remmel, Lee. "Curly Lambeau, 1898–1965." *Green Bay Packer Yearbook 1965* (1965): 22–26.

———. "Greatest Packer Games: No. 9." *Pro* (9 August 1975): 52–55.

Reyburn, Susan. *Football Nation: Four Hundred Years of America's Game, from the Library of Congress*. New York: Abrams, 2013.

Reynolds, Dick. *The Steam Roller Story*. Self-published, 1989.

Reynolds, Quentin. "Football Town." *Collier's* 100 (6 November 1937): 62+.

Richman, Michael. *The Redskins Encyclopedia*. Philadelphia, Pa.: Temple University Press, 2008.

Roberts, Howard. *The Chicago Bears*. New York: Putnam, 1947.

———. *The Story of Pro Football*. New York: Rand McNally, 1953.

Rockne, Knute. *The Autobiography of Knute K. Rockne*. Ed. Bonnie Skiles Rockne. Indianapolis, Ind.: Bobbs-Merrill, 1931.

Roper, William W. *Football, Today and Tomorrow*. New York: Duffield & Co., 1927.

Ruck, Rob. *Rooney: A Sporting Life*. Lincoln.: University of Nebraska Press, 2010.

Savener, Dorothy Chamberlin. Interview with E. A. Kral, 23 May 1996, Guy Chamberlin file, Gage County Historical Society.

Schubert, Bill. "Jimmy Conzelman." *Coffin Corner* 19, no. 1 (1997): 1–3.

Scott, Harry G. *Jock Sutherland: Architect of Men*. New York: Exposition, 1954.

Sears, Vic. *NFL Films Interview*. NFL Films, 1999.

Shaughnessy, Clark. "Football for Morale." *Esquire* (August 1942): 22+.

———. *Football in War and Peace*. Clinton, S.C.: Jacobs Press, 1943.

Shaughnessy, Clark, Ralph Jones, and George Halas. *The Modern "T" Formation with Man-in-Motion*. Chicago: Shaughnessy, Jones, and Halas, 1941.

Smith, Don. "Ray Flaherty." *Coffin Corner* 6, no. 5/6 (1984): 7–8.

Smith, Robert. *Pro Football: The History of the Game and the Great Players*. Garden City, N.Y.: Doubleday, 1963.

Soar, Hank. *NFL Films Interview*. NFL Films, 1999.

Sperber, Murray. *Shake Down the Thunder: The Creation of Notre Dame Football*. New York: Henry Holt, 1993.

Stagg, Amos Alonzo, and Henry Llewellyn Williams. *A Scientific and Practical Treatise on American Football for Schools and Colleges*. Hartford, Conn.: Press of the Case, Lockwood & Brainard Co., 1893.

Stagg, Amos Alonzo, and Wesley Winans Stout. *Touchdown!* New York: Longmans, Green, 1927.

Stinson, Steve. *"Bullet" Bill Dudley: The Greatest 60-Minute Man in Football*. Lanham, Md.: Taylor Trade, 2016.

Stockton, J. Roy. "The Browns' Secret Weapon." *Saturday Evening Post* 217 (30 September 1944): 18+.

Strickler, George. "Defense Came First with Steve Owen." *Football Digest* 1 (November 1971): 86–94.

Strother, Shelby. *NFL's Top 40: The Greatest Pro Football Games Ever Played*. New York: Viking, 1988.

Sutherland, John B., and William S. Maulsey. "Those Pro's Can Point." *American Legion Magazine* 29 (November 1940): 12+.

Terrill, John. "Man in Motion." *Collier's* 108 (25 October 1941): 20+.

Terzian, James P. *New York Giants*. New York: Macmillan, 1973.

Trippi, Charley. *Backfield Play*. Chicago: Ziff-Davis, 1948.

———. *NFL Films Interview*. NFL Films, 1999.

Tunnell, Emlen, and William Gleason. *Footsteps of a Giant*. Garden City, N.Y.: Doubleday, 1966.

Turner, Clyde. *Playing the Line*. Chicago: Ziff-Davis, 1948.

Twombly, Wells. *Blanda: Alive and Kicking*. Los Angeles, Calif.: Nash Publishing, 1973.

Van Buren, Steve. *NFL Films Interview*. NFL Films, 1997.

Walker, Sam. *The Captain Class: The Hidden Force That Creates the World's Greatest Teams*. New York: Random House, 2017.

Warner, Glenn S. *A Course in Football for Players and Coaches*. Carlisle, Pa.: Carlisle, 1912.

———. *Football for Coaches and Players*. Palo Alto, Calif.: Stanford University, 1927.

Washington Post. *Redskins: A History of Washington's Team*. *Washington Post*, www.washingtonpost.com/wp-srv/sports/redskins/longterm/book/skinbook.htm (9 April 2018).

Whittingham, Richard. *What a Game They Played: Stories of the Early Days of Pro Football by Those Who Were There*. New York: Harper & Row, 1984.

Willis, Chris. *Dutch Clark: The Life of an NFL Legend and the Birth of the Detroit Lions*. Lanham, Md.: Scarecrow, 2012.

———. *The Man Who Built the National Football League: Joe Carr*. Lanham, Md.: Scarecrow, 2010.

———. *Old Leather: An Oral History of Early Pro Football in Ohio, 1920–1935*. Lanham, Md: Scarecrow, 2005.

Wistert, Al. *NFL Films Interview*. NFL Films, 2008.

Ziegler, Jack. "Jock Sutherland: Forgotten Coaching Great." *Coffin Corner* 13, no. 4 (1991): 1–7.

———. "Podunk versus Gotham: The 1946 Browns–Yankees Rivalry." *Coffin Corner* 16, no. 2 (1994): 1–5.

Ziemba, Joe. *When Football Was Football*. Chicago: Triumph, 1999.

Zimmerman, David. *Curly Lambeau: The Man behind the Mystique*. Hales Corner, Wisc.: Eagle Books, 2003.

Zimmerman, Paul. *A Thinking Man's Guide to Pro Football*. New York: Dutton, 1970.

Zimmerman, Paul, and Peter King. *Dr. Z: The Lost Memoirs of an Irreverent Football Writer.* Chicago: Triumph, 2017.
Zuppke, Robert C. *Football Technique and Tactics.* Champaign, Ill.: Bailey and Himes, 1924.

NEWSPAPERS

The following newspapers were examined thoroughly:
Baltimore Sun
Boston Globe
Brooklyn Eagle
Canton Daily News
Canton Repository
Chicago Tribune
Cleveland Plain Dealer
Detroit Free Press
Green Bay Press-Gazette
Los Angeles Times
New York Times
Philadelphia Inquirer
Pittsburgh Post-Gazette
St. Louis Post-Dispatch
Washington Post

INDEXES USED TO CONSULT DAILIES

Newspapers Archive
Newspapers.com
Genealogy Bank

ARCHIVAL MATERIAL

Clark Shaughnessy Notebooks, Pro Football Hall of Fame
Dutch Sternaman Collection, Pro Football Hall of Fame

GAME FILM

I was able to study more than 100 full game films from the time period involving the coaches included aside from Guy Chamberlin.

INDEX

Acme Packing Company, 23
Akron Pros, 6, 7, 9, 10, 11, 51, 224
Albert, Frankie, 154–155, 167
Aldrich, Ki, 129
Alexander, Joe, 90, 113
Alexander, John, xx, xxi–xxii
Alford, Bruce, 120
All-America Football Conference, x, xxi,
    xxviii, 185, 205, 206, 215, 218, 220
Allen, George, 162, 163, 170, 228
Anderson, Eddie, 22
Anderson, Heartley "Hunk", xviii, xix, 22,
    157–158, 159, 161, 174, 175
Andrew, Dal, 24–25, 26, 30, 44
Andrew, Helen Hampson, 30
Andrew, Len, 30
Andrew, LeRoy, xxv, 2, 19–22, 24–30,
    33–35, 40–42, 44, 47, 50, 90, 91, 110,
    218, 227
Andrew, Mack, 30
Angsman, Elmer, 159, 185, 190, 191, 192,
    193, 204
Arians, Bruce, xxv
Armstrong, Neill, 204, 207
Artoe, Lee, 129
Ashmore, Roger, 111
Atkins, Doug, 169
Auburn University, 167

Bach, Joe, xviii
Badgro, Red, 42, 64, 105

Baker, Roy "Bullet", 114
Ball, Herman, 170
Baltimore Colts (AAFC), 122, 123
Banonis, Vince, 185, 189, 190, 193
Barber, Jim, 114, 123
Barnes, Don, 184
Barnes, Piggy, 205, 211, 212
Barnum, Len, 95, 202
Barry, Norm, xvii, 22
Barwegan, Dick, 121, 122
Batterson, George "Dim", 113
Battles, Cliff, 115, 116, 121, 124, 128
Baugh, Sammy, 43, 58, 104, 110, 115, 116,
    118, 125–127, 127–129, 146, 171, 174
Baumgartner, Stan, 202
Bausch, Frank, 114
Baylor University, 99
Bednarik, Chuck, 205, 211
Behman, Bull, 10
Beinor, Ed, 183
Belichick, Bill, xxviii, 217, 228
Bell, Bert, 30, 137, 139, 200, 206, 215
Bengtson, Phil, 154
Bennett, Chuck, 209
Bergman, Dutch, xviii, 62, 82, 101, 115
Berry, Charlie, 23–24
Berwanger, Jay, 153
Bezdek, Hugo, 131
Bible, Dana X., xviii
Bidwill, Charley, 184, 185, 193
Billick, Brian, 228

Biola, John, 38

Bleeker, Mal, 209

Blood, Johnny (McNally), xxi, 24, 27, 31, 39, 41–43, 179, 188

Boston Braves/Redskins. *See* Washington Redskins

Boston College, 61, 199

Boston Yanks, 104, 156, 167, 204, 205

Bowdoin, Jim, 40

Bowles, Todd, 225–226

Boyette, Garland, 225

Brandy, Joe, xvii

Brill, Marty, xviii

Brito, Gene, 32

Britt, Eddie, 114

Brock, Charley, 40

Brooklyn Dodgers (AAFC), 122

Brooklyn Dodgers (NFL), xxvi, 28, 31, 72, 74, 75, 76, 77–79, 80, 82, 83, 92, 114–115, 118, 119, 120, 121, 131, 135, 136–139, 142, 143, 144, 145–146, 202

Bross, Mal, 111–112

Brown, Brother, 152

Brown, Mike, 219

Brown, Paul, x, xxviii, 88, 104, 107, 121, 122, 131, 132, 155, 175, 211, 213, 215–221, 228

Brown, Rosey, 225

Brown University, 223–224

Bruder, Hank, 36

Brumbaugh, Carl, 57, 58, 62, 65, 106, 150, 157, 185

Buchanan, Buck, 225

Buffalo All-Americans, 6, 8, 9, 52, 113

Bulger, Chet, 185

Bumgardner, Rex, 216

Burkett, Jeff, 185

Burnett, Dale, 65

Burns, Robert, 133

Butler University, 54, 71

Cabrelli, Larry, 202

Caddell, Ernie, 84

Cafego, George, 146

Cahoon, Ivan "Tiny", 111

Calac, Pete, 4

Calgary Stampeders, 100

Calhoun, George Whitney, 22

California Western University, 80

Camp, Walter, xvi–xvii, xviii, 47–48, 67

Camp Funston, 50, 70

Camp Kearny, 4

Campbell, Jim, xx

Cannon, Jimmy, 107

Canton Bulldogs, xxv, 4–8, 10, 13–14, 15, 16, 51, 52, 134, 197

Canton Noakers (baseball), 5

Carlisle Industrial School, xvii, 48, 150

Carr, Joe, xxiii, 73

Carroll, Bird, 6, 16

Carroll, Pete, xxv, 228

Cavanaugh, Frank, 61

Cavosie, John, 63

Chamberlin, Bernyce Weeks, 12

Chamberlin, Anna Tobyne, 2

Chamberlin, Bill, 2, 3

Chamberlin, Elmer, 2

Chamberlin, Frances, 2

Chamberlin, Guy, xi, xxv, 1–18, 19, 24, 30, 51, 52, 91, 218, 227

Chamberlin, Lucille Lees, 4

Chamberlin, Patricia, 4

Chamberlin, Ramona, 2

Chamberlin, Truman, 2

Chamberlin, Warren, 2

Chamberlin, William, 2

Cheatham, Lloyd, 120

Cherundolo, Chuck, 140

Chevigny, Jack, xviii

Chicago Bears/Staleys, xvi, xix, xxiii–xxiv, xxv, xxvii, 1, 5, 6, 7, 9, 10–11, 12, 16–17, 32, 33, 38, 42–43, 49, 51–53, 55–65, 69, 72–74, 75, 76–77, 79, 92, 93, 97, 98, 101, 103, 105–106, 113, 114, 116, 118–120, 127–129, 137, 138, 141, 153, 155–158, 159, 160, 161–163, 163, 165, 165–166, 166, 168–169, 169–173, 174, 175, 177, 185–186, 188, 190, 192–193, 195, 199, 201–202, 204–205, 208–209, 212

Chicago Black Hawks (football), 224

Chicago Bulls (AFL), 52, 53, 111

Chicago Cardinals, xvi, xxv, xxvii, 7, 11–12, 21, 27, 29, 32, 68, 72, 73, 76, 76–77, 114, 123, 128, 132, 143, 156, 157, 159, 173, 177, 178, 179, 182–183, 184–186, 187–193, 203, 204–205, 209, 212–213

Chicago Hornets, 109, 122
Chicago Rockets, 121, 122–123, 156
Chicago White Sox, 197
Christensen, George, 72, 84
Christl, Cliff, 23, 40
Christman, Paul, 159, 185, 186, 189, 190,
191, 192, 193
Cincinnati Reds (baseball), 112, 197–198,
199
Cincinnati Reds (football), 30, 75
Clair, Emmett, 23
Clair, John, 23
Clark, Algy, xxi
Clark, Earl "Dutch", xxi, 63, 72, 74, 75,
77, 78, 81, 82, 84
Clark, George "Potsy", xviii, xxviii, 29, 49,
67–84, 88, 94, 137–138, 145, 219, 228
Clark, James, 205, 206
Clark, Jane, 68
Clark, Janet Mahon, 70–71
Clark, Mary, 71
Clark, Stuart, 72
Clarke, Harry, 166
Clement, Johnny, 140, 142, 146, 188
Cleveland Browns, xxviii, 33, 99, 104,
106–107, 121–123, 206, 213, 215–219,
220
Cleveland Bulldogs, xxv, 8–10, 13, 17, 19,
20, 25–26, 40, 90, 91
Cleveland Collegians, 12
Cleveland Indians (football), 8, 9
Cleveland Rams. *See* Los Angeles Rams
Cochran, Red, 185, 187, 189, 193
Cochrane, Mickey, 75
Cofall, Stan, xviii
Colgate University, 12, 164
College All-Stars, 33, 40, 96, 166
Collier, Blanton, 220, 221, 227
Colorado College, 63, 75, 79
Columbia University, 29, 58, 98, 149, 167
Columbus Panhandlers, 8, 9
Comerford, Tony, 61
Comp, Irv, 32
Comstock, Rudy, 7, 11
Conerly, Charlie, 98, 101, 102, 106–107
Conover, Larry, 7, 9
Considine, Bob, 177
Conti, Enio, 210
Conzelman, Anne Forestal, 182

Conzelman, James, xxvii, 2, 21, 37, 50, 51,
129, 159, 165, 167, 177–193, 207, 209,
219, 228
Conzelman, James, Jr., 182, 186–187
Conzelman, John, 182
Conzelman, Lillian Granzon, 181
Conzelman, Margaret Ryan Dunn, 178
Conzelman, Oscar, 178, 179
Conzelman, Robert, 182
Cope, Frank, 95
Cope, Myron, 144–145
Cornell University, 156, 164
Corum, Bill, 93
Coryell, Don, 228
Coughlin, Frank, xviii, 179
Coughlin, Tom, 228
Courtright, R. O., 21
Cowher, Bill, 228
Craft, Russ, 204, 209, 213, 216
Craig, Larry, 38
Craigue, Paul, 114
Creighton, Milan, xxi
Crennell, Romeo, 225
Crosby, Bing, 110–111, 117
Cross, Irv, 225
Crowe, Clem, xviii
Crowley, Jim, xviii, 78
Cuff, Ward, 94, 97
Cunningham, Bill, 141
Curran, Bob, 179, 201
Cyre, Hec, 111

Daley, Arthur, 31, 118, 170, 205
Damn Yankees (musical), 182
Danowski, Ed, 84, 93, 94, 102, 106, 116,
117
Daugherty, Duffy, 78
Daugherty, Russ, xviii
Davis, Al, 227
Dayton Triangles, 7, 9, 197
Decatur Staleys. *See* Chicago Bears
defensive formations: 4-3 defense, 104,
155, 210, 211; Eagle defense, xxvii,
195, 204, 209, 210, 217; five-man line,
x, 103, 116, 127, 208, 210, 213; seven-
man line, 38, 40, 82, 91, 103, 210; six-
man line, 29, 40, 82, 91, 101, 103,
106–107, 129; umbrella defense, 99,
104, 106, 118

DeGroot, Dudley, xxvii, 132, 154, 159
DeHart, Jimmy, 218
Depler, Jack, xviii
Detroit Lions, xxvii, 42, 62, 75–78, 79,
    82–83, 84, 93, 113, 156, 163, 193, 204.
    See also Portsmouth Spartans
Detroit Panthers, 180
Detroit Tigers (baseball), 75
Detroit Tigers (football), 58
Detroit Wolverines, xxv, 19, 20, 26, 27, 91
Deutsch, Sam, 8, 9–10, 25, 26
Dewell, Billy, 185, 190
DeWitt, Bill, 184
Dietrich, John, 37
Dilweg, Lavvie, 24
Dimancheff, Babe, 186, 188, 190
DiMeolo, Luby, 135
Ditka, Mike, 163
Doane College, 4
Dobie, Gil, xviii
Dorais, Gus, xviii, 111, 113, 132
Douds, Forrest "Jap", xxi, 72, 73
Douglass, William O., 187
Dove, Bob, 189
Driscoll, Paddy, 21, 50–51, 157, 159, 161,
    174, 179
Dudley, Bill, 140, 142, 144–145
Duff, Joe, 134
Duke University, 218
Duluth Kelleys, 52
Dungy, Tony, 225, 227
Dunn, James Gleason, 178
Dunn, Red, 23–24, 27, 30, 36, 42
Durden, Chauncey, 57
Durden, Earnell, 225

Earpe, Jug, 42
Edwards, Bill, 132
Edwards, Howard "Cap", xviii
Edwards, Turk, 116, 159
Effrat, Louis, 104
Emerson, Ox, 72
Espy, Jack, 137
Ewbank, Weeb, 221, 227

Falaschi, Nello, 95
Famiglietti, Gary, 171
Farkas, Andy, 116, 127, 129
Farman, Dick, 117

Farrell, Scrapper, 79
Faurot, Don, 167
Fears, Tom, 160, 173, 213
Feather, Tiny, 40
Feathers, Beattie, 58, 62, 105
Ferrante, Jack, 146, 202, 212
Fewell, Perry, 226
Filchock, Frank, 98, 102, 116, 117, 118,
    125, 126, 145, 158, 171, 173
Finks, Jim, 163
Fisher, Elliott, 26
Flaherty, Alice M., 110
Flaherty, Eugene, 110
Flaherty, Jackie, 123
Flaherty, Ray, xxvi, xxviii, 31, 34, 41, 43,
    97, 103, 109–129, 145, 170, 188, 218,
    220, 228
Flaherty, Ray, Jr., 123
Flaherty, Richard, 110, 111
Flaherty, Rose, 110
Flaherty, Thomas J., 110
Flaherty, Wilfrid, 110
Flanigan, Walter, 179–180
Fleckenstein, Bill, 34
Flournoy, Peggy, 152
Folwell, Robert, 131
Ford, Gerald, 79
Fordham University, 136
Fort Greenleaf, 134
Fort Riley, 70
Fox, John, 228
Francis, Sam, 137
Frank, Clint, 200
Frankford Yellow Jackets, xvi, xxv, 9,
    10–12, 14, 17, 28, 111, 181
Frankian, Ike, 106
Frazier, Leslie, 225
Friedman, Benny, xxv, 20, 25–26, 27,
    28–29, 33–35, 40–42, 68, 91–92, 112,
    115
Fritsch, Ted, 43
Fullerton, Hugh, Jr., 189
Furlong, Bill, 169

Gallerneau, Hugh, 151, 157
Gantenbein, Milt, 43
Garrett, Budge, 224
George, Bill, 162, 169
Georgia Tech, xviii

Getto, Mike, 135
Gianelli, Mario, 205, 210–211
Gibbs, Joe, xxviii, 227
Giddins, Gary, 110
Gifford, Frank, 99
Gilbertson Cadamounts, 224
Gillies, Fred, 157
Gillman, Sid, xxviii, 162, 228
Gipp, George, 21
Glamp, Joe, 141
Glassgow, Willis, 209
Gleason, Bill, 162
Goldberg, Marshall, 136–137, 178, 183, 185, 187, 189
Goldenberg, Charles "Buckets", 40
Goldston, Ralph, 225
Gonzaga University, 110–112, 113, 120
Good News (musical), 182
Gottehrer, Barry, 28–29
Governali, Paul, 98
Graham, Otto, 106–107, 121, 206, 216, 217, 220
Grange, Red, xvi, xxiii, 10, 52–53, 55, 56, 57, 62, 65, 74, 111–112, 157, 180–181, 216
Grant, Bud, 84, 228
Grateful Dead, 163
Grayson, Harry, 183–184
Great Lakes Naval Training Station, 21, 50, 178, 218, 219
Green, Dennis, xxv, 225
Green, Ernie, 225
Green, Johnny, 204, 210
Green Bay Packers, xxiii, xxv, 19, 22–24, 27–28, 29, 30–33, 34–44, 53, 72, 73–74, 76–77, 79, 82, 83–84, 96, 97–98, 104, 106, 111–112, 114–115, 117, 119, 123, 127, 137, 149, 157, 158, 161, 162, 170, 172, 180
Grier, Rosey, 224
Griffith, Clark, 70
Griffith, Major John, 67, 70, 81
Grigg, Cecil "Tex", 4
Grosshandler, Stan, 101, 103
Gruden, Jon, 228
Guderian, General Heinz, 169
Gulyanics, George, 193
Gutowsky, Ace, 63, 75, 84, 163
Guyon, Joe, 4

Hachten, William, 99
Halas, Barbara, 49–50
Halas, Frank, 49
Halas, Frank, Jr., 49
Halas, George, xviii, xxi, xxv, xxv–xxvi, xxvii, 1, 2, 5, 9, 11, 13, 16–17, 21, 33–34, 35, 47, 49–53, 54–55, 56–60, 61–63, 64–65, 67, 68, 70, 74, 87–88, 98, 116, 137, 143, 149–150, 153, 157–158, 159, 161–163, 165, 165–166, 168, 170, 172, 174–175, 177, 179–180, 183, 185, 186, 190, 209, 218, 220, 227
Halas, George, Jr., 50
Halas, Lillian, 49
Halas, Minerva Bushing, 50
Halas, Walter, 49, 158
Halloran, Bill, 117
Hamer, Tex, 17
Hammond Pros, 7, 51, 224
Handler, Phil, 185, 192, 193
Hanley, Dick, 54
Hapes, Merle, 98, 158
Harbaugh, Jim, xxiv, 227
Harbaugh, John, 228
Harder, Pat, 159, 185, 190, 193, 212
Hare, Ray, 120, 145
Harlem Brown Bombers, 224
Harper, Jess, xviii, 3–4
Harvard University, 48, 58–59, 67, 70, 76, 132, 151, 153, 154
Haughton, Percy, 67, 68, 70, 74, 81
Hay, Ralph, 4–5, 51
Healy, Ed, 179
Hein, Mel, 64–65
Heisman, John, xviii
Heller, Warren, 133
Helms Foundation Hall of Fame, 12
Henderson, Gus, 131
Hendrian, Dutch, 7
Henry, Wilbur "Pete" "Fats", 6, 8, 9, 15, 17
Herber, Arnie, 30, 31–32, 36, 43, 44, 83, 97
Herzog, Buck, 197
Hess, Wally, 224
Hewitt, Bill, 57, 65, 76
Hickok, Ralph, 38
Hinkle, Clarke, 36–37, 39, 73, 76, 83
Hinkle, Jack, 202

Hirsch, Elroy, 160, 168, 213
Hoeffel, Joe, 23
Hoernschemeyer, Bob, 122
Hoffman, Bill, 14
Holmgren, Mike, 228
Holovak, Mike, 186, 190
Holt, Zelda, 21
Homan, Henry "Two Bits", 17
Horween, Arnold, 132
Horween, Ralph, 132
Howell, Jim Lee, 94, 227
Hubbard, Cal, 24, 30, 38–39, 40
Hubert, Pooley, 164
Huff, George, 54
Huggins, Miller, 69
Hughitt, Tommy, 52
Humbert, Dick, 202, 208, 210
Hunsinger, Chuck, 161
Hutson, Don, 30–32, 33, 35, 37–39, 42–43, 104, 206

Indian Packing Company, 20, 22
Indiana Basketball Hall of Fame, 57
Iowa State University, 156
Ironton Tanks, 72, 199, 209
Irwin, Don, 114
Isbell, Cecil, 31, 32, 36, 43
Ivy, Pop, 185, 189

Jackson, General Stonewall, 196
Jackson, Hue, 225
Jacobs, Jack, 40
Johnson, Chuck, 162
Johnson, Jimmy, xxv, xxviii, 228
Johnson, Nate, 122
Johnson, Pearce, 224
Johnsos, Luke, 57, 129, 155, 157–158, 159, 161, 173, 174, 175, 202
Jolley, Al, xxi, 30
Jones, Ben, 10
Jones, Dub, 216
Jones, Howard, xviii
Jones, Ralph, xxv–xxvi, xxvii, 47, 49, 50, 54–57, 60–61, 63–64, 68, 156, 157, 173, 218–219, 227
Joseph, Vance, 226
Justice, Ed, 114, 116, 117, 127, 128

Kansas City Blues/Cowboys, 20, 24–25, 40, 90, 91
Karcher, Jim, 114
Karr, Bill, 57, 65
Kavanaugh, Ken, 171, 190, 212
Kelley, Larry, 200
Kellison, John, 197, 199, 200, 203, 207, 208
Kelly, Chip, xxv
Kelly, Shipwreck, 31
Kercheval, Ralph, 137, 142
Kerr, Andy, 164
Kieran, John, 31
Kiesling, Walt, 203
Kilroy, Bucko, 191, 203, 211, 212
Kinard, Bruiser, 79, 120, 121, 137
Kinard, George, 120, 121
King, Joe, 127
Kipkuth, Bob, 200
Kirksey, George, 188
Kizer, Noble, 218
Klewicki, Ed, 84
Kline, Bill, 3, 13
Kmetovic, Pete, 154
Knox, Chuck, 228
Kopf, Herb, 167, 198
Kopf, Larry, 198
Kotal, Eddie, 40
Kraehe, Ollie, 22
Krause, Max, 65, 125
Kreutzmann, Bill, 163
Kryk, John, xix
Kuechle, Ollie, 40
Kuharich, Joe, 183
Kutner, Mal, 185, 189, 190, 191

Lafayette College, 134–135
Lake Forest Academy, 54
Lake Forest College, 56–57, 156
Lambeau, Don, 23
Lambeau, Earl "Curly", xviii, xxv, 1–2, 19–21, 22–24, 30–33, 35–44, 47, 53, 73, 74, 76, 78, 88, 91, 116, 137, 149, 167, 218, 220, 227
Lambeau, Marcel, 22
Lambeau, Marguerite Van Kessell, 22–23, 31
Lambeau, Marie, 22
Lambeau, Mary, 22

Lambeau, Susan Johnson, 30
Lambeau, Victor, 22
Landry, Tom, xxviii, 99, 104, 228
Lauer, Dutch, 180
Lautenschlager, Lester, 151
Lavan, Al, 225
Lavelli, Dante, 121, 216
Laws, Joe, 36, 43–44
Lawson, Jim, 112, 154
Leahy, Frank, xviii
LeBaron, Eddie, 32
Ledbetter, Bob, 225
Leemans, Tuffy, 97, 100
Lees, James Thomas, 4
Leonard, Jim, 139
Levy, Marv, 227
Lewellen, Verne, 23, 36, 41–42
Lewis, Art, xxi
Lewis, Marvin, 225
Lincoln University, 223
Lindskog, Vic, 203
Little, Lou, 29, 30, 78, 94, 167
Livingston, Howie, 97
Loebs, Frank, 182
Lombardi, Vince, xxvi, xxviii, 2, 14, 33,
    82, 123, 136, 162, 227
Los Angeles Dons (AAFC), 156
Los Angeles Rams, xxvii, 40, 91, 141, 156,
    160–161, 163, 164, 167–168, 173–174,
    203, 205, 210, 213, 219, 225
Los Angeles Wildcats (AFL), 109
Louisville Brecks, 7
Loyola of New Orleans, 152
Luckman, Sid, 98, 104, 129, 149–150,
    153–154, 157, 166–167, 171, 173, 190,
    193, 212
Lujack, Johnny, 173, 192, 193, 212
Lumpkin, Father, 72, 83
Lunday, Kayo, 94
Lundy, Lamar, 225
Lyle, Dewey, 180
Lyman, Link, 6, 10–11, 15–16, 57, 101
Lynn, Anthony, 225

Mackrides, Bill, 212, 216
MacMonnies, Frederick, 180
Madden, John, 228
Maes, Homer, Jr., 33
Magee, John, 205

Mallouf, Ray, 185, 186, 193, 212
Malone, Charley, 114, 127, 128, 171
Mandel, Fred, 79
Manders, Jack, 64, 128, 158
Manders, Pug, 120, 121, 137, 146
Manhattan University, 105
Maniaci, Joe, 78, 171
Manske, Eggs, 128, 149
Mara, Tim, 20, 26–27, 28, 35, 91, 99–100,
    112, 113, 120
Mara, Wellington, 99–100, 112, 113
March, Harry, 27, 68, 94, 132
Mare Island Marines, 21, 50
Marietta College, 197
Marquette University, 23, 111
Marshall, George Preston, 30, 32, 42, 109,
    113, 114, 116–117, 118, 120, 172
Martz, Mike, 228
Massillon Tigers, xvi, 5, 134
Masterson, Bernie, 58, 62, 128, 150, 155
Masterson, Bob, 116, 117, 120
Mathys, Charles, 36
Matthews, Billie, 225
Maubetsch, John, 89–90
Mauldin, Stan, 185, 186, 190
McAfee, George, 170, 171
McBride, Jack, 92
McCaskey, Virginia Halas, 50
McChesney, Bob, 114
McCrary, Herdis, 41
McFadden, Banks, 138
McGraw, John, 70
McGugin, Dan, xviii
McHugh, Pat, 191
McIlwain, Wally, xviii
McIntyre, Monty "Tubby", 90
McKay, John, 131, 228
McKenney, Joe, 61
McLain, Chief, 209
McLean, Scooter, 166
McMillan, Ernie, 225
McMillen, Jim, 91
McMillin, Bo, 132
McPhail, Larry, 120
Meagher, Jack, xviii, 167
Meehan, Chick, 78
Mehre, Harry, xviii
Melrose Athletic Club, 8
Metzger, Sol, 61

Meyers, Billy, 55
Miami of Ohio University, 217
Michalske, Mike, 24, 38, 39
Michelosen, John, 136, 139, 147
Michigan State University, 70, 78
Milner, Wayne, 114, 127, 128
Milwaukee Badgers, xvi, 7, 9, 23, 180, 224
Minneapolis Marines, xvi
Molenda, Bo, 41–42, 97
Molesworth, Keith, 57, 62, 64
Monnett, Bob, 36, 43
Montgomey, General Bernard, 159
Moore, Red, 140
Moore, Wilbur, 117, 126, 129
Mora, Jim, Sr., 228
Moran, Hap, 28
Morze, Frank, 162
Motley, Marion, 219
Muha, Joe, 204
Muncie Flyers, xvi
Munn, Lyle, 42
Muskingum College, 197
Musso, George, 57
Myers, Denny, 199–200

Nagurski, Bronko, xxiii–xxiv, 57, 58, 62, 63–64, 65, 74, 76
Naismith, James, 54
Nash, Tom, 42
National Association of Intercollegiate Athletics Hall of Fame, 57
Neale, Adelaide Bray Donahoe, 207
Neale, Earle "Greasy", xxvii, 98, 102, 132, 160, 186, 190, 192, 193, 195–213, 215, 219, 220, 228
Neale, Genevieve Horner, 197, 207
Neale, Irene, 196
Neale, Julia Anne, 196
Neale, Ola Maurice, 207
Neale, Tom, 196
Neale, Widdy, 199
Neale, William, 196
Nebraska Wesleyan University, 3
Nesbit, Dick, 63
Nevers, Ernie, xvii, 29–30, 182
New York Bulldogs, 123
New York Giants (baseball), 77
New York Giants (football), xxv, xxvi, 19, 20, 24, 26–29, 31, 32, 40–42, 43–44,

57, 64–65, 68, 72, 74, 77, 79, 83, 84, 88, 90–107, 109, 110, 112–113, 115–119, 120, 122, 138, 139, 153, 156–157, 158, 172, 173, 185, 187, 188, 199, 202, 206, 208, 224–225
New York Yankees (AAFC), 24, 109, 120–124, 185
New York Yankees (AFL), 53, 111–112
New York Yankees (baseball), 51, 120
Newman, Harry, 64, 65, 84, 92, 93, 94, 101, 102, 105
Newsome, Ozzie, 226
Nied, Frank, 224
Nix, Emery, 102
Nixon, Mike, 135, 144
Noll, Chuck, xxviii, 221, 228
Nolting, Ray, 170–171
North Carolina Pre-Flight, 79
North Central Association of Colleges, 71
North Park College, 56
Northeastern University, 77
Northwestern University, 54, 154
Notre Dame University, xvii–xviii, xviii, 3, 21, 22, 28, 35, 37, 40, 48–49, 51, 59, 62, 68, 90, 91, 102, 111, 131, 149, 151, 152, 153, 156, 167, 180, 183, 188

Oakland Raiders, 211, 223
Obelin Prep Academy, 133–134
Oberlin College, 154
O'Brien, Chris, 12
O'Brien, Davey, 118
Oden, Curly, 181
O'Donnell, Dick, 40
offensive formations: wing T, 98, 102, 167; A formation, 95, 97, 101, 102, 115; Harvard shift, 58–59; Minnesota Shift, xvii, 58, 151; Notre Dame box, xvii, 35–36, 40, 49, 59–60, 62, 68, 102, 111, 149, 166, 188; pro set, 168, 174; short punt, 40, 49, 69, 82, 110, 124, 127, 144, 201, 209, 218; single wing, xvii, xviii, xxvi, xxvi–xxvii, xxviii, 1, 14, 19, 29, 35, 36, 40, 48–49, 58, 62, 67, 68–69, 74, 81, 82, 95, 98, 101, 102, 109–110, 114, 116, 119, 120, 123, 124, 125, 127, 132, 134, 141–142, 143, 146–147, 149, 154, 156, 159, 163–164, 167, 181, 182, 188, 201, 202, 209, 210,

218; T formation, xvii, xxvi, xxvii, 1, 31, 35–36, 47–49, 55–56, 57–58, 58–61, 62, 65, 67, 68, 69, 97, 98, 102, 103, 110, 119, 121, 123, 125, 129, 143, 146, 147, 149–150, 151, 153–157, 157–158, 159–160, 163–168, 170–172, 174, 175, 178, 188, 189, 191, 195, 201–202, 208–209, 210, 218, 219

Ohio State University, 153, 217, 218
Olderman, Murray, 38
Oorang Indians, 6, 8
Orange Tornadoes, 27
Oriard, Michael, xv–xvi
O'Rourke, Charley, 129
Osborn, Duke, 6, 14
Osmanski, Bill, 155, 170–171
Owen, Bill, 89, 91, 98
Owen, Florence Carr, 92
Owen, Isabella Doak, 88–89, 96–97
Owen, James Rufus, 88–89
Owen, Miriam Sweeny, 93, 94
Owen, Paul, 89
Owen, Steve, xxvi, 17, 24, 27, 28, 31, 32, 40, 43, 65, 68, 78, 87–107, 109, 109–110, 112–113, 114, 115–116, 118, 126, 188, 198, 206, 209, 219, 220, 228

Palmer, Derrell, 120
Parcells, Bill, 228
Parker, Ace, 78, 120, 121, 137–138, 139, 141, 142, 145–146, 193
Parker, Buddy, xxviii, 84, 188
Parseghian, Ara, 221
Paschal, Bill, 97, 101
Patton, Cliff, 204, 212
Peck, Frank, 22
Penn State University, 59
Perry, Joe, 225
Perry, Lowell, 224
Pershing, General John, 70
Peterson, Robert, 94
Petitbon, Richie, 169–170
Phelan, Jimmy, xviii, 132
Phelps, Don, 216
Philadelphia Bell (WFL), 225
Philadelphia Eagles, xxvii, 68–69, 76, 98, 100, 104, 118, 119, 138, 141, 146–147, 156, 160, 173, 186, 191–192, 193, 195, 200–206, 207–213, 215–217

Philadelphia Phillies (baseball), 197–198
Philadelphia Quakers (AFL), 53
Phillips, Bum, 228
Phillips, Wade, 228
Phillips University, 89–90, 101, 198
Pihos, Pete, 146, 204, 212, 216
Pinckert, Erny, 114, 116
Pitts, Elijah, 225
Pittsburg State University, 21
Pittsburgh Steelers/Pirates, xxvi, 68–69, 75–76, 79, 114, 116, 123, 126, 129, 135, 136, 139–141, 143, 144, 146–147, 149, 156, 200, 202–203, 204, 210, 224, 225
Pittser, Chester, 217
Plansky, Tony, 42
Pogue, Harold, 70
Pollard, Frederick "Fritz", xxviii, 51, 223–224, 225, 226
Pollock, Ed, xxiv
Pond, Ducky, 200
Pool, Hampton, 168, 171
Poole, Jim, 94
Portsmouth Spartans, xxiii–xxiv, xxvi, 29, 63–64, 71–75, 76, 82, 83–84, 199, 209. See also Detroit Lions
Potteiger, Earl, 90
Pottsville Maroons, xvi, 9, 11, 24
Povich, Shirley, 103, 121, 124, 184, 209
Presnell, Glenn, 72, 75, 81, 82, 84, 199, 209
Price, Eddie, 101
Princeton University, 159
Pritchard, Bosh, 146, 203
Pro Football Hall of Fame, 13, 33, 56, 100, 123, 169, 187, 207, 223, 226
Proctor, Dewey, 120
Prokop, Eddie, 120, 122
Providence Grays (baseball), 112
Providence Steam Roller, xvi, xxvii, 11, 112, 132, 181, 188, 223, 224
Provost, Wally, 2
Purdue University, 31, 54, 135, 218
Pyle, C. C., 52–53, 92, 111–112

Ragazzo, Phil, 201
Ramsey, Buster, 185, 191
Rankin, Walt, 185
Ranney, Art, 224

Raye, Jimmy, 225
Reed, Cameron, 24, 30
Reed, Eddie, 152
Reeves, Dan (coach), 228
Reeves, Dan (owner), 160
Reid, Andy, 228
Remmel, Lee, 20, 44
Rennie, Rud, 106
Rentner, Pug, 114
Rhodes, Ray, 225
Richards, George A., 75, 76, 77–78, 79
Robb, Harry, 6, 9
Roberts, Wooky, 6, 11
Robeson, Paul, 21
Robinson, Eddie, 131
Rochester Jeffersons, 9
Rock Island Independents, xvi, 22,
    179–180
Rockne, Knute, xvii, xviii, 3–4, 22, 28, 35,
    67, 111, 131, 151, 152
Roland, Johnny, 225
Ronzani, Gene, 157, 161
Rooney, Art, 135, 136, 139, 143, 149–150,
    187, 200, 224
Rooney, Jimmy, 135
Roosevelt, Franklin D., 21
Roper, Bill, 67
Rose Bowl, xv, xxvii, 21, 31, 50, 132,
    135–136, 152, 154, 155–156, 157, 195,
    198, 206, 223
Rowe, Harmon, 99
Ruck, Rob, 136
Russell, Bo, 117
Russell, Jack, 120
Rutgers University, 21
Ryan, Bill, 23
Ryan, Buddy, 228

Saban, Lou, 221, 228
Saban, Nick, xxiv
Sacrinty, Nick, 190
Sallee, Slim, 198
Sampson, Arthur, 3
San Francisco 49ers, 122, 123, 162, 215
San Jose State University, 154
Sanders, Spec, 120, 121
Santa Clara University, 154, 155
Saskatchewan Roughriders, 100
Sauer, George, 99

Savitsky, George, 205
Schmidt, Francis, 218
Schnellbacher, Otto, 99
Schottenheimer, Marty, 228
Schramm, Tex, 161
Schwartz, Marchy, 79, 154
Schwartz, Perry, 120, 121, 137
Schwartzwalder, Ben, 199
Schwenk, Bud, 183, 188
Sears, Vic, 202, 203, 209
Sedbrook, Len, 42
Senn, Bill, 17
Seymour, Bob, 145
Shanahan, Mike, 227
Shaughnessy, Clark, xxvii, 57, 68, 132,
    150–157, 158–163, 164, 165, 167–170,
    173–175, 213, 218, 219, 228
Shaughnessy, Edward, 150
Shaughnessy, Edward, Jr., 150
Shaughnessy, Louvania Mae Hamilton,
    151
Shaughnessy, Lucy Ann, 150
Shaughnessy, Percy, 150
Shaw, Bob, 173
Shaw, Buck, xviii, 154
Shaw, Pete, 16
Shell, Art, xxviii, 223, 225
Sherman, Allie, 102, 203, 227
Shetley, Rhoten, 146
Shugart, Clyde, 117
Shula, Don, xxviii, 88, 221, 228
Sivell, Jim, 137
Skladany, Joe, 75, 135
Skorich, Nick, 140, 144
Slivinski, Steve, 117
Smith, Andy, 14
Smith, Lovie, 225
Smith, Maurice "Clipper", xviii, 22, 111,
    132
Smith, Pete, 31
Smith, Red, 78
Smith, Riley, 114
Smyth, Lou, 10
Snavely, Carl, 164
Snyder, Bob, 40, 160
Soar, Hank, 94, 97, 103, 106
Sonnenberg, Gus, 181
Southworth, Billy, 199
Spears, Clarence "Doc", 71

Speedie, Mac, 216
St. Louis All-Stars, 22
St. Louis Browns, 184
St. Louis Cardinals (baseball), 184, 199
St. Louis Gunners, 68, 76, 182
St. Louis Rams. *See* Los Angeles Rams
St. Mary's College, 123
St. Mary's Pre-Flight, 79
Stagg, Amos Alonzo, xvi–xvii, xviii, xix, 61, 67, 151, 153
Staley, A. E., 51
Standlee, Norm, 154, 157
Stanford University, xvii, xxvii, 31, 135, 154–157, 165, 167, 175
Stansbury, Harry, 196, 197
Stanton, Homer, 196
Staten Island Stapetons, 28, 74, 92
Stebbins, Harold, 136
Steele, Ernie, 203, 209
Steers, Bill, 5
Stephens, Ray, 112
Sternaman, Edward "Dutch", xviii, xxv, xxv–xxvi, 16, 33, 47, 49, 50–55, 56, 58, 59, 67, 157, 179, 188, 218
Sternaman, Florence, 56
Sternaman, Joey, xviii, 16, 17, 52, 53
Stevens, Mal, 78
Stewart, Dave, 217–218, 220
Stiehm, Ewald "Jumbo", 3, 13
Stockton, Houston, 17, 111
Stockton, John, 111
Storck, Carl, xvi, 137
Stram, Hank, 227
Strode, Woody, 219
Strong, Ken, 27, 28, 65, 84, 92, 94, 97, 106
Stydahar, Joe, 158, 160–161, 168, 170, 199
Sugar Bowl, 152
Sutherland, Archibald, 133
Sutherland, Archie, 133
Sutherland, Jessie, 133
Sutherland, John "Jock", xviii, xxvi, 110, 118, 131–147, 158, 204, 218, 219, 228
Sutherland, Louisa, 133
Sutherland, Margaret, 133
Sutherland, Marion, 133
Sutherland, Mary Burns, 133
Sutherland, William, 133
Sweiger, Bob, 122
Syracuse Stormers, 100

Taylor, Lionel, 225
Taylor, Tarzan, 6, 16
Texas Christian Univesity, 110
Thayer, Harry, 201, 203
Thomas, Emmitt, 226
Thomason, Bobby, 174
Thompson, Alexis "Lex", 200, 205
Thompson, Tommy, 146, 191–192, 201, 202–203, 204, 208, 212–213, 216
Thornhill, Tiny, 154
Thorpe, Jim, xvii, 4, 6, 13, 51, 90, 134, 150, 197
Tidwell, Travis, 107
Tobin, Elge, 224
Todd, Dick, 117, 129, 145
Toledo Maroons, 7, 8, 90
Tomasetti, Lou, 201
Tomlin, Mike, 225
Toney, Fred, 197
Topping, Dan, 78, 120, 122, 137
Toronto Argonauts, 100, 225
Trafton, George, 51
Trippi, Charlie, 159, 185, 191–192, 193, 204
Troup, T. J., 103
Tucker, Mel, 226
Tufts University, 113
Tulane University, 151–152
Tunnell, Emlen, 99, 225
Tunney, Gene, 120
Turnbull, Andrew, 23
Turner, Bulldog, 171

UCLA, 155
Udell, Peggy, 180, 181
Union College, 97
University of Alabama, 31, 35
University of California, 14, 155, 198
University of Chicago, 153–154
University of Dayton, 183, 184
University of Denver, 72
University of Detroit, 111, 113
University of Georgia, 157
University of Grand Rapids, 79
University of Hawaii, 163
University of Illinois, xviii, xxv–xxvi, 3, 49, 50–51, 54, 55, 61, 67, 69–70, 70
University of Indiana, 75, 154, 207
University of Iowa, 150, 209

University of Kansas, 70, 71
University of Maryland, 158, 159
University of Michigan, xviii, xix, 25, 34, 89, 92, 133, 153
University of Minnesota, 58, 70, 71, 135, 150–151, 155
University of Missouri, 167
University of Nebraska, xviii, 3–4, 12–13, 23, 51, 79–80, 155, 156
University of Oregon, 5
University of Pacific, 153
University of Pennsylvania, 30, 131, 151, 159, 205
University of Pittsburgh, xxvi, 133–136, 143–144, 159, 198, 218
University of Southern California, 135
University of Texas, xviii, 89, 101
University of Virginia, 140, 199
University of Washington, 111, 136
University of West Virginia, 199
University of Wisconsin, 22, 23, 154
Urban, Luke, 6

Van Brocklin, Norm, 160, 173–174
Van Buren, Steve, 146–147, 203–204, 209, 212, 213, 215
Van Dyse, Mary Jane, 33
Vaughan, Harp, 75
Vermeil, Dick, 227
Vince, Ralph, 13, 17
Virginia Military Institute, 163

Wabash College, 54, 154
Waddell, Chauncey, 30
Walker, Sam, 18
Walls, Will, 100
Walsh, Adam, xviii, xxvii, 160
Walsh, Bill, xxviii, 221, 228
Walsh, Charles "Chile", xviii, 183
Walters, Bucky, 112
Walton, Frank, 135
Ward, Arch, 95
Ward, Grant P., 83
Warner, Glenn "Pop", xvii, xviii, 48, 61, 67, 132–133, 134–135, 141, 143, 154, 156, 164, 167, 183, 188, 198
Washington, Kenny, 219
Washington & Jefferson University, 198–199, 206

Washington Redskins, xxvi, xxvii, 30, 31, 32, 42–43, 58, 68, 74, 76, 79, 97, 98, 100, 103, 104, 109–110, 113–120, 121, 123–127, 127–129, 137, 138, 141, 145–146, 149, 155, 156–157, 158, 159, 160, 166, 170–172, 173–174, 175, 185, 187, 188, 195, 204, 207, 208, 209
Washington Senators (baseball), 70
Washington State University, 111, 112
Washington University (Missouri), 51, 132, 178, 179, 182, 183
Waterfield, Bob, 160, 173–174, 213
Watkins, Foster, 201
Webb, Allan, 225
Webb, Del, 120
Weinmeister, Arnie, 99
West, Charlie, 198
West Point, 156
West Virginia Wesleyan, 196–197
White, Byron "Whizzer", 79
White, Tarzan, 94
Whittingham, Richard, 144
Widseth, Ed, 94, 117
Wilkin, Wee Willie, 116
Wilks, Steve, 226
William and Vashti College, 69
Williams, Henry L., xvi–xvii, xviii, 67, 151, 152
Willis, Bill, 219
Wills, Bob, 167
Wilson, George "Wildcat", 111, 181, 188
Wilson, Mule, 64
Wistert, Al, 203, 206, 207
Withington, Paul, 70
Wojciechowicz, Alex, 204, 205, 207–208, 210
Wolfner, Walter, 32
Wood, Willie, 225
Woodruff, George, xviii, 132
Woodward, Stanley, 67, 81, 138, 164
Workman, Hoge, 9, 17
Wray, Lud, 30
Wydo, Frank, 140

Yale University, xvi, 48, 92, 199–200, 206
Yost, Fielding, xviii, xix, 25, 34, 131
Young, Buddy, 121
Young, Waddy, 146

Ziemba, Joe, 183
Zimmerman, Leroy, 118, 171, 203, 204
Zimmerman, Paul, 153, 165

Zuppke, Bob, xviii, xxv–xxvi, 49, 50, 51, 54, 58, 61, 67, 68, 69–70, 70, 82, 125, 150

ABOUT THE AUTHOR

John Maxymuk is a reference librarian at Rutgers University, where he has worked for 28 years. He has written four books on libraries and computers, and more than a dozen on professional football history. He has appeared in the NFL Films *Top 10* series on the NFL Network and written more than 25 articles for *Coffin Corner*, the newsletter of the Professional Football Researchers Association. He has written for the *New York Times* football blog and has his own blog on Green Bay Packers history called *Packers Past Perfect*, consisting of Packers-related posts and illustrations. Maxymuk lives with his wife in Cherry Hill, New Jersey, and is the proud father of two beautiful, intelligent grown daughters.